BOYS' & GIRLS'
BOOK SERIES
REAL WORLD ADVENTURES

IDENTIFICATION & VALUES

Diane McClure Jones & Rosemary Jones

COLLECTOR BOOKS

A Division of Schroeder Publishing Co., Inc.

On the Cover
Bunny Brown, Bobbsey Twins, Nathalie,
Linger-Nots, and Black Stallion.

Cover design: Beth Summers
Book design: Joyce Cherry

Searching For A Publisher?

We are always looking for people knowledgeable within their fields. If you feel that there is a real need for a book on your collectible subject and have a large comprehensive collection, contact Collector Books.

Collector Books
P.O. Box 3009
Paducah, KY 42002-3009

www.collectorbooks.com

CONTENTS

ACKNOWLEDGMENTS

Thanks to Lynn, Karyl, Kirk, Evie, and all the rest of the Oz gang for book loans and suggestions. And a big thank you to our readers for their letters and e-mail.

EXPLANATION OF PRICING

Prices of collectible books vary dramatically, due to changes in popularity of items. The revival of interest in an old novel for any reason, such as the production of a film based on the story, can create or increase demand.

We have based our prices on suggested prices received from a number of antiquarian book dealers.

ALL QUOTED PRICES are for individual hardcover books in good condition but WITHOUT dust jackets. When dust jacket pricing information is available, it is included and identified.

BOOK CLUB EDITIONS are quite common for this period and usually command one-third to one-half of the listed price depending upon their rarity. For a few exceptional titles from this period, book club editions may be the only hardcover editions available and in those instances, command a higher price.

EX-LIBRARY EDITIONS are not considered desirable by most collectors and all book dealers, and therefore are generally sold as reading copies and priced in the $5.00 to $20.00 range with a good dust jacket.

GOOD CONDITION means clean, sound cover and spine without breaks or furred edges, clean undamaged pages, all pages and illustrations tightly attached. Price adjustments should be made for fingerprints, small tears, and loose pages. Large reductions are made for broken and seriously damaged covers, loose and missing pages, torn pages, water stains, and mold. In the case of children's books, other common damage found includes pencil and crayon marks.

FIRST EDITIONS are noted. Series books often do not identify editions on the copyright page, and so collectors then have to depend on the "list-to-self" method. On the dust jacket flap or on an interior advertising page in the book, titles of books in the series may be listed. If the book's title is the last title on the list, this is called a "list-to-self" book. Because this information is not 100% reliable, collectors and dealers refer to such a book as a "probable first."

RARE BOOKS are designated as such in the listings and not priced. A rare book is one that is extremely difficult to find, and the price is usually determined at the time of the sale. It will often depend solely on how much an individual collector wants the book. Auction prices can go into the thousands of dollars for a particular sale to a particular customer, but that price may never be paid again for an identical volume and is therefore not a reliable guide to pricing.

INVESTMENTS. Because of the fragile nature of paper and the "well-handled" condition of most children's books, most collectors collect children's books for the joy of finding and owning them. Some of them may be excellent investments. Some may lose value. As we cannot guess which books will increase in value and which will decrease, we have in our own collections books that we acquired and love for their content rather than their potential monetary value.

INTRODUCTION TO CHILDREN'S SERIES IN AMERICAN PUBLISHING

From dime novels to Harry Potter, the series novel has dominated children's publishing in this country for the last 150 years. Children like nothing better than to read and then read some more about favorite characters.

Collectors of series books spring from the readers of series books. As children grow up (but never grow old), they remember their favorite series with great affection. Today, on auction sites like e-Bay and at any bookstore specializing in out-of-print children's books, the series book enjoys a special place.

While librarians and other literary mavens tend to shove the series book into the footnotes of literary history, a number of American publishing houses got their start or derived their main income from the series book (see Publishers and Identifying First Editions for the history of individual companies).

Henty, Optic, Alger & Castlemon

British author G.A. Henty really didn't set out to create a children's series. He primarily wrote rousing military histories about British lads going off to the colonies and whacking the enemy. As the British empire in the mid-nineteenth century was spread across the entire globe and involved in numerous military engagements wherever they went, former war correspondent Henty had lots of material. He even dipped back into history for past British exploits and other ancient battles.

Young gentlemen (and older ones) on both sides of the Atlantic quickly decided that Henty's books were a lively good read and made his books best-sellers. Henty's publishers grabbed onto the notion of making the books look uniform as well as giving them very similar sounding titles. A series was born even though there were no real continuing characters (see HENTY in series list). However, young readers could count on fairly similar plots and action from each of Henty's novels.

In America, William T. Adams used the pen name of Oliver Optic and created dozens of juvenile books which were eventually packaged or repackaged as series by his publishers.

But for both collectors and series publishers, Optic was quickly overshadowed by the creator of the Upward and Onward theory: Horatio Alger. Oddly enough, Alger got his start by writing for Adams' own boys' periodical, *Student and Schoolmate*.

Although one unkind historian said that Alger wrote one book and then rewrote it 118 times, Alger created a formula for series books that continues today. In an Alger novel, a plucky orphan boy triumphs over adverse circumstances through his own innate virtue and rises to the top of his profession. Substitute a wizard orphan for the nineteenth century newsboy, and the distance between Harry Potter and Ragged Dick is not so very far (although the authors of this book will be the first to admit that writing for children has vastly improved since Alger's day!).

Ragged Dick sold thousands of copies and inspired Alger to repeat his formula in 118 other novels. By the late nineteenth century, Alger dominated children's series novels. Because publishing records are rather vague, nobody knows how many Alger books were sold, but various publishing histories list the probable total at close to 250 million copies.

Another popular boys' novelist of the day, Harry Castlemon, created a number of series based on his own experiences in the Civil War as well as the country's increasing interest in the West. Indians, cowboys, and the Gold Rush can all be found in Castlemon's books.

Henty, Optic, Alger, and Castlemon all wrote sound sermons on the value of manly virtues in defeating villainy while delivering vigorous adventure stories. Early editions of their books are charming examples of Victorian book art, lavishly decorated with gilt on the covers, and illustrated with black-and-white etchings. Today, collectors of these novels seek out the earliest editions for their look as much as their story.

Dime Novels & Frank Merriwell

In 1860, Erastus Beadle had the brilliant idea of printing *Malaeska: The Indian Wife of the White Hunter* on cheap paper with a paper binding and selling it for one thin dime. His advertisements trumpeted: "A dollar book for a dime! 128 pages complete, only ten cents!"

Malaeska became a smashing success. Beadle went on to sell more than 4 million dime novels during the Civil War to the young men of the Union Army.

Because nothing in publishing inspires copying more than financial success, a number of other publishers immediately launched their own dime novels after the Civil War.

Among those watching the dime novel's rise was a young magazine publisher, Ormond Smith. At the age of 28, Ormond entered the dime novel field with several lines including a series called the Nugget Library for children (priced at a very reasonable 5 cents). At the time, his best-selling dime novels were the Nick Carter Library, based on the popular detective stories that originally appeared in the *New York Weekly*.

The weekly Nick Carter series was really meant for adults (although boys liked the stories too!). The Frank Merriwell series was specifically written for boys.

Merriwell author Gil Patten loved adventure stories. As a young man of 15, he'd discovered Beadle's tales of pirates, cowboys, and other daring young men. While still in his teens, Patten began submitting his own adventure tales to Beadle's editor Orville Victor.

Patten earned six dollars for his first story. Eventually he went to New York to meet the editor and join the stable of writers churning out tales of derring-do for the company. By 1894, Patten earned $100 a novel. However, despite both the popularity of his tales and his speed in writing them, Beadle's president William Adams refused to pay Patten's full fee when Patten asked for an advance.

Furious, Patten marched over to Beadle's rival, Street & Smith. After some serious selling, he managed to convince editor Edward Stratemeyer to pay him $150 for a story. Following that promising start, Patten wrote 20 million words over 20 years for Street & Smith. Under the pseudonym Burt L. Standish, Patten's popular Merriwell stories quickly took the magazine *Tip Top Quarterly* into a circulation of 750,000.

Unlike the other boys' series of the time, the Merriwell series relied more on the character than the action. Protagonist Frank Merriwell had a few more vices than his contemporaries (he liked to gamble), but he loved his horse and was always loyal to his friends. He also aged, eventually graduating from Yale despite the author's sending him off for a year to work on the railroad. Author Patten eventually turned to Frank's younger brother Dick for further school adventures.

Smith took the stories from *Tip Top*, repackaged them, and then sold them for 15 cents as the Frank Merriwell Series.

The dime novels eventually faded away at the beginning of the twentieth century. However, the original idea of exciting fiction at a reasonable price continued to power the children's series publishers for decades to come.

Today, dime novels appeal to collectors of Victoriana, magazines, and children's stories. Fragile reminders of a time when adventures seemed to lurk around every corner, they still turn up at auctions and antique shows, often lovingly preserved by a reader captured by the romance of a dime novel.

Edward Stratemeyer

In the 1890s, Edward Stratemeyer worked as a jack-of-all-trades for Street & Smith. He edited the boy's magazine, *Good News*, wrote dime novels as Jim Bowie or Nat Woods, and even did a serial story for the female readers under the pseudonym Julie Edwards.

When Horatio Alger died in 1899, Stratemeyer finished some Alger manuscripts (or wrote them totally from scratch, depending on the biographer) to keep the Alger stories continuing.

While working at Street & Smith, Stratemeyer learned that series sell. Also, he learned that the author's name on the cover of the book may stay the same, but you can always change the actual writer behind it.

In the early 1900s, Stratemeyer launched a triple threat of pseudonyms and series: The Rover Boys by Arthur M. Winfield; Motor Boys by Clarence Young; and Tom Swift by Victor Appleton.

These early series alone sold several million copies. Tom Swift endured for generations (quite literally for both the character and his fans). Masked by the pseudonyms, dozens of writers ghosted over the decades for the Stratemeyer Syndicate. One family, the Garis family, accounted for hundreds of titles.

The series reflected the changes in publishing for children. The message, which was always dominant in the fiction of Alger, got muted under the action and the characters. Like the Frank Merriwell series, once Stratemeyer found an appealing character like Tom Swift, that character stayed pretty much the same from book to book. And so did the character's friends, parents, faithful servants, and home town, so that readers always knew right where they were when they visited their favorite series.

Unlike earlier series, the Stratemeyer characters were less likely to be orphaned, but they did suffer from a rash of widowed fathers (mothers, one suspects, might have curbed the adventure too much!).

The rest of American publishing, recognizing financial success when they saw it, copied Stratemeyer and launched their titles of continuing characters for their children's lines. L.C. Page credited his financial well-being to *Pollyanna* and *Anne of Green Gables.*

In the 1930s, the depression hit American publishing hard. The "serious" New York houses had to cut back their lists and institute policies that allowed bookstores to return books for full credit just to keep the bookselling trade afloat.

But the series publishers just rolled along, somewhat protected by the arrival of the "fifty center" for children. Once again, the cheap houses like A.L. Burt, Cupples & Leon, and Grosset & Dunlap turned to their enormous backlist of series books to re-release them in new, uniform editions for a new low price. *Elsie Dinsmore, Anne of Green Gables,* and *Pollyanna* all reappeared in the fifty cent format. Catalogs like Sears or Montgomery Ward featured series books along with dry goods.

Even the head librarian of the Boy Scouts, Franklin K. Mathiews, praised the fity cent books as stepping stones to more serious literature. Again, literally millions of series books were sold to children who really didn't care about literature but knew a good story when they read it.

The 1930s also saw the introduction of the two most popular Stratemeyer series: *Hardy Boys* by Franklin Dixon and *Nancy Drew* by Carolyn Keene.

Nancy Drew, a blonde teenage female detective, raced around in her convertible, solved mysteries, reported in (occasionally) to her widowed father, and came with a whole crew of friends who continued to share her adventures. Despite Nancy's early tendency towards car crashes and being hit over the head, she's survived into the twenty-first century and a whole new generation of fans.

When Stratemeyer died in 1930, his daughters, particularly Harriet Adams, and a crew of editors and ghost writers kept the Syndicate afloat. New series were created, old characters got various remakes (Nancy's hair color changes shades a few times!), and the series rolled merrily along.

In the 1950s and 1960s, librarians often banned the Stratemeyer books from the shelves on the basis that they lacked literary quality. But children kept buying them with their pocket money.

Other publishers were quick to note Stratemeyer's success and series continue as an important part of the overall children's book market. In 1955, more than 125 series were listed in the new books section of *Publishers' Weekly*

The Stratemeyer Syndicate rewrote their most popular older books, updating references for a new generation of readers.

After Grosset & Dunlap sold the rights to Nancy and the Hardy Boys to Simon & Schuster in 1979, those series eventually dropped their hardback editions and became paperbacks, providing readers once again with the modern equivalent of a dime novel.

At the bigger New York publishers, children's authors continued to create their own series characters, often sticking with them for years, if not decades. A few series drifted across the Atlantic, although authors like W.E. Johns or Enid Blyton never received the popularity here that they enjoyed in Great Britain.

American publishers still rely on series books, either with continuing characters or look-alike covers, for a substantial portion of their children's book sales. Go into any children's section in a bookstore and you can probably discover a dozen or more new series represented on the shelves.

A Note About Series Listed

This price guide lists series by series name except for those series best known by the author's name such as Horatio Alger, Harry Castlemon, G.A. Henty, and Oliver Optic.

The series covered in this book are real world adventures such as Ragged Dick or Nancy Drew. In a future book, we will explore fantasy, science fiction and fairy tale series.

We're always interested in hearing from collectors. The best way to reach us is by e-mail: lostlvs@aol.com. You may also write to Rosemary Jones, PO Box 9432, Seattle, WA 98109. For a reply, please enclosed a self-addressed, stamped envelope.

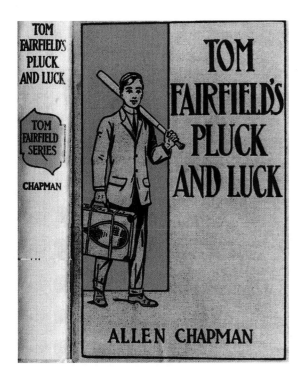

STRATEMEYER SYNDICATE, see p. 176 for series.

PUBLISHERS AND IDENTIFYING FIRST EDITIONS

Identifying First Editions: More on American and British Publishers

Because many series were in print for decades, identifying first editions can be the trickiest part of collecting. Many experienced collectors and book dealers rely on factors other than copyright information to tell the age of their books or document a possible first edition.

One useful clue can be found in the publisher's advertisments. Early editions of a series generally include advertisements that "list-to-self" or list to the titles published in the same year as the first edition. Collectors should remember that many planned series, such as Nancy Drew or Hardy Boys, were often started with two or three books. Thus the first book in the series will show an advertisement for all the books that were planned for the first year of publication. The Horatio Alger series, such as Ragged Dick, often carried information on future titles.

Often, children's books were reproduced without crediting the earlier editions or, in some cases, the author. Both British and American writers of the Victorian age frequently complained about transatlantic piracy. Later, publishers like Grosset or Donohue might buy the actual printing plates from the original publisher and not alter the copyright page.

British publishers rarely identified the date of publication or distinguished first editions from later editions prior to the adoption of the International Copyright Convention of 1957.

Collectors of first editions usually want "first state" or "first printing" editions. In the nineteenth and early twentieth century books, the best way to identify a first printing is errors, incorrect text placement, changes in the binding colors, or other "points" of identification. Fan club magazines such as *Whispered Watchword*, auction catalogs of well-documented collections or other specialized reference material list these points for specific titles.

For some books, one of the best clues to age is the publisher's name. Although many publishers stuck with the same name for a century or more, some companies, like Scribner's, changed names or shuffled names as business partners quit or died. Major name changes are noted below.

Starting in the 1970s, American publishers adopted a numeric or alphabetic system such as 1 2 3 4 5 6 7 8 9 or A B C D E to identify printings. This information usually appears on the copyright page. In most cases, the 1 or the A indicates a first printing. The "1" was removed, as in 2 3 4 5 6 7 8 9, to indicate a second printing and so on. Sometimes publishers used numbers in a reverse pattern such as 10 9 8 7 6 5 4 3 2 1 or in an alternating pattern of odds and evens. In most cases, the appearance of the "1" or "A" still indicated a first printing, and a line starting or ending with the "2" or "B" a second printing and so on.

Collectors can also date books through the appearance of publishing codes such as Library of Congress markings (see glossary for dates), ISBN, and bar codes. For example, ISBN numbers started appearing on book jackets or copyright pages in the late 1960s (see glossary for further explanation), and bar codes appeared even later.

There are always exceptions to any rule, and not all publishers adhered to the same system for all books. If the printing makes a significant difference in price, a careful collector should ask for an explanation of dating from the dealer.

The bibliography at the back of this book lists several additional resources. For further information on identifying first editions, see Volumes 1 and 3 of our *Collector's Guide to Children's Books.*

Altemus & Company, Henry Altemus
Prior to 1950, first editions from this Philadelphia publisher show the first edition date with no additional printings indicated on the back of the title page.

Applewood Books
This American publisher reprints rare children's books such as early titles in the Nancy Drew, Hardy Boys, and Tom Swift series. These reissues are currently in print, clearly identified as Applewood Books on the title page, and should not cost more than the retail price in the secondary market.

Atheneum
Formed in 1959, this New York publisher stated on the copyright page "First Edition" or "First American Edition." They did not adopt a numeric system for printings until the mid-1980s.

Beadle and Company; Beadle & Adams
This early American publisher of dime novels sold more than 4 million copies of their books during the Civil War, and their style had a strong influence on

such series writers as Gil Patten (pseudonym Burt Standish). By the late nineteenth century, the company operated under the name Beadle & Adams.

A.L. Burt

Founded by Albert Burt, this reprint house issued many series and was considered a major rival of Grosset & Dunlap. Their best-selling children's books included the works of Horatio Alger, G. A. Henty, Edward S. Ellis, and James Otis. In 1925, Burt started printing the Elsie Dinsmore series in a new fifty cents format and sold literally thousands of copies. Harry P. Burt sold the company in 1937 to Blue Ribbon Books. In 1939, Doubleday bought Blue Ribbon and the extensive backlist of titles acquired by the company. Like G&D, Burt books rarely indicated the year of printing (copyright usually refers to the original date that the work was copyrighted, not the date published).

Bobbs-Merrill Company

This Indianapolis publisher was founded in 1885 by two booksellers, Silas Bowen and Samual Merrill, and used the imprint Bowen-Merrill Company. In 1903, the name was changed to Bobbs-Merrill. Early first editions may only show the month of publication on the copyright page. Starting in the 1920s, some books carried the words "first edition," and, in the 1930s, some first editions were identified with a bow-and-arrow symbol on the copyright page. However, for reprints, first editions may not be clearly marked, and the copyright dates often refer to the original copyright rather than the year printed by Bobbs-Merrill. In general, this publisher was a reprint publisher, but they did issue first American editions of a few British series.

Bowen-Merrill Company
See Bobbs-Merrill

Blackie & Sons

This British publisher began printing children's books during the 1800s. Early books usually do not have a printing date indicated. Collectors generally rely on publisher's advertisements, inscriptions or other factors to date books. The words "First published" followed by the year and no other information may indicate a first edition.

Buccaneer

A reprint house, Buccaneer started reissuing a number of hard-to-find children's books in the 1990s. Their books are clearly marked, lack dust jackets, and should be priced as modern reprints in the secondary market.

Henry T. Coates
See Porter & Coates

Copp, Clark Company, Ltd.

This Toronto publisher issued the Canadian editions of several children's books and series. They often bought printing plates from American publishers, such as Reilly & Lee, and would make only minor changes to cover art and title page (usually substituting their name for the American publisher).

Thomas Y. Crowell

A New York publisher who entered the business in the 1870s with a series of reprints of poetry given the title *Crowell's Red Line Poets*. In the 1880s, the firm entered the Sunday School market by acquiring the backlist of the bankrupt Warren and Wyman. Early first editions varied, with the publisher using the words "first edition" or no additional printing dates on the copyright page. Starting in the 1940s, first editions were identified with a numerical code.

Chatterton & Peck

An early publisher of Stratemeyer's series, their backlist of children series was acquired by Grosset & Dunlap in 1908.

Cupples & Leon Company

A New York publishing house, Cupples & Leon specialized in series books and reprints of newspaper cartoons such as Buster Brown. The company was started in 1902 by Victor Cupples and Arthur Leon. By the late 1920s, company catalogs listed more than 240 books in 28 series including such titles as Motor Boys and Ruth Fielding. First editions were not distinguished from other printings.

Dean & Son

This London firm was one of the first English publishers to make extensive use of lithography and chromo-lithography for printing illustrations. Starting in the 1840s, they began making movable and flap books. The movable books were often published under their own name such as *Dean's New Book of Dissolving Pictures*. The firm adopted the name Dean & Son in 1846.

J.M. Dent

This English publisher began printing children's books in the nineteenth century. Prior to the 1930s, Dent did not identify the date of printing. After 1929, books began appearing with the words "first published" followed by the year of publication.

Dodd, Mead & Company (Dodd)

The original publisher of the Elsie Dinsmore novels released the first title in 1867. The series lasted for 26 volumes, taking Elsie from childhood to old age, and sold over 5 million copies in a period of 70 years. A relative, Edward Mead, joined the firm in 1870, which led to the name Dodd and Mead and later Dodd, Mead & Company. The Dinsmore titles were reprinted by A.L. Burt in the 1920s.

M.A. Donohue & Co.

This Chicago publisher generally did not identify the dates of their publications. They bought or leased printing plates of books first published by other publishers. Donohue also issued a number of reprints of Victorian children's series (see Goldsmith and Porter & Coates).

George H. Doran

Doran, a salesman for Fleming Revell, decided to start his own company in the 1890s. Based in New York, he made an arrangement with the British company Hodder & Stoughton in 1908 to reprint their most popular titles for the American market. The company merged with Doubleday in 1927. Early first editions show a GHD symbol on the title page or copyright page. After 1921, the GHD symbol appears on the copyright page under the copyright notice.

Doubleday

Beginning in the late 1890s, Doubleday went through a number of acquisitions and mergers. At various times, the company was called Doubleday, McClure & Co. (ca. 1897); Doubleday, Page & Co. (ca. 1900) and Doubleday, Doran (ca. 1927). This old New York publisher finally consolidated their various holdings as Doubleday & Company in 1945.

E.P. Dutton & Company

Established in the1850s, Dutton was both a publisher and a bookstore in their early years. The company moved from Boston to New York in the 1860s. E. P. Dutton worked in the firm until 1923 when he died at the age of 92. Until 1928, Dutton first editions generally have a single date on the copyright page. After 1928, the words "first edition" or "first published" may appear on the copyright page.

Garden City Publishing Co.

This New Jersey publisher reprinted other publishers' originals. Many of their reprints appear to have been made from the original publisher's plates and may not show the actual date of printing. Other Garden City editions may carry the date in the artwork, on the frontispiece, or on the back of the title page.

Goldsmith

In the 1930s, this imprint of the M.A. Donohue company produced children's books for the five-and-dime stores. *Five Little Peppers* and *Heidi* were two of their top-selling titles. Goldsmith tried out new series, designing a colorful dust jacket, and putting a series name on the spine. Some were successful, others include the first book only, and several, like the Herb Kent series, died after the second title.

Golden Press

In the 1940s, Western Publishing's Artist and Writer's Guild created the Little Golden Books line for New York publisher Simon & Schuster. A phenomenal success from the beginning, Western quickly decided that they could make more money if they controlled the books. So, in 1958, Western and paperback publisher Pocket Books established a partnership to buy back Little Golden Books. Golden Press was formed and placed under the control of former Simon & Schuster president A. R. Leventhal. By the early 1960s, Golden Press was selling more than 5 million books a year. Western bought out Pocket Books' interest and Golden Press became a wholly owned subsidiary in 1964. Golden Press generally uses an alphabetic printing code with an "A" indicating a first printing. See also Little Golden and Western.

Grosset & Dunlap

Alexander Grosset and George Dunlap launched their company in 1898 by buying the left-over stock of the bankrupt American Publishers Corporation. For the next several decades, cheap editions of popular works remained the mainstay of the company, whether through rebinding other publisher's sheets (pages of a book) in cheaper materials; buying up printer's plates to produce their own editions; or pirating the works of British authors such as Rudyard Kipling. The company's original name was Dunlap & Grosset, but Dunlap left for a brief spell. The company continued as Alexander Grosset & Co. until Dunlap's return in 1900 when the new name of Grosset & Dunlap was adopted. In 1908, salesman John May persuaded the partners to take over the children's line previously published by Chatterton & Peck. Along with C&P's many boys' books came several series by Edward Stratemeyer. From then until the 1970s, Grosset & Dunlap would enjoy enormous success with Stratemeyer's many series including Tom Swift, Hardy Boys, and Nancy Drew. Although called a reprinter of children's books in many histories of American publishing, Grosset & Dunlap actually printed the first editions of the majority of the Stratemeyer titles. The publisher kept the most popular series in print for decades, reprinting titles as quickly as they could sell them (and they sold millions). Following the death of the original partners and eventual decline of the Stratemeyer Syndicate, G&D sold the rights for the Hardy Boys and Nancy Drew to Simon & Schuster in the late 1970s. Collectors of G&D books rely on advertisements, changes in binding, and dust jacket art to date their books. The copyright date only refers to the date of original publication and cannot be used to reliably date the work.

Harper & Brothers, Harper & Row (Harper)

The two eldest Harper brothers published their first book in 1819. Although they'd started out as printers, they quickly realized the potential profit in publishing popular English authors for the growing American market. By 1833, all four brothers were involved in the business, leading to the name Harper & Brothers (who was Harper and who were the Brothers was the source of a number of family jokes). In 1962, Harper merged with the textbook publisher Row, Peterson & Company and began using the imprint Harper & Row. From the late 1800s through 1911, this publisher generally used a single date on the back of the title page to indicate a first edition. From 1912 to 1922, they used an alphabetic code to identify the first editions. After 1922, the words "first edition" appeared on the copyright page. For the Harper & Row imprint, "first edition" was printed on the back of the title page for firsts published in the early 1960s. The company started using a numeric code for printings in the late 1960s which would appear on the last page of the text.

Harper & Row, Peterson
See Harper & Row

Henry Holt & Company

In 1873, Holt & Leypoldt became Henry Holt & Company. By the 1890s, the company had a strong textbook division as well as publishing a wide variety of other books. First editions should have no additional printing date on copyright page or back of title page. After 1944, the words "first edition" or "first printing" may appear on copyright page.

Houghton Mifflin

Originally called Hurd & Houghton, Hurd retired in 1878 and Houghton went through a number of name changes as he changed business partners, finally settling on Houghton Mifflin in 1880. First editions may have a single date on the title page.

John Martin's Book

This publishing company was founded in 1912 by Morgan Shepard, who had previously written a newsletter for children and signed himself "John Martin." The hardcover publication was sold by subscription as a monthly publication for children and contained stories, puzzles, games, and various illustrations. Shepard hired a variety of freelance artists and writers for his books, and many later achieved fame in their own right. The value of the books varies according to the talent or later fame of the contributors.

Alfred A. Knopf, Inc.

Starting out as a clerk for Doubleday, young Alfred quickly decided that he could run his own business. In 1915, he persuaded future wife Blanche Wolf to help him start a publishing company. Until 1933, the first edition's copyright page or the back of the title page would have only a single date or no additional printing dates. After 1934, the words "first edition" may appear on the copyright page with no

additional printing dates.

Lee & Shepard

The company was founded in 1861. See also Lothrop.

Frank Leslie

In the 1870s, *Frank Leslie's Boys Library Series* was a popular softcover series for boys, sold through newsstands. Following Leslie's near bankruptcy and death in 1880, his wife took over the business and legally changed her name to Frank Leslie (she also called herself the Baroness de Bazus in later years). Mrs. Leslie launched a number of new books under the Frank Leslie title. She scandalized New York society with her frequent marriages and divorces, and left an estate of $2 million in 1914 to Carrie Chapman Catt to promote the cause of women's suffrage.

J.B. Lippincott and Company;
J. B. Lippincott Company

In 1827, thirteen-year-old Joshua B. Lippincott got his first job working in a bookstore. By the 1850s, he owned one of the largest bookselling emporiums in Philadelphia and established his own publishing company under the name Lippincott, Grambo and Company. Grambo retired in 1855 and the name changed to J.B. Lippincott and Company. The firm dropped the "and" in their name in 1885, becoming J.B. Lippincott Company. Until 1924, Lippincott used a single date on the copyright page or copyright date one year later than the title page date to designate their first editions. After 1925, the words "first edition" may appear, or a numerical code, or the words "published" followed by the month and year.

Little, Brown

Established by a pair of Boston booksellers as Charles Little and Company, this publisher then changed the name to Little, Brown and Company in 1847. Through 1929, first editions had only a single date on the back of the title page. Later first editions may be designated by the words "first edition" or "first printing."

Little Golden Books

Originally created for Simon & Schuster's juvenile division in the 1940s, this popular line of early books sold millions of copies of their titles from their earliest years. In 1958, Western purchased the Little Golden line and formed Golden Press. First editions of these books generally had an "A" printed on the first, second or last page. Sometimes the "A" is hidden by the binding. The authors of this book highly recommend Steve Santi's bibliography of Little Golden Books for any serious collector. See also Western Printing.

Longmans Green Co.

Established in 1724 in London, Longmans formed

a New York branch in 1887. Until the 1920s, first editions generally had the same date on the back of the title page as the front. In the 1920s, the company switched to using the words "first edition" or "first published" to designate first editions.

A.K. Loring
See Porter & Coates

D. Lothrop & Co.; Lothrop, Lee & Shepard Company, Inc.

Founded in Boston in 1850, the company incorporated in 1887 as D. Lothrop Co. In 1880, Lothrop bought *Five Little Peppers and How They Grew*, a children's book that went on to sell millions of copies. By 1894, the publisher used the name Lothrop Publishing Company. In 1904, Lothrop consolidated with Lee & Shepard. In 1947, the company was purchased by Crown. First editions may be designated in a variety of ways including no additional publishing dates on the copyright page.

Macmillan Company

In 1859, the British publisher Macmillan began distributing popular titles in the United States through arrangements with Scribner & Welford. In 1869, British bookseller George Edward Brett established a Macmillan office in New York. Following his death in 1890, his son George Platt Brett agreed to continue the office if the Macmillans made him a partner. In 1896, the younger Brett reorganized the American branch as a separate company under his control. Through the 1930s, first editions of the American Macmillan generally stated the month and year of publication with a single date on the copyright page. After 1936, the words "first published" may appear on the copyright page.

McLoughlin Bros.

Scottish immigrant John McLoughlin established his New York printing company in 1828. He also wrote and printed sermons for children, which were eventually issued as the series *McLoughlin's Books for Children*. In the 1840s, the firm was known as John Elton and Co. for a time. In 1848, McLoughlin's sons took over the business and renamed it McLoughlin Bros. The company specialized in books for children, first issuing hand-colored picture books and later investing in new methods of printing. In 1869, they established a major printing plant in Brooklyn and eventually employed a staff of 75 artists to create books and games for children. The company was sold to Milton Bradley in 1920 but continued to publish under the McLoughlin name. In the 1950s, revenues began to dwindle and the company was sold again to Kushner & Jacobs. The firm eventually ceased publishing by 1970.

William Morrow and Company (Morrow)

Established in 1926, this New York publisher's books generally have no additional printing dates indicated on the back of the title page of first editions. Occasionally, the words "first printing" may also appear, followed by the year, and with no additional dates indicated. Starting in the 1950s and 1960s, subsequent printings or editions were clearly marked "Second Printing" or "Second Edition" and so on. First printings usually had no additional information on the copyright page. In 1973, the publisher started using a numeric sequence where the "1" indicated a first edition.

Oxford University Press

This British publisher has had an American branch since 1896. In 1958, publisher Henry Z. Walck bought the American OUP's list of juvenile titles. First editions may have the words "first edition" on the back of the title page or may be designated by a single date on the copyright page with no additional dates. Collectors of the British Biggles series have reported a number of discrepancies in the labeling of first editions, indicating that OUP may have been more casual about their juveniles.

L. C. Page & Company Publishers

This Boston company was founded in 1892. In 1913, they bought *Pollyanna*, a book that had begun as a serial in the *Christian Herald*. Pollyanna and her many sequels, published as the Glad Books, cemented the company's financial success. Some estimates put the sale of the first book into well over one million copies. In 1914, Page changed their name to Page Company, but by 1923 had resumed the L.C. Page name. Page also published other children's series including Anne of Green Gables and Little Colonel. L.C. Page often stated that the House of Page owed its long history to the success of Pollyanna and Anne. He died at the age of 86 at Page Court in 1956, and the company was eventually sold to Farrar, Straus & Giroux.

Parents' Magazine Press

Many Parents' books were reprints (see also Weekly Reader Club) although they did some originals as well as the first hardcover editions of works originally published in softcover. Later printings should be indicated on copyright page. A numeric system was not adopted until after 1975.

Platt & Munk

Founded in 1920 by a pair of former Saalfield salesmen, the Munk brothers, and investor George E. Platt, this company focused on colorful books for younger readers. House pseudonym Watty Piper accounted for a number of bestselling titles including the *Brimful Book* and the Piper edition of *Little Engine that Could*. Although the firm's greatest successes came in the 1920s and 1930s, they continued to publish into the 1970s and eventually became part of the conglomerate that owned Grosset & Dunlap.

Porter & Coates, Henry T. Coates

This Philadelphia publisher issued first editions of several Castlemon and Alger books as well as other juvenile series. Formed in 1848 as Davis & Porter, Coates became a junior partner in 1866 and eventually the sole owner in 1895. The company acquired several Alger titles from A.K. Loring. In 1899, Coates began to let Hurst and Donohue reissue the popular but aging Alger titles in cheap twenty-five cent editions. In 1904, Coates sold the company to John C. Winston and that company took over the publication of Coates' extensive backlist of juvenile titles. Coates' first editions may say "published" followed by the month and year or have only a single date on the copyright page (however, collectors have noted a number of discrepancies over the years).

G.P. Putnam, G.P. Putnam's Sons

George Palmer Putnam established his New York firm in 1848, publishing both books and magazines like many early American publishers. Financial difficulties forced Putnam to take a job as a collector of Internal Revenue in the 1860s, but his sons joined the business and the company continued. In the 1890s, Putnam's son, George Haven, was a major supporter of international copyright laws to protect the rights of publishers and authors. France even awarded him a Cross of the Legion of Honor for his work. An American and a British Putnam's were established. The American company designated first editions by the words "first American edition" followed by the year or by showing no additional printing dates on the copyright page. In the 1920s and 1930s, some American books might also state "first edition" on the copyright page. By the 1950s, Putnam also used other systems. If the date on the title page and the date on the copyright page match, it is probably a first edition. Later printings may be indicated by such terms as "second impression" and so on appearing on the copyright page.

Rand McNally

This Chicago firm started in the 1870s as a publisher of business directories and maps. The book division was formed in the 1880s, but they didn't really start publishing juveniles until later. The Elf books and Elf Junior books were small books aimed at the same market as the Little Golden Books. Early first editions of Rand McNally chapter books might have the letters "MA" on the copyright page or would show no additional printing dates. After 1937, the words "first published" followed by the year or an alphabetical code might indicate a first edition.

Random House

In the 1950s, New York publisher Random considerably expanded its juvenile list. The popular Landmark series sold more than 6 million copies in its first five years. Random House editor Bennett Cerf was a major influence on children's publishing in the mid-twentieth century, especially for his promotion of the works of Dr. Seuss and the creation of I-Can-Read books. This publisher used a variety of systems for identifying first editions of its children's books. The Black Stallion series clearly state "first printing" or subsequent printings on the copyright page. After 1968, the words First Printed or First Edition appear in the copyright page of many Random House books (and disappear from subsequent printings). The number sequence adopted in the 1970s, unlike that of most publishers, uses the words "First Edition" and a "2" in the number line to indicate first editions (the "1" never appears). Picture books published for the youngest readers may not have editions clearly marked, and collectors rely on advertisements or title lists to date these books.

Reilly & Britton or Reilly & Lee

This Chicago company published a variety of children's books and series. In 1919, they changed their name to Reilly & Lee. Under the Reilly & Lee name, they continued to publish children's books into the 1960s. For any series book, the publisher's advertisements generally end with or before that edition's title. As both Reilly & Britton and Reilly & Lee, they rarely updated copyright information and most dealers disregard this information when dating their books.

George Routledge & Sons

This British publisher began printing children's books in the 1800s. They are rarely dated.

Roberts Brothers

In 1864, the brothers started publishing children's books as well as their popular photograph albums. In 1868, editor Thomas Niles bought *Little Women* by Louisa May Alcott, which inspired a number of sequels. Niles and Alcott had a long and satisfactory business relationship, partially inspired by Niles' early advice to Alcott to hang onto her copyrights and his highly ethical accounting of her royalties. Little, Brown bought the company in 1898.

Saalfield Publishing Co.

Started in 1899 by Arthur J. Saalfield, this firm's early publishing success came from the *White House Cookbook* and other reprint titles. In 1919, Saalfield's son Albert started a children's book division and concentrated on issuing beautiful books to compete with the European imports. However, in the 1930s, the company entered into the "ten cent" trade along with Goldsmith, McLoughlin, and Whitman. The most successful of the Saalfield titles in this period featured

Shirley Temple. The company also created a line of boxed books and picture puzzles for sale to the toy stores and variety chains. In the 1960s, Saalfield did very well with a Peanuts coloring book, but the company eventually went out of business in the 1970s.

Scribner & Company, Scribner and Welford, Charles Scribner's Sons (Scribner)

This leading New York publisher had multiple name changes through the nineteenth century. In 1846, Charles Scribner and Isaak D. Baker formed a partnership and bought the publishing business of John Taylor. In 1850, Baker's death and the acquisition of new junior business partners caused the firm's name to change to Scribner, Armstrong and Company. Scribner and Englishman Charles Welford created a second company to import English books under the name Scribner and Welford or Scribner, Welford and Company (see G.A. Henty). The Welford company operated during the same time as the other Scribner company continued to publish original works, primarily by American authors. In 1879, the Armstrong was dropped in favor of Charles Scribner's Sons. The separate company of Scribner and Welford was absorbed by Charles Scribner's Sons in 1891. Early first editions of Scribner's own books have a single date on the title page or no additional printings indicated on the back of the title page or copyright page. Starting in 1930, an "A" may be printed on the copyright page to designate the first edition. The company went to a numeric system in the mid-1970s.

Simon & Schuster

This New York publisher started in 1925 and derived their early success from a series of popular crossword books. In 1942, firm salesman Albert Leventhal launched Little Golden Books, a wise decision that eventually led to his leaving Simon & Schuster to head up Golden Press. See also Western.

Stratemeyer Syndicate

Not a publisher but an important force in children's series books, the Stratemeyer Syndicate was started by Edward Stratemeyer. An early example of a book packager, Stratemeyer would design a series, coming up with titles, plot outlines, and pseudonyms and then parcel out the work to a large stable of ghost writers. Following Stratemeyer's death in 1930, his daughters continued the company. The majority of Stratemeyer's lines were published by Grosset & Dunlap. See Resources at the back of this book for several websites devoted to the history of the Syndicate.

Street & Smith

In 1889, Ormond Smith entered the dime novel trade. This publisher issued a number of magazines and weekly titles. The books had soft cardboard covers, were about 4¼" x 6¼", about 250 pages, and printed on cheap paper. Popular series included the Frank and Dick Merriwell series, Nick Carter series, Jack Lightfoot series, Young Railroader series, and novels written by Horatio Alger and Oliver Optic. Popular stories were frequently repackaged into sturdier book formats. Street & Smith went on to become one of the largest publishing firms in the United States, launching a number of famous pulp magazines in the 1930s, such as the *Shadow* and *Doc Savage*, and later creating fashion magazines such as *Mademoiselle*.

Viking Press

In 1925, Harold K. Guizburg and George S. Oppenheimer established Viking Press. In 1933, editor May Massee started Viking's children's book division. First editions published prior to 1937 usually had no additional printing dates on the back of the title page. Later, the words "first published" or "first edition" with no additional printing dates might be used. Viking was an early supporter of the book club idea. Book club editions may have "first edition" printed on the copyright page and may only be identified as book club editions on the dust jacket (front flap).

Weekly Reader's Children's Book Club

These book club editions show the original publisher on the spine, such as Doubleday or Scribners, but are clearly marked in several places: back cover, title page, and copyright page. They are considered book club editions (reprints) by collectors and not true first editions, even when this is the first time that the book appeared in hardcover.

Western Printing & Lithographing Company; Western Publishing

As their early name indicates, this publisher really started out as a printer. In 1916, the partners entered the publishing business when the Hemming-Whitman Publishing Company defaulted on their bills. As the bankrupt company's chief creditor, Western took the Hemming-Whitman's stock and started Whitman Publishing Company to liquidate the assets. As that venture proved profitable, Western continued to expand into the juvenile market. They formed an agreement in 1933 with Walt Disney Productions for the exclusive right to create books based on the Disney cartoon characters. By 1935, the company opened a second printing plant in New York. In the early 1940s, the Artists and Writers Guild was started to serve as an early book packager. The editors would generate the idea for a book and then hire writers and artists to create it. An early and highly successful venture was the creation of Little Golden Books for Simon & Schuster. Western bought the Golden Books line back in 1958. Western also launched the Golden Key Comics. In 1960, the company went public and changed their name to Western Publishing. See also Golden Press and Whitman.

Whitman Publishing Co.

This Racine, Wisconsin, publisher was formed by Western Printing (see earlier listing). They issued the Big Little Books and the Better Little Books as well as a variety of series books based on comic strip characters or popular movie stars. The early Big Little Books had print runs of 250,000 and 350,000 with no reprints. By the 1960s, changes in endpapers indicate that Whitman would do more than one printing of popular titles. They also reprinted various children's classics. Like Grosset & Dunlap, the copyright date only refers to the original copyright of the material. Collectors rely on other information, such as advertise-

ments and price, to date their books.

John C. Winston Company

Harvard graduate Winston launched his Philadelphia publishing company by creating a subscription book called *The Crown Book of the Beautiful, the Wonderful, and Wise.* Another successful subscription venture was a memorial edition of *Uncle Tom's Cabin* but the company depended on printing nearly 500 varieties of Bibles for financial success. In 1904, Winston bought Henry Coates' backlist of Alger and other juvenile titles and began bringing out their own cheap reprints. In 1940, Winston hit it big again with Eric Knight's *Lassie Come Home* which sold more than one million copies in various editions.

GOLDSMITH: 1930s Goldsmith dust jacket

DONOHUE: Ca. 1900 Donohue cover

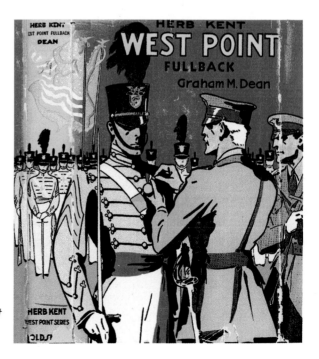

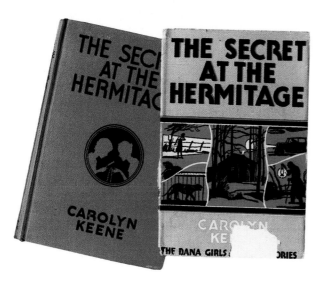

GROSSET: Grosset World War II edition

PORTER & COATES: Ca. 1908 Henry T. Coates edition endpapers

STREET & SMITH: Tip Top Weekly

Book List by Series

Prices are for each hardcover book in good condition but without dust jacket, except when noted.

— A —

ABBEY SCHOOL SERIES, Elsie J. Oxham, 1920s through 1960s Collins, London, hardcover with frontispiece. First edition dates are shown with the titles, however, this series was constantly reprinted, and printing dates are often difficult to identify. First edition values are therefore vague, but generally higher in England, and with a good dust jacket can be in the $100.00 range. Later printings: ($25.00 with dust jacket) $10.00

Abbey Girls, 1920
Abbey Girls Go Back to School, 1922
New Abbey Girls, 1923
Abbey Girls in Town, 1926
Queen of the Abbey Girls, 1926
Jen of the Abbey School, 1927
Abbey Girls Win Through, 1928
Abbey School, 1928
Abbey Girls At Home, 1930
Abbey Girls Play Up, 1930
Abbey Girls On Trial, 1931
Biddy's Secret, 1932
Rosamund's Victory, 1933
Call of the Abbey School, 1934
Maidlin to the Rescue, 1934
Joy's New Adventure, 1935
Rosamund's Tuckshop, 1936
Maidlin Bears the Torch, 1937
Schooldays at the Abbey, 1938
Rosamund's Castle, 1938
Secrets of the Abbey, 1939
Two Joans at the Abbey, 1945
An Abbey Champion, 1946
Abbey Girls at Home, 1947
Fiddler for the Abbey, 1948
Guardians of the Abbey, 1950
Schoolgirl Jen at the Abbey, 1950
Stowaways at the Abbey, 1951
Dancer from the Abbey, 1953
Rachel in the Abbey, 1954
Strangers at the Abbey, 1960
Abbey Girls in Town, 1967

ADELE DORING SERIES, Grace North, 1919 – 23 Lothrop, Lee & Shepard, illustrated with color plates by Florence Liley Young. $25.00

Adele Doring of the Sunnyside Club
Adele Doring on a Ranch
Adele Doring at Boarding-School
Adele Doring in Camp
Adele Doring at Vineyard Valley

ADVENTURE BOYS or JEWEL SERIES, Ames Thompson (Josephine Chase) 1927 Cupples & Leon, hardcover, 5 titles. $15.00

ADVENTURE GIRLS SERIES, Clair Blank, 1920 Burt, hardcover. ($25.00 with dust jacket) $10.00

Adventure Girls at K-Bar-O
Adventure Girls in the Air
Adventure Girls at Happiness House

ADVENTURE AND MYSTERY SERIES FOR GIRLS, 1930s Burt, hardcover. ($15.00 with dust jacket) $10.00

Phantom Yacht, Carol Norton
Bobs, a Girl Detective, Carol Norton
Seven Sleuths Club, Carol Norton
Phantom Treasure, Harriet Grove
Mystery of the Sandalwood Boxes, Harriet Grove
Secret of Steeple Rock, Harriet Grove
Black Box, Thelma Lientz
Kay and the Secret Code, Thelma Lientz

ADVENTURE SERIES, Enid Blyton, ca. 1944 – 55, Macmillan, UK, hardcover, illustrated by Stuart Tresilian, featuring four children and Kiki the parrot. Early British editions featured hardcover with contrasting picture stamped on cover, and colorful wraparound dust jacket illustration by Tresilian. First editions: ($100.00 with dust jacket) $30.00. Later editions: ($35.00 with dust jacket) $15.00

Island of Adventure
Castle of Adventure
Valley of Adventure
Sea of Adventure
Mountain of Adventure
Ship of Adventure
Circus of Adventure
River of Adventure

ADVENTUROUS ALLENS SERIES, Harriet Grove, ca. 1932 Burt, hardcover, frontispiece. ($15.00 with dust jacket) $10.00

Adventurous Allens
Adventurous Allens Afloat
Adventurous Allens' Treasure Hunt
Adventurous Allens Find Mystery
Adventurous Allens Marooned

AEROPLANE BOYS SERIES, John Langworthy, ca. 1912 Donohue, also published as BIRD BOYS (heroes are Frank and Andy Bird) and AIRPLANE BOYS, with variations of the following titles. $20.00

Aeroplane Boys' First Air Voyage

Aeroplane Boys on the Wing
Aeroplane Boys Among the Clouds
Aeroplane Boys' Flight
Aeroplane Boys on a Cattle Ranch

AGATON SAX SERIES, Nils-Olof Franzen, Andre Deutsch, London, translated from Swedish, hardcover, illustrated endpapers, humorous b/w drawings throughout by Quentin Blake, adventures of Swedish "arch-enemy of the criminal" Agaton Sax, master of disguises and numerous other weird and wonderful skills. ($25.00 with dust jacket) $10.00 Delacorte edition: ($15.00 with dust jacket) $10.00

Agaton Sax and the Diamond Thieves, 1967
Agaton Sax and the Scotland Yard Mystery, 1969
Agaton Sax and the Incredible Max Brothers, 1970
Agaton Sax and the Criminal Doubles, 1971
Agaton Sax and the Colossus of Rhodes
Agaton Sax and the London Computer Plot, 1973
Agaton Sax and the League of Silent Exploders, 1974
Agaton Sax and the Haunted House, 1975
Agaton Sax and the Lispington's Grandfather Clock, 1978
Agaton Sax and the Big Rig, 1981

AIR COMBAT STORIES FOR BOYS SERIES, Thomson Burtis, Adams, Avery (Rutherford Montgomery), stories of aerial combat in World War I (1914 – 18) and World War II (1939 – 45), Grosset and Dunlap, green hardcover, black illustration of plane, pictorial endpapers of air battle, b/w frontispiece. 1930s titles, World War I

stories: ($30.00 with dust jacket) $15.00
Daredevils of the Air
Four Aces
Wing for Wing
Flying Blackbirds
Doomed Demons
Wings of the Navy
War Wings
1940s titles, World War II stories: ($20.00 with dust jacket) $10.00
Yankee Flier with the R.A.F.
Yankee Flier in the Far East
Yankee Flier in the South Pacific
Yankee Flier in North Africa
Yankee Flier in Italy
Yankee Flier Over Berlin
Yankee Flier in Normandy
Yankee Flier on a Rescue Mission
Yankee Flier Under Secret Orders

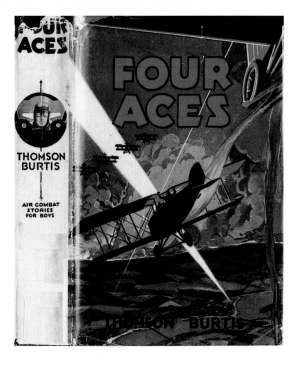

AIR MYSTERY SERIES, A. Van Buren Powell, 1932 Saalfield, reprints of SKY SCOUT SERIES, hardcover, boys' mystery-adventure stories, frontispiece. ($15.00 with dust jacket) $10.00
Mystery Crash
Haunted Hanger
Vanishing Airliner
Ghost of Mystery Airport

AIR SERVICE BOYS SERIES, Charles Amory Beach (Stratemeyer Syndicate pseudonym), 1918 – 1920 Sully, hardcover. $20.00. Reprints by Goldsmith, Saalfield, World: ($20.00 with dust jacket) $10.00
Flying for France
Flying for Victory
In the Big Battle

Over the Atlantic
Over the Enemy's Lines
Over the Rhine

AIR STORIES, Covington Clarke, ca. 1930 Reilly & Lee, hardcover. ($20.00 with dust jacket) $15.00

AIRPLANE BOYS SERIES, Edith Janice Craine, 1932 World, hardcover, also called SKY BUDDIES, 5 titles, early editions. ($25.00 with dust jacket) $10.00
Titles include:
Airplane Boys at Cap Rock
Airplane Boys Discover the Secrets of Cuzco
Airplane Boys at Platinum River

AIRPLANE GIRL SERIES, Harrison Bardwell (Edith Craine), ca. 1930 World Syndicate, hardcover, four titles. ($25.00 with dust jacket) $10.00

AIRSHIP BOYS SERIES, H. L. Sayler, ca. 1910 Reilly & Britton, cloth-over-board hardcover with impressed illustration, 300+ pages, b/w frontispiece by Riesenberg. $20.00
Airship Boys
Airship Boys Adrift
Airship Boys Due North
Airship Boys in the Barren Lands
Airship Boys in Finance
Airship Boys' Ocean Flyer

AL SERIES, Constance Greene, Viking, hardcover, illustrated by Byron Barton. ($20.00 with dust jacket) $10.00
Girl Called Al, 1969
I Know You, Al, 1975
Your Old Pal Al, 1979
Al(exandra) the Great, 1982
Just Plain Al, 1986
Al's Blind Date, 1989

ALDEN FAMILY MYSTERIES see BOXCAR CHILDREN

ALDO SERIES, Johanna Hurwitz, Morrow, hardcover, b/w illustrations by Diane deGroat. ($25.00 with dust jacket) $10.00
Much Ado About Aldo, 1978
Aldo Applesauce, 1979
Aldo Ice Cream, 1981
Tough-Luck Karen, 1982
Aldo Peanut Butter, 1990

ALEXANDER SERIES, Marjorie Knight, Dutton.
Alexander's Christmas Eve, 1938 Dutton, cloth-over-board cover, small, 93 pages, color endpapers, b/w and color illustrations by Howard Simon. First edition with dust jacket: $70.00. Later printings: ($40.00 with dust jacket) $20.00

Alexander's Birthday, 1940 Dutton, cloth-over-board cover, illustrated endpapers, b/w and color illustrations by Howard Simon. ($40.00 with dust jacket) $20.00

Alexander's Vacation, 1943 Dutton, blue hardcover, 106 pages, first edition, illustrated by Howard Simon. ($40.00 with dust jacket) $20.00

ALFRED HITCHCOCK AND THE THREE INVESTIGATORS SERIES, Random House, color illustrated paper-over-board covers, graveyard illustration endpapers, b/w full page illustrations, about 150 pages, series titles listed on back cover. First editions generally list-to-self.

Three teens investigate crimes at the instigation of movie director Alfred Hitchcock (1899 – 1980), who appears briefly in the introduction or closing chapters. Robert Arthur (1909 – 1969), an editor at the *Alfred Hitchcock Mystery Magazine,* wrote ten of the early titles in the 43 book series.

Following Hitchcock's death, books #31 through #43 used a fictional film director named Hector Sebastian. Later titles are the most difficult to find, due to the limited number of printings.

After 1979 the series name changed to Three Investigators and reprints of earlier stories had the titles revised, dropping the Hitchcock reference.

Probable firsts: $40.00

Early printings, hardcovers: $20.00

Later reprints: $10.00

1970s Scholastic paperbacks: $5.00

Secret of Terror Castle, Robert Arthur, 1964
Mystery of the Stuttering Parrot, Robert Arthur, 1964
Mystery of the Whispering Mummy, Robert Arthur
Mystery of the Green Ghost, Robert Arthur, 1965
Mystery of the Vanishing Treasure, Robert Arthur, 1966
Secret of Skeleton Island, Robert Arthur, 1966
Mystery of the Fiery Eye, Robert Arthur, 1967
Mystery of the Silver Spider, Robert Arthur, 1967
Mystery of the Screaming Clock, Robert Arthur, 1968
Mystery of the Moaning Cave, William Arden, 1968
Mystery of the Talking Skull, Robert Arthur, 1969
Mystery of the Laughing Shadow, William Arden, 1969
Secret of the Crooked Cat, William Arden, 1970
Mystery of the Coughing Dragon, Nick West, 1970
Mystery of the Flaming Footprints, M. V. Carey, 1971
Mystery of the Singing Serpent, Carey, 1972
Mystery of the Shrinking House, Arden, 1972
Mystery of Monster Mountain, Carey, 1973
Secret of Phantom Lake, Arden, 1973
Secret of the Haunted Mirror, Carey, 1974
Mystery of the Dead Man's Riddle, Arden, 1974
Mystery of the Invisible Dog, Carey, 1975
Mystery of Death Trap Mine, Carey, 1976
Mystery of the Dancing Devil, Arden, 1976
Mystery of the Headless Horse, Arden, 1977
Mystery of the Magic Circle, Carey, 1978
Mystery of the Deadly Double, Arden, 1978
Mystery of the Sinister Scarecrow, Carey, 1979

Secret of Shark Reef, Arden, 1979
Mystery of the Scar-Faced Beggar, Carey, 1981
Mystery of the Blazing Cliffs, Carey, 1981
Mystery of the Purple Pirate, Arden, 1982
Mystery of the Wandering Cave Man, Carey, 1982
Mystery of the Kidnapped Whale, Marc Brandel, 1983
Mystery of the Missing Mermaid, Carey, 1983
Mystery of the Two-Toed Pigeon, Brandel, 1984
Mystery of the Smashing Glass, Arden, 1984
Mystery of the Trail of Terror, Carey, 1984
Mystery of the Rogues' Reunion, Brandel, 1985
Mystery of the Creep-Show Crooks, Carey, 1985
Mystery of Wreckers' Rock, Arden, 1986
Mystery of the Cranky Collector, Carey, 1987

More: Three Investigators Crimebusters Series, the boys are now teenagers and continue to solve crimes, ca. 1989 – 1990 in pictorial hardcovers published by Knopf, and library editions by Random House, as well as paperback editions. Hardcovers: $15.00

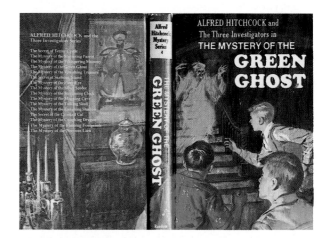

ALFRED HITCHCOCK ANTHOLOGIES, 1960s Random House, oversize illustrated hardcover, illustrated endpapers, 200+ pages, two-color illustrations, collections of short stories by noted mystery writers matching the title theme. ($20.00 with dust jacket) $10.00

Alfred Hitchcock's Haunted Houseful, 1961
Alfred Hitchcock's Ghostly Gallery, 1962
Alfred Hitchcock's Monster Museum, 1965
Alfred Hitchcock's Sinister Spies, 1966
Alfred Hitchcock's Spellbinders in Suspense, 1967
Alfred Hitchcock's Daring Detectives, 1969

ALGER BOOKS, Horatio Alger Jr. (1834 – 1899). Alger's first published work appeared in 1856, and new titles continued even after his death. Many of the titles originally published between 1900 and 1908 were written by Edward Stratemeyer, who later created his own profitable syndicate of boys and girls series books. Alger wrote both series and individual titles. The value varies depending on the presentation of the book (the more elaborate the binding and illustrations, the greater the appeal to many collectors); the printing (first printings can command double to triple the price of early editions); and the rarity of the title. Nineteenth century wrappers (dust jackets) also add considerably to the desirablity of the book.

Loring of Boston published most of Alger's earliest titles, 1860s through 1870s, with other publishers printing his books after 1880. Points for first editions are discussed in *First Printings of American Authors v5*, edited by Philip Eppard (Gale Research 1987) with additional research available through the Alger Society.

Alger books, Bound to Win Series, 1930s edition Grosset, illustrated by Ernest Townsend. $10.00

Phil Hardy's Struggle

Phil Hardy's Triumph

Alger books, Boy's Own Library, 1880s Burt, books generally dated by collectors through advertisements and publisher's address rather than copyright dates. Early editions $100.00, later editions, $20.00

Tom Temple's Career (BOL #7), 1888, publisher's address listed as 162 William St.

Errand Boy (BOL #14), 1888, publisher's address changes to 56 Beekman St.

Alger books, Boy's One At A Time Library, 1880s Aldine (London), British pirated editions of Alger's titles reprinted in this series, published without crediting the author. See also Garfield Library. RARE

Alger books, Brave and Bold Series, 1870s Loring, first editions generally dated by books appearing in advertisments. Early editions $150.00, later editions $50.00

1890s Winston editions, illustrated $20.00

1900s Street & Smith editions, originally sold for a nickel. Several titles also reprinted in Medal Library. RARE

Brave and Bold, 1874, title listed as "Bold and Brave" in first printing, corrected in later editions.

Jack's Ward, 1875

Shifting for Himself, 1876, next title listed as "Work and Hope" in first edition and corrected in later editions.

Wait and Hope, 1877

Alger books, Campaign Series, 1890s Winston, small size, illustrated $20.00

Frank's Campaign

Charlie Codman's Cruise

Paul Prescott's Charge

Alger books, Frank and Fearless Series, 1890s Winston, small size, illustrated $20.00

Frank Hunter's Peril

Frank and Fearless

Young Salesman

Alger books, Garfield Library, 1880s Aldine (London), British pirated editions of Alger's titles appeared in this series. RARE

Alger books, Go Ahead Series, 1880s Porter & Coates, Philadelphia. In 1888, the price for series

was shown as $3.75 per book. Later advertisements show increases to $4.50 per book. Collectors also use title lists in the advertisements to date books. Early editions $125.00, later editions $50.00

Alger books, Good Fortune Library Series, 1890s Winston, small size, illustrated $20.00

Alger books, Leather Clad Tales, 1890s United States Book Company, first publication of many Alger stories and some Alger stories written under the pseudonym of Arthur Lee Putnam. RARE

Alger books, Luck and Pluck Series, Second Luck and Pluck Series, 1860s – 1870s Loring, first appearance of these titles. First editions generally identified by advertisements announcing the next book in series. Early editions $150.00, later editions $50.00

1890s Winston editions, small size, illustrated $20.00

Luck and Pluck, 1869, first printing lists only this title in series.

Sink or Swim, 1870

Strong and Steady, 1871, ads announce Strive (1872) and Phil (1872). Early editions have five full-page illustrations plus frontispiece. Later editions had four illustrations.

Strive and Succeed, 1872

Try and Trust, 1873, earliest editions have four illustrations, later editions had three.

Bound to Rise, 1873

Risen from the Ranks, 1874

Herbert Carter's Legacy, 1875

Alger books, Medal Library, 1900s Street & Smith, small size, dime novels with printed covers. See also *Brave and Bold*. RARE

Alger books, New World Series, 1890s Winston, small size, illustrated $20.00

Digging Gold

Facing the World

In a New World

Alger books, Pacific Series (reprinted as Young Adventurers, Winston), 1870s Loring. First printings identified through advertisements. Early editions $150.00, later editions $50.00, Winston editions $25.00

Young Adventurer, 1878

Young Miner, 1879

Young Explorer, 1880

Alger books, Ragged Dick Series, Second Ragged Dick Series, 1868 – 1870 Loring, first appearance of these titles. First editions generally identified by advertisements announcing the next book in series. Early editions $150.00, later printings $50.00 (see exceptions below).

1890s Winston editions, small size, illustrated $15.00

Ragged Dick: or Street Life in New York with the Boot-Blacks, 1868 Loring. First edition ad announces *Fame and Fortune* to be published next. First series book written by Alger. First printing RARE, early printings $750.00, later printings $75.00

Fame and Fortune, 1868 Loring, advertisement

announces Mark (May 1869) and Rough (Dec 1869).

Mark the Match Boy, 1869
Rough and Ready, 1869
Ben the Luggage Boy, 1870
Rufus and Rose, 1870

Alger books, Tattered Tom Series, Second Tattered Tom Series, 1870s Loring, original publication of these titles. Most first printings identified through advertisments. Early printings, $150.00, later editions $50.00

Early Winston edition, small size, illustrated $15.00
Tattered Tom, 1871
Paul the Peddler, 1872
Phil the Fiddler, 1872
Slow and Sure, 1872
Julius, 1874
Young Outlaw, 1875
Sam's Chance, 1876
Telegraph Boy, 1879

Alger books, Victory Series, early Winston edition, small size, illustrated $20.00

Alger books, ca. 1930 Whitman, small paper-over-board hardcover with wraparound illustration and cloth spine, b/w illustrated endpapers. $20.00

1907 Federal, 1910 NY Book

Whitman editions

ALICE AND JERRY READERS Row, Peterson and Co., ca. 1930s – 1940s, illustrated hardcover school readers for early grades, color illustrations. Less popular than the Dick and Jane readers, the Alice and Jerry books and workbooks can usually be purchased in the $15.00 to $25.00 range.

ALL ABOUT BOOKS, Random House, hardcover, pictorial boards, illustrations. ($15.00 with dust jacket) $10.00
All About Dinosaurs, R. C. Andrews, 1953
All About the Sea, F. Lane, 1953
All About Whales, R. C. Chapman, 1954
All About the Insect World, Lane, 1954
All About Famous Inventors and Their Inventions, Pratt, 1955
All About our Changing Rocks, White, 1955
All About the Flowering World, Lane, 1956
All About Moths and Butterflies, Lemmon, 1953
All About Famous Inventors and their Inventions, Fletcher, 1955
All About Strange Beasts of the Present, Lemmon, 1957
All About Animals and Their Young, McClung, 1958
All About Monkeys, Lemmon, 1958
All About Rockets and Jets, Pratt, 1958
All About the Ice Age, Patricia Lauber, 1959
All About Fish, Carl Burger, 1960
All About Undersea Exploration, Ruth Brindze, 1960
All About Aviation, Loomis, 1964

ALL AMERICAN SPORT SERIES, Harold Sherman, ca. 1930 Goldsmith, hardcover. ($25.00 with dust jacket) $10.00
Over the Line
Down the Ice
It's a Pass
Strike Him Out
Interference and Other Football Stories

ALL-OF-A-KIND FAMILY SERIES, Sidney Taylor, various publishers and illustrators. Early printings: ($75.00 with dust jacket) $20.00
All-of-a-Kind Family, 1951 Wilcox and Follett, illustrated by Helen John
More All-of-a-Kind Family, 1954 Wilcox, illustrated by Mary E. Stevens
All-of-a-Kind Family Uptown, 1958 Wilcox, illustrated by Mary E. Stevens
All-of-a-Kind Family Downtown, 1972, b/w illustrations by Beth and Joe Krush, oversize, 187 pages, wraparound illustration dust jacket
Ella of All-of-a-Kind Family, 1978 Dutton, illustrated by Gail Owens

ALVIN FERNALD SERIES, Clifford B. Hicks, 1970s Holt, Weekly Reader edition, illustrated hardcover, illustrated by Bill Sokol. $15.00
Marvelous Inventions of Alvin Fernald, 1960

Alvin's Secret Code, 1963 Houghton
Alvin Fernald, Foreign Trader, 1966
Alvin Fernald, Mayor for a Day, 1970
Alvin Fernald, Superweasel, 1974
Alvin's Swap Shop, 1976
Alvin Fernald, TV Anchorman, 1980
Wacky World of Alvin Fernald, 1981
Alvin Fernald, Master of a Thousand Disguises, 1986

AMELIA BEDELIA SERIES, Peggy Parish, Harper & Row, Weekly Reader Book Club, "An I Can Read Book", 64 pages, pictorial hardcover, illustrated by Fritz Siebel or Wallace Tripp. Early editions: ($35.00 with dust jacket) $20.00 Later printings: $10.00
Amelia Bedelia, 1963
Thank You, Amelia Bedelia, 1964
Amelia Bedelia and the Surprise Shower, 1969
Come Back, Amelia Bedelia, 1971
Play Ball, Amelia Bedelia, 1972
Amelia Bedelia's Family Album, 1988 Greenwillow, first edition, illustrations by Lynn Sweat, 48 pages. ($15.00 with dust jacket) $10.00

AMELIARANNE SERIES, originated by Constance Heward and illustrator Susan Pearce, 1920 – 40 McKay, London and U. S., small hardcover, color illustrations throughout. ($85.00 with dust jacket) $30.00
Ameliaranne and the Green Umbrella, 1920
Ameliaranne Keeps Shop, 1928
Ameliaranne, Cinema Star, 1929
Ameliaranne at the Circus, Margaret Gilmour, 1931 McKay
Ameliaranne at the Farm, 1937
Ameliaranne Gives a Christmas Party, 1938

Ameliaranne Camps Out, 1939
Ameliaranne Keeps School, 1940

AMERICAN ADVENTURE SERIES, Margaret Trent, 1932 Burt, hardcover, 3 titles. $10.00

AMERICAN BOYS see PAN-AMERICAN

AMERICAN BOYS SPORTS SERIES, Mark Overton, ca. 1919 Donohue, cloth-over-board cover, b/w illustrations. $15.00
Jack Winters' Baseball Team
Jack Winters' Campmates
Jack Winters' Gridiron Chums
Jack Winters' Iceboat Wonder

AMERICAN GIRLS SERIES, Mary Darling, ca. 1900 Lee & Shepard, 35 unrelated titles, hardcover. $15.00

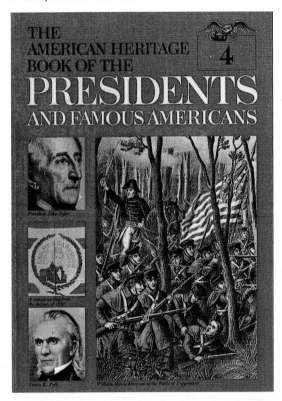

AMERICAN HERITAGE BOOK OF THE PRESIDENTS SERIES, ca. 1976 Dell, 12 volume series, oversize, glossy illustrated hardcover, color illustrated endpapers, color and b/w illustrations throughout. Each: $20.00

AMERICAN HERITAGE LANDMARK BOOKS see LANDMARK BOOKS

AMERICAN HERITAGE SERIES, Aladdin Books, hardcover. ($20.00 with dust jacket) $10.00
Titles include:
Back of Beyond, George Franklin, 1952
Wildcat, the Seminole, Electa Clark, 1956

King of the Clippers, Edmund Collier, 1955
Pirates of the Spanish Main, Hamilton Cockran, 1961

AMERICAN REGIONAL STORIES SERIES, Lois Lenski, Lippincott, hardcover, illustrated endpapers, b/w illustrations by author.
First edition: ($150.00 with dust jacket) $35.00
Later printings: ($40.00 with dust jacket) $15.00
Bayou Suzette, 1943
Strawberry Girl, 1945
Blue Ridge Billy, 1946
Judy's Journey, 1947
Boom Town Boy, 1948
Cotton in My Sack, 1949
Texas Tomboy, 1950
Prairie School, 1951
Mama Hattie's Girl, 1953
Corn-Farm Boy, 1954
San Francisco Boy, 1955
Houseboat Girl, 1957
Coal Camp Girl, 1959
Shoo-Fly Girl, 1963
To Be a Logger, 1967
Deer Valley Girl, 1968

TO BE A LOGGER
LOIS LENSKI

AMERICAN TRAIL BLAZERS see TRAIL BLAZERS

AMY AND LAURA see VERONICA GANZ

ANASTASIA KRUPNIK SERIES, Lois Lowry, Houghton, hardcover, illustrations by Diane De Groat. ($20.00 with dust jacket) $10.00
Anastasia Krupnik, 1979
Anastasia Again, 1981
Anastasia at Your Service, 1982
Anastasia, Ask Your Analyst, 1984
Anastasia on Her Own, 1985

Anastasia Has the Answers, 1986
Anastasia's Chosen Career, 1987
Anastasia at This Address, 1991
Anastasia Absolutely, 1995

ANDY BLAKE SERIES, Leo Edwards, ca. 1928 – 30 Grosset & Dunlap, illustrated by Bert Salg. ($40.00 with dust jacket) $15.00
Andy Blake
Andy Blake's Comet Coaster
Andy Blake's Secret Service
Andy Blake and the Pot of Gold

ANDY LANE FLIGHT SERIES, Eustace Adams, 1928 – 1932 Grosset & Dunlap. Andy and his dog Scotty, fly with friends Sam and Sonny in this early air adventure series. ($25.00 with dust jacket) $10.00
Fifteen Days in the Air
Over the Polar Ice
Racing Around the World
Runaway Airship
Pirates of the Air
On the Wings of Flame
Mysterious Monoplane
Flying Windmill
Plane Without a Pilot
Wings of Adventure
Across the Top of the World
Prisoners of the Clouds

ANGELA BRAZIL BOOKS FOR GIRLS, Angela Brazil, ca. 1915 Burt, hardcover, "for girls 12 to 16." ($20.00 with dust jacket) $10.00
Luckiest Girl in School
Princess of the School
Popular Schoolgirl
Jolliest School of All
Marjorie's Best Year
Schoolgirl Kitty

ANGUS THE DOG SERIES, Marjorie Flack (1897 – 1958)
Angus and the Cat, 1931 Doubleday, 32 pages, illustrations by author $40.00
Angus and the Ducks, 1930 Doubleday, color illustrations by author $45.00
Angus Lost, 1932 Doubleday, 32 pages, illustrations by author $40.00

ANN BARTLETT SERIES, Martha Johnson, ca. 1940s Crowell, adventures of a Navy nurse, hardcover. ($40.00 with dust jacket) $15.00
Ann Bartlett: Navy Nurse
Ann Bartlett at Bataan
Ann Bartlett in the South Pacific
Ann Bartlett Returns to the Philippines

ANN STERLING SERIES, Harriet Grove, 1926 Burt, seven books, "stories of ranch life." ($15.00 with dust jacket) $10.00

Ann Sterling
Courage of Ann
Ann and the Jolly Six
Ann Crosses a Secret Trail
Ann's Search Rewarded
Ann's Ambitions
Ann's Sterling Heart

ANNA SERIES, Judith Kerr, Coward McCann, hardcover, b/w illustrations by author. ($25.00 with dust jacket) $10.00
When Hitler Stole Pink Rabbit, 1971
Other Way Around, 1975
Small Person Far Away, 1978

ANNAPOLIS SERIES see DICK PRESCOTT

ANNE SHIRLEY SERIES (see also EMILY), L. M. Montgomery, novels for girls, written as individual novels with a continuing character by the same author, originally published in U. S. by L. C. Page, Boston, hardcover, paste-on pictorial, gilt lettering on some titles, illustrators include Geoge Gibbs and Maria Kirk. Page first editions: $250.00 Early reprints: $50.00
Burt hardcover with paste-on-pictorial early reprints: $50.00
Grosset & Dunlap pictorial hardcover reprints: $10.00
Anne of Green Gables, 1908
Anne of Avonlea, 1909
Chronicles of Avonlea, 1912
Anne of the Island, 1915
Anne's House of Dreams, 1917
Further Chronicles of Avonlea, 1920
Anne of Windy Poplars, 1936
Anne of Ingleside, 1939

ANNETTE see WALT DISNEY

ANNIE OAKLEY, Doris Schroeder, Whitman. This series is based on the TV series about the famous sharpshooter, wraparound color illustration on laminated hardcover (laminate tends to peel), illustrated endpapers, two-color illustrations throughout by Tony Sgroi and Harlan Young. $10.00

Annie Oakley in Danger at Diablo, 1955
Annie Oakley in Ghost Town Secret, 1957
Annie Oakley in Double Trouble, 1958

ANNUALS, these are usually large volumes containing collections of stories, articles, games, illustrations, originally printed in magazines and put together in a yearly hardcover edition. Annuals are especially popular in UK, still in production, and often feature popular TV cartoon stories or comic strip characters.
Typical examples include:
Australian Children's Annual, 1960s Angus and Robertson, Sydney, first edition, oversize, color and b/w plates plus text illustrations, approximately 180+ pages. ($85.00 in dust jacket)
Chatterbox, first published in the mid-1800s, at various times published by 4 or 5 different publishers in UK, NY, Boston, and Chicago. *Chatterbox* was a gathering of materials from a children's magazine, put out sometimes as an annual, sometimes as a quarterly. Oversize brown hardcovers with paste-on-pictorial, color and b/w illustrations. Prices range all over the map because price really depends on condition, and most are in very poor condition. $20.00 to $80.00
Chummy Books, undated ca. 1915 – 20 Sully and Kleinteich, NY, oversize, color illustrated paper-over-board cover, 300+ pages, annual, collected stories, poems, large print, 12 color plates plus b/w illustrations. $45.00 each
Herbert Strang's Annual, early 20th century, oversize volumes with paste-on-pictorial covers, 200+ pages, color endpapers and frontispiece, b/w

and color illustrations. $25.00 each

St. Nicholas Magazine was founded ca. 1870 by Scribner's as an illustrated magazine for children, and its first editor was Mary Mapes Dodge, author of *Hans Brinker*. It published work by a wide selection of writers, some famous at the time, some who went on to fame, including Edna St. Vincent Millay, Emily Dickinson, Louisa May Alcott, Rudyard Kipling, and Jack London. The magazine was bound into annuals, with cloth hardcovers and paste-on-pictorial covers. $30.00 to $50.00

Tiny Tots Annual, Amalgamated Press, London, color illustrated paper-over-board cover, oversize, about 134 pages, collection of stories, articles, poems, games, connected to *Little Folks* magazine, color and b/w illustrations throughout. $45.00

APPLE MARKET STREET SERIES, Betsy Mabel Hill, author-illustrator, 1934 – 43 Stokes and Lippincott, b/w and color illustrations by author.
Early printings, plain cover: ($40.00 with dust jacket) $15.00
Early printings with paste-on-pictorial: $35.00
Judy Jo's Magic Island, 1953
Along Comes Judy-Jo, 1943
Down Along Apple Market Street, 1934
Surprise for Judy-Jo, 1939
Judy Jo's Winter in Ducklight Cove, 1951
Snowed In Family, 1951

ARMY BOY SERIES, Charles Kilbourne, 1913 – 16 Penn, hardcover. $30.00
Army Boy in Pekin, 1912
Army Boy in the Philippines, 1913
Army Boy in Mexico, 1914
Army Boy in Alaska, 1915

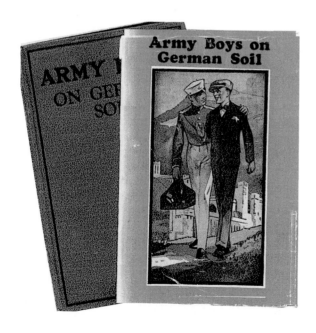

ARMY BOYS SERIES, Homer Randall, ca. 1920 World, hardcover, b/w frontispiece, illustrated by Robert Gaston Herbert. ($30.00 with dust jacket) $15.00
Army Boys in France
Army Boys in the French Trenches
Army Boys on the Firing Line
Army Boys in the Big Drive
Army Boys Marching into Germany
Army Boys on German Soil

ARTHUR SERIES, Alan Coren, ca. 1970s Little, Brown Weekly Reader editions, pictorial hardcover, two-color illustrations throughout by John Astrop. Tales of a boy dropped into well-known historical or fictional problems which he solves by wit and humor. $10.00
Railroad Arthur
Arthur the Kid
Buffalo Arthur
Lone Arthur
Klondike Arthur
Arthur's Last Stand

AUGUSTUS SERIES, Le Grand (Henderson), 1940s Bobbs Merrill, oversize, about 130 pages, pictorial endpapers, three-color illustrations by author. ($35.00 with dust jacket) $25.00
Reprints by Grosset, oversize, about 130 pages, pictorial endpapers, b/w illustrations. ($25.00 with dust jacket) $15.00
Augustus and the River, 1939
Augustus Goes South, 1940
Augustus and the Mountains, 1941
Augustus Helps the Navy, 1942
Augustus Helps the Army, 1943
Augustus Helps the Marines, 1943
Augustus Flies, 1944
Augustus Drives a Jeep, 1944
Augustus Saves a Ship, 1945
Augustus Hits the Road, 1946
Augustus Rides the Border, 1947
Augustus and the Desert, 1948

AUNT JANE'S NIECES, Edith Van Dyne (L. Frank Baum), novels for girls, created as a series for Reilly, Chicago, and Copp Clark, Canada, small size, cloth covers, impressed and color paste-on cover illustration, illustrations E. A. Nelson. Firsts are usually identified by list-to-self method, with book being the last title listed on advertising page.

Firsts: ($150.00 with dust jacket) $55.00
Later editions: ($60.00 with dust jacket) $25.00
Aunt Jane's Nieces, 1906
Aunt Jane's Nieces Abroad, 1906
Aunt Jane's Nieces at Millville, 1908
Aunt Jane's Nieces at Work, 1909
Aunt Jane's Nieces in Society, 1910
Aunt Jane's Nieces and Uncle John, 1911
Aunt Jane's Nieces on Vacation, 1912
Aunt Jane's Nieces on the Ranch, 1913
Aunt Jane's Nieces Out West, 1914
Aunt Jane's Nieces in the Red Cross, 1915

AUSTIN BOYS SERIES, Ken Anderson, 1940s – 50s Zondervan, hardcover. $10.00
Austin Boys
Austin Boys Marooned
Austin Boys Adrift

AUSTIN CHRONICLES, Madeleine L'Engle, hardcover novels that fall between real world adventures and fantasy. The first title was first published by Vanguard. The other titles were first published by Farrar, and all have been reprinted by Farrar.
Meet the Austins, 1960 Vanguard, first edition: ($50.00 with dust jacket) $15.00
Moon by Night, 1963, first edition: ($100.00 with dust jacket) $20.00
Twenty-Four Days before Christmas, 1964, first, red hardcover, color illustrations by Inge. ($100.00 with dust jacket) $20.00
Young Unicorns, 1968, first: ($50.00 with dust jacket) $15.00
Ring of Endless Light, 1980, first: ($50.00 with dust jacket) $15.00
Austin Chronicles, related books, O'Keefe Family Chronicles, Farrar, hardcover, generally categorized as fantasy. Crossover characters appear in the O'Keefe and Austin Chronicles, later printings: ($20.00 with dust jacket) $10.00
Wrinkle in Time, 1962
Wind in the Door, 1973
Swiftly Tilting Planet, 1978
Many Waters, 1986

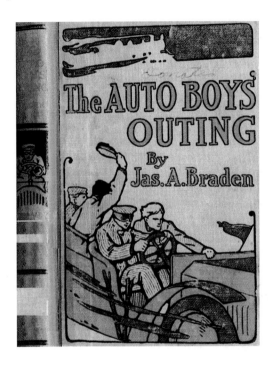

AUTO BOYS SERIES, James A. Braden, ca. 1908 – 1927 Saalfield, printed illustration on tan cloth hardcover, b/w frontispiece by Arthur DeBebian. ($25.00 with dust jacket) $15.00
Auto Boys
Auto Boys' Adventure
Auto Boys' Outing
Auto Boys' Race
Auto Boys' Quest
Auto Boys' Camp
Auto Boys' Vacation
Auto Boys' Big Six
Auto Boys' Mystery
Auto Boys on the Road

AUTOMOBILE GIRLS SERIES, Laura Crane, 1910 Altemus, 6 books ($30.00 with dust jacket) $10.00
Automobile Girls at Newport
Automobile Girls in the Berkshires
Automobile Girls Along the Hudson
Automobile Girls at Chicago

Automobile Girls at Palm Beach
Automobile Girls at Washington

AVIATOR SERIES, Captain Frank Cobb, ca. 1927 Saalfield, impressed illustration on cloth-over-board cover, frontispiece illustration. ($20.00 with dust jacket) $10.00
Battling the Clouds, or For the Comrade's Honor
Aviator's Luck, or The Camp Knox Pilot
Dangerous Deeds, or Flight in the Dirigible

AVIATOR SERIES see BILL BRUCE

AZOR BOOKS, Maude Crowley, Oxford and Walck, small hardcover, about 70 pages, b/w illustrations by Helen Sewell.
First editions: ($50.00 with dust jacket) $20.00
Later editions: ($30.00 with dust jacket) $10.00
Azor, 1948
Azor and the Haddock, 1949
Azor and the Blue Eyed Cow, 1951
Tor and Azor, 1955, illustrated by Veronica Reed

———— **B** ————

BABS SERIES, Alice Colver, 1917 Penn Publishing, hardcover, illustrations by Donaldson. ($25.00 with dust jacket) $10. 00
Babs
Babs at College
Babs at Birchwood

BAGTHORPES SERIES, Helen Cresswell, Macmillan, hardcover, humorous tales of an eccentric family with an "ordinary" son. ($35.00 with dust jacket by Trina Schart Hyman) $15.00
Ordinary Jack, 1977
Absolute Zero, 1978
Bagthorpes Unlimited, 1978
Bagthorpes vs. the World, 1979
Bagthorpes Abroad, 1984
Bagthorpes Haunted, 1985
Bagthorpes Liberated, 1989
Bagthorpes Triangle, 1993

BANNER BOY SCOUTS SERIES, George Warren, ca. 1912 Cupples & Leon, hardcover with impressed design, some with gilt lettering. ($20.00 with dust jacket) $15.00
Banner Boy Scouts
Banner Boy Scouts on Tour
Banner Boy Scouts Afloat
Banner Boy Scouts Snowbound

BANNER CAMPFIRE GIRLS SERIES, Julianne DeVries, 1933 World, hardcover, 6 titles. ($20.00 with dust jacket) $10.00
Banner Campfire Girls as Detectives

Banner Campfire Girls Flying Around the Globe
Banner Campfire Girls as Federal Investigators
Banner Campfire Girls at the White House
Banner Campfire Girls on Caliban Island
Banner Campfire Girls at Holly House

BARBARA HALE see GARIS

BARBIE BOOKS, Cynthia Lawrence and Bette Lou Maybee, stories based on the Mattel Barbie doll.
Barbie's New York Summer, 1962 Random House, first edition, small hardcover. ($35.00 with dust jacket) $15.00
World of Barbie, 1962 Random House, first edition, pictorial hardcover, illustrated by Clyde Smith. $35.00
Barbie and Ken, 1963 Random House, pictorial hardcover, illustrated by Clyde Smith. $25.00
Here's Barbie, 1963 Random House, first edition, 3-in-1 hardcover, 186 pages, illustrated. $35.00
Barbie Solves a Mystery, 1963 Random House, hardcover, illustrations by Clyde Smith. $15.00
Barbie, Midge and Ken, 1964 Random House, illustrated by Robert Patterson. $25.00
Barbie Books, Little Golden Books: $5.00
Barbie, Betty Biesterveld, 1974
Superstar Barbie, Anne Foster, 1977

BARKHAM STREET SERIES, M. S. Stolz, Harper, hardcover, humorous b/w illustrations by Leonard Shorthall. ($20.00 with dust jacket) $10.00
Dog on Barkham Street, 1960
Bully on Barkham Street, 1963
Explorer of Barkham Street, 1984

BARNEY JUNIOR MYSTERY SERIES, Enid Blyton, ca. 1950 – 70s Collins Adventure Library reprints, hardcover, illustrations by Gilbert Dunlop. ($20.00 with dust jacket) $10.00
Rockingdown Mystery
Rilloby Fair Mystery
Ring O'Bells Mystery
Rubadub Mystery
Rat-A-Tat Mystery
Ragamuffin Mystery

BARTON BOOKS, May Hollis Barton (Stratemeyer Syndicate pseudonym), ca. 1920 Cupples & Leon, small size, cloth cover stamped in color. $10.00
Girl from the Country
Three Girl Chums at Laurel Hall
Nell Grayson's Ranching Days
Four Little Women of Roxby
Plain Jane and Pretty Betty

BASEBALL JOE SERIES, Lester Chadwick (pseudonym of Edward Stratemeyer), Cupples & Leon, gray hardcover with red/black printed illustration and lettering, 4 b/w plates.

Early editions, titles through *Home Run King*: ($65.00 with dust jacket) $25.00
Early editions, titles after *Home Run King*: ($150.00 with dust jacket) $35.00
Later editions: ($50.00 with dust jacket) $15.00
Baseball Joe of the Silver Stars, 1912
Baseball Joe on the School Nine, 1912
Baseball Joe at Yale, 1913
Baseball Joe in the Central League, 1914
Baseball Joe in the Big League, 1915
Baseball Joe on the Giants, 1916
Baseball Joe in the World Series, 1917
Baseball Joe around the World, 1918
Baseball Joe: Home Run King, 1922
Baseball Joe: Saving the League, 1923
Baseball Joe: Captain of the Team, 1924
Baseball Joe: Champion of the League, 1925
Baseball Joe: Club Owner, 1926
Baseball Joe: Pitching Wizard, 1928

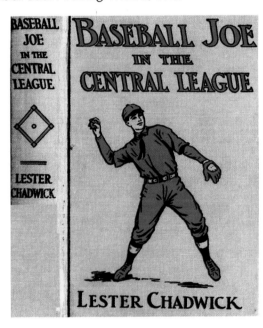

BASKETBALL SERIES, Harold M. Sherman, first two titles published by Appleton, third title and reprints by Grosset & Dunlap, hardcover. $45.00

BASTABLES see TREASURE SEEKERS

BATTLESHIP BOYS SERIES, Frank Patchin, ca. 1911 Saalfield, hardcover, b/w illustrations, usually a frontispiece and two or three additional full-page b/w illustrations. The illustrations appear to be the work of John Neill, illustrator of the Oz books, though they are unsigned, which gives the books collectible value for Neill and Oz collectors.
Silver cloth-over-board hardcover: $25.00
Gray, blue, green, purple and brown hardcovers: ($25.00 with dust jacket) $15.00
Battleship Boys at Sea
Battleship Boys in Foreign Service

Battleship Boys' First Step Upward
Battleship Boys on the Sky Patrol

BAUM BOOKS, L. Frank Baum. Baum wrote numerous series under pseudonyms, as well as his famous Oz books. Those series that are real world adventures rather than stories set in fantasy lands can be found in this volume under the following listings:
AUNT JANE'S NIECES, pseudonym Edith Van Dyne
BOY FORTUNE HUNTERS (including the SAM STEELE books), pseudonym Floyd Akers
MARY LOUISE, pseudonym Edith Van Dyne
Baum Books, Daring Series, L. Frank Baum, written under his own name, hardcover with printed illustration on cloth. Dust jacket is RARE. Hardcover without dust jacket: $250.00
Daring Twins, 1911
Phoebe Daring, 1912

BEANY MALONE SERIES, Lenora Mattingly Weber, Crowell, hardcover. These hard-to-find books are favorites of those who read them as teenagers in the 1950s. First edition with dust jacket: $225.00
Later printings: ($50.00 with dust jacket) $25.00
Meet the Malones, 1943
Beany Malone, 1948
Leave it to Beany!, 1950
Beany and the Beckoning Road, 1952
Beany Has a Secret Life, 1955
Make a Wish for Me, 1956
Happy Birthday, Dear Beany, 1957
More the Merrier, 1958
Bright Star Falls, 1959
Welcome Stranger, 1960
Pick a New Dream, 1961

Tarry Awhile, 1962
Something Borrowed, Something Blue, 1963
Come Back, Wherever You Are, 1969
Related title:
Beany Malone Cookbook, 1972

BELL HAVEN SERIES, George Barton (1866 – 1940), 1914 John C. Winston, sports series covering baseball, basketball, etc., hardcover, illustrated by Charles Paxon Gray. $25.00
Bell Haven Eight, 1914
Bell Haven Nine, 1914
Bell Haven Five, 1915
Bell Haven Eleven, 1915

BERT WILSON SERIES, J. W. Duffield, ca. 1910 – 1915 Sully & Kleintech, hardcover with gilt, four b/w plates. $35.00
Ca. 1924 Western Printing reprints: ($30.00 with dust jacket) $10.00
Bert Wilson at the Wheel, 1913
Bert Wilson, Wireless Operator, 1913
Bert Wilson's Fadeaway Ball, 1913
Bert Wilson, Marathon Winner, 1913
Bert Wilson at Panama, 1914
Bert Wilson in the Rockies, 1914
Bert Wilson on the Gridiron, 1914

BESSIE BOOKS, Joanna H. Matthews, ca. 1870s Robert Carter & Brothers, reprints by Platt & Peck Company, continuing titles by Stokes, hardcover. $25.00

Bessie
Bessie in the City
Bessie's Friends
Bessie in the Mountains
Bessie on Her Travels

BETH ANNE SERIES, Mary Pemberton Ginther, ca. 1916 – 1920 Penn, hardcover, illustrations by author, 4 books. $35.00
Beth Anne Herself
Beth Anne Really-for-Truly
Beth Anne's New Cousin
Beth Anne Goes to School

BETSY HALE SERIES, Mary Pemberton Ginther, ca. 1920s Winston, hardcover, illustrations by author. $35.00
Betsy Hale
Betsy Hale Tries
Betsy Hale Succeeds

BETSY SERIES, (also see EDDIE), Carolyn Haywood, Harcourt Brace, cloth-over-board oversize cover, illustrated endpapers, b/w illustrations by author. ($40.00 with dust jacket.) $20.00
"B" is for Betsy, 1939
Betsy and Billy, 1941
Back to School with Betsy, 1943
Betsy and the Boys, 1945
Betsy and the Circus, 1954
Snowbound with Betsy, 1962
Betsy and Mr. Kilpatrick, 1967
Merry Christmas from Betsy, 1970
Betsy's Play School, 1977

BETSY-TACY SERIES, Maud Hart Lovelace, Crowell, cloth-over-board hardcover, b/w illustrations by Lois Lenski, becoming highly collectible.
First editions: ($150.00 with dust jacket) $40.00
Early printings: ($60.00 with dust jacket) $20.00
Betsy-Tacy, 1941
Betsy-Tacy and Tib, 1941
Betsy and Tacy Go Over the Big Hill, 1942
Betsy and Tacy Go Down Town, 1943
Heaven to Betsy, 1945
Betsy in Spite of Herself, 1946
Betsy was a Junior, 1947
Betsy and Joe, 1948
Betsy-Tacy hard-to-find titles: First editions with dust jacket: $300.00 and up. Early printings: (over $100.00 with dust jacket) $50.00
Emily of Deep Valley, 1950
Betsy and the Great World, 1952, b/w illustrations by Vera Neville
Winona's Pony Cart, 1953, b/w illustrations by Vera Neville
Betsy's Wedding, 1955

BETTER LITTLE BOOKS (also see BIG LITTLE), 1930s on, Whitman Publishing, extension of Whitman's successful Big Little Books line, advertised as "Better Little Books feature your favorite characters," small, pictorial cardboard covers, b/w illustrations. Most are priced in the $20.00 to $40.00 range. See Bibliography.

BETTY SERIES, Alice Hale Burnett, New York Book Company, small size, 84 pages, color paste-on-pictorial covers, 3 color plates by Charles Lester, advertised as "40 cents postpaid" apiece. $20.00
Betty and Her Chums
Betty's Attic Theatre
Betty's Carnival
Betty's Orphans

BETTY GORDAN SERIES, Alice B. Emerson (Stratemeyer pseudonym), ca. 1920s – 1930s, Cupples & Leon, small size, hardcover. $10.00
Betty Gordan at Bramble Farm
Betty Gordan in Washington
Betty Gordan in the Land of Oil
Betty Gordan at Boarding School
Betty Gordan at Mountain Camp
Betty Gordan at Ocean Park
Betty Gordan and Her School Chums
Betty Gordan at Rainbow Ranch
Betty Gordan in the Mexican Wilds
Betty Gordan and the Lost Pearls
Betty Gordan on the Campus
Betty Gordan and the Hale Twins
Betty Gordan at Mystery Farm
Betty Gordan on No-Trail Island
Betty Gordan and the Mystery Girl

BETTY LEE SERIES, Harriet Pyne Grove, ca. 1931 World, hardcover. $10.00
Betty Lee, Freshman
Betty Lee, Sophomore
Betty Lee, Junior
Betty Lee, Senior
Betty Lee, Freshman and Betty Lee, Sophomore, 1931 World, Jumbo Books: two complete books in one, hardcover. $20.00

BETTY WALES SERIES, Margaret Warde (Edith K. Dunton), ca. 1910 – 1930 Penn, 10 titles, hardcover. $20.00
Grosset & Dunlap reprints: ($30.00 with dust jacket) $10.00
Titles include:
Betty Wales
Betty Wales, Girls and Mr. Kidd
Betty Wales, Freshman
Betty Wales, Sophomore
Betty Wales, Junior
Betty Wales, Senior

BEVERLY GRAY COLLEGE MYSTERY SERIES, Clair Blank (1915 – 1965), girl sleuth series. The first eight books were published by Burt, hardcover, illustrated endpapers, frontispiece. *World's Fair* was published only by Burt, the others were reprinted by Grosset.
1934 – 1937 Burt editions, except *World's Fair:* ($50.00 with dust jacket) $15.00
1935 Burt, *Beverly Gray at the World's Fair,* hard-to-find: ($200.00 with dust jacket) $50.00
1930s Grosset, hardcover, reprints of Burt titles: ($30.00 with dust jacket) $10.00
1930s Grosset, hardcover, new titles beginning with *Orient:* ($40.00 with dust jacket) $10.00
1940s Grosset, hardcover, new titles: ($30.00 with dust jacket) $10.00
1950 – 54 Grosset, hardcover, new titles: ($40.00 with dust jacket) $10.00
Ca. 1955, McLoughlin Clover books, glossy illustrated covers, reprints of last seven titles, plus new title *Beverly Gray's Surprise:* $15.00
Beverly Gray, Freshman, 1934
Beverly Gray, Sophomore, 1934
Beverly Gray, Junior, 1934
Beverly Gray, Senior, 1934
Beverly Gray's Career, 1935
Beverly Gray at the World's Fair, 1935 Burt, no Grosset reprint
Beverly Gray on a World Cruise, 1936
Beverly Gray in the Orient, 1937
Beverly Gray on a Treasure Hunt, 1938
Beverly Gray's Return, 1939
Beverly Gray, Reporter, 1940
Beverly Gray's Romance, 1941
Beverly Gray's Quest, 1942
Beverly Gray's Problem, 1943
Beverly Gray's Adventure, 1944
Beverly Gray's Challenge, 1945

Beverly Gray's Journey, 1946
Beverly Gray's Assignment, 1947
Beverly Gray's Mystery, 1948
Beverly Gray's Vacation, 1949
Beverly Gray's Fortune, 1950
Beverly Gray's Secret, 1951
Beverly Gray's Island Mystery, 1952
Beverly Gray's Discovery, 1953
Beverly Gray's Scoop, 1954

BIFF BREWSTER SERIES, Andy Adams (Walter B. Gibson/Maxwell Grant), ca. 1960 Grosset, blue-gray hardcover. First editions are not clearly marked, but are usually judged by title being last on title list.
Early editions: ($25.00 with dust jacket) $10.00
1960s Grosset pictorial hardcover edition, illustrated endpapers, b/w plates: $15.00
Brazilian Gold Mine Mystery, 1960
Mystery of the Chinese Ring, 1960
Hawaiian Sea Hunt Mystery, 1960.
African Ivory Mystery, 1961. First edition: $50.00 with dust jacket
Mystery of the Ambush in India, 1962. First edition: $75.00 with dust jacket
Mystery of the Tibetan Caravan, 1963. First edition: $65.00 with dust jacket

Egyptian Scarab Mystery, 1963. First edition: $65.00 with dust jacket

BIG FOUR SERIES, Ralph Henry Barbour, ca. 1905 Appleton Boys Library, 3 titles, hardcover. $15.00
Four Afoot
Four Afloat
Four in Camp

BIG LEAGUE SERIES, Burt L. Standish, ca. 1920s Barse, cloth-over-board cover with logo of baseball and player's face on front, logo of baseball on spine, b/w frontispiece. First edition with dust jacket: $100.00 Later printings: ($40.00 with dust jacket) $15.00
Lefty o' the Bush
Lefty o' the Big League
Lefty o' the Blue Stockings
Lefty o' the Training Camp
Brick King, Backstop
Making of a Big Leaguer
Courtney of the Center Garden
Covering the Look-in Corner
Lefty Locke, Pitcher-Manager
Guarding the Keystone Sack
Man on First
Lego Lamb, Southpaw
Grip of the Game
Lefty Locke, Owner
Lefty Locke Wins Out

BIG LITTLE BOOKS, Whitman, series introduced in 1933, approximately 4½" high x 3½" wide x 1½" thick, color illustrated paper-over-cardboard covers, b/w illustrations facing each page of text, stories generally based on newspaper comic strips. Generally, greatest demand is for Dick Tracy, science fiction characters such as Flash Gordon and John Carter of Mars, and for specific collector favorites such as Mickey Mouse and Tarzan. Condition affects value dramatically, and so does changing popularity with collectors of specific characters or titles. Low-end price is about $25.00, with prices ranging up to $200.00 for hard-to-find titles.

BIG RED SERIES, Jim Kjelgaard, Holiday House book club editions: hardcover, frontispiece. These popular dog stories were reprinted in several editions, some with illustrated endpapers. ($20.00 with dust jacket) $10.00
Grosset, pictorial hardcover editions: $15.00
Big Red, 1954
Irish Red, Son of Big Red, 1951
Outlaw Red, 1953

BIGGLES SERIES, Captain W.E. Johns (1893 – 1968), 1938 – 1970, 96 titles. Along with the prolific Enid Blyton and Frank Richards (see BILLY BUNTER),

Johns was one of the bestselling authors of children's series in Great Britain, with some 167 books credited to him. His longest and most popular series was Biggles, based originally on his own aviation exploits in WWI. As the series continued, Biggles moved forward in time, fighting in WWII and later running his own air company or solving aviation mysteries. Various publishers issued Biggles books, and first editions were rarely identified as such. Collectors rely on such clues as the publishers' advertisements to identify probable publication date.

Biggles book were issued by various publishers, including Hodder & Stoughton, Oxford, Brockhampton, Dean, Thames, or Marks and Spencer. Johns continued to write new books until his death in 1968, while working on the uncompleted *Biggles Does Some Homework*, the book in which Biggles was supposed to retire.

Probable first editions: ($50.00 with dust jacket) $15.00
Later editions: ($25.00 with dust jacket) $10.00
Dean laminated pictorial hardcovers, probable first editions of later 1960s titles: $35.00
Dean pictorial hardcovers, other editions: $10.00

Camels Are Coming, 1932
Cruise of the Condor, 1933
Biggles of the Camel Squadron, 1934
Biggles Flies Again, 1934
Biggles Learns to Fly, 1935
Black Peril, 1935
Biggles Flies East, 1935
Biggles Hits the Trail, 1935
Biggles in France, 1935
Biggles & Co., 1936
Biggles in Africa, 1936
Biggles: Air Commodore, 1937
Biggles Flies West, 1937
Biggles Flies South, 1938
Biggles Goes to War, 1938
Rescue Flight, 1939
Biggles in Spain, 1939
Biggles Flies North, 1939
Biggles: Secret Agent, 1940
Biggles in the Baltic, 1940
Biggles in the South Seas, 1940
Biggles Defies the Swastika, 1941
Biggles Sees It Through, 1941
Spitfire Parade, 1941
Biggles in the Jungle, 1942
Biggles Sweeps the Desert, 1942
Biggles: Charter Pilot, 1943
Biggles in Borneo, 1943
Biggles Fails to Return, 1943
Biggles in the Orient, 1945
Biggles Delivers the Goods, 1946
Sergeant Bigglesworth CID, 1947
Biggles' Second Case, 1948
Biggles Hunts Big Game, 1948
Biggles Takes a Holiday, 1948

Biggles Breaks the Silence, 1949
Biggles Gets His Men, 1950
Another Job for Biggles, 1951
Biggles Goes to School, 1951
Biggles Works It Out, 1952
Biggles Takes the Case, 1952
Biggles Follows On, 1952
Biggles, Air Detective, 1952
Biggles and the Black Raider, 1953
Biggles in the Blue, 1953
Biggles in the Gobi, 1953
Biggles of the Special Air Police, 1953
Biggles Cuts It Fine, 1954
Biggles and the Pirate Treasure, 1954
Biggles Foreign Legionnaire, 1954
Biggles Pioneer Airfighter, 1954
Biggles in Australia, 1955
Biggles' Chinese Puzzle, 1955
Biggles of 266, 1956
No Rest for Biggles, 1956
Biggles Takes Charge, 1956
Biggles Makes Ends Meet, 1957
Biggles of the Interpol, 1957
Biggles on the Home Front, 1957
Biggles Presses On, 1958
Biggles on Mystery Island, 1958
Biggles Buries a Hatchet, 1958
Biggles in Mexico, 1959
Biggles' Combined Operation, 1959
Biggles at the World's End, 1959
Biggles and the Leopards of Zinn, 1960
Biggles Goes Home, 1960
Biggles and the Poor Rich Boy, 1960
Biggles Forms a Syndicate, 1961
Biggles and the Missing Millionaire, 1961
Biggles Goes Alone, 1962
Orchids for Biggles, 1962
Biggles Sets a Trap, 1962
Biggles Takes It Rough, 1963
Biggles Takes a Hand, 1963
Biggles' Special Case, 1963
Biggles and the Plane That Disappeared, 1963
Biggles Flies to Work, 1963
Biggles and the Lost Sovereigns, 1964
Biggles and the Black Mask, 1964
Biggles Investigates, 1964
Biggles Looks Back, 1965
Biggles and the Plot That Failed, 1965
Biggles and the Blue Moon, 1965
Biggles Scores a Bull, 1965
Biggles in the Terai, 1966
Biggles and the Gun Runners, 1966
Biggles Sorts It Out, 1967
Biggles and the Dark Intruder, 1967
Biggles and the Penitent Thief, 1967
Biggles and the Deep Blue Sea, 1967
Boy Biggles, 1968
Biggles in the Underworld, 1968
Biggles and the Little Green God, 1969

Biggles and the Noble Lord, 1969

Biggles Sees Too Much, 1970

Biggles related titles, fiction:

Biggles Breaks the Silence, Brockhampton Press, ca. 1960, W.E. Johns. Small (48 pages). Illustrated by "Kay." Hardcover:($25.00 with dust jacket) $12.00

Daily Mail Boy's Annual, John Bellamy, editor, ca. 1950s, hardcover collections of stories printed in the boy's magazine. Editions with "Biggles" stories: ($30.00 with dust jacket) $12.00

Biggles, related books, nonfiction:

Biggles Book of Heroes, 1959 Max Parrish, (with dust jacket $85.00) $40.00

Biggles Book of Treasure Hunting, 1962 Max Parrish, very hard to find, (one dealer listed this as $200.00 in 2001).

Biggles Omnibuses, collections of short stories originally published in magazines, or later collections of various out-of-print books. Various publishers.

Biggles Omnibus, 1938 Oxford University Press, RARE

Biggles Flying Omnibus, 1940 Oxford University Press, RARE

Third Biggles Omnibus, 1941 Oxford University Press, RARE

First Biggles Omnibus, 1953 Hodder & Stoughton, $35.00

Biggles Air Detective Omnibus, 1956 Hodder & Stoughton, $35.00

Biggles Adventure Omnibus, 1965, $25.00

Bumper Biggles, 1983, Chancellor Press (with dust jacket $20.00) $10.00

Best of Biggles, 1985, Chancellor Press, pictorial hardcover $20.00

Biggles Omnibus, 1994, Cresset (with dust jacket $15.00) $5.00

Biggles reprints, ca. 1950 – 1970, titles originally issued prior to 1950. Various publishers including Hodder & Stoughton, who took over from Oxford University Press in the 1940s (Oxford also continued to reprint titles that they had first issued). Other publishers include Brockhampton, Dean, Thames, or Marks and Spencer. Hardcover: ($25.00 with dust jacket) $10.00

BILL BERGSON SERIES, Astrid Lindgren, Viking, hardcover, illustrations by Don Freeman. ($35.00 with dust jacket) $15.00

Bill Bergson, Master Detective, 1952

Bill Bergson Lives Dangerously, 1954

Bill Bergson and the White Rose, 1965

BILL BOLTON AVIATION SERIES, Lt. Noel Sainsbury, Jr., ca. 1933 Goldsmith, hardcover, about 250 pages. ($20.00 with dust jacket) $15.00

Bill Bolton and Hidden Danger

Bill Bolton and the Flying Fish

Bill Bolton, Flying Midshipman

Bill Bolton and Winged Cartwheels

BILL BRUCE AVIATOR SERIES, Maj. Henry H. Arnold "of the U.S. Army Air Corps," ca. 1928 Burt, hardcover with print illustration, "for boys 12 to 16 years." ($25.00 with dust jacket) $15.00

Bill Bruce and the Pioneer Aviators

Bill Bruce, the Flying Cadet

Bill Bruce Becomes an Ace

Bill Bruce on Border Patrol

Bill Bruce in the Trans-Continental Race

Bill Bruce on Forest Patrol

BILLABONG SERIES, Mary Grant Bruce (1878 – 1927), 1910 – 1942 Ward Lock Publishers, hardcover. Fifteen fictional novels based on the author's memories of childhood in Australia. These are ever-popular and reappear regularly in paperback editions.

Australian first editions, hardcover: ($80.00 with dust jacket) $25.00

London hardcover editions: ($30.00 with dust jacket) $15.00

Little Bush Maid, 1910

Mates at Billabong

Norah of Billabong, 1913

From Billabong to London

Jim and Wally

Captain Jim

Back To Billabong, 1921

Billabong's Daughter

Billabong Adventures

Bill of Billabong, 1931

Billabong's Luck

Wings above Billabong, 1935

Billabong Gold, 1937

Son of Billabong, 1939

Billabong Riders, 1942

BILLIE BRADLEY SERIES, Janet D. Wheeler, ca. 1920s Cupples & Leon, small size, cloth covers, illustrations. ($25.00 with dust jacket) $10.00

Billie Bradley and Her Inheritance

Billie Bradley at Three-Towers Hall

Billie Bradley on Lighthouse Island

Billie Bradley and Her Classmates

Billie Bradley at Twin Lakes

Billie Bradley at Treasure Cove

Billie Bradley at Sun Dial Lodge

Billie Bradley and the School Mystery

Billie Bradley Winning the Trophy

BILLY BUNTER SERIES, Frank Richards (pseudonym of Charles Harold St. John Hamilton, 1876 – 1961), 1947 – 1965 Skilton or Cassells, 38 titles. Bunter stories began as magazine pieces for "The Magnet" (1908 to 1940). English publisher Skilton printed the books through 1952, after which Cassells took over the series. Another English publisher, Hawk, began printing fascimile hardcovers of early titles in the 1990s. Early editions were issued with color frontispiece and black-and-white illustrations. Illustrators included R. J. MacDonald and C.H. Chapman. Some books issued after Hamilton's death were finished by other authors. Prices in England tend to be much higher than US prices.

Billy Bunter, Charles Skilton editions, 1947 – 1952: ($35.00 with dust jacket) $15.00

Cassell hardcover reprints, ca. 1950 – 1960s, same titles: ($20.00 with dust jacket) $10.00

Billy Bunter of Greyfriars School, 1947
Billy Bunter's Banknote, 1948
Billy Bunter's Barring Out, 1948
Billy Bunter in Brazil, 1949
Billy Bunter's Christmas Party, 1949
Bessie Bunter of Cliff House School, 1949
Billy Bunter's Benefit, 1950
Billy Bunter Among the Cannibals, 1950
Billy Bunter's Postal Order, 1951
Billy Bunter Butts In, 1951
Billy Bunter and the Blue Mauritius, 1952 Skilton, harder-to-find because it is the last Skilton title, hardcover: ($60.00 with dust jacket) $20.00

Billy Bunter, Cassell, titles first published by Cassell, hardcover: Firsts with dust jacket, $30.00. Later editions: ($20.00 with dust jacket) $10.00

Billy Bunter's Beanfeast, 1952
Billy Bunter's Brainwave, 1953
Billy Bunter's First Case, 1953
Billy Bunter the Bold, 1954
Bunter Does His Best, 1954
Billy Bunter's Double, 1955
Backing Up Billy Bunter, 1955
Lord Billy Bunter, 1956
Banishing of Billy Bunter, 1956
Billy Bunter's Bolt, 1957
Billy Bunter Afloat, 1957
Billy Bunter's Bargain, 1958
Billy Bunter the Hiker, 1958
Bunter Out of Bounds, 1959
Bunter Comes for Christmas, 1959
Bunter the Bad Lad, 1960
Bunter Keeps It Dark, 1960
Billy Bunter's Treasure Hunt, 1961
Billy Bunter at Butlins, 1961
Bunter the Ventriloquist, 1961
Bunter the Caravanner, 1962
Billy Bunter's Bodyguard, 1962
Big Chief Bunter, 1963
Just Like Bunter, 1963
Bunter the Stowaway, 1964
Thanks to Bunter, 1964
Bunter the Sportsman, 1965
Bunter's Last Fling, 1965

BILLY TO-MORROW SERIES, Sarah Pratt Carr, ca. 1910 A. C. McClurg, hardcover, b/w plates by Charles Relyea. $50.00

Billy To-morrow
Billy To-morrow in Camp
Billy To-morrow Stands the Test
Billy To-morrow's Chums

BIRD BOYS SERIES see AEROPLANE BOYS

BIRDY JONES SERIES, E. W. Hildick (Edmund Wallace, b. 1925), Stackpole and Doubleday, hardcover, illustrated by Richard Rose, English teen pursues a pop music career. ($15.00 with dust jacket) $10.00

Birdy Jones, 1969
Birdy and the Group, 1969
Birdy Swings North, 1971
Birdy in Amsterdam, 1971
Birdy Jones and the New York Heads, 1974

BLACK RIDER SERIES, Saalfield reprints from Burt Company's Adventure and Mystery Series, hardcover. ($30.00 with dust jacket) $10.00

Camp of the Black Rider, Capwell Wycoff
Mystery of Lake Retreat, Capwell Wycoff
Tom Blake's Mysterious Adventure, Milton Richards

BLACK STALLION SERIES and **ISLAND STALLION SERIES,** Walter Farley, ca. 1941 – 1971 Random House, hardcover, 18 books. By the 1950s, Random House generally identified books in both of Farley's horse series as belonging to the Black Stallion series, with some novels featuring characters from both series. First editions (first printing) are clearly marked on the copyright page.

1950s first edition hardcover: ($25.00 with dust jacket) $15.00

1960s first edition hardcover: ($20.00 with dust jacket) $15.00

Later hardcover editions: ($15.00 with dust jacket) $10.00

Black Stallion, 1941, illustrations by Keith Ward

Black Stallion Returns, 1945, illustrated by Harold Eldridge

Son of Black Stallion, 1947, illustrated by Milton Menasco

Island Stallion, 1948

Black Stallion and Satan, 1949

Blood Bay Colt, 1950

Island Stallion's Fury, 1951

Black Stallion's Filly, 1952

Black Stallion Revolts, 1953

Black Stallion's Sulky Colt, 1954

Island Stallion Races, 1955

Black Stallion's Courage, 1956

Black Stallion Mystery, 1957

Horse Tamer, 1958

Black Stallion and Flame, 1960

Black Stallion Challenged, 1964

Black Stallion's Ghost, 1969

Black Stallion and the Girl, 1971

Black Stallion, related books, Farley, Random House (I Can Read Beginner Books), color endpapers and full-color illustrations by James Schucker. Hard-to-find with dust jacket. (List from $50.00 to $95.00 with dust jacket) $15.00

Little Black, a Pony, 1961

Little Black Goes to the Circus, 1963

BLACK TIGER SERIES, Patrick O'Connor (Leonard Wibberley, author of *Mouse that Roared*), Washburn, (also Hale library bindings which did not have dust jackets), hardcover. Also issued in paperback. Black Tiger is a racecar. Hardcover: ($20.00 with dust jacket) $10.00

Black Tiger, 1956

Mexican Roadrace, 1957

Black Tiger at Le Mans, 1958

Black Tiger at Indianapolis, 1962

Black Tiger at Bonneville, 1960

Car Called Camellia, 1970

BLAZE SERIES, Clarence W. Anderson (1891 – 1971), Macmillan, oversize hardcover, horse stories, full page b/w illustrations by author. Early editions: ($35.00 with dust jacket) $10.00

Book Club editions with illustrated hardcover, no dust jacket: $15.00

Billy and Blaze, 1936

Blaze and the Gypsies, 1937

Blaze and the Forest Fire, 1938

Blaze Finds a Trail, 1950

Blaze and Thunderbolt, 1955

Blaze and the Gray Spotted Pony, 1968

Blaze Shows the Way, 1969

Blaze Finds Forgotten Roads, 1970

BLOSSOM SHOP SERIES, Isla May Mullins, 1913 – 22 Page, hardcover with gilt lettering and circular pictorial paste-on, illustrated by John Goss, 6 titles. Early editions: $25.00

Titles include:

Blossom Shop: A Story of the South, 1913

Anne of the Blossom Shop, 1914

Anne's Wedding, 1916

Mt. Blossom Girls, 1918

BLUE BIRDS SERIES, Lillian Elizabeth Roy (1868 – 1932), (first published ca. 1919 Platt & Nourse) ca. 1930s edition Burt, blue pictorial hardcover, illustrated. ($30.00 with dust jacket) $15.00

Blue Birds of Happy Time Nest

Blue Birds' Winter Nest

Blue Birds' Uncle Ben

Blue Birds at Happy Hills

BLUE BONNET SERIES, Lela Horn Richards, 1910 – 29 Page, decorated hardcover, b/w plates by John Goss. $20.00

Texas Blue Bonnet

Blue Bonnet's Ranch Party

Blue Bonnet in Boston

Blue Bonnet Keeps House

Blue Bonnet – Debutante

Blue Bonnet of Seven Stars

Blue Bonnet's Family

BLUE DOMERS SERIES, Jean Finley, ca. 1920s Burt, pictorial boards, small, color illustrated endpapers, color illustrations. ($50.00 with dust jacket) $30.00

Blue Domers

Blue Domers' Alphabet Zoo

Blue Domers in the Deep Woods

Blue Domers and the Wishing Tree

Blue Domers Under Winter Skies
Blue Domers and the Magic Flute

BLUE GRASS SEMINARY GIRLS SERIES, Carolyn J. Burnett, ca. 1916 Burt, pictorial tan cloth-over-board cover, about 250 pages. ($20.00 with dust jacket) $15.00
Blue Grass Seminary Girls' Vacation Adventures
Blue Grass Seminary Girls' Christmas Holidays
Blue Grass Seminary Girls in the Mountains
Blue Grass Seminary Girls on the Water

BLYTHE GIRLS SERIES, Laura Lee Hope, 1925 – 32 Grosset, illustrations by Thelma Gooch, advertised as "The Blythe girls were left alone in New York City...," Grosset & Dunlap: ($25.00 with dust jacket) $10.00
Whitman, pictorial hardcover: $15.00
Blythe Girls, Helen, Margy and Rose
Blythe Girls, Margy's Queer Inheritance
Blythe Girls, Rose's Greatest Problem
Blythe Girls, Helen's Strange Boarder
Blythe Girls, Three on a Vacation
Blythe Girls, Margy's Secret Mission
Blythe Girls, Rose's Odd Discovery
Blythe Girls, Disappearance of Helen
Blythe Girls, Snowbound in Camp
Blythe Girls, Margy's Mysterious Visitor
Blythe Girls, Rose's Hidden Talent
Blythe Girls, Helen's Wonderful Mistake

BOB AND BETTY SERIES, Boyd E. Smith (b. Canada, 1860 – 1943), illustrator-author, paper-over-board hardcover with cloth spine, illustrated endpa-pers, beautiful full-page watercolor illustrations by the author.
Farm Book: Bob and Betty Visit Uncle John, 1910 Houghton, oblong oversize, pictorial boards, illus-trated endpapers, 12 color plates. $65.00
Railroad Book, Bob and Betty's Summer on the Rail-road, 1913 Houghton, oblong oversize, pictorial boards, illustrated endpapers, 12 color plates. $65.00
Seashore Book: Bob and Betty's Summer with Cap-tain Hawes, 1912 Houghton, oblong oversize, pic-torial boards, illustrated endpapers, 12 color plates. $65.00

BOB AND JUDY SCHOOL READERS, Grace Storm and Berenice Maloney, 1930s Lyons and Carnahan Publishers, Basic Reading Program, color illustra-tions by Vera Norman. $25.00

BOB CHASE SERIES, Frank Warner (Stratemeyer Syn-dicate pseudonym), ca. 1930 Barse, hardcover, illustrations by David Randolph. $30.00, Grosset & Dunlap reprints, ($20.00 with dust jacket) $15.00
Bob Chase with the Big Moose Hunters
Bob Chase after Grizzly Bears
Bob Chase in the Tiger's Lair
Bob Chase with the Lion Hunters

BOB COOK see FLAG AND COUNTRY

BOB DEXTER SERIES, Willard F. Baker, ca. 1920 Cup-ples, hardcover. ($40.00 with dust jacket) $20.00
Bob Dexter and the Club-House Mystery, 1925
Bob Dexter and the Beacon Beach Mystery, 1925
Bob Dexter and the Storm Mountain Mystery, 1925
Bob Dexter and the Aeroplane Mystery, 1930
Bob Dexter and the Seaplane Mystery, 1931
Bob Dexter and the Red Auto Mystery, 1932

BOB FLAME SERIES, Dorr Yeager, Sears Books or Dodd, cloth-over-board cover, photo plate illustrations. ($30.00 with dust jacket) $20.00
Bob Flame Ranger, 1934
Bob Flame Rocky Mountain Ranger, 1935
Bob Flame in Death Valley, 1937

BOB HANSON SERIES, Russell Carter, ca. 1920s Penn, hardcover, illustrated by Gordon Smyth, 4 books. $20.00
Bob Hanson, Tenderfoot
Bob Hanson, Scout
Bob Hanson, First Class Scout
Bob Hanson, Eagle Scout

BOB HUNT SERIES, George W. Orton, (ca. 1915 George W. Jacobs), hardcover, Whitman reprints: ($25.00 with dust jacket) $10.00
Bob Hunt at Camp Pontiac
Bob Hunt, Senior Camper

Bob Hunt in Canada

BOB STEELE SERIES (also called MOTOR POWER SERIES), Donald Grayson (pseudonym), 1909 McKay, yellow-beige pictorial hardcover, with wheel-shaped logo inscribed Motor Power Series, frontispiece by George Avison. $50.00

Bob Steele's Motorcycle, or True to His Friends
Bob Steele on High Gear, or Prize Worth Winning
Bob Steele From Auto to Airship, or Strange Adventure in the Air
Bob Steele Afloat in the Clouds, or Boy Who Owned an Airship
Bob Steele's Submarine Cruiser, or Captain Nemo's Friend
Bob Steele in Strange Waters, or Aboard a Strange Craft
Bob Steele's Motorboat, or Fellow They Could Not Beat
Bob Steele's Winning Race, or Fearless and True
Bob Steele's New Aeroplane, or Bird Man
Bob Steele's Last Flight, or Sail of the "Comet"

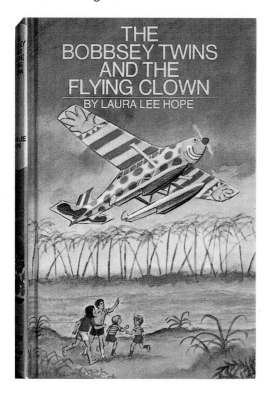

BOBBSEY TWINS, Laura Lee Hope (Stratemeyer Syndicate pseudonym), Chatterton-Peck and Mershon, hardcover novels about two sets of twins, b/w illustrations. The series was created in 1904 by the Stratemeyer Syndicate, became one of its best sellers, and has been reprinted numerous times. Grosset first editions appeared after 1913. By 1950 Grosset began re-issuing the earlier books, sometimes with text revisions, often with title revisions to appeal to the contemporary market.

Chatterton-Peck and Mershon hardcovers: $35.00
Bobbsey Twins, Grosset, prices:
Pre-1920 hardcovers with paste-on pictorial: $25.00
Post-1920 hardcovers with paste-on pictorial: $20.00
Plain hardcover with illustrated (non-paper doll) dust jacket: $20.00
Plain hardcover with illustrated dust jacket and 2 paper dolls on back of jacket (1930s reprints): $35.00
Plain green hardcover without dust jacket: $15.00
Pictorial hardcovers (no dust jackets): $15.00
Bobbsey Twins, titles:
Bobbsey Twins, or Merry Days Indoors and Out, 1904
Bobbsey Twins in the Country
Bobbsey Twins at the Seashore
Bobbsey Twins at School
Bobbsey Twins at Snow Lodge
Bobbsey Twins on a Houseboat, 1915
Bobbsey Twins at Meadow Brook
Bobbsey Twins at Home
Bobbsey Twins in a Great City
Bobbsey Twins on Blueberry Island
Bobbsey Twins on the Deep Blue Sea
Bobbsey Twins in Washington
Bobbsey Twins in the Great West, 1920
Bobbsey Twins at Cedar Camp
Bobbsey Twins at the County Fair
Bobbsey Twins Camping Out
Bobbsey Twins and Baby May
Bobbsey Twins Keeping House, 1925
Bobbsey Twins at Cloverbank
Bobbsey Twins at Cherry Corners
Bobbsey Twins and their Schoolmates
Bobbsey Twins Treasure Hunting
Bobbsey Twins at Spruce Lake, 1930
Bobbsey Twins' Wonderful Secret
Bobbsey Twins at the Circus
Bobbsey Twins on an Airplane
Bobbsey Twins on a Ranch, 1935
Bobbsey Twins on Eskimo Island
Bobbsey Twins in a Radio Play
Bobbsey Twins at Windmill Cottage
Bobbsey Twins at Lighthouse Point
Bobbsey Twins at Indian Hollow, 1940
Bobbsey Twins at the Ice Carnival
Bobbsey Twins in the Land of Cotton
Bobbsey Twins in Echo Valley
Bobbsey Twins on the Pony Trail
Bobbsey Twins at Mystery Mansion, 1945
Bobbsey Twins at Sugar Maple Hill
Bobbsey Twins in Mexico
Bobbsey Twins' Toy Shop
Bobbsey Twins in Tulip Land
Bobbsey Twins in Rainbow Valley, 1950
Bobbsey Twins Own Little Railroad
Bobbsey Twins at White Sail Harbor
Bobbsey Twins at Horseshoe Riddle
Bobbsey Twins at Big Bear Pond
Bobbsey Twins on a Bicycle Trip

Bobbsey Twins' Own Little Ferryboat, 1956
Bobbsey Twins at Pilgrim Rock
Bobbsey Twins' Forest Adventure
Bobbsey Twins at London Tower
Bobbsey Twins in the Mystery Cave, 1960
Bobbsey Twins in Volcano Land
Bobbsey Twins and the Goldfish Mystery
Bobbsey Twins and the Big River Mystery
Bobbsey Twins and the Greek Hat Mystery
Bobbsey Twins Search for the Green Rooster, 1965
Bobbsey Twins and their Camel Adventure
Bobbsey Twins Mystery of the King's Puppet
Bobbsey Twins and the Secret of Candy Castle
Bobbsey Twins and the Doodlebug Mystery
Bobbsey Twins and the Talking Fox Mystery, 1970
Bobbsey Twins and the Red, White and Blue Mystery
Bobbsey Twins, Dr. Funnybone's Secret
Bobbsey Twins and the Tagalong Giraffe
Bobbsey Twins and the Flying Clown
Bobbsey Twins and the Sun-Moon Cruise, 1975
Bobbsey Twins, the Freedom Bell Mystery
Bobbsey Twins and the Smoky Mountain Mystery
Bobbsey Twins in a TV Mystery Show
Bobbsey Twins and the Coral Turtle Mystery, 1979
Bobbsey Twins, continued publication into the 1980s in Wanderer paperbacks.
Bobbsey Twins, related book:
Bobbsey Twins Coloring 4 Fun, 1954 Whitman coloring book. $40.00

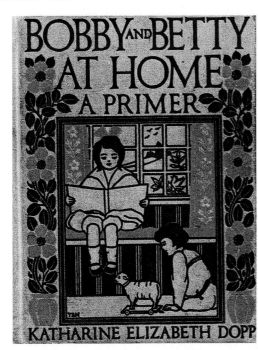

BOBBY AND BETTY SERIES, Katharine Dopp, 1917 – 27 Rand McNally, school readers, b/w/orange illustrations by Mary Spoor Brand. $30.00
Bobby and Betty at Home
Bobby and Betty with the Workers
Bobby and Betty at Play

Bobby and Betty in the Country

BOBBY BLAKE SERIES, Frank Warner, ca. 1920s Barse, cloth-over-board cover, b/w illustrations. Titles are slightly altered in the 1930s Grosset listings. ($20.00 with dust jacket) $10.00
Bobby Blake at Rockledge School
Bobby Blake at Bass Cove
Bobby Blake on a Cruise
Bobby Blake and His Chums
Bobby Blake on a Ranch
Bobby Blake on an Auto Tour
Bobby Blake in the Frozen North
Bobby Blake at Snowtop Ranch
Bobby Blake on the School Nine
Bobby Blake on the School Eleven
Bobby Blake on a Plantation
Bobby Blake on Mystery Mountain

BOBBY BREWSTER SERIES, H. E. Todd, 1954 – 1974 Hodder and Stoughton, and Edmund Ward, illustrators include Lilian Buchanan, Bryan Ward. $15.00
Also reprinted in paperback by Knight, UK, and Scholastic, US.
Bobby Brewster
Bobby Brewster Bus Conductor
Bobby Brewster's Shadow
Bobby Brewster's Bicycle
Bobby Brewster Camera
Bobby Brewster's Wallpaper
Bobby Brewster's Conker
Bobby Brewster Detective
Bobby Brewster's Potato
Bobby Brewster and the Ghost
Bobby Brewster's Kite
Bobby Brewster's Scarecrow
Bobby Brewster's Torch
Bobby Brewster's Balloon Race
Bobby Brewster's Typewriter
Bobby Brewster's Bee
Bobby Brewster's Wishbone

BONES SERIES, Jean Caryl, Funk & Wagnalls, hardcover, b/w illustrations by Jessica Zemsky. ($20.00 with dust jacket) $10.00
Bones and Smiling Mackerel, 1964
Bones and the Black Panther, 1963
Bones and the Pointed House, 1968

BONNIE AND DEBBIE SERIES, Rebecca Caudill, 1950 – 60 Winston, small hardcover, b/w illustrations by Decie Merwin. ($35.00 with dust jacket) $15.00
Schoolhouse in the Woods
Up and Down the River
Happy Little Family
Schoolhouse in the Parlor

BOOKSHELF FOR BOYS AND GIRLS, 1948 University

Society, NY, color paste-on-pictorial on cloth hardcover. This series combines material from *Boys and Girls Bookshelf*, *Young Folks Treasury*, and *Modern Boy's Activity*. Per volume: $10.00

BOONE AND KENTON see ELLIS

BORDER BOYS SERIES, Fremont B. Deering, ca. 1911 A. L. Burt, tan pictorial cloth-over-board cover, also ca. 1911 Hurst, illustrated cloth-over-board cover, illustrated by Charles Wrenn. $20.00
Border Boys on the Trail
Border Boys across the Frontier
Border Boys with the Mexican Rangers
Border Boys with the Texas Rangers
Border Boys in the Canadian Rockies
Border Boys along the St. Lawrence River

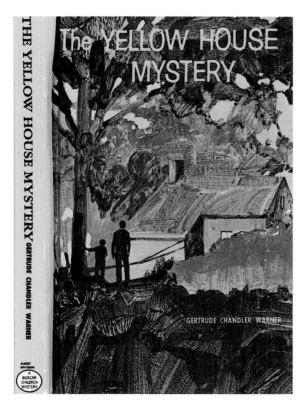

BOXCAR CHILDREN MYSTERIES, also called ALDEN FAMILY MYSTERIES, Gertrude Chandler Warner, ca. 1950s – 60s Whitman Pilot Books, b/w illustrations, color illustrated boards. $15.00
Boxcar Children
Surprise Island
Yellow House Mystery
Mystery Ranch
Mike's Mystery
Blue Bay Mystery
Woodshed Mystery
Lighthouse Mystery
Mountain Top Mystery
Schoolhouse Mystery
Caboose Mystery

Houseboat Mystery
Snowbound Mystery
Tree House Mystery
Bicycle Mystery
Mystery in the Sand
Mystery Behind the Wall
Bus Station Mystery
Benny Uncovers a Mystery

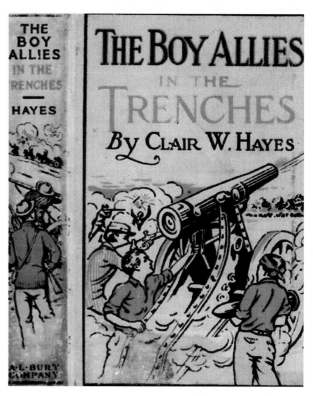

BOY ALLIES WITH THE ARMY SERIES, Clair W. Hayes, ca. 1915 – 1919 A. L. Burt, illustrated cloth-over-board cover, frontispiece illustration. Advertised as, "In this series we follow the fortunes of two American lads unable to leave Europe after war is declared. They meet the soldiers of the Allies and decide to cast their lots with them. Their experiences and escapes are many, and furnish plenty of good, healthy action that every boy loves." ($35.00 with dust jacket) $15.00
Boy Allies at Liege
Boy Allies on the Firing Line
Boy Allies with the Cossacks
Boy Allies in the Trenches
Boy Allies in Great Peril
Boy Allies in the Balkan Campaign
Boy Allies on the Somme
Boy Allies at Verdun
Boy Allies under the Stars and Stripes
Boy Allies with Haig in Flanders
Boy Allies with Pershing in France
Boy Allies with Marshall Foch

BOY ALLIES WITH THE NAVY SERIES, Ensign Robert L. Drake, ca. 1915 – 1919 A. L. Burt. Advertised as

"Frank Chadwick and Jack Templeton, young American lads, meet each other in an unusual way soon after the declaraton of war. Circumstances place them on board the British cruiser *The Sylph* and from there on, they share adventures..." ($35.00 with dust jacket) $15.00

Boy Allies with the North Sea Patrol
Boy Allies Under Two Flags
Boy Allies with the Flying Squadron
Boy Allies with the Terror of the Sea
Boy Allies under the Sea
Boy Allies in the Baltic
Boy Allies at Jutland
Boy Allies with Uncle Sam's Cruisers
Boy Allies with the Submarine D-32
Boy Allies with the Victorious Fleets

BOY AVIATORS SERIES, Captain Wilbur Lawton, 1910 Hurst, green pictorial hardcover. $12.00
Boy Aviators in Nicaragua, or Leagued with Insurgents
Boy Aviators on Secret Service, or Working with Wireless
Boy Aviators in Africa, or Aerial Ivory Trail
Boy Aviators in Record Flight, or Rival Aeroplane
Boy Aviators on Polar Dash, or Facing Death in the Antarctic

BOY CHUMS SERIES, Wilmer M. Ely, ca. 1909 Burt, cloth-over-board cover with paste-on-pictorial. $15.00
Boy Chums on the Indian River
Boy Chums on Haunted Island
Boy Chums in the Forest
Boy Chums' Perilous Cruise
Boy Chums in the Gulf of Mexico
Boy Chums in Florida Waters
Boy Chums in the Florida Jungle
Boy Chums in Mystery Land

BOY DONALD SERIES, Penn Shirley, pseudonym (Sarah J. Clarke), ca. 1900 Lee & Shepard, hardcover, illustrated by Bertha G. Davidson. $25.00
Boy Donald
Boy Donald and His Chum
Boy Donald and His Hero

BOY EXPLORERS SERIES, Warren H. Miller, ca. 1920s Harper & Brothers, 5 titles, hardcover. $20.00
In Darkest New Guinea
In the Pirate Archipelago
On Tiger Trails
Ape-Man of Sumatra
In Borneo

BOY FORTUNE HUNTERS SERIES, Floyd Akers (L. Frank Baum), ca. 1908 Reilly and Britton, hardcover. Publisher launched the Boy Fortune Hunter series in 1908, using the two Sam Steele books under new titles.

Sam Steele titles, by Capt. Hugh Fitzgerald (L. Frank Baum):
Sam Steele's Adventures on Land and Sea, 1906 Reilly, first edition, color paste-on-pictorial and gilt cover decorations $300.00. Later editions $120.00
Sam Steele's Adventures in Panama, 1907 Reilly, paste-on-pictorial, gilt lettering $300.00
Boy Fortune Hunter titles, first editions of Boy Fortune Hunters: $400.00 Early editions: $150.00
Boy Fortune Hunters in Alaska, (first titled: *Sam Steele's Adventures on Land and Sea*)
Boy Fortune Hunters in Panama, (first titled: *Sam Steele's Adventures in Panama*)
Boy Fortune Hunters in Egypt
Boy Fortune Hunters in China
Boy Fortune Hunters in the Yucatan
Boy Fortune Hunters in the South Seas

BOY HUNTER SERIES, Capt. Ralph Bonehill, ca. 1900 Donohue, hardcover, b/w frontispiece, title crossovers with Young Sportsman's series. $20.00
Four Boy Hunters
Guns and Snowshoes
Young Hunters in Porto Rico
Young Hunters of the Lake
Boy Hunters in the Mountains

BOY INVENTORS SERIES, Richard Bonner, ca. 1912 Hurst, Donohue $15.00
Boy Inventors' Wireless Triumph
Boy Inventors' and the Vanishing Sun
Boy Inventors' Diving Torpedo Set
Boy Inventors' Flying Ship
Boy Inventors' Electric Ship
Boy Inventors' Radio Telephone

BOY PIONEER see ELLIS

BOY RANCHERS SERIES, Willard F. Baker, ca. 1920s Cupples & Leon, small size, cloth cover with printed illustration, b/w illustrations $15.00
Boy Ranchers
Boy Ranchers in Camp
Boy Ranchers on the Trail
Boy Ranchers among the Indians
Boy Ranchers at Spur Creek
Boy Ranchers in the Desert
Boy Ranchers on Roaring River

BOY SCOUT see PEE WEE HARRIS, ROY BLAKELY, TOM SLADE, WESTY MARTIN, WORLD WAR SERIES

BOY SCOUT EXPLORERS SERIES, Don Palmer (Mildred Wirt), Cupples and Leon, hardcover. ($20.00 with dust jacket) $10.00
Boy Scout Explorers at Emerald Valley, 1955
Boy Scout Explorers at Treasure Mountain, 1955
Boy Scout Explorers at Headless Hollow, 1957

BOY SCOUT SERIES, Maj. Robert Maitland, ca. 1910 Saalfield, small, impressed cover illustration, 150+ pages, illustrated endpapers, 20 or more volumes. $15.00

Boy Scout in Camp
Boy Scout to the Rescue
Boy Scout on the Trail
Boy Scout Fire-Fighters
Boy Scout Afloat
Boy Scout Pathfinders
Boy Scout Automobilists
Boy Scout Aviators
Boy Scouts with King George
Boy Scouts at Liege
Boy Scouts with the Cossacks
Boy Scouts before Belgrade

BOY SCOUTS OF THE AIR SERIES, Gordan Stuart, ca. 1912 Reilly & Britton, then Reilly and Lee, printed illustration on hardcover, b/w frontispiece for Reilly & Britton titles by Norman Hall. ($45.00 with dust jacket) $15.00

Boy Scouts of the Air at Greenwood School, 1912 Reilly & Britton
Boy Scouts of the Air in Indian Land, 1912 Reilly & Britton
Boy Scouts of the Air in Northern Wilds, 1912 Reilly & Britton
Boy Scouts of the Air at Eagle Camp, 1912 Reilly & Britton
Boy Scouts of the Air in the Lone Star Patrol, 1916 Reilly & Britton
Boy Scouts of the Air in the Dismal Swamp, 1920 Reilly & Lee, frontispiece by Kirke Bride
Boy Scouts of the Air on Baldcrest, 1922 Reilly & Lee, illustrated by Harry W. Armstrong

BOY SCOUTS SERIES, Crowell Publishers, small pictorial hardcover, novels by three different writers, packaged as a series in matching formats. $15.00

Boy Scouts in the Maine Woods, James Otis, 1911
Boy Scouts on Lake Champlain, Fitzhugh, 1912
Boy Scouts in the Rockies, Sabin, 1912
Boy Scouts of Panama, Fitzhugh, 1913
Boy Scouts in a Lumber Camp, James Otis, 1913
Boy Scouts on the Mississippi, Fitzhugh, 1914

BOY SCOUTS SERIES, Herbert Carter, ca. 1913 Burt, mustard cloth-over-board cover with illustration, illustrations by J. Watson Davis, "new Boy Scout stories of camp life." ($25.00 with dust jacket) $15.00

Boy Scouts' First Campfire
Boy Scouts in the Blue Ridge
Boy Scouts on the Trail
Boy Scouts in the Maine Woods
Boy Scouts through the Big Timber
Boy Scouts in the Rockies
Boy Scouts on Sturgeon Island

Boy Scouts Down in Dixie
Boy Scouts at the Battle of Saratoga
Boy Scouts along the Susquehanna
Boy Scouts on War Trails in Belgium
Boy Scouts afoot in France

BOY SCOUTS SERIES, Maj. Archibald Lee Fletcher, ca. 1913 Donohue, small, impressed illustration on cover, b/w frontispiece. $20.00

Boy Scout Pathfinders
Boy Scout Signal Senders
Boy Scouts in the Everglades

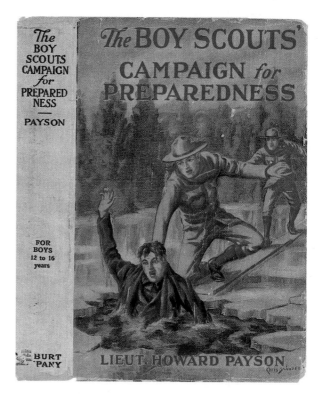

BOY SCOUTS SERIES, Lieut. Howard Payson, ca. 1910 Hurst and Burt, color printed cover illustration, b/w illustrations by R. M. Brinkerhoff, "a series of stories in which self-reliance and self-defense through organized athletics are emphasized." ($50.00 with dust jacket) $25.00

Boy Scouts of Eagle Patrol
Boy Scouts on the Range
Boy Scouts and the Army Airship
Boy Scouts' Mountain Camp
Boy Scouts for Uncle Sam
Boy Scouts at the Panama Canal
Boy Scouts under Fire in Mexico
Boy Scouts on Belgian Battlefields
Boy Scouts with the Allies in France
Boy Scouts at the Pan-Pacific Exposition
Boy Scouts under Sealed Orders
Boy Scouts Campaign for Preparedness

BOY SCOUTS SERIES, G. Harvey Ralphson, ca. 1920s – 30s Donohue, printed illustration on hardcover,

illustrated endpapers, b/w frontispiece. ($30.00 with dust jacket) $15.00
Boy Scouts in Mexico
Boy Scouts in the Canal Zone
Boy Scouts in the Philippines
Boy Scouts in the Northwest
Boy Scouts in a Motor Boat
Boy Scouts in an Airship
Boy Scouts in a Submarine
Boy Scouts on Motorcycles
Boy Scouts beyond the Arctic
Boy Scout Camera Club
Boy Scout Electricians
Boy Scouts in California
Boy Scouts on Hudson Bay
Boy Scouts in Death Valley
Boy Scouts on Open Plains
Boy Scouts in Southern Waters
Boy Scouts in Belgium
Boy Scouts in the North Sea
Boy Scouts Mysterious Signal
Boy Scouts with the Cossacks

BOY SCOUTS SERIES, Capt. V. T. Sherman, ca. 1910 Donohue, unrelated books about scouting adventures, printed illustration on tan hardcover, b/w frontispiece. ($30.00 with wraparound illustration dust jacket) $15.00
Titles include:
Boy Scouts with Joffre
Scouting the Balkans in a Motor Boat
Capturing A Spy

BOY SCOUTS SERIES, Ralph Victor, ca. 1910 Burt or Chatterton, reprints by Platt & Peck, and Hurst, eight titles. ($25.00 with dust jacket) $10.00

BOY TRAVELLERS, Thomas Knox, ca. 1890s Harper & Brothers, oversize, coveted by collectors for the deluxe hardcovers with leather-like look and ornamental gilt trim and lettering, detailed map endpapers for each journey, color frontispiece, b/w illustrations. $75.00 to $150.00
South America
Great Britain and Ireland

Russian Empire
Mexico
Far East
Egypt and the Holy Land
Australia
Japan and China
Ceylon and India
Northern Europe
Central Europe
Southern Europe
Central Africa
Congo
Levant
Far East

BOY TROOPERS SERIES, Clair W. Hayes, ca. 1920 A. L. Burt, cloth-over-board cover, frontispiece illustration, b/w illustrations, advertised as "adventures of two boys with the Pennsylvania State Police." ($40.00 with dust jacket) $15.00
Boy Troopers on the Trail
Boy Troopers in the Northwest
Boy Troopers on Strike Duty
Boy Troopers among the Wild Mountaineers

BOY VOLUNTEERS SERIES, Kenneth Ward, ca. 1915 New York Book Co., hardcover with printed illustration, b/w illustrations. $20.00
Boy Volunteers on the Belgian Front
Boy Volunteers with the French Airmen
Boy Volunteers with the British Artillery
Boy Volunteers with the Submarine Fleet

BOYS' ADVENTURE BOOKS SERIES, E. Keble Chatterton, 1927 – 1930 Lippincott, small pictorial hardcovers, 4 plates. $20.00
Across the Seven Seas
King of the Air
In Great Waters
Through the Sea and Sky
Adventurers of the Air
Sky Riders

BOYS AND GIRLS BOOKS, undated ca. 1910 – 20 Goldsmith, books are packaged uniformly in hardcover, each has 256 pages, b/w illustrated endpapers, individually designed four-color dust jackets. Fifty-one titles are listed on the back cover of *S.W.F Club*. This collection of authors and unrelated titles is a publisher's put-together series for marketing purposes; many of the titles are books from other series. ($15.00 with dust jacket) $8.00
Titles include:
Big Leaguer
Bobbsey Twins
Captain of the Eleven
Circus Dan
Connie at Rainbow Ranch
Dixie School Girl

Girls of Silverspur Ranch
Herb Kent, Fullback
Janet Hardy in Hollywood
Mimi at Camp
Nobody's Buddy
Penny Nichols Finds a Clue
Phantom Whale
Polly What's Her Name
Sacred Scimiter
Secret of Tibet
S.W.F. Club
Unseen Enemy
Whispering Rails

Young Express Agent
Two Boy Publishers
Mail Order Frank
Business Boy

BOYS' BOOK SERIES, Irving Crump, 1916 – 1934 Dodd Mead, cloth-over-board cover, non-fiction, photo illustrations. ($25.00 with dust jacket) $15.00

Boys' Book of Firemen
Boys' Book of Policemen
Boys' Book of Mounted Police
Boys' Book of Railroads
Boys' Book of Forest Rangers
Boys' Book of Arctic Exploration
Boys' Book of the U. S. Mails
Boys' Book of Airmen
Boys' Book of Coast Guards
Boys' Book of Fisheries
Boys' Book of Newsreel Hunters
Boys' Book of Cowboys

BOYS OF BUSINESS SERIES, Allen Chapman, ca. 1910 Cupples & Leon, cloth-over-board cover with impressed illustration, b/w plates. ($25.00 with dust jacket) $15.00

BOYS OF COLUMBIA HIGH SERIES, Graham B. Forbes, 1912 – 1920 Grosset, impressed illustration on cover, b/w illustrations, advertised as "never was there a cleaner, brighter, more manly boy than Frank Allen, the hero of this series of boys' tales, and never was there a better crowd of lads to associate with than students of the school." ($25.00 with dust jacket) $15.00

Boys of Columbia High
Boys of Columbia High on the Diamond
Boys of Columbia High on the River
Boys of Columbia High on the Gridiron
Boys of Columbia High on the Ice
Boys of Columbia High in Track Athletics
Boys of Columbia High in Winter Sports

Boys of Columbia High, Frank Allen series, Graham Forbes (Stratemeyer Syndicate pseudonym), ca. 1925 Garden City, cloth-over-board cover. These are crossover books re-titled from BOYS OF COLUMBIA HIGH SERIES. $15.00

Frank Allen's Schooldays
Frank Allen Playing to Win
Frank Allen in Winter Sports
Frank Allen and his Rivals
Frank Allen, Pitcher
Frank Allen, Head of the Crew
Frank Allen in Camp
Frank Allen at Rockspur Ranch
Frank Allen at Gold Fork
Frank Allen and His Motor Boat
Frank Allen, Captain of the Team

Frank Allen at Old Moose Lake
Frank Allen at Zero Camp
Frank Allen Snowbound
Frank Allen after the Big Game
Frank Allen with the Circus
Frank Allen Pitching His Best

BOYS OF LIBERTY LIBRARY, ca. 1905 David McKay Publishers, small tan hardcover with impressed illustration, b/w frontispiece, adventure novels with patriotic themes, authors include John De Morgan, T. C. Harbaugh, Irving Hancock, Lt. Lounsberry, Frank Sheridan. $20.00
Titles include:
First Shot for Liberty
Hero of Ticonderoga
Young Guardsman
Washington's Young Spy
Captain of the Minute Men
By Order of the Colonel
Cruise of the Essex
Under Greene's Banner

BOYS OF THE ROYAL MOUNTED POLICE SERIES, Milton Richards, ca. 1920s Burt, illustrated cloth-over-board cover, b/w frontispiece. ($35.00 with dust jacket) $15.00
Dick Kent with the Mounted Police
Dick Kent in the Far North
Dick Kent with the Eskimos
Dick Kent, Fur Trader
Dick Kent and the Malemute Mail
Dick Kent on Special Duty
Dick Kent at Half Way House
Dick Kent, Mounted Police Deputy
Dick Kent's Mysterious Mission
Dick Kent and the Mine Mystery

BRAD FORREST ADVENTURE SERIES, Hugh Maitland, Longmans, Canada, hardcover, 8 titles. A young Canadian's adventures in other parts of the world. ($15.00 with dust jacket) $10.00
Brad Forrest's Calgary Adventure, 1964
Brad Forrest's Hong Kong Adventure, 1964
Brad Forrest's Los Angeles Adventure, 1964
Brad Forrest's Madagascar Adventure, 1964
Brad Forrest's New York Adventure, 1965
Brad Forrest's Yucatan Adventure, 1965
Brad Forrest's Halifax Adventure, 1965
Brad Forrest's London Adventure, 1965

BRAINS BENTON SERIES, Charles Spain Verral and George Wyatt, 1959 – 60 Whitman, hardcover, pictorial hardcovers. $20.00
Ca. 1960s Golden Press, yellow spine, slightly wider than Whitman editions, illustrated hardcover. $15.00
Case of the Missing Message
Case of the Counterfeit Coin
Case of the Stolen Dummy
Case of the Roving Rolls
Case of the Waltzing Mouse
Case of the Painted Dragon

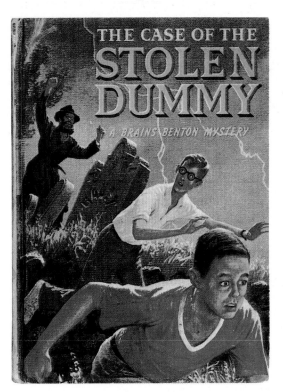

BRANDEIS DOCUMENTARY SERIES, Madeline Brandeis, film producer, ca. 1930s Grosset, hardcovers with printed illustration on paper-over-board cover, cloth spine, illustrated endpapers, b/w documentary-type photo illustrations from Pathe

films. $15.00
Sample titles:
Little Anne of Canada
Little Dutch Tulip Girl
Little Indian Weaver
Little Spanish Dancer
Little Swiss Wood Carver
Wee Scotch Piper

BRAVE HEART SERIES, Adele E. Thompson, ca. 1900 Lee & Shepard, ca. 1930s Grosset & Dunlap, illustrations by Lillian Crawford True.
Lee & Shepard edition: $40.00
Grosset & Dunlap edition: ($15.00 with dust jacket) $10.00
Betty Seldon, Patriot
Brave Heart Elizabeth
Lassie of the Isles

BRET KING MYSTERY SERIES, Dan Scott, ca. 1960s Grosset, pictorial hardcover, illustrated endpapers, b/w illustrations by Joe Beeler. $15.00
Mystery of Ghost Canyon
Secret of Hermit's Peak
Range Rodeo Mystery
Mystery of Rawhide Gap

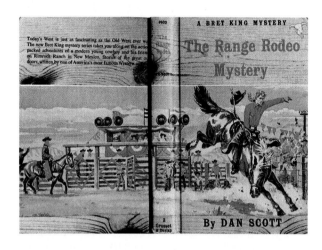

BRICK HOUSE BOOKS, Nina Rhoades, ca. 1915 Lothrop, unrelated novels for small girls packaged in hardcovers with printed or impressed illustrations that featured a brick pattern either in the illustration or as edge trim. Most have b/w illustrations by Bertha Davidson. $15.00
Only Dollie
Little Girl Next Door
Winifred's Neighbors
Children on the Top Floor
How Barbara Kept Her Promise
Little Miss Rosamond
Priscilla of the Doll Shop
Brave Little Peggy
Other Sylvia

BRIGHTON BOYS SERIES, Lt. James R. Driscoll, undated Winston ca. WW 1, hardcover, four b/w plates. $15.00
Brighton Boys with the Flying Corps
Brighton Boys in the Trenches
Brighton Boys with the Battle Fleet
Brighton Boys with the Radio Service
Brighton Boys with the Submarine Fleet
Brighton Boys at Chatieu-Thierry
Brighton Boys at St. Mihiel
Brighton Boys with the Engineers

BRILLSTONE MYSTERIES SERIES, Florence Heide, Whitman, oversize pictorial hardcover. $15.00
Brillstone Break-in, 1977
Burning Stone at Brillstone, 1978
Fear at Brillstone, 1978
Face at the Brillstone Window, 1979
Black Magic at Brillstone, 1981
Time Bomb at Brillstone, 1982
Body in the Brillstone Garage, 1988

BRONC BURNETT SERIES, Wilfred McCormick, late 1948 – 1960s Grosset, (some by Putnam), tweed hardcover, high school sports stories centered around sixteen-year-old Bronc. ($20.00 with dust jacket) $10.00
Three-Two Pitch
Legion Tourney
Fielder's Choice
Bases Loaded
Eagle Scout
Grand Slam Homer
Rambling Halfback
Flying Tackle
Quick Kick
Stranger in the Backfield
Go-Ahead Runner
Big Ninth
Last Put-Out

One O'Clock Hitter
No Place for Heroes
Tall at the Plate
One Bounce Too Many
Incomplete Pitcher

BRONCHO RIDER BOYS SERIES, Frank Fowler, ca. 1914
– 16 Burt, hardcover with illustration of three cow-
boys, frontispiece, illustration by Walton Davis.
Dust jacket same as cover. ($30.00 with dust jack-
et) $15.00
Broncho Rider Boys at Keystone Ranch, or Three
Chums of the Saddle and Lariat
Broncho Rider Boys down in Arizona, or A Struggle for
the Great Copper Lode
Broncho Rider Boys along the Border, or The Hidden
Treasure of the Zuni Medicine Man
Broncho Rider Boys on the Wyoming Trail, or The Mys-
tery of the Prairie Stampede
Broncho Rider Boys with the Texas Rangers, or The
Smugglers of the Rio Grande
Broncho Rider Boys with Funston at Vera Cruz, or
Upholding the Honor of the Stars and Stripes

BROTHER AND SISTER SERIES, Josephine Lawrence,
ca. 1920 Cupples & Leon, small size, illustrations
by Julia Greene ($30.00 with dust jacket) $15.00
Brother and Sister
Brother and Sister's Schooldays
Brother and Sister's Holidays
Brother and Sister's Vacation

BROWNIE SCOUTS SERIES, Mildred Wirt, ca. late 1940s
Cupples & Leon, cloth-over-board cover in bright
colors. ($35.00 dust jacket) $15.00
Brownie Scouts at Snow Valley, 1949
Brownie Scouts in the Circus, 1949
Brownie Scouts in the Cherry Festival, 1950
Brownie Scouts and Their Tree House, 1951
Brownie Scouts at Silver Beach, 1952
Brownie Scouts at Windmill Farm, 1953

BUCK AND LARRY BASEBALL STORIES, Elmer Dawson
(Stratemeyer Syndicate pseudonym) ca. 1930
Grosset & Dunlap, hardcover, illustrations by Wal-
ter Rogers, stories of the Chester boys. ($30.00
with dust jacket) $15.00
Pick-Up Nine
Buck's Winning Hit
Larry's Fadeaway
Buck's Home Run Drive
Larry's Speedball

BUCKSKIN SERIES, ca. 1960s Macmillan, hardcover.
($15.00 with dust jacket) $10.00
Danger in the Cove, Thompson
Heroine of Long Point, Benham
Boy and the Buffalo, Wood
Scout Who Led an Army, Ballantyne

Adventure at the Mill, Barbara and Heather Bramwell
Man with the Yellow Eyes, Catherine Clark
Escape from Grand Pre, Thompson

BUD BRIGHT SERIES, A. Van Buren Powell, ca. 1930
Penn, cloth-over-board cover, 200+ pages, b/w
illustration. $15.00
Bud Bright, Boy Detective
Bud Bright and the Bank Robbers
Bud Bright and the Counterfeiters
Bud Bright and the Drug Ring

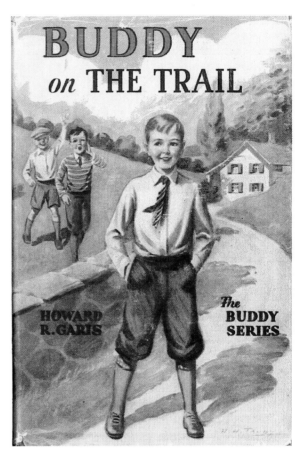

BUDDY SERIES, Howard Garis, ca. 1930s Cupples &
Leon, small, approximately 210 pages, impressed
illustration on red cloth-over-board cover, b/w,
illustrated endpapers, b/w illustrated frontispiece
advertised as "a really fascinating character-
study of an up-to-date young lad..." ($25.00 with
single-illustration-for-series dust jacket designed
by Russell Tandy) $15.00
Buddy on the Farm
Buddy at School
Buddy's Winter Fun
Buddy at Rainbow Lake
Buddy and His Chums
Buddy at Pine Beach
Buddy and His Flying Balloon
Buddy on Mystery Mountain
Buddy on Floating Island
Buddy and the Secret Cave

Buddy and His Cowboy Pal
Buddy and the Indian Chief
Buddy and the Arrow Club
Buddy at Lost River
Buddy on the Trail
Buddy in Deep Valley
Buddy at Red Gate

BUNGALOW BOYS SERIES, Dexter J. Forrester, ca. 1912 Hurst, hardcover, six titles. $20.00

BUNNY BROWN SERIES, Laura Lee Hope, 1916 – 31 Grosset, 20 books, advertised as "eagerly welcomed by the little folks," green hardcover with paste-on-pictorial, b/w plates by Florence Nosworthy. $30.00
1930s Grosset reprints: ($30.00 with dust jacket) $15.00
The following title order appeared on an early 1930s dust jacket, but we have seen slightly different listings on other books.

Bunny Brown and His Sister Sue
Bunny Brown and His Sister Sue on Grandpa's Farm
Bunny Brown and His Sister Sue Playing Circus
Bunny Brown and His Sister Sue at Camp Rest-A-While
Bunny Brown and His Sister Sue at Aunt Lu's City Home
Bunny Brown and His Sister Sue in the Big Woods
Bunny Brown and His Sister Sue on an Auto Tour
Bunny Brown and His Sister Sue and Their Shetland Pony
Bunny Brown and His Sister Sue Giving a Show
Bunny Brown and His Sister Sue at Christmas Tree Cove
Bunny Brown and His Sister Sue in the Sunny South
Bunny Brown and His Sister Sue Keeping Store
Bunny Brown and His Sister Sue and Their Dog Trick
Bunny Brown and His Sister Sue at a Sugar Camp
Bunny Brown and His Sister Sue on the Rolling Ocean
Bunny Brown and His Sister Sue on Jack Frost Island
Bunny Brown and His Sister Sue at Shore Acres
Bunny Brown and His Sister Sue at Berry Hill
Bunny Brown and His Sister Sue at Sky Top
Bunny Brown and His Sister Sue at the Summer Carnival

BURGESS NATURE BOOKS, Thornton Burgess, Little, Brown, hardcover.
Burgess Animal Book for Children, ca. 1920, full-page color and b/w illustrations by Louis Fuertes. First edition: $95.00 with dust jacket Later printings: ($35.00 with dust jacket) $15.00
Burgess Animal Book for Children, 1950 edition, color paste-on pictorial on cover, full-page color and b/w illustrations by Louis Fuertes First edition: $50.00 with dust jacket Later printings: ($20.00 with dust jacket) $15.00
Burgess Bird Book for Children, 1919, color plate illustrations by Fuertes. First edition: $80.00 with dust jacket Later printings: ($20.00 with dust jacket) $15.00

Burgess Flower Book for Children, color and b/w illustrations First edition: $85.00 with dust jacket Later printings: ($20.00 with dust jacket) $15.00
Burgess Seashore Book for Children, color and b/w illustrations b W. H. Southwick. First edition: $90.00 with dust jacket Later printings: ($20.00 with dust jacket) $15.00

BUSTER BROWN SERIES, R. F. Outcault, oversize, color and b/w illustrations by author, ca. 1900 London and Stokes NY. Buster Brown, a saucy lad with a clever dog, became a logo for children's shoes.
Buster Brown, His Dog Tige and Their Troubles, 1900 London, color illustrations $85.00
Buster Brown Abroad, 1904 Stokes, oversize dark blue hardcover: $80.00, Chambers, London edition: $200.00
Buster Brown, My Resolutions, 1906 Stokes, small red hardcover with white lettering. (A signed copy lists for $350.00) $85.00

Buster Brown Nugget Series, R. F. Outcault, ca. 1905 Cupples & Leon, small paper-over-board hardcovers, 36 pages, full-color full-page illustrations by author. $75.00
Buster Brown Goes Fishing
Buster Brown Goes Swimming
Buster Brown Plays Indian
Buster Brown Goes Shooting
Buster Brown Plays Cowboy
Buster Brown on Uncle Jack's Farm
Buster Brown, Tige, and the Bull
Buster Brown and Uncle Buster
Buster Brown, related items:
Buster Brown Playing Cards, 1904 U. S. Play Card Co., deck of 52 cards with a different picture on each

card telling a story of Buster and Tige, in a leather and fur case. $250.00
Buster Brown's Painting Book, 1916 Cupples and Leon, color and b/w illustrations. $50.00

BUTTONS SERIES, Edith McCall, 1950s Beckley-Cardy, also Benefic Press, church school books, hardcover, illustrated. $15.00
Bucky Buttons, 1953
Buttons at the Farm, 1955
Buttons at the Soap Box Derby, 1957
Buttons and the Boy Scouts, 1958
Buttons Go Camping, 1960
Buttons and the Whirlybird, 1960
Buttons and the Little League, 1961
Buttons and the Pet Parade, 1961
Buttons Take a Boat Ride, 1961

— C —

CAMPBELL SERIES, Janet Lambert, ca. 1958 – 1960 Dutton, hardcover, popular teen romance novels. ($100.00 with dust jacket) $35.00
Precious Days
For Each Other
Forever and Ever
Five's a Crowd
First of All

CAMP FIRE AND TRAIL SERIES, Lawrence J. Leslie, ca. 1910 – 15 New York Book Co., small, about 185 pages, color paste-on-pictorial on cover, b/w frontispiece. $15.00
In Camp on the Big Sunflower
Rivals of the Trail
Strange Cabin on Catamount Island
Lost in the Great Dismal Swamp
With Trapper Jim in the North Woods
Caught in a Forest Fire

CAMP FIRE BOYS SERIES, Oliver Clifton, ca. 1920s Barse, cloth-over-board cover, b/w illustrations. ($20.00 with dust jacket) $10.00
Camp Fire Boys at Log Cabin Bend
Camp Fire Boys in Muskrat Swamp
Camp Fire Boys at Silver Fox Farm
Camp Fire Boys' Canoe Cruise
Camp Fire Boys' Tracking Squad

CAMP-FIRE BOYS SERIES, Lotharo Hoover, ca. 1930 A.L. Burt , hardcover, six titles. $15.00
Titles include:
Camp-fire Boys in the Philippines
Camp-fire Boys in the African Jungles
Camp-fire Boys in Australian Gold Fields
Camp-fire Boys in the Brazilian Wilderness
Camp-fire Boys in the South Seas
Camp-fire Boys in Borneo
Camp-fire Boys' Treasure Quest

CAMP FIRE GIRLS SERIES, Amy Blanchard, ca. 1915 Wilde, hardcover. $25.00
Camp Fire Girls of Brightwood
Fagots and Flames; A Story of Winter Campfires
In Camp with the Muskoday Camp Fire Girls

CAMP FIRE GIRLS SERIES, Hildegarde Frey, 1916 – 20 Burt, 10 books. ($25.00 with dust jacket) $10.00
Camp Fire Girls in the Maine Woods
Camp Fire Girls at School
Camp Fire Girls at Onoway House
Camp Fire Girls Go Motoring
Camp Fire Girls' Larks and Pranks
Camp Fire Girls on Ellen's Isle
Camp Fire Girls on the Open Road
Camp Fire Girls Do Their Bit
Camp Fire Girls Solve a Mystery
Camp Fire Girls at Camp Keewaydin

CAMP FIRE GIRLS SERIES, Isabel Hornibrook, 1916 – 1919 Lothrop, Lee & Shepard, hardcover, illustrations by Nana French Bickford. $25.00
Camp Fire Girls and Mr. Greylock
Pemrose Lorry, Camp Fire Girl
Camp Fire Girls in War and Peace
Girls of the Morning Glory Camp Fire

CAMP FIRE GIRLS SERIES, Margaret Sanderson, 1913 thru 1917 Reilly & Britton, 1918 – on Reilly & Lee, hardcover. $20.00
Camp Fire Girls at Pine-Tree Camp, 1914
Camp Fire Girls at Top o' the World, 1916
Camp Fire Girls at Lookout Pass, 1917
Camp Fire Girls at Driftwood Heights, 1918
Camp Fire Girls in Kentucky, 1919
Camp Fire Girls on a Yacht, 1920

CAMP FIRE GIRLS SERIES, Margaret Vandercook, ca. 1915 Winston, hardcover. ($25.00 with dust jacket) $10.00
Camp Fire Girls at Sunrise Hill
Camp Fire Girls amid the Snows
Camp Fire Girls in the Outside World

Camp Fire Girls across the Seas
Camp Fire Girls' Careers
Camp Fire Girls in After Years
Camp Fire Girls on the Edge of the Desert
Camp Fire Girls at the End of the Trail
Camp Fire Girls behind the Lines
Camp Fire Girls on the Field of Honor
Camp Fire Girls in Glorious France
Camp Fire Girls in Merrie England
Camp Fire Girls at Half Moon Lake
Camp Fire Girls at Blue Lagoon

CAMPFIRE GIRLS, LUCILE SERIES, Elizabeth M. Duffield, 1915 – 1918
Sully & Kleinteich, hardcover, illustrations by M. P. Taylor. ($30.00 with dust jacket) $15.00
Lucile, the Torch Bearer
Lucie, Bringer of Joy
Lucile of the Heights
Lucile Triumphant

CAMPFIRE GIRLS SERIES, Irene Elliott Benson, 1912 – 1918 Donohue, hardcover, b/w frontispiece, titles vary in later editions. ($25.00 with dust jacket) $10.00
Titles include:
Campfire Girls in thhe Allegheny Mountains, or A Christmas Success against Odds
Campfire Girls in the Country, or The Secret Aunt Hannah Forgot
Campfire Girls Trip Up the River, or Ethel Hollister 's First Lesson
Campfire Girls' Outing, or Ethel Hollister's Second Summer as a Campfire Girl
Campfire Girls on a Hike, or Lost in the Great North Woods
Campfire Girls' Lake Camp, or Searching for New Adventures

Campfire Girls at Twin Lakes, or Quest of a Summer Vacation

CAMPFIRE GIRLS SERIES, Margaret Penrose, 1930 Goldsmith Publ, 4 books, (first published as Radio Girls.) ($20.00 with dust jacket) $10.00
Campfire Girls at Roselawn
Campfire Girls on the Program
Campfire Girls on the Station
Campfire Girls at Forest Lodge

CAMPFIRE GIRL SERIES, Jane Stewart, 1914 Saalfield, 6 books, hardcover, b/w frontispiece. ($20.00 with dust jacket) $10.00
Campfire Girl's First Council Fire
Campfire Girl's Chum
Campfire Girl in Summer Camp
Campfire Girl's Adventure
Campfire Girl's Test of Friendship
Campfire Girl's Happiness

CANDY KANE SERIES, Janet Lambert, Dutton, hardcover. First edition: ($150.00 with dust jacket) $35.00
Grosset & Dunlap reprints: ($35.00 with dust jacket) $15.00
Candy Kane, 1943
Whoa, Matilda, 1944
One for the Money, 1946

CANOE AND CAMPFIRE SERIES, St. George Rathborne, ca. 1910 Donohue, printed illustration on

hardcover, illustrated endpapers, b/w frontispiece. $15.00
Canoemates in Canada
Young Fur-Takers
House-Boat Boys
Chums in Dixie

CAREER SERIES see DODD, MEAD

CAREER SERIES, Sara Ware Bassett, Little Brown, cloth-over-board hardcover, 250+ pages, plates. $20.00
Titles include:
Paul and the Printing Press, 1920
Steve and the Steam Engine, 1921
Ted and the Telephone, 1922
Walter and the Wireless, 1923
Carl and the Cotton Gin, 1924
Christopher and the Clockmakers, 1925

CAREER SERIES, Carla Greene, Children's Press, Chicago, hardcover. ($20.00 with dust jacket) $10.00
Titles include:
I Want to be a Nurse, illustrated by Krehbiel.
I Want to be a Train Engineer, 1956, illustrated by V. Havel.
I Want to be a Bus Driver, 1957, illustrated by Katherine Evans.
I Want to be a Dairy Farmer, 1957, illustrated.
I Want to be a Teacher, 1957, illustrated.
I Want to be an Airplane Hostess, 1960
I Want to be a Scientist, 1961, illustrated by Janet LaSalle.
I Want to be a Musician, 1962, illustrated.
I Want to be a Pilot, 1964, illustrated by Janet LaSalle.
I Want to be an Orange Grower/Storekeeper, 1969, illustrated by Audrey Williamson.
I Want to be a Zoo-Keeper, 1969, illustrated by Frances Eckert.

CARTER GIRLS SERIES, Nell Speed, ca. 1915 Burt, hardcover, advertised as "High School age stories." ($20.00 with dust jacket) $10.00
Carter Girls
Carter Girls' Weekend Camp
Carter Girls' Mysterious Neighbors
Carter Girls of Carter House

CASTLEMON BOOKS, Harry Castlemon (pseudonym of Charles A. Fosdick), 1842 – 1915. This prolific American writer turned out numerous adventure stories for boys, some written during his service in the US Navy from 1862 – 1867. Many of his short stories and early works first appeared in magazines such as *Golden Days* and *Golden Argosy*. Like other Victorian series, first printings are difficult to distinguish from later printings of the first editions. Jacob Blanck did an extensive bibliography and history of Castlemon's work, including probable variations in printings. Publishers and descriptions listed for first editions. For more information, see Bibliography.

Castlemon books, Afloat and Ashore Series, 1897 – 1898, Henry T. Coates. Cover illustrations printed on cloth in yellow, orange, and gold with gilt lettering on spine, frontispiece, and three plates. Early editions, $30.00; later reprints $10.00.
Rebellion in Dixie, 1897
Ten Ton Cutter, 1897. Cover states that title is *"The"* *Ten Ton Cutter;* the title page calls it *"A" Ten Ton Cutter,* and *Rebellion in Dixie* lists title as *"Cruise of the Ten-Ton Cutter"* in the last chapter.
Sailor in Spite of Himself, 1898, story originally serialized in *New York Weekly* in 1877 and introduces characters of *Rebellion in Dixie.* Usually listed as first book in series despite later publishing date.

Castlemon books, Boy Trapper Series, 1877 – 1879, Porter & Coates. Cloth binding with printed decorative type and title; spine decorated in gilt with small illustrations; frontispiece and three full-page plates. Porter & Coates editions $30.00; later reprints $10.00
Buried Treasure or Old Jordan's "Haunt," 1877
Boy Trapper, 1878
Mail Carrier, 1879

Castlemon books, Castlemon's War Series, 1889 – 1893, Porter & Coates. Three-color plus gilt cover illustration printed on light brown cloth shows two cadets struggling for American flag (same cover illustration used for all titles). Spine also decorated. Illustrations by George G. White. Porter & Coates early editions, $35.00; Winston reprints $10.00.
True to His Colors, 1889, 8 illustrations
Rodney the Partisan, 1890, 4 illustrations
Marcy the Blockade-Runner, 1891, 4 illustrations
Marcy the Refugee, 1892, 4 illustrations
Rodney the Overseer, 1892, 4 illustrations
Sailor Jack the Trader, 1893, 4 illustrations

Castlemon books, Castlemon Series, 1900 – 1902, Saalfield Publishing Company.
First Capture, 1900, red, white and blue cover illustration printed on cloth binding with gilt type on spine, four plates. Early editions, $35.00; later reprints $10.00
Winged Arrow's Medicine, 1901, three-color illustration of Indian printed on cloth with gilt type of spine, four plates. Illustrated by W. H. Fry. Early editions, $45.00; later reprints $10.00
Struggle for Fortune, 1902, three-color illustration printed on cloth with gilt type on spine, four plates. Illustrated by W.H. Fry. Early editions, $35.00; later reprints $10.00

Castlemon books, Forest & Stream Series, 1886 – 1888, Porter & Coates. Cloth binding stamped in black and gold. Frontispiece and three plates. Early editions, $35.00; later reprints $10.00

Joe Wayring at Home or *The Adventures of a Fly-Rod*
Snagged and Sunk or *The Adventures of a Canvas Canoe*
Steel Horse or *The Rambles of a Bicycle*

Castlemon books, Frank Nelson Series, 1876 – 1877, Porter & Coates (original copyright held by R.W. Carroll but first editions issued by P&C). Both Porter and Carroll's names appear in earliest editions, see Jacob Blanck's book (listed in Bibliography) for variations in printings of the first edition. Issued in same format as *Sportsman's Club* with cloth binding, spine heavily decorated in gilt, and four plates including frontispiece. Early editions, $45.00; H.T. Coates reprints $20.00; reprints by other publishers, $10.00

Snowed Up or *The Sportman's Club In the Mountains,* 1876

Frank Nelson in the Forecastle or *The Sportman's Club Among the Whalers,* 1876

Boy Traders or *The Sportmans's Club Among the Boers,* 1877

Castlemon books, Gun-Boat Series, also listed as the Gunboat series (no hyphen) by publishers. 1865 – 1868 R.W. Carroll. The first series written by Castlemon and first issued by R.W. Carroll & Co of Ohio. Later editions published by Porter & Coates; Henry T. Coates; and the John C. Winston Company under the series name "Frank and Archie." First printings not distinguished by Carroll, but Jacob Blanck's bibliography of Castlemon claims that the titles of the first three books in the series appeared in the probable first edition of *Frank the Young Naturalist.*

R.W. Carroll probable firsts: RARE, later editions $75.00

Porter & Coates editions: $35.00, H.T. Coates editions, $20.00, later reprints (Winston, Hurst and others), $10.00

Frank the Young Naturalist, 1865 R.W. Carroll, author's name shown as H.C. Castlemon, cloth binding stamped with all-over arabesque design and gilt decoration on spine. Decorative title page states "by a Gunboat Boy" (author was serving in the Navy at that time). Two full-page illustrations .

Frank on a Gun-Boat, 1865 R.W. Carroll, author's name shown as H.C. Castlemon, cloth binding with gilt decorations on spine, two full-page illustrations.

Frank in the Woods, 1866 R.W. Carroll, author's name shown as H.C. Castlemon, cloth binding with gilt decorations on spine, two full-page illustrations

Frank before Vicksburg, 1866 R.W. Carroll, author's name shown as H.C. Castlemon, cloth binding with gilt decorations on spine, two full-page illustrations.

Frank on the Lower Mississippi, 1867 R.W. Carroll, author's name shown as Harry Castlemon, cloth binding with gilt decorations on spine, two full-page illustrations.

Frank on the Lower Mississippi, ca. 1910 edition Burt, tan hardcover, paste-on-pictorial showing Frank in his blue uniform. $25.00

Frank on the Prairie, 1868 R.W. Carroll, author's name shown as Harry Castlemon, cloth binding with gilt decorations on spine, two full-page illustrations. Earliest editions end with Frank and Archie returning home. Starting in late 1869, the final chapter concludes with the heroes going West to San Diego to have more adventures (the ROCKY MOUNTAIN series).

Castlemon books, House-Boat Series, 1895 – 1896, Henry T. Coates. Front cover two-color illustrations printed on cloth with gilt type on spine. frontispiece and three full-page illustrations. Early editions, $35.00; later reprints by other publishers, $10.00

House-Boat Boys, 1895, earliest editions retain Porter & Coates monogram on title page but spine has HTC imprint.

Mystery of the Lost River Canyon, 1896

Young Game-Warden, 1896

Castlemon books, Hunter Series, 1892, Porter & Coates. Cover illustrations printed on cloth binding in black, gray, and gold. Illustrated with frontispiece and three full-page plates. Early editions, $30.00; reprints by other publishers such as Winston, $10.00

Two Ways of Becoming a Hunter, 1892

Camp in the Foothills (spelled Foot-Hills on title page), 1893

Oscar in Africa, 1894. First edition, fourth printing, shows Henry T. Coates on spine but retains Porter & Coates on title-page (see Blanck in Bibliography), later printings eventually drop P&C information.

Castlemon books, Lucky Tom Series, 1887 – 1895,

Porter & Coates or Henry T. Coates as listed (see also PUBLISHERS). Early editions, $30.00; reprints by other publishers such as Winston, $10.00

Our Fellows or *Skirmishes with the Swamp Dragoons*, 1887 Porter, cloth binding stamped in black and gold, frontispiece and three plates.

Elam Storm, The Wolfer or *The Lost Nugget*, 1895 Porter, cloth stamped in black, gold, and yellow; frontispiece and three plates.

Missing Pocket-Book or *Tom Mason's Luck*, 1895 Henry T. Coates & Co (copyright notice and title page of earliest editions still show Porter monogram and information). Cloth binding stamped in black, gold, and yellow; frontispiece and three plates.

Castlemon books, Pony Express Series, 1898 – 1900, Henry T. Coates & Co., cloth binding stamped in black and gold, frontispiece and three plates. Early editions, $30.00; reprints by other publishers, $10.00

Pony Express Rider, 1898
White Beaver, 1899
Carl the Trailer, 1900

Castlemon books, Rocky Mountain Series, 1871, R.W. Carroll. Continuing adventures of the heroes of the Gun-Boat series. Earliest Carroll editions issued with pebbled cloth binding, blind-stamped on front; spine heavily decorated in gilt with decorative scrolls, title, author's name and publisher's logo; decorative title page and two full-page illustrations on coated paper. Starting in 1872, reissued by Porter & Coates under a joint imprint: R.W. Carroll & Company-Porter & Coates. See also PUBLISHERS. Carroll editions, RARE; P&C early editions, $35.00; later reprints by other publishers, $10.00.

Frank Among the Rancheros, 1871
Frank at Don Carlos' Rancho, 1871
Frank in the Mountains, 1871

Castlemon books, Rod and Gun Series, 1883 – 1885, Porter & Coates. Continues adventures of Don Gordon, first introduced in *Boy Trapper*. Cloth binding stamped black and gold (gilt) or brown and gold. Early editions, $45.00; later reprints by other publishers, $10.00

Don Gordon's Shooting-Box, 1883, frontispiece and two full-page illustrations
Rod and Gun Club, 1883, frontispiece and three full-page illustrations
Young Wild-Fowlers, 1885, frontispiece and three full-page illustrations

Castlemon books, Rolling-Stone Series (also called "Go-Ahead" after 1872), 1869 – 1871, R.W. Carroll. Earliest Carroll editions issued with pebbled cloth binding, blind-stamped on front; spine heavily decorated in gilt with decorative scrolls, title, author's name and publisher's logo; frontispiece, decorative title page and two full-page illustrations on coated paper. Starting in 1872,

reissued by Porter & Coates under a joint imprint: R.W. Carroll & Company-Porter & Coates. See also PUBLISHERS. Carroll imprint: RARE; P&C early editions, $30.00; other reprints, $10.00.

Tom Newcombe or *The Boy of Bad Habits*, 1869
Go Ahead or *The Fisher-boy's Motto*, 1870
No Moss or *Career of a Rolling Stone*, 1871

Castlemon books, Roughing It Series, 1879 – 1882, Porter & Coates, continuing adventures of George Ackerman introduced in the Boy Trapper series. Cloth binding with printed decorative type and title; spine decorated in gilt with small illustrations; frontispiece and three full-page plates. Early editions, $30.00; Winston reprints, $10.00.

George in Camp or *Life on the Plains*, 1879
George at the Wheel or *Life in the Pilot-House*, 1881
George at the Fort or *Life Among the Soldiers*, 1882

Castlemon books, Sportsman Club Series, 1873 – 1874, Porter & Coates (original copyright held by R.W. Carroll but first editions issued by P&C). Both Porter and Carroll's names appear in earliest editions, see Blanck (Bibliography) for variations in printings of the first edition. Cloth binding with spine heavily decorated in gilt, four plates including frontispiece. See also Frank Nelson titles. Porter early editions, $40.00; H.T. Coates reprints, $15.00; other reprints, $10.00.

Sportsman's Club in the Saddle, 1873
Sportsman's Club Afloat, 1874
Sportsman's Club Among the Trappers, 1875

CATHY AND CARL SERIES, Dorothy Grunbock Johnston, Scripture Press, illustrated hardcover. ($15.00 with dust jacket) $10.00

Cathy and Carl Captured, 1954
Cathy and Carl of the Covered Wagon, 1954
Cathy and Carl Join the Gold Rush!, 1955
Cathy and Carl Shipwrecked, 1956
Cathy and Carl Ride the Pony Express, 1958

CATHY LEONARD SERIES, Catherine Woolley, 1970s Morrow, hardcover. ($20.00 with dust jacket) $10.00

Cathy and the Beautiful People, illustrated by Paul Frame
Cathy Leonard Calling, illustrated by Liz Dauber
Cathy Uncovers a Secret, illustrated by Don Almquist
Cathy's Little Sister, illustrated by Liz Dauber
Chris in Trouble, illustrated by Paul Frame
Room for Cathy, illustrated by Veronica Reed

CAVALCADE BOOKS, Doubleday, hardcover, historical fiction by a variety of authors. ($20.00 with dust jacket) $10.00

Sample titles:

Eagle of Niagara, John Brick, 1955
Witch of Merthyn, Llewellyn, 1954
Flame of Hercules, Richard Llewellyn, 1955
Mississippi Pilot: With Mark Twain on the Great River, Phil Stong, 1954

CHALET SCHOOL, Elinor Brent-Dyer (1894 – 1969), W.R. Chambers, UK, hardcover. Original dust jacket illustrations from 1925 through 1950 drawn by Nina K. Brisley; dust jackets in the 1950s through the 1970s illustrated by Walter Spence and later D. Brooks (both artists also did revised dust jacket illustrations for earlier titles). Most collectors prefer the hardcover editions because the later paperback reprints were often abridged or adapted from the earlier books. Brent-Dyer also wrote a number of individual titles as well as LA ROCHELLE and CHUDLEIGH series. Books command highest prices from British and Canadian collectors.

First editions of 1920s and 1930s titles: RARE

1940s – 1960s first editions: ($150.00 with dust jacket) $50.00

1950s – 1960s reprints: ($100.00 with dust jacket) $25.00

School at the Chalet, 1925
Jo of the Chalet School, 1926
Princess of the Chalet School, 1927
Head-Girl of the Chalet School, 1928
Rivals of the Chalet School, 1929
Eustacia Goes to the Chalet School, 1930
Chalet School and Jo, 1931
Chalet Girls in Camp, 1932
Exploits of the Chalet Girls, 1933
Chalet School and the Lintons, 1934 (split into 2 paperbacks: *Chalet School and the Lintons; Rebel at the Chalet School*)
New House at the Chalet School, 1935
Jo Returns to the Chalet School, 1936
New Chalet School, 1938 (split into 2 paperbacks: *New Chalet School; United Chalet School*)
Chalet School in Exile, 1940
Chalet School Goes to It, 1941
Highland Twins at the Chalet School, 1942
Lavender Laughs in the Chalet School, 1943
Gay From China at the Chalet School, 1944
Jo to the Rescue, 1945
Three Go to the Chalet School, 1949
Chalet School and the Island, 1950
Peggy of the Chalet School, 1950
Carola Storms the Chalet School, 1951

Wrong Chalet School, 1952
Shocks for the Chalet School, 1952
Chalet School in the Oberland, 1952
Bride Leads the Chalet School, 1953
Changes for the Chalet School, 1953
Joey Goes to the Oberland, 1954
Chalet School and Barbara, 1954
Tom Tackles the Chalet School, 1955
Chalet School Does it Again, 1955
Chalet Girl from Kenya, 1955
Mary-Lou of the Chalet School, 1956
Genius at the Chalet School, 1956 (split into 2 paperbacks: *Genius at the Chalet School; Chalet School Fete*)
Problem for the Chalet School, 1956
New Mistress at the Chalet School, 1956
Excitements at the Chalet School, 1957
Coming of Age of the Chalet School, 1957
Chalet School and Richenda, 1958
Trials for the Chalet School, 1958
Theodora and the Chalet School, 1959
Joey and Co. in Tirol, 1960
Ruey Richardson – Chaletian, 1960
Leader in the Chalet School, 1961
Chalet School Wins the Trick, 1961
Future Chalet School Girl, 1962
Feud in the Chalet School, 1962
Chalet School Triplets, 1963
Chalet School Reunion, 1963
Jane and the Chalet School, 1964
Redheads at the Chalet School, 1964
Adrienne and the Chalet School, 1965
Summer Term at the Chalet School, 1965
Challenge for the Chalet School, 1966
Two Sams at the Chalet School, 1967
Althea Joins the Chalet School, 1969
Prefects of the Chalet School, 1970

Chalet School, related titles: Chalet Books, Chambers, UK. Three collections of short stories or novellas (some stories later released as individual paperback titles). Also reprinted in the 1970s as part of the My Treasure Hour annuals. Hardbacks (with dust jacket $150.00) $50.00

Chalet Book for Girls, 1947
Second Chalet Book for Girls, 1948
Third Chalet Book for Girls, 1949

Chalet School, nonfiction title:
Chalet Girls' Cookbook, 1953 Chambers, hardback with dust jacket, RARE

CHAMPION SPORTS SERIES, Noel Sainsbury, Jr., 1934 Cupples & Leon, hardcover, 5 titles. ($20.00 with dust jacket) $10.00

Fighting Five
Gridiron Grit
Winning Forward Pass
Homerun Hennessey
Touchdown to Victory

CHARLIE SERIES, Helen Hill and Violet Maxwell, 1920s Macmillan, cloth-over-board cover with small impressed illustration, small, illustrated endpapers, color illustrations by authors. ($65.00 with dust jacket) $30.00

Charlie and His Kitten Topsy, 1922
Charlie and His Coast Guards, 1925
Charlie and His Surprise House, 1926
Charlie and His Friends, 1927
Charlie and His Puppy Bingo, 1929

CHATTERBOX BOOKS see ANNUALS

CHERRY AMES SERIES, Helen Wells or Julie (Campbell) Tatham, Grosset. There were 27 books written between 1943 and 1968. A planned 28th book was not published. A few of the later books had small printings and therefore command a higher price, which is listed after the title.

Most plain hardcovers: ($30.00 with dust jacket) $15.00
Illustrated hardcover: $20.00
Student Nurse, 1943
Senior Nurse, 1944
Army Nurse, 1944
Chief Nurse, 1944
Flight Nurse, 1945
Veterans' Nurse, 1946
Private Duty Nurse, 1946
Visiting Nurse, 1947
Cruise Nurse, 1948
At Spencer, 1949
Night Supervisor, 1950
Mountaineer Nurse, 1951

Clinic Nurse, 1952
Dude Ranch Nurse, 1953
Rest Home Nurse, 1954
Country Doctor's Nurse, 1955
Boarding School Nurse, 1955
Department Store Nurse, 1956
Camp Nurse, 1957
At Hilton Hospital, 1959 ($40.00 with dust jacket) $15.00
Book of First Aid & Home Nursing, 1959, grey tweed hardcover, first edition: $150.00
Island Nurse, 1960
Rural Nurse, 1961
Staff Nurse, 1962
Companion Nurse, 1964
Jungle Nurse, 1965
Mystery in the Doctor's Office, 1966, illustrated hardcover, hard-to-find. $50.00
Ski Nurse Mystery, 1968, illustrated hardcover, hard-to-find. $50.00

CHESTER BOYS see BUCK AND LARRY

CHICKEN LITTLE JANE SERIES, Lily Munsel Ritchie, Britton, hardcover, illustrations. $30.00
Barse & Hopkins, hardcover, illustrated frontispiece. $20.00
Chicken Little Jane, 1918
Adventures of Chicken Little Jane, 1920
Chicken Little Jane Comes to Town, 1921
Chicken Little Jane in the Rockies, 1926

CHILDHOOD OF FAMOUS AMERICANS SERIES, Bobbs-Merrill, hardcover, illustrated. ($30.00 with dust jacket) $15.00
Titles include:
George Dewey: Vermont Boy, Laura Long, ca. 1952
Zeb Pike: Boy Traveller, Augusta Stevenson, 1953
Nancy Hanks, Kentucky Girl, Augusta Stevenson, 1954
Daniel Boone, Boy Hunter, Augusta Stevenson, 1961

CHILDREN'S FRIEND SERIES, ca. 1905 Little, Brown, small hardcover with impressed illustration or design, some with gilt lettering or trim, uncredited b/w illustrations, included titles by Louisa May Alcott, Susan Coolidge, Louise Chandler Moulton, Nora Perry, Laura Richards. $25.00
Hole in the Wall
Marjorie's Three Gifts
May Flowers
Poppies and Wheat
Candy Country
Christmas Dream
Little Button Rose
Pansies and Water-Lilies
Doll's Journey
Little Women at Play
Little Men at Play

Mountain Laurel and Maiden Hair
Susan Coolidge titles:
Little Knight of Labor
Curly Locks
Two Girls
Little Tommy Tucker
Little Bo-Peep and Queen Blossom
Uncle and Aunt

CHIP HILTON SPORTS SERIES, Clair Bee, Grosset & Dunlap, red tweed hardcover, sport design endpapers, b/w illustrations. Probable first edition with dust jacket: $75.00 ($30.00 with dust jacket) $15.00
Touchdown Pass, 1948
Championship Ball, 1948
Strike Three, 1949
Clutch Hitter, 1949
Hoop Crazy, 1950
Pitchers' Duel, 1950
Pass and a Prayer, 1951
Dugout Jinx, 1952
Freshman Quarterback, 1952
Backboard Fever, 1953
Fence Busters, 1953
Ten Seconds to Play, 1955
Fourth Down Showdown, 1956
Tournament Crisis, 1957
Hardcourt Upset, 1957
Pay-Off Pitch, 1958
No-Hitter, 1959
Triple-Threat Trouble, 1960
Backboard Ace, 1961
Buzzer Basket, 1962
Comeback Cagers, 1963
Home Run Feud, 1964
Hungry Hurler, 1966

CHLORIS SERIES, Kin Platt, Bradbury Press, hardcover. Chloris has her own opinions of her mother and sister's friends. Dust jacket by Bernard Colonna. ($25.00 with dust jacket) $10.00
Chloris and the Creeps, 1973

Chloris and the Freaks, 1975
Chloris and the Weirdos, 1978

CHRISTIE DRAYTON SERIES see LAMBERT

CHRISTOPHER COOL, TEEN AGENT SERIES, Jack Lancer, Grosset, illustrated hardcover. $15.00
X Marks the Spy, 1967
Mission: Moonfire, 1967
Department of Danger, 1967
Ace of Shadows, 1968
Heads You Lose, 1968
Trial by Fury, 1969

CHUDLEIGH HOLD SERIES, Elinor Brent-Dyer (see also CHALET SCHOOL, LA ROCHELLE). W.R. Chambers, UK, hardcover, hard-to-find: ($100.00 with dust jacket) $50.00
Chudleigh Hold, 1954
Condor Crags Adventure, 1954
Top Secret, 1955
Chudleigh related titles, some of the same characters also appear in:
Fardingales, 1950
Susannah Adventure, 1953

CINDA HOLLISTER SERIES, Janet Lambert, Dutton, hardcover: $150.00 with dust jacket
Grosset & Dunlap tweed hardcover reprint: ($50.00 with dust jacket) $25.00
Cinda, 1954
Fly Away Cinda, 1956
Big Deal, 1958
Triple Trouble, 1965
Love to Spare, 1967

CIRCUS BOYS SERIES, Edgar B. P. Darlington, ca. 1910 Altemus, print illustration on cloth-over-board cover, about 250 pages, b/w illustrations. ($25.00 with dust jacket) $15.00
Circus Boys on the Flying Rings
Circus Boys across the Continent
Circus Boys in Dixie Land
Circus Boys on the Mississippi
Circus Boys on the Plains

CLARENCE THE DOG SERIES, Patricia Lauber, Cow-ard-McCann, illustrated hardcover, b/w illustra-tions. $20.00
Clarence, the TV Dog, 1955, illustrated by Leonard Shortall
Clarence Turns Sea Dog, 1959, illustrated by Leonard Shortall
Clarence and the Burglar, adapted by Monjo, 1973, illustrated by Paul Galdone
Clarence and the Cat, adapted from a chapter in first book, 1977, illustrated by Paul Galdone

CLEO SERIES see GARIS

CLINT WEBB SERIES, W. Bert Foster, ca. 1914 M.A. Donohue, hardcover, four titles. $15.00

CLOUD PATROL SERIES, Irving Crump, ca. 1930s Gros-set & Dunlap, hardcover, flying stories. ($25.00 with dust jacket) $15.00
Cloud Patrol
Pilot of the Cloud Patrol
Craig of the Cloud Patrol

CLOVERFIELD FARM SERIES, Helen Fuller Orton, 1922 – 26 Stokes, hardcover, illustrated. $10.00
Prince and Rover of Cloverfield Farm
Summer at Cloverfield Farm
Bobby of Cloverfield Farm

Winter at Cloverfield Farm
Cloverfield Farm related title:
Cloverfield Farm Stories, 1947 Lippincott

COLLEGE LIFE SERIES, Gilbert Patten (see also FRANK MERRIWELL SERIES), ca. 1920s Barse, cloth-over-board cover, b/w illustrations. ($20.00 with dust jacket) $10.00
Boltwood of Yale
College Rebel
On College Battlefields
Call of the Varsity
Sons of Old Eli
Ben Oakman, Stroke

COLLEGE SPORTS SERIES, Lester Chadwick, ca. 1925 Cupples & Leon, hardcover, b/w plates. ($35.00 with dust jacket) $10.00
Rival Pitchers
Quarterback's Pluck
Batting to Win
Winning Touchdown
For the Honor of Randall
Eight-Oared Victors

COLONIAL SERIES, Edward Stratemeyer, ca. 1910 Lothrop, Lee, printed illustration on hardcover, b/w frontispiece. $25.00
With Washington in the West
Marching on Niagara
At the Fall of Montreal
On the Trail of Pontiac
Fort in the Wilderness
Trail and Trading Post

COLONY SERIES, James Otis, 1910 American Book Company, green hardcover, b/w illustrations. $25.00
Calvert of Maryland: A Story of Lord Baltimore's Colony
Mary of Plymouth: A Story of the Pilgrim Settlement
Peter of New Amsterdam: A Story of Old New York
Richard of Jamestown: A Story of the Virginia Colony
Ruth of Boston: A Story of the Massachusetts Bay Colony
Stephen of Philadelphia: A Story of the Penn's Colony

COLOSSAL CORCORAN SERIES, W. Ingram Morgan (pseudonym of R.G. Campbell), 1952 Cole Pub-lishing, Australia, hardcover, illustrated by Wally Driscoll. ($20.00 with dust jacket) $10.00
Colossal Corcoran in Mystery Valley
Colossal Corcoran on Skull Atoll
Colossal Corcoran in the Caribbean
Colossal Corcoran on Smoke Island
Colossal Corcoran in the Hindu Kush Mountains

CONNIE BLAIR MYSTERY SERIES, Betsy Allen, ca. 1940s Grosset, cloth-over-board cover, advertised as "Connie is a career girl with a job in an advertising agency ...you can identify A Connie Blair Mystery at a glance because a color is always in the title." Last titles are hard-to find. Earlier titles: ($35.00 with dust jacket) $15.00

Clue in Blue
Riddle in Red
Puzzle in Purple
Secret of Black Cat Gulch
Green Island Mystery
Ghost Wore White
Yellow Warning
Gray Menace
Brown Satchel Mystery
Peril in Pink
Silver Secret, 1956, $70.00 with dust jacket
Mystery of the Ruby Queens, 1958, $150.00 with dust jacket

CONNIE LORING SERIES see GARIS

CONNIE MORGAN SERIES, James Hendryx, pseudonym (James Beardsley, 1880 – 1963). Putnam and Doubleday, hardcover, b/w illustrations by W. W. Clarke, first edition: $100.00
Connie Morgan in Alaska, 1916
Connie Morgan with the Mounted, 1918
Connie Morgan in the Lumber Camps, 1919
Connie Morgan in the Fur Country, 1921
Connie Morgan in the Cattle Country, 1923, illustrations by Frank E. Schoonover.
Connie Morgan with the Forest Rangers, 1925
Connie Morgan Hits the Trail, 1929
Connie Morgan in the Arctic, ca. 1936

CORALLY CROTHERS SERIES, Romney Gay and Phyllis Britcher, Grosset, easy reader, small, color illustration on paper-over-board cover, illustrated endpapers, color illustrations by author. ($75.00 with dust jacket) $30.00
Tale of Corally Crothers, 1932
Come Play with Corally Crothers, 1943
Corally Crothers' Birthday, 1944

CORNER HOUSE GIRLS SERIES, Grace Brooks Hill, Barse, illustrated cloth-over-board cover, illustrated endpapers, 4 b/w illustrations by Emmett Owen. ($30.00 with dust jacket) $20.00
Undated Grosset reprints, b/w illustrations by Hastings. ($20.00 with dust jacket) $15.00
Corner House Girls, 1915
Corner House Girls at School, 1915
Corner House Girls Under Canvas, 1915
Corner House Girls Odd Find, 1916
Corner House Girls in a Play, 1916
Corner House Girls on Tour, 1917
Corner House Girls Growing Up, 1918
Corner House Girls Snowbound, 1920
Corner House Girls with the Gypsies, 1921
Corner House Girls on Palm Island, 1922
Corner House Girls Solve a Mystery, 1923
Corner House Girls Facing the World, 1926

CORNERSTONES OF FREEDOM SERIES, 1960s Children's Press, hardcover, numerous titles, illustrated, by various authors. ($15.00 with dust jacket) $10.00
Story of the Statue of Liberty
Story of the Lewis & Clark Expedition
Story of the USS Arizona
Story of the Constitution
Story of the Declaration of Independence
Story of the Supreme Court
Story of the Alamo
Story of the Gettysburg Address
Story of the Conestoga Wagon
Story of the Mayflower
Story of Monticello
Story of the Bonhomme Richard

COUSIN LUCY SERIES, Jacob Abbott (1803 – 1879), NY, ca. 1840s, small hardcover (see ROLLO series), b/w plates. Ca. 1870s Clark & Maynard reprints: $20.00
Titles included:
Cousin Lucy at Play
Cousin Lucy Among the Mountains
Cousin Lucy at the Sea-Shore
Cousin Lucy's Conversations

COWBOY SAM SERIES, Edna Walker Chandler, Beckley-Cardy, Benefic Press, small pictorial hardcover, 64 pages, illustrated by Jack Merryweather. $20.00

Cowboy Sam and Freddy, 1951
Cowboy Sam and the Fair, 1951
Cowboy Sam and the Rodeo, 1952
Cowboy Sam and Flop, 1958
Cowboy Sam and the Rustlers, 1959
Cowboy Sam and Big Bill, 1961
Cowboy Sam and the Indians, 1962
Cowboy Sam and Shorty, 1971

CRANBERRYPORT SERIES, Wende and Harry Devlin, oversize color illustrated books for young readers, featuring Maggie and her grandmother and a variety of town residents, delightfully presented in full-page and double-page color illustrations by the authors and including a cranberry recipe. Prices are for early edition hardcover.

Cranberry Thanksgiving, 1971 Parents, Maggie's grandmother's Cranberry Bread recipe is featured on the back cover. $20.00

Cranberry Christmas, 1976 Parents, Maggie's Favorite Cranberry Cookies recipe is featured on the back cover. $20.00

Cranberry Mystery, 1978 Four Winds Press. $30.00

Cranberry Halloween, 1982 Four Winds Press, includes recipe for Cranberry Dessert. $30.00

Cranberry Valentine, 1986 Four Winds Press. $30.00

Cranberry Easter, 1990 Four Winds Press, includes recipe for Cranberry Cobbler. ($65.00 with dust jacket) $30.00

Cranberry Summer, 1992 Four Winds Press. ($50.00 with dust jacket) $20.00

Cranberry Birthday, 1993 Four Winds Press. $30.00

Cranberry Autumn, 1993 Four Winds Press. ($40.00 with dust jacket) $20.00

Cranberry First Day of School, 1995 Four Winds Press. $30.00

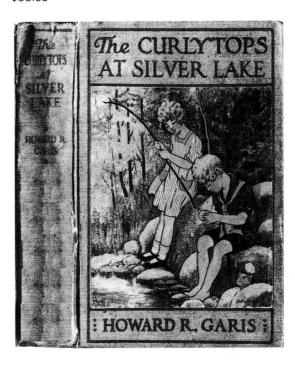

CURLYTOPS SERIES, Howard R. Garis, ca. 1920s Cupples & Leon, paste-on-pictorial, hardcover, b/w illustrations by Julia Greene, 14 books including the titles listed. $30.00

Curlytops at Cherry Farm
Curlytops on Star Island
Curlytops Snowed In
Curlytops at Uncle Frank's Ranch
Curlytops at Silver Lake
Curlytops and Their Pets
Curlytops and Their Playmates
Curlytops in the Woods
Curlytops at Sunset Beach
Curlytops at Happy House
Curlytops at the Circus
Curlytops Growing Up

— D —

DADDY SERIES, Howard Garis (1914 – 20 Fenno), 1920s edition Donohue, small size hardcover with paste-on-pictorial, two-color illustrations by Louis Wisa, Edyth Powers, Eva Dean. $35.00

Daddy Takes Us Camping
Daddy Takes Us Fishing
Daddy Takes Us to the Circus
Daddy Takes Us Skating
Daddy Takes Us Coasting
Daddy Takes Us to the Farm
Daddy Takes Us to the Garden
Daddy Takes Us Hunting Birds
Daddy Takes Us Hunting Flowers

Daddy Takes Us to the Woods

DAN CARTER SERIES, Mildred Wirt, Cupples & Leon, 200+ pages, red cloth-over-board cover, b/w frontispiece. Individually illustrated dust jackets. ($20.00 with dust jacket) $10.00

Dan Carter, Cub Scout, and the River Camp, 1949
Dan Carter and the Money Box, 1950
Dan Carter and the Haunted Castle, 1951
Dan Carter and the Great Carved Face, 1952
Dan Carter and the Cub Honor, 1953

DANA GIRLS MYSTERY SERIES, Carolyn Keene (Stratemeyer Syndicate pseudonym), ca. 1930s Grosset & Dunlap, hardcover, various illustrators.
Early editions: ($35.00 with dust jacket) $15.00
1950s reprints: ($25.00 with dust jacket) $15.00

By the Light of the Study Lamp, 1934
Secret at Lone Tree Cottage
In the Shadow of the Tower
Three-Cornered Mystery
Secret at the Hermitage
Circle of Footprints
Mystery of the Locked Room
Clue in the Cobweb
Secret at the Gatehouse, 1940
Mysterious Fireplace
Clue of the Rusty Key
Portrait in the Sand
Secret in the Old Well
Clue in the Ivy, 1952
Secret of the Jade Ring
Mystery at the Crossroads
Ghost in the Gallery
Clue of the Black Flower
Winking Ruby Mystery
Secret of the Swiss Chalet
Haunted Lagoon
Mystery of the Bamboo Bird, 1960
Sierra Gold Mystery
Secret of Lost Lake
Mystery of the Stone Tiger
Riddle of the Frozen Fountain
Secret of the Silver Dolphin, 1965
Mystery of the Wax Queen

Secret of the Minstrel's Guitar
Phantom Surfer, 1968

Dana Girls, 1970s illustrated white hardcovers, Grosset & Dunlap renumbered series, including new titles. Price through *Swiss Chalet:* $10.00
The last five titles are more difficult to find, each: $20.00 to $40.00

Mystery of the Stone Tiger
Riddle of the Frozen Fountain
Secret of the Silver Dolphin
Mystery of the Wax Queen
Haunted Lagoon
Mystery of the Bamboo Bird
Sierra Gold Mystery
Secret of Lost Lake
Winking Ruby Mystery
Secret of the Swiss Chalet
Ghost in the Gallery
Curious Coronation
Hundred Year Mystery
Mountain-Peak Mystery
Witch's Omen

DANCING PEEL SERIES, Lorna Hill, 1954 – 1962, Thomas Nelson, hardcover, 6 titles. See also MARJORIE, PATIENCE, SADLER'S WELLS, and VICARAGE CHILDREN. ($20.00 with dust jacket) $10.00

Dancing Peel, 1954
Dancer's Luck, 1955
Little Dancer, 1956
Dancer in the Wings, 1958
Dancer in Danger, 1960
Dancer on Holiday, 1962

DANDELION COTTAGE SERIES, Carroll Watson Rankin, 1904-21 Holt, 5 titles. $20.00
Titles include:
Dandelion Cottage, (1904) 1936 edition Henry Holt, b/w plates by Florence Shinn and Elizabeth Finley. $20.00

Dandelion Cottage, (1904) 1946 edition Henry Holt, b/w drawings by Mary Stevens. ($35.00 with dust jacket) $15.00

Adopting of Rosa Marie, 1908 Henry Holt, hardcover with impressed design, color frontispiece, b/w illustrations by Florence Shinn. $20.00

Castaways of Pete's Patch, 1911 Henry Holt, hardcover with impressed design, b/w illustrations by Ada Williamson. $20.00

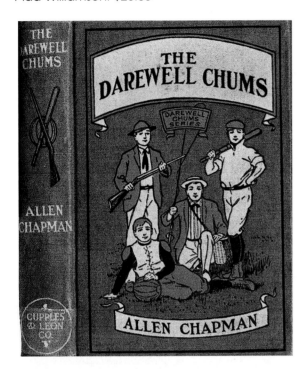

DAREWELL CHUMS SERIES, Allen Chapman, ca. 1908 Cupples & Leon, illustrated brown cloth-over-board cover, "telling the doings of four chums at school and elsewhere," b/w illustrations by Boehm. ($25.00 with dust jacket) $15.00
Goldsmith reprints: ($15.00 with dust jacket) $10.00
Darewell Chums
Darewell Chums in the City
Darewell Chums in the Woods
Darewell Chums in a Winter Camp
Darewell Chums on a Cruise

DAUNTLESS SERIES, Peter Dawlish, mid-1950s Oxford University Press, hardcover, illustrated by Jobson. ($25.00 with dust jacket) $10.00
Dauntless and the Mary Baines
Dauntless Takes Recruits
Dauntless Finds Her Crew
Dauntless in Danger

DAVE DARRIN SERIES see DICK PRESCOTT

DAVE DASHAWAY SERIES, Roy Rockwood, ca. 1915 Cupples & Leon, printed illustration on hardcover, b/w frontispiece. ($25.00 with dust jacket) $15.00

Dave Dashaway, the Young Aviator
Dave Dashaway and His Hydroplane
Dave Dashaway Around the World
Dave Dashaway and His Giant Airship
Dave Dashaway, Air Champion

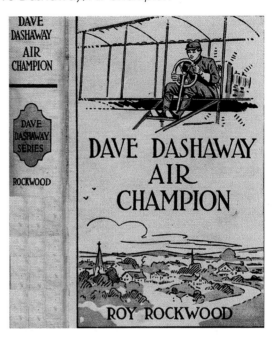

DAVE DAWSON SERIES, Sidney Bowen, ca. 1940s Saalfield, hardcover. ($30.00 with dust jacket) $15.00
Dave Dawson with the Air Corps
Dave Dawson, Flight Lieutenant
Dave Dawson at Dunkirk
Dave Dawson with the R.A.F.
Dave Dawson with the Commandos
Dave Dawson with the Pacific Fleet
Dave Dawson on Convoy Patrol
Dave Dawson at Singapore
Dave Dawson in Libya
Dave Dawson with the Flying Tigers
Dave Dawson on Guadalcanal
Dave Dawson on the Russian Front

DAVE FEARLESS see DEEP SEA

DAVE PORTER, Edward Stratemeyer, ca. 1905 – 1920 Lothrop, Lee & Shepard, hardcover, some of the titles reissued in the STRATEMEYER POPULAR SERIES. ($35.00 with dust jacket) $20.00
Dave Porter at Oak Hill
Dave Porter in the South Seas
Dave Porter's Return to School
Dave Porter in the Far North
Dave Porter and his Classmates
Dave Porter at Star Ranch
Dave Porter and his Rivals
Dave Porter on Cave Island
Dave Porter in the Gold Fields
Dave Porter at Bear Camp

Dave Porter and His Double
Dave Porter's Great Search
Dave Porter Under Fire
Dave Porter's War Honors

DAVID SERIES, David Binney, 1925 – 1931 Putnam, small hardcover, illustrated endpapers, photo illustrations, Arctic adventures. ($25.00 with dust jacket) $15.00
David Goes Voyaging
David Goes to Greenland
David Goes to Baffin Island
David Sails the Viking Trail

DAVY SERIES, Lois Lenski, published by Oxford University and Walck.
Surprise for Davy, 1947 Oxford, hardcover. ($50.00 with dust jacket) $25.00
Dog Came to School, a Davy Book, 1955 Walck, first edition. ($25.00 with dust jacket) $15.00
Big Little Davy, 1956 Walck, first edition, 48 pages. ($25.00 with dust jacket) $15.00
Davy and His Dog, 1957 Oxford, dark pink hardcover, 39 pages. ($25.00 with dust jacket) $15.00

DEAR LITTLE GIRL SERIES, Amy Ella Blanchard (1856-1926), G.W. Jacobs, small hardcover. $20.00
Dear Little Girl at School, 1910
Dear Little Girl's Summer Holidays, 1911
Dear Little Girl's Thanksgiving Holidays, 1912

DEEP SEA SERIES, Roy Rockwood, 1905 – 1908 Stitt, also published by Chatterton-Peck, Mershon, and Grosset & Dunlap, hardcover adventure novels written under a Stratemeyer Syndicate pseudonym. The first three titles were reprinted as Dave Fearless Series in 1918 by Sully, and ten years later Garden City picked up the Dave Fearless name and continued the series in paperback.
Hardcover: ($40.00 with dust jacket) $20.00
Rival Ocean Divers, or *After a Sunken Treasure,* 1905
Cruise of the Treasure Ship, or *Castaways of Floating Island,* 1906
Adrift on the Pacific, or *Secret of the Island Cave,* 1908
Jack North's Treasure Hunt, or *Daring Adventures in South America,* 1907

DEEP SEA HUNTERS SERIES, A. Hyatt Verrill, 1922 – 1924 Appleton, red or blue hardcover with clipper ship design, frontispiece. $60.00
Deep Sea Hunters Adventures on a Whaler
Deep Sea Hunters in the Frozen Seas
Deep Sea Hunters in the South Seas

DEER LODGE SERIES, W. Gordon Parker, 1898 – 1900 Lee and Shepard, pictorial hardcover, illustrations throughout, adventure novels. $20.00
Six Young Hunters, or *Adventures of the Greyhound Club,* 1898
Grant Burton the Runaway, or *The Mishaps of a School Boy,* 1899
Rival Boy Sportsmen, or *Mink Lake Regatta,* 1900

DEERFOOT SERIES see ELLIS

DESMOND THE DOG SERIES, Herbert Best, Viking, hardcover, b/w illustrations by Lilian Obligado or Ezra Jack Keats. ($25.00 with dust jacket) $10.00
Desmond's First Case, 1961
Desmond the Dog Detective: the Case of the Lone Stranger, 1962
Desmond and the Peppermint Ghost: The Dog Detective's Third Case, 1965
Desmond and Dog Friday, 1968

DICK SERIES, Anthony Weston Dimock, ca. 1909 Stokes, illustrated hardcover, fictional stories with photo illustrations. $15.00
Dick in the Everglades
Dick among the Lumberjacks
Dick among the Seminoles
Dick among the Miners

1962 edition

DICK AND JANE BOOKS, William Gray and others, 1927 – 1970 Scott, Foresman and Company. The first-grade primers featuring Dick and Jane were updated every five years to reflect changes in clothing, automobiles, and American lifestyles. Last update occurred in 1965. Original illustrations of early books are by Eleanor Campbell. Prices given show the date of publication of that particular book, not its original date of copyright.

"Ex-school copies" are the most commonly available types, stamped with school names, room numbers, and so forth.

Because these first-grade readers are almost always ex-schoolroom books, prices vary widely, depending on condition. Condition varies from a neatly written room number to heavy stamping and wear. Prices given are for clean copies with few marks and need to be discounted for condition.

Dick and Jane paperbound hardcover pre-primers, 1950s and 60s editions: $50.00 to $100.00

Dick and Jane
More Dick and Jane Stories
We Come and Go
We Look and See
We Work and Play
Sally, Dick and Jane
Fun With Our Family
Fun Wherever We Are

Dick and Jane clothbound hardcovers, 1950s and 60s editions: $30.00 to $65.00

Fun with Dick and Jane
New Fun with Dick and Jane
Fun with Our Friends

John and Jean hardcover readers:

Fun with John and Jean, 1951, same story as *Fun with Dick and Jane,* but revised for Catholic schools and labeled "New Cathedral Basic Reader," light green hardcover, 159 pages, illustrated by Eleanor Campbell. $50.00

Dick and Jane hardcover readers, 1950s – 1960s, first printings: $60.00 to $100.00 range

Our New Friends, 1950s edition

Good Times With Our Friends, Dorothy Baruch, 1948 edition

Happy Days with Our Friends, Elizabeth Montgomery, Bauer, Gray, 1954, blue hardcover, illustrated by Ruth Steed.

More Fun with Our Friends, Helen Robison, 1962 edition

Meet Our New Friends, 1956, brown hardcover

New Fun with Dick and Jane, William Gray, 1956 first printing

New More Streets and Roads, William Gray, 1956

Fun with Our Friends, Robinson, Monroe, Artley, 1963 edition

Friends New and Old, Helen Robinson, 1963

Dick and Jane workbook, 1950s – 1960s, workbooks vary widely in condition, some heavily marked, some unused, and this greatly affects value. $50.00 to $100.00

Dick and Jane "Before We Read" Picture Books, oversize oblong hardcover, also softcover workbook editions, b/w and color illustrations, no words. $40.00 to $100.00 range

Before We Read
We Read Pictures
We Read More Pictures

Dick and Jane teacher's edition, 1940s:

Guidebook to Our New Friends, 1946 – 47. $125.00
Guidebook to Fun With Dick and Jane, 1946 – 47. $125.00

Dick and Jane teacher's edition, 1950s and 1960s:

New Guess Who, 1962 teacher's edition, hardcover, guide to preprimers. $85.00

We Read Pictures, 1963 Cathedral Basic Reader teacher's edition, oblong oversize hardcover, 48 pages, with instructions to teacher to use John, Jean, Judy names. $60.00

We Read More Pictures, 1951 teacher's edition, oblong oversize hardcover, 48 pages. $75.00

We Read More Pictures, 1962 teacher's edition, oblong oversize softcover, 78 page "teacher notes" section precedes 48 story pages. $75.00

Dick and Jane related books:

White House Murder Case and *Dick and Jane,* Jules Feiffer, 1970 Grove, hardcover, illustrated by Feiffer. First edition: $40.00 with dust jacket

DICK AND JANET CHERRY SERIES, Howard Garis, 1930 McLoughlin, small size, 264 pages, wraparound color illustration on cover boards, b/w endpaper and frontispiece illustrations $30.00

Dick and Janet Cherry Shipwrecked on Christmas Island
Dick and Janet Cherry in the Gypsy Camp
Dick and Janet Cherry Saving the Old Mill
Dick and Janet Cherry on a Bear Hunt

DICK ARNOLD SERIES, Earl Silvers, Appleton, hardcover with paste-on-pictorial by Varian, college stories. $15.00

Dick Arnold of Raritan College, 1920
Dick Arnold Plays the Game, 1920
Dick Arnold of the Varsity, 1921

DICK HAMILTON SERIES, Howard R. Garis, 1909 – 1914 Grosset & Dunlap, brown hardcover with color illustration, frontispiece and three plates. ($30.00 with dust jacket) $15.00

Goldsmith, World, and Saalfield reprints, 1925 and later: ($20.00 with dust jacket) $15.00

Fortune, or *Stirring Doings of a Millionaire's Son*
Cadet Days, or *Handicap of a Millionaire's Son*
Steam Yacht, or *Young Millionaire and the Kidnappers*
Football Team, or *Young Millionaire on the Gridiron*
Touring Car, or *Young Millionaire's Race for a Fortune*
Airship, or *Young Millionaire in the Clouds*

DICK KENT SERIES see BOYS OF THE ROYAL MOUNTED POLICE

DICK PRESCOTT SERIES, Irving Hancock, a continuing saga in which Dick Prescott and/or his friends, including Greg Holmes, Dave Darrin, Dan Dalzell, Harry Hazeling, and Tom Reade, expand their adventures. The following series take these characters from grammar school through college, war service, and careers.

Published by Altemus, also Donohue, hardcover, black and white line drawing illustrations in many of these books attributed to John R. Neill. ($35.00 with dust jacket) $20.00

Saalfield reprints: ($15.00 with dust jacket) $10.00

Dick Prescott, Grammar School Boys Series, 1911
Grammar School Boys of Gridley
Grammar School Boys Snowbound
Grammar School Boys in the Woods
Grammar School Boys in Summer Athletics

Dick Prescott, High School Boys Series, 1910
High School Freshmen, or Dick & Co.'s First Year Pranks and Sports
High School Pitcher, or Dick & Co. on Gridley Diamond
High School Left End, or Dick & Co. on the Football Gridiron
High School Captain of the Team, or Leading the Athletic Vanguard

Dick Prescott, High School Boys Vacation Series, 1913
High School Boys' Canoe Club, or Dick & Co.'s Rivals on Lake Pleasant, High School Boys in Summer Camp, or *Dick Prescott Six Training for the Gridley Eleven*
High School Boys' Fishing Trip, or *Dick & Co. in the Wilderness*
High School Boys' Training Hike, or *Making Themselves "Hard as Nails"*

Dick Prescott, Annapolis Series, 1910 – 1911
Dave Darrin's First Year at Annapolis
Dave Darrin's Second Year at Annapolis
Dave Darrin's Third Year at Annapolis
Dave Darrin's Fourth Year at Annapolis

Dick Prescott, West Point Series, 1910 – 1911
Dick Prescott's *First Year at West Point, or Two Chums in Cadet Gray*
Dick Prescott's *Second Year at West Point, or Finding the Glory in a Soldier's Life*
Dick Prescott's *Third Year at West Point, or Standing Firm for Flag and Honor*
Dick Prescott's *Fourth Year at West Point, or Dropping the Gray for Shoulder Straps*

Dick Prescott, Dave Darrin Series, 1918
Dave Darrin at Vera Cruz
Dave Darrin on Mediterranean Service
Dave Darrin's South American Cruise
Dave Darrin on the Asiatic Station
Dave Darrin and the German Submarines
Dave Darrin after the Mine Layers

Dick Prescott, Boys of the Army, or Uncle Sam's Boys Series, 1912
Uncle Sam's Boys in the Philippines
Uncle Sam's Boys at the Capture of Boston

Dick Prescott, Young Engineers Series, *1912 – 1920*
Young Engineers in Colorado
Young Engineers in Arizona
Young Engineers in Nevada
Young Engineers in Mexico

Young Engineers on the Gulf

DICK TRAVERS SERIES, Adelaide Samuels, 1870s Lee & Shepard, small size, cloth with gilt covers, line drawings. $25.00
Dick Travers in Africa
Dick Travers in the Chagos Islands
Dick Travers in London

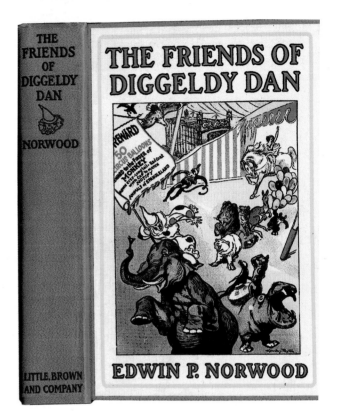

DIGGELDY DAN SERIES, Edwin Norwood, circus adventures.
Adventures of Diggeldy Dan, 1922 Little Brown , color paste-on-pictorial cover, 240 pages, 8 color plate illustrations by A. Conway Peyton. $45.00
Friends of Diggeldy Dan, 1924 Little Brown, color paste-on-pictorial cover, 240 pages, 8 color plate illustrations by A. Conway Peyton. $35.00
In *the Land of Diggeldy Dan,* 1923 Little Brown, color paste-on-pictorial cover, 240 pages, 8 color plate illustrations by A. Conway Peyton. $35.00

DIMSIE SERIES, Dorita Fairlie Bruce, Oxford U Press, pictorial hardcover with gilt, illustrated by Gertrude Hammond. First edition: $60.00 There have been several reprintings, and occasionally titles are changed. Later printings: $20.00
Dimsie Moves Up, 1921
Dimsie Moves Up Again, 1922
Dimsie, Head Girl, 1925
Dimsie Goes Back, 1927
Dimsie among the Prefects, 1927
Dimsie Carries On, last book in series, ca. 1940s

DING DONG SCHOOL BOOKS, 1953 – 1956 Rand McNally, 25 titles. Small hardcover books with pictorial covers and silver foil spines, 28 pages, color illustrations, various illustrators. Covers state "By Miss Frances" (Dr. Frances Horwich), the host of the NBC television series. $12.00
Your Friend the Policeman, 1953
Debbie and Her Nap, 1953
Suitcase with a Surprise, 1953
Big Coal Truck, 1953
I Decided, 1953
Day Downtown with Daddy, 1953
Dressing Up, 1953
Daddy's Birthday's Cakes, 1953
Baby Chipmunk, 1953
Peek In, 1954
Growing Things, 1954
My Goldfish, 1954
In My House, 1954
Dolls of Other Lands, 1954
My Big Brother, 1954
Robin Family, 1954
Grandmother Is Coming, 1954
Looking Out the Window, 1954
Our Baby, 1955
Jingle Bell Jack, 1955
Mr. Meyer's Cow, 1955
Lucky Rabbit, 1955
Magic Wagon, 1955
My Daddy Is a Policeman, 1956
Here Comes the Band, 1956
We Love Grandpa, 1956

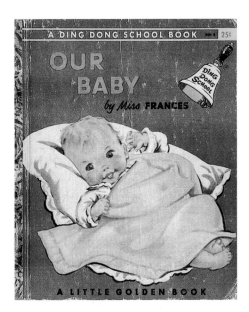

Ding Dong School Books, ca. 1959 – 1960 Golden Press, 8 titles. Reprints of the earlier Rand McNally titles done as part of the standard Little Golden Book format, 24 pages. Gold foil spines, pictorial covers state "Golden Press" or "A Little Golden Book." $10.00

DINNY GORDON SERIES, Anne Emery, MacRae, hardcover. First edition: $65.00 with dust jacket
Later printings: ($35.00 with dust jacket) $20.00
Dinny Gordon, Freshman, 1959
Dinny Gordon, Sophomore, 1961
Dinny Gordon, Junior, 1964
Dinny Gordon, Senior, 1967

DISNEY see LITTLE GOLDEN BOOKS
DIVINE CORNERS see HEADLINE BOOKS

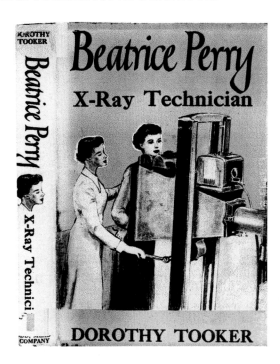

DODD, MEAD CAREER BOOKS, ca. 1940s – 1950s Dodd, Mead, hardcover, about 250 pages, written by professionals in each field. ($20.00 with dust jacket) $10.00
Titles include:
Beatrice Perry, X-Ray Technician, Dorothy Tooker
Betty Blake, O. T., Edith Stern and Meta Cobb, O.T.R.
Cadet Derry, West Pointer, Lt. Col. John B. Stanley, US Army
Carol Brant, Picture Magazine Reporter, Margit Varga
Come Soon Tomorrow, singer Gladys Swarthout
Diane Corbin, Decorator, Ina Germaine, A.I.D.
Dr. Kay Winthrop, Intern, Caroline Chandler, M. D.
Four Young Teachers, Genevieve Chase
Frills and Thrills, Lois Barnes Gallagher, fashion design
Front Page Story, Robert van Gelder
Full Ahead!, Felix Riesenberg, Jr.
Hostess of the Skyways, Dixie Willson
Ice Patrol, Lt. Kensil Bell, Coast Guard
Marian-Martha, Lucile F. Faro, librarianship
Opera Ballerina, Marie-Jeanne
Patsy Succeeds in Advertising, Evalyn Grumbine
Peggy Goes Overseas, Emma Rugby, journalism
Penny Marsh, Public Health Nurse, Dorothy Deming, R. N.
Penny Marsh, Supervisor of Public Health Nurses

Penny Marsh, Finds Adventure in Public Health Nursing
Penny and Pam, Nurse and Cadet
Phil Sterling, Salesman, Michael Gross
Polly Tucker, Merchant, Sara Penoyer
Press Box, Robert Kelley
Shirley Clayton, Secretary, Gibbs and Adams
Stand By – Mark!, Lt. Commander F. M. Gardiner, US Navy
Star on Her Forehead, actress Helen Hayes and Mary Kennedy
Susie Steward, M. D.
Touch of Parsley, May Worthington, home economics
Tune in for Elizabeth, Mary Margaret McBride, radio interviewer

DOGTOWN SERIES, Frank Bonham, Dutton, hardcover, first edition: ($30.00 with dust jacket) $10.00
Mystery of the Fat Cat, 1968
Nitty-Gritty, 1968
Vivi Chicano, 1970
Cool Cat, 1971
Hey, Big Spender, 1972

DOLLY AND MOLLY SERIES, Elizabeth Gordon, 1914 Rand McNally, small hardcover, 60 pages, illustrations by Frances Beem. $75.00
1930s reprints, pictorial hardcover, illustrations: $40.00
Dolly and Molly at the Circus
Dolly and Molly at the Seashore
Dolly and Molly and the Farmer Man

DON HALE SERIES, W. Crispin Sheppard, Penn, red hardcover with paste-on-pictorial, First World War stories, b/w plates by Bodine. $20.00
Don Hale in the War Zone, 1917
Don Hale Over There, 1918
Don Hale with the Flying Squadron, 1919
Don Hale with the Yanks, 1919

DON STURDY SERIES, Victor Appleton, ca. 1925 Grosset & Dunlap, small, cloth-over-board cover, illustrated by Walter Rogers. ($25.00 with dust jacket) $12.00
On the Desert of Mystery
With the Big Snake Hunters
In the Tombs of Gold
Across the North Pole
In the Land of Volcanoes
In the Port of Lost Ships
Among the Gorillas
Captured By Head Hunters
In Lion Land
In the Land of Giants
On the Ocean Bottom
In the Temples of Fear
Lost in Glacier Bay
Trapped in the Flaming Wilderness
With the Harpoon Hunters

DON WINSLOW SERIES, Frank Martinek, 1940 – 1941 Grosset & Dunlap, blue hardcover with yellow lettering, based on the comic strip character "Don Winslow of the Navy," frontispiece by Warren. This character was also featured in a radio series and later on TV. ($30.00 with dust jacket) $15.00
Don Winslow of the Navy
Don Winslow Face to Face with the Scorpion
Don Winslow Breaks the Spy Net
Don Winslow Saves the Secret Formula
Don Winslow, Whitman Big Little Books, ca. 1938 – 40: $45.00
Don Winslow of the Navy versus the Scorpion Gang
Don Winslow of the Navy and the Great War Plot
Don Winslow, Navy Intelligence Ace
Don Winslow of the Navy and the Secret Enemy Base
Don Winslow, Whitman Authorized Edition: ($25.00 with dust jacket) $10.00
Don Winslow and the Scorpion's Stronghold, 1946

DONNA PARKER SERIES, Marcia Martin, 1957 – 64 Whitman, glossy pictorial hardcover, plaid endpapers, 2-color illustrations. $15.00
Donna Parker at Cherrydale
Donna Parker, Special Agent
Donna Parker on Her Own
Donna Parker, Spring to Remember
Donna Parker in Hollywood
Donna Parker, Mystery at Arawak
Donna Parker Takes a Giant Step

DORIS FORCE SERIES, Julia K. Duncan (Stratemeyer Syndicate pseudonym), ca. 1930 Altemus, reprinted by Goldsmith and Donohue, cover illustration by Thelma Gooch. ($20.00 with dust jacket) $10.00

Doris Force at Locked Gates
Doris Force at Cloudy Cove
Doris Force at Raven Rock
Doris Force at Barry Manor

DOROTHY SERIES, Evelyn Raymond, 1907 – 13 Chatterton-Peck, impressed illustration on hardcover, b/w plates by R. Menck. ($20.00 with dust jacket) $10.00
Dorothy
Dorothy at Skyrie
Dorothy's Schooling
Dorothy's Travels
Dorothy's House Party
Dorothy in California
Dorothy on the Ranch
Dorothy's House Boat
Dorothy at Oak Knowe
Dorothy's Triumph
Dorothy's Tour

DOROTHY DAINTY SERIES, Amy Brooks (b. Boston) author-illustrator, 1902 – 23 Lothrop-Lee, small hardcovers with illustrations by Brooks, 22 titles.
Early edition hardcovers, except as noted after individual titles: (up to $100.00 with dust jacket) $25.00
Dorothy Dainty, 1902
Dorothy Dainty at School, 1904
Dorothy Dainty at the Shore, 1905
Dorothy Dainty at Home, 1907
Dorothy Dainty in the Country, 1909
Dorothy Dainty at the Mountains, 1911
Dorothy Dainty in the City, 1912
Dorothy Dainty at Glenmore, 1917, green and black hardcover, hard-to-find. $100.00
Dorothy Dainty at Foam Ridge, 1918
Dorothy Dainty at Stone House, 1919
Dorothy Dainty at Gem Island, 1920

DOROTHY DALE SERIES, Margaret Penrose (Stratemeyer Syndicate pseudonym), ca. 1910 – 1920s Cupples & Leon, small size tan hardcover, illustrated, 13 books, advertised as "Dorothy Dale is the daughter of an old Civil War veteran who is running a weekly newspaper in a small Eastern town...her trials and triumphs make clean, interesting and fascinating reading." ($25.00 with dust jacket) $10.00
Dorothy Dale: A Girl of To-Day
At Glenwood School
Great Secret
And Her Chums
Queer Holidays
Camping Days
School Rivals
In the City
Dorothy Dale's Promise
In the West

Strange Discovery
Engagement
To the Rescue

DOROTHY DIXON SERIES, Dorothy Wayne, ca. 1933 Goldsmith, hardcover, about 250 pages, mysteries for girls. ($20.00 with dust jacket) $10.00
Dorothy Dixon Wins Her Wings
Dorothy Dixon and the Mystery Plane
Dorothy Dixon Solves the Conway Case
Dorothy Dixon and the Double Cousin

DOT AND DASH SERIES, Dorothy West (Mildred Wirt), Cupples & Leon, hardback. ($30.00 with dust jacket) $15.00
Dot and Dash at the Sugar Maple Camp, 1938
Dot and Dash at Happy Hollow, 1938
Dot and Dash in the North Woods, 1938
Dot and Dash at the Seashore, 1940

DOTTY DIMPLE see LITTLE PRUDY

DRAGON THE HORSE SERIES, Lynn Hall, ca. 1970s Follett, glossy illustrated hardcover, b/w illustrations by Joseph Cellini. $15.00
Horse Called Dragon
New Day for Dragon
Dragon's Delight
Dragon Defiant

DREADNOUGHT BOYS SERIES, Capt. Wilbur Lawton, ca. 1910 Hurst, cloth-over-board cover, 4 full-page illustrations. ($20.00 with dust jacket) $15.00
Dreadnought Boys on Battle Practice
Dreadnought Boys aboard a Destroyer

Dreadnought Boys in a Submarine
Dreadnought Boys on Aero Service
Dreadnought Boys' World Cruise
Dreadnought Boys Home Waters

DRIA MEREDITH SERIES, Janet Lambert, ca.1952 Dutton, hardcover. ($75.00 with dust jacket) $30.00
1950s Grosset & Dunlap reprints: ($40.00 with dust jacket) $20.00
Star Dream
Summer for Seven
High Hurdles

DULCIE SERIES, by Jack Bechdolt and Decie Merwin, Dutton, small size, illustrated, paper-over-board hardcover, 64 pages, 2-color illustrations by author. $25.00
Dulcie and Half a Yard of Linsey Woolsey, 1943
Dulcie and Her Donkey, 1944
Dulcie Sews a Sampler, 1945
Dulcie and the Gypsies, 1948

———— E ————

EAGLE SCOUT SERIES, Norton Jonathan, ca. 1934 Donahue, hardcover. Goldsmith reprints: ($30.00 with dust jacket) $15.00
Movie Scout
Speedway Cyclone
Lost Empire

EASTERN INDIAN SERIES, Elmer Russell Gregor, Appleton, decorated hardcover, novels of East Coast

Indians, frontispiece. $20.00
Running Fox, 1918
White Wolf, 1921
Spotted Deer, 1922
War Eagle, 1926
Mystery Trail, 1927
Spotted Pony, 1930

EDDIE SERIES (also see BETSY), Carolyn Haywood, Morrow, hardcover, b/w illustrations throughout by author. First editions: ($45.00 in dust jacket) $15.00
Later editions: ($25.00 in dust jacket) $10.00
Little Eddie, 1947
Eddie and the Fire Engine, 1949
Eddie and Gardenia, 1951
Eddie's Pay Dirt, 1953
Eddie and His Big Deals, 1955
Eddie Makes Music, 1957
Eddie and Louella, 1959
Annie Pat and Eddie, 1960
Eddie's Green Thumb, 1964
Eddie the Dog Holder, 1966
Ever-Ready Eddie, 1968
Eddie's Happenings, 1971
Eddie's Valuable Property, 1975
Eddie's Menagerie, 1978
Merry Christmas from Eddie, 1986
Eddie's Friend Boodles, 1991

EDITHA SERIES, began with:
Editha's Burglar, Frances Burnett, 1888 Caldwell, cloth-over-board cover with gilt, photo frontispiece, b/w plates by Henry Sandham. $45.00
Burnett's book was so popular that the name Editha was then used for a series of children's books by various authors, often reprints.
Editha Series, ca. 1900 Caldwell, hardcover, color paste-on-pictorial and/or gilt decoration, illustrat-

ed frontispiece. $25.00 to $60.00 range
Titles include:
Adventures of a Brownie, Mulock
Brownies, Juliana Horatia Ewing
Burglar's Daughter, Margaret Penrose, illustrated by Frank Merrill
Little Professor, Ida Cash
Little Prudy's Story Book, Sophie May, illustrated by Amy Brooks and Birtha Davidson
Little Prudy's Captain Horace, Sophie May, illustrated by Amy Brooks and Birtha Davidson
Rab and his Friends, Brown
Pygmies and Other Stories, Nathaniel Hawthorne
Wonder Book Stories, Hawthorne, illustrated by Eliot Keen

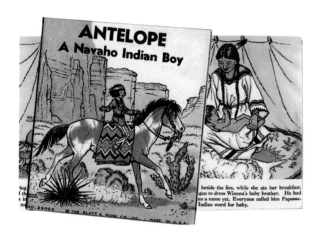

EIGHT LITTLE INDIAN SERIES, Josephine Lovell, 1935 Platt Munk, small, illustrated paper cover, 12 pages, b/w and color illustrations by Roger Vernam, books numbered 3300 A thru H. $20.00
Antelope, A Navaho Boy
Gray Bird, A Little Plains Indian
Leaping Trout, A Little Iroquois Boy
Micco, A Seminole Indian Boy
Morning Star, A Little Pueblo Girl
Nigalek, A Little Eskimo Boy
Watlala, An Indian of the Northwest
Winona, A Little Indian of the Prairies

ELIZABETH ANN SERIES, Josephine Lawrence, 1923 – 29 Barse, hardcover. $15.00
Grosset reprints, blue hardcover with orange lettering, illustrated endpapers. ($35.00 with dust jacket) $15.00
Adventures of Elizabeth Ann
Elizabeth Ann at Maple Spring
Elizabeth Ann, Six Cousins
Elizabeth Ann and Doris
Elizabeth Ann's Borrowed Grandma
Elizabeth Ann's Spring Vacation
Elizabeth Ann and Uncle Doctor
Elizabeth Ann on the Houseboat

ELLEN GRAE SERIES, Bill and Vera Cleaver, Lippincott,

hardcover, first edition. ($25.00 with dust jacket) $10.00
Ellen Grae, 1967
Lady Ellen Grae, 1968
Grover, 1970

ELLERY QUEEN JR. MYSTERY SERIES, Ellery Queen Jr. (pseudonym for Frederick Dannay, and Manfred B. Lee), 1940 titles first published by Lippincott, titles added in the 1950s by Little Brown, complete series reprinted in hardcover by Grosset & Dunlap. Paperback editions published later by Berkley and Scholastic Book Service.

Ellery Queen Jr. 1940s Grosset, also Stokes, cloth-over-board hardcover, illustrated endpapers with map, b/w illustrations. ($25.00 with dust jacket) $15.00
Black Dog Mystery, 1941, illustrations by William Sanderson
Golden Eagle, 1942
Green Turtle, 1944, illustrations by E. A. Watson
Red Chipmunk, 1946
Brown Fox, 1948

Ellery Queen Jr. 1950s Grosset, cloth-over-board hardcover, illustrated endpapers with map, b/w illustrations, hard-to-find. ($150.00 with dust jacket) $40.00
White Elephant Mystery, 1950
Yellow Cat Mystery, 1952
Blue Herring Mystery, 1954

Ellery Queen, Jr. 1961 – 1962 Golden Press, pictorial hardcover, 2 titles, illustrations by Robert Magnusen. New series started by authors of orignal Ellery Queen Jr. Series for Golden Press. This series featured different characters. Reissued in 1969 as

part of the "Golden Griffon Detective Stories."
$15.00.

Mystery of the Merry Magician, 1961
Mystery of the Vanished Victim, 1962
Ellery Queen, Jr. 1965 Putnam, purple hardcover.
Purple Bird Mystery $35.00

ELLIS BOOKS, Edward Ellis, numerous books for boys with two or more volumes on a theme or using the same characters. Hardcover, usually with printed decoration: $15.00 to $25.00 range

Ellis Books, Boone and Kenton Series, ca. 1890s Winston
Shod With Silence
In the Days of the Pioneers
Phantom of the River
Ellis books, Boy Pioneers, ca. 1890s Winston
Ned in the Block-House
Ned on the River
Ned in the Woods
Ellis books, Deerfoot Series, ca. 1890s Winston
Hunters of the Ozark
Last War Trail
Camp in the Mountains
Ellis books, Flying Boys Series, featuring Harvey Hamilton and Bohunkus Johnson, 1911 Winston, pictorial hardcover shows a plane flying above the clouds, 4 b/w plates.
Flying Boys in the Sky
Flying Boys to the Rescue
Ellis Books, Forest and Prairie Series, 1894 Winston, illustrations by White.
Great Cattle Trail
Ellis books, Launch Boys Series, 1912 Winston
Launch Boys' Cruise in the Deerfoot
Launch Boys in Northern Waters
Ellis books, Log Cabin Series, ca. 1890s Winston
Lost Trail
Footprints in the Forest
Camp-Fire and Wigwam

ELOISE SERIES, Kay Thompson (1909 – 1998, b. St. Louis, Mo., famous musical performer and voice coach), Simon and Schuster, oversize hardcover, illustrations by Hilary Knight. The first book was reprinted continually, but the others had limited printings. (First new editions for all titles issued in 1999 and 2000.)
Eloise, 1955, first edition, ($200.00 with dust jacket) $50.00 Later editions: ($35.00 with dust jacket) $15.00
Eloise in Paris, 1957, first edition. ($300.00 with dust jacket) $50.00
Eloise at Christmastime, 1958, first edition. ($300.00 with dust jacket) $50.00
Eloise in Moscow, 1959, first edition. ($300.00 with dust jacket) $50.00

ELSIE DINSMORE SERIES, Martha Finley, 1867 – 1905

Dodd, 28 titles, also see MILDRED series, 1880s printings: $40.00
Burt reprints, ca. 1910, advertised as "the famous Elsie books," plain hardcover. Dust jacket by Jessie Willcox Smith. ($25.00 with dust jacket) $10.00
Titles include:
Elsie Dinsmore
Elsie's Holiday at Roseland
Elsie's Motherhood
Elsie's Children
Elsie's Widowhood
Grandmother Elsie
Elsie's New Relations
Elsie at Nantucket
Two Elsies
Elsie's Kith and Kin
Elsie's Friends at Woodburn
Christmas with Grandmother Elsie
Elsie Yachting with the Raymonds
Elsie at Viamede
Elsie's Vacation
Elsie at Ion
Elsie's Journey on Inland Waters
Elsie at the World's Fair
Elsie, related books:
Elsie Dinsmore on the Loose, Josie Turner (Phyllis Crawford), 1930 Jonathan Cape, hardcover, b/w illustrations by Eldon Kelley, a parody of the Elsie stories. First edition: $65.00

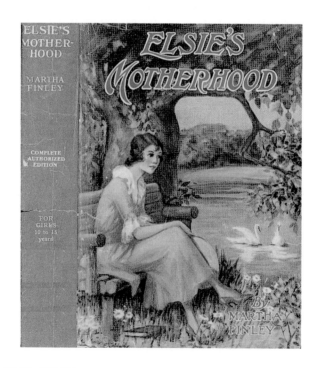

EMIL SERIES, Astrid Lindgren, hardcover, illustrations by Bjorn Berg. Emil is a small Scandanavian boy whose pranks turn into disasters for everyone else.
Brockhampton English translations, first editions: ($70.00 with dust jacket) $20.00

Follett, American editions: ($20.00 with dust jacket)
$10.00
Emil in the Soup Tureen, 1963
Emil's Pranks, 1971
Emil and the Piggy Beast, 1973 Follett
Emil and His Clever Pig, 1974 Brockhampton
That Emil, 1973 Brockhampton, oblong oversize hardcover with glossy boards: $75.00

EMILY KIMBROUGH see HEART

EMILY SERIES, L. M. Montgomery, 1920s George G. Harrap, hardcover, less famous than the author's *Anne of Green Gables* series, this series is thought to be closer to the author's own life story.
McClelland and Stewart, hardcover with paste-on-illustration by M. L. Kirk, color frontispiece, first edition Canada: ($75.00 with dust jacket) $30.00
Stokes, hardcover with paste-on-illustration by M. L. Kirk, color frontispiece, first edition US: ($125.00 with dust jacket) $30.00
Ca. 1930 Grosset reprints: ($30.00 with dust jacket) $10.00
1970s reprints by Harrap with photo illustrated dust jacket by Charlie Stebbings. ($25.00 with dust jacket) $10.00
Emily of New Moon, 1923
Emily Climbs, 1925
Emily's Quest, 1927 Stokes

EMMA AND RICHARD SERIES, Honor Arundel, Hamish, UK, hardcover, and the following first American editions: ($25.00 with dust jacket) $10.00
High House, 1967 Meredith
Emma's Island, 1968 Hawthorne
Emma in Love, 1970 Nelson

ENCYCLOPEDIA BROWN SERIES, Donald J. Sobol, 1963 – 1980s Thomas Nelson, tweed hardcover with gilt emblem in corner which reads "America's Sherlock Holmes in Sneakers," each book

contains four mysteries, b/w illustrations by Leonard Shortall, titles through *Encyclopedia Brown and the Case of the Dead Eagles,* 1975.
Other publishers extended the series and reprinted titles, including Four Winds, Morrow, Macmillan, Delacorte, Lodestar. Later illustrators include Lillian Brandy and Gail Owens.
Early printings, tweed hardcovers with Shortall illustrations: ($35.00 with dust jacket) $15.00
Weekly Reader editions, illustrated hardcovers, other illustrators: $20.00
Encyclopedia Brown, Boy Detective
Encyclopedia Brown and the Case of the Secret Pitch
Encyclopedia Brown Finds the Clues
Encyclopedia Brown Gets His Man
Encyclopedia Brown Solves Them All
Encyclopedia Brown Keeps the Peace
Encyclopedia Brown Saves the Day
Encyclopedia Brown Tracks Them Down
Encyclopedia Brown Shows the Way
Encyclopedia Brown Takes the Case
Encyclopedia Brown Lends a Hand
Encyclopedia Brown and the Case of the Dead Eagles
Encyclopedia Brown and the Case of the Midnight Visitor
Encyclopedia Brown Carries On
Encyclopedia Brown Sets the Pace
Encyclopedia Brown Takes the Cake
Encyclopedia Brown and the Case of the Exploding Plumbing
Encyclopedia Brown and the Case of the Disgusting Sneaker
Encyclopedia Brown and the Case of the Two Spies
Encyclopedia Brown and the Case of Pablo's Nose
Encyclopedia Brown's Record Book of Weird and Wonderful Facts
Encyclopedia Brown's Book of Wacky Crimes
Encyclopedia Brown's Book of Wacky Sports
Encyclopedia Brown's Book of Wacky Animals

ESPIE SANCHEZ SERIES, Terry Dunnahoo, Dutton, hardcover. ($25.00 with dust jacket) $10.00
Who Cares about Espie Sanchez?, 1975
Who Needs Espie Sanchez?, 1975
This is Espie Sanchez, 1976

ETHEL HOLISTER see CAMPFIRE GIRLS

ETHEL MORTON SERIES, Mabell Smith, 1915 Goldsmith, 1930s reprints World Books and Donohue, hardcover, 6 titles. ($20.00 with dust jacket) $10.00
Ethel Morton at Rose House
Ethel Morton at Sweet Briar Lodge
Ethel Morton's Holidays
Ethel Morton's Enterprise
Ethel Morton and the Christmas Ship
Ethel Morton at Chautauqua

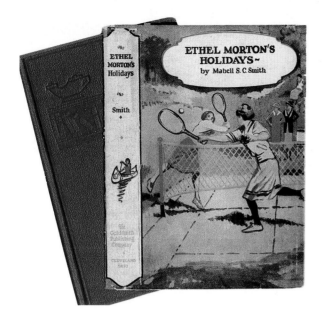

Everett Anderson's Goodbye

by Lucille Clifton

illustrated by Ann Grifalconi

EVERETT ANDERSON SERIES, Lucille Clifton, Holt, Rinehart and Winston, oblong or square hardcover, lifelike situations told in verse with full-page b/w illustrations. Early editions: ($25.00 with dust jacket) $15.00

Some of the Days of Everett Anderson, 1970, illustrated Evaline Ness. First edition: $200.00 with dust jacket

Everett Anderson's Christmas Coming, 1971, illustrated Evaline Ness. First edition: $150.00 with dust jacket

Everett Anderson's Year, Holt, 1974, illustration by Ann Grifalconi.

Everett Anderson's Friend, Holt, 1976, Illustrated by Ann Grifalconi.

Everett Anderson's Nine Month Long, 1978, Illustrated by Ann Grifalconi.

Everett Anderson's Goodbye, 1983, illustrated by Ann Grifalconi.

Everett Anderson's 1, 2, 3, 1992, illustrated

EVERY GIRL'S SERIES, ca. 1920s – 30s Goldsmith, a put-together (wannabe?) group of unrelated titles, in matching covers for marketing purposes, poor quality paper but colorful dust jackets. ($20.00 with dust jacket) $8.00

S.W.F. Club, Caroline E. Jacobs

Jane Lends a Hand, Shirley Watkins

Nancy of Paradise College, Shirley Watkins

Georgina Finds Herself, Shirley Watkins

Helen in the Editor's Chair, Ruthe Wheeler

Jane, Stweardess of the Airlines, Ruthe Wheeler

Cheer Leader, Janet Singer

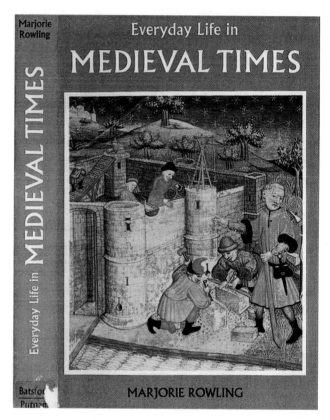

EVERYDAY LIFE SERIES, ca. 1960s Batsford, London/Putnam, NY, hardcover with gilt lettering, b/w illustrations. ($20.00 with dust jacket) $10.00

Titles include:

Everyday Life in Prehistoric Times, M. and C. H. B. Quennell

Everyday Life in Ancient Egypt, Jon Manchip White

Everyday Life in Babylonia and Assyria, H. W. F. Saggs

Everyday Life in Ancient Greece, M. and C. H. B. Quennell

Everyday Life in Ancient Rome, F. R. Cowell

Everyday Life in Roman and Anglo-Saxon Times, M. and C. H. B. Quennell

Everyday Life in Byzantium, Tamara Talbot Rice
Everyday Life in the Viking Age, Jacqueline Simpson
Everyday Life in Medieval Times, Marjorie Rowling
Everyday Life in Renaissance Times, E. R. Chamberlin

EXPLORATION SERIES, James H. Foster, ca. 1935 A.L. Burt, reprints by Saalfield. ($25.00 with dust jacket) $10.00
Lost in the Wilds of Brazil
Captured by the Arabs
Secret of the Andes
Forest of Mystery

--- F ---

FAIRMOUNT GIRLS SERIES, Etta Iva Anthony Baker, 1904 – 14 Little, Brown, pictorial boards, 4 titles. $10.00
Girls of Fairmount, 1909, illustrated by Maud Tousey
Frolics at Fairmount, 1910
Fairmount's Quartette, 1914, with illustrations by Charles M. Belyea

FAITH PALMER SERIES, Lazelle Thayer Woolley, ca. 1912 Penn, hardcover. $10.00
Faith Palmer at the Oaks, 1912, illustrated by A. Edwin Kromer
Faith Palmer at Fordyce Hall, 1913, illustrated by A. Edwin Kromer
Faith Palmer in New York, 1914, illustrated by Paula B. Himmelsbach
Faith Palmer in Washington, 1915, illustrated by Paula B. Himmelsbach

FAIRVIEW BOYS SERIES, Frederick Gordon (Stratemeyer Syndicate), ca. 1914 Graham and Matlock, hardcover, illustrated. There are cross-over titles with Stratemeyer's UP AND DOING series. ($30.00 with dust jacket) $10.00
Fairview Boys Afloat and Ashore
Fairview Boys on Eagle Mountain
Fairview Boys and their Rivals
Fairview Boys at Camp Mystery
Fairview Boys at the Lighthouse Cove
Fairview Boys on a Ranch

FAMOUS AMERICANS SERIES, collection of separate novels, ca. 1920s edition Barse, cloth-over-board cover, b/w illustrations. ($20.00 with dust jacket) $10.00
Story of George Washington, J. W. McSpadden
Story of John Paul Jones, C. C. Fraser
Story of Benjamin Franklin, C. T. Major
Story of David Crockett, J. Corby
Story of Thomas Jefferson, G. Stone
Story of Abraham Lincoln, J. W. McSpadden
Story of Robert Fulton, I. N. McFee
Story of Thomas A. Edison, I. N. McFee

Story of Harriet B. Stowe, R. B. MacArthur
Story of Mary Lyon, H. O. Stengel
Story of Theodore Roosevelt, J. W. McSpadden

FAMOUS DOG STORIES, ca. 1940s Grosset & Dunlap, plain tan cover. Collection of dog novels, mainly reprints, by various authors, b/w illustrations. Individually illustrated dust jackets. ($20.00 with dust jacket) $7.00
Sample titles:
Lassie Come Home, Eric Knight
Silver Chief, Dog of the North, Jack O'Brien
Silver Chief to the Rescue, Jack O'Brien
Baree, Son of Kazan, James Oliver Curwood
Beautiful Joe, Marshall Saunders
Big Red, Jim Kjelgaard
Bob, Son of Battle, Alfred Ollivant
Boru: Story of an Irish Wolfhound, J. Allen Dunn
Call of the Wild, Jack London
Greyfriars Bobby, Eleanor Atkinson
Juneau, the Sleigh Dog, West Lathrop
Kazan, the Wolf Dog, James Oliver Curwood
White Fang, Jack London
Wild Dog of Edmonton, David Grew
Snow Dog, Jim Kjelgaard
Derry: Airedale of the Frontier, Hubert Evans

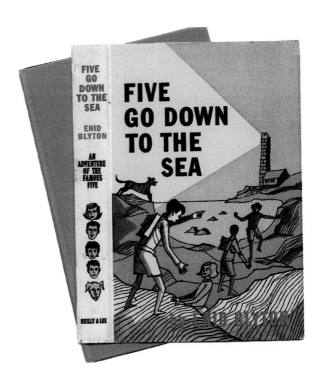

FAMOUS FIVE SERIES, Enid Blyton, 1942 – 1970s Hodder and Stoughton, hardcover, illustrated. This series was reprinted regularly in paperback.
Pre-1950 early hardcover editions: ($65.00 with dust jacket) $30.00
1950 – 1960s first edition: ($55.00 with dust jacket) $15.00
Later hardcover printings: ($20.00 with dust jacket) $10.00

Five on a Treasure Island
Five Go Adventuring Again
Five Run Away Together
Five Go to Smuggler's Top
Five Go Off in a Caravan
Five on Kirrin Island Again
Five Go Off to Camp
Five Get into Trouble
Five Fall into Adventure
Five on a Hike Together, 1950
Five Have a Wonderful Time
Five Go Down to the Sea
Five Go to Mystery Moor, 1954
Five Have Plenty of Fun
Five on a Secret Trail
Five Go to Billycock Hill
Five Get into a Fix
Five on Finniston Farm
Five Go to Demon's Rocks
Five Have a Mystery to Solve
Five Are Together Again
Famous Five Big Book, 1964 Hodder & Stoughton, first edition thus, *Five on a Treasure Island*, *Five Go Adventuring Again*, *Five Run Away Together*. $15.00

Famous Five, 1960s Reilly & Lee editions, hardcover, b/w illustrations by Frank Aloise. ($25.00 with dust jacket) $10.00
Five Go Down to the Sea
Five Run Away Together
Five Go to Smuggler's Top

FAMOUS HORSE STORIES, ca. 1940s Grosset & Dunlap, plain cloth-over-board cover. Collection of horse novels, mainly reprints, by various authors. Individually illustrated dust jackets. ($20.00 with dust jacket) $7.00
Sample titles:
Mountain Pony and the Pinto Colt, Henry V. Larom
Cinchfoot, Thomas C. Hinkle
Frog: the Horse That Knew No Master, Col. S. P. Meek
Indian Paint, Glenn Balch
Kentucky Derby Winner, Isabel McMeekin
Magnificent Barb, Dana Faralla
Midnight, Rutherford Montgomery
Mountain Pony, Henry V. Larom
Sorrel Stallion, David Grew
Wild Palomino, Stephen Holt
Ticktock and Jim, Keith Robertson
Hoofbeats, John T. Foote
Mountain and the Rodeo Mystery, Henry Larom
Bluegrass Champion, Dorothy Lyons
Strawberry Roan, Don Lang
Lost Horse, Glenn Balch
Beyond Rope and Fence, David Grew
Prairie Colt, Stephen Holt
Capture of the Golden Stallion, Rutherford Montgomery
Golden Stallion's Revenge, Rutherford Montgomery

Golden Stallion to the Rescue, Rutherford Montgomery
Mountain Pony and the Elkhorn Mystery, Henry Larom
Golden Stallion's Victory, Rutherford Montgomery
Phantom Roan, Stephen Holt

FAMOUS SPORT SERIES, Grosset & Dunlap, collection of sports novels for boys, numerous titles in matching hardcover format with colorful dust jackets. ($20.00 with dust jacket) $10.00
Sample titles:
High, Inside!, Emery, 1948
Fighting Southpaw, Flood, 1949
Club Team, Richard, 1950
College Slugger, Fitzgerald, 1950
Never Come Back, O'Rourke, 1952
Yankee Rookie, Ed Fitzgerald, 1952

FAMOUS TRAMP SERIES, signed "A. No. 1" (Leon Ray Livingston), ca. 1910 – 20 A. No. 1 Publishing Co., Erie, Pa., black/red/orange illustrated paper cover, small, approximately 135 pages, b/w drawings, advertised as "books on tramp life" with the warning "To Restless Young Men and Boys who read this book, the author, who has led for over a quarter of a century the pitiful and dangerous life of a tramp, gives this well-meant advice: Do not jump on moving trains or street cars, even if only to ride to the next street crossing, because this might arouse the Wanderlust..."
Most titles: $35.00
Life and Adventures of a No. 1 Hobo
Hobo Camp Fire Tales
Curse of Tramp Life
Trail of the Tramp

Adventures of a Female Tramp
Ways of the Hobo
Snare of the Road
From Coast to Coast with Jack London, includes a
    photo of London. $70.00
Mother of the Hoboes
Wife I Won
Traveling with Tramps

FATHER TAKES US SERIES, Grace Humphrey, 1927
    Penn, hardcover, illustrated with b/w photos.
    ($25.00 with dust jacket) $15.00
Father Takes Us to New York
Father Takes Us to Boston
Father Takes Us to Philadelphia
Father Takes Us to Washington

FELICIA SERIES, Elizabeth Gould, 1908 – 11 Penn,
    impressed illustration on cover, b/w illustrations by
    Mary Price or Josephine Bruce. $15.00
Felicia
Felicia's Friends
Felicia Visits
Felicia's Folks

FERRY HILL SERIES, Ralph Henry Barbour, 1926 – 1929
    Dodd, Mead, hardcover, four titles: $25.00
 Reprints by Grosset & Dunlap: $20.00
Titles include:
Crimson Sweater

FIGHTERS FOR FREEDOM SERIES, ca. 1943 Whitman,
    plain hardcover, illustrated endpapers, b/w illus-
    trations. ($20.00 with dust jacket) $10.00
Barry Blake and the Flying Fortress, DuBois
Norma Kent of the WAACS
Sally Scott of the WAVES, Snell
Sparky Ames of the Ferry Command, Snell
March Anson and Scoot Bailey of the U. S. Navy,

Duncan
Dick Donnelly of the Paratroops, Duncan
Kitty Carter, Canteen Girl, Ruby Radford

FIGHTING FOR THE FLAG SERIES, Charles Norton,
    1890s Wilde, cloth-over-board cover with gilt
    design, b/w plate illustrations by George Gibbs.
    $20.00
Midshipman Jack
Jack Benson's Log
Medal of Honor Man

FIRST BOOK SERIES, Watts Publishing, hardcover, b/w
    illustrations, numerous titles by various authors.
    ($20.00 with dust jacket) $10.00
Titles include:
First Book of Indians, 1950
First Book of Baseball, 1950
*First Book of Cowboys,*1950
First Book of Birds, 1951
*First Book of Eskimos,*1952
First Book of Eskimos, 1952
First Book of Chess, 1953
First Book of Magic, 1953
First Book of Boats, 1953
First Book of Conservation, 1954
First Book of Rhythms, 1954
*First Book of Holidays,*1955
First Book of Canada, 1955
First Book of Gardening, 1956
First Book of Codes and Ciphers, 1956
First Book of Antarctic, 1956
First Book of Snakes, 1956
First Book of Submarines, 1957
First Book of American History, 1957
*First Book of Tropical Mammals,*1958
First Book of Airplanes, 1958
First Book of Measurement, 1960
First Book of Hiking, 1965
First Book of Congress, 1965
First Book of the Cliff Dwellers, 1968

FIRST GOLDEN LEARNING LIBRARY see LITTLE GOLD-
    EN BOOKS

FIVE FIND-OUTERS SERIES, Enid Blyton, ca. 1950
    Methuen, gray hardcover, 170+ pages, b/w illus-
    trations by Treyer Evans. ($40.00 with dust jacket)
    $20.00
Mystery of the Burnt Cottage
Mystery of the Disappearing Cat
Mystery of the Secret Room
Mystery of the Hidden House
Mystery of the Spiteful Letters
Mystery of the Pantomime Cat
Mystery of the Missing Necklace
Mystery of the Invisible Thief
Mystery of the Vanished Prince
Mystery of the Strange Bundle

Mystery of Holly Lane
Mystery of the Strange Messages
Mystery of Tally-Ho Cottage
Mystery of the Missing Man

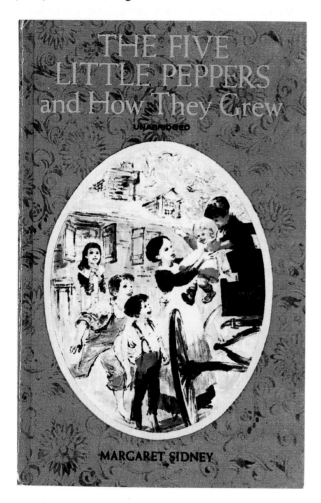

FIVE LITTLE PEPPERS SERIES, Margaret Sidney (Harriet Lothrop) 1880 – 1916 Lothrop, hardcover with gilt trim, b/w plates. Price range for first editions: $60.00 to $200.00

1965 edition Whitman, blue hardcover with cameo illustration, illustrated endpapers and color illustrations by Tom O'Sullivan. $20.00

Numerous reprints in hardcover: $5.00 to $10.00 range

Five Little Peppers and How They Grew
Five Little Peppers at School
Stories Dolly Pepper Told, illustrated by Jessie McDermott and Ethelred Barry
Five Little Peppers Midway, illustrated by W. L. Taylor
Five Little Peppers Grown Up
Five Little Peppers Abroad, illustrated by Fanny Cory
Ben Pepper

FIVE LITTLE STARRS SERIES, Lillian Elizabeth Roy, 1913 Platt & Peck, small, illustrated cloth-over-board cover, 190+ pages, b/w frontispiece. $15.00

Burt editions, ca. 1915: ($20.00 with dust jacket)

$10.00
Five Little Starrs
Five Little Starrs on a Canal Boat
Five Little Starrs on a Ranch
Five Little Starrs in an Island Cabin
Five Little Starrs in the Canadian Forest
Five Little Starrs on a Motor Tour
Five Little Starrs in Alaska
Five Little Starrs in Hawaii

FLAG AND COUNTRY SERIES, Paul Tomlinson, Barse and Hopkins, red hardcover, illustrated endpapers, 4 b/w plates by Charles Wrenn, First World War series. $25.00

Bob Cook and the German Spy, 1917
Bob Cook and the German Air Fleet, 1918
Bob Cook's Brother in the Trenches, 1918
Bob Cook and the Winged Messenger, 1919
Bob Cook and the Bomb Plot, 1919

FLAG OF FREEDOM, Captain Ralph Bonehill (Stratemeyer Syndicate pseudonym), ca. 1900 Mershon Company between 1899 and 1902. Later reprints by George M. Hill, Stitt. $15.00

FLAXIE FRIZZLE SERIES, Sophie May, ca. 1870s Lee & Shepard, b/w illustrations by Elizabeth Tucker. $35.00

1910 edition Lothrop, Lee & Shepard, small size, printed illustration on cover. $20.00

Flaxie Frizzle
Little Pitcher, Flaxie Frizzle Stories
Kittyleen, Flaxie Frizzle Stories
Flaxie Growing Up

FLICKA THE HORSE SERIES, Mary O'Hara (1885 – 1980), Lippincott, numerous editions and print-

ings, hardcover, novels about the McLaughlin family, their son Ken, and their horse ranch.
Early Lippincott editions: $45.00 with dust jacket
My Friend Flicka, 1941
Thunderhead, 1943
Green Grass of Wyoming, 1946

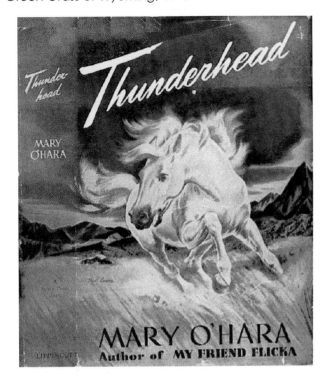

FLICKA, RICKA AND DICKA SERIES, written and illustrated by Maj Lindman, Whitman, oversize hardcover books with bright cover illustrations, color illustrations throughout, first edition: ($175.00 with

dust jacket) $100.00
Flicka, Ricka, Dicka and the New Dotted Dresses, 1939
Flicka, Ricka, Dicka and the Girl Next Door, 1940
Flicka, Ricka, Dicka and the Three Kittens, 1941
Flicka, Ricka, Dicka and their New Friend, 1942
Flicka, Ricka, Dicka and the Strawberries, 1944
Flicka, Ricka, Dicka and their New Skates, 1950
Flicka, Ricka, Dicka Bake a Cake, 1955
Flicka, Ricka, Dicka Go to Market, 1958
Flicka, Ricka, Dicka and the Big Red Hen, 1960

FLIP SERIES, Wesley Dennis, Viking, hardcover, 63 pages, illustrations by author, first edition: ($35.00 with dust jacket) $20.00
Flip, 1941
Flip and the Cows, 1942
Flip and the Morning, 1951

FLYING BOYS SERIES see ELLIS

FLYING MACHINE BOYS SERIES, Frank Walton, ca. 1913 Burt, illustrated cloth-over-board cover, frontispiece illustration. ($45.00 with dust jacket) $20.00
Flying Machine Boys in Deadly Peril, or Lost in the Clouds
Flying Machine Boys in Mexico, or Secret of the Crater
Flying Machine Boys in the Wilds, or Mystery of the Andes
Flying Machine Boys on Duty, or Clue Above the Clouds
Flying Machine Boys on Secret Service, or Capture in the Air

FLYING U RANCH SERIES, B.M. Bower, Grosset & Dunlap, also Triangle Books. ($25.00 with dust jacket) $10.00
Titles include:
Flying U's Last Stand
Chip of the Flying U
Flying U Ranch
Flying U Omnibus
Flying U Rodeo
Flying U's Dark Horse

FLYING WHEELS SERIES, W.E. Butterworth, ca. 1960 Grosset & Dunlap, hardcover. 1970s pictorial hardcover edition: $15.00
Fast Green Car
Crazy to Race
Return to Racing
Return to Daytona

FOOTBALL ELEVEN SERIES, Ralph Henry Barbour, 1914 and 1925 Dodd Mead, hardcover, eleven titles: ($50.00 with dust jacket) $20.00
Reprints by Grosset & Dunlap: ($35.00 with dust

jacket) $10.00
Left End Edwards
Left Tackle Thayer
Left Guard Gilbert
Center Rush Rowland
Full-Back Foster
Quarter-Back Bates
Left Half Harmon
Right End Emerson
Right Guard Grant
Right Tackle Todd
Right Half Hollins

FORTUNE HUNTERS SERIES, Frank Gee Patchin, 1928 Altemus, hardcover with paste-on illustration, 4 b/w plates, South Seas adventure series, same-as-cover dust jacket. ($50.00 with dust jacket) $15.00
Ted Jones, Fortune Hunter, or *Perilous Adventures with a Chinese Pearl Trader*
Ted Jones at Desperation Island, or *Affair with the Yellow Coral Prince*
Ted Jones' Weeks of Terror, or *Luckless Three's Revolt Against the Sandalwood Sharpers*
Ted Jones Under Sealed Orders, or *Mysterious Treasure Trail to the Red Lagoon*

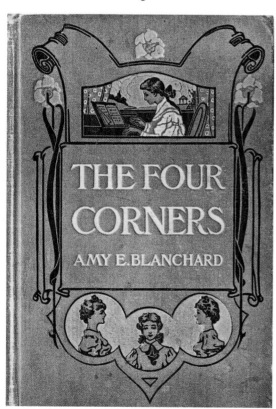

FOUR CORNERS SERIES, Amy Ella Blanchard (1856 – 1926), 1906 – 13 Jacobs, hardcover with gilt. $25.00
Four Corners, 1906
Four Corners in California, 1907
Four Corners at School, 1908

Four Corners Abroad, 1909
Four Corners in Camp, 1910
Four Corners at College, 1911
Four Corners in Japan, 1912
Four Corners in Egypt, 1913, last title, hard-to-find: $50.00

FOUR LITTLE BLOSSOMS SERIES, Mabel C. Hawley 1920 – 30 Cuples & Leon, small, cloth hardcover with color imprint. ($40.00 with dust jacket) $15.00
Saalfield edition: ($20.00 with dust jacket) $10.00
Four Little Blossoms at Brookside Farm
Four Little Blossoms at Oak Hill School
Four Little Blossoms and their Winter Fun
Four Little Blossoms on Apple Tree Island
Four Little Blossoms Through the Holidays
Four Little Blossoms at Sunrise Beach
Four Little Blossoms Indoors and Out

FRANK ALLEN see BOYS OF COLUMBIA HIGH

FRANK AND ANDY SERIES see RACER BOYS

FRANK ARMSTRONG SERIES, Matthew Colton, 1911 – 1914 Hurst, illustrated green cloth-over-board cover, frontispiece illustration. $15.00
Frank Armstrong's Vacation
Frank Armstrong at Queens
Frank Armstrong's Second Term
Frank Armstrong, Drop Kicker
Frank Armstrong, Captain of the Nine
Frank Armstrong at College

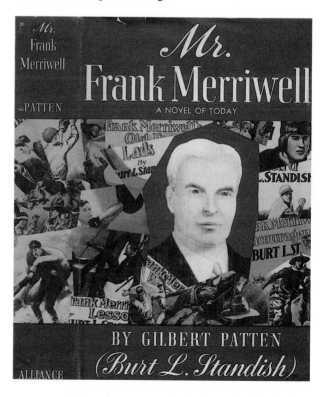

FRANK MERRIWELL, JR. SERIES, by Burt Standish (Gilbert Patten, 1866 – 1945), adventures of Frank and Dick Merriwell, hundreds of titles. These stories were great favorites of early 20th century boys. Merriwell first appeared in 1896 in *Tip Top Weekly*, a magazine for boys. Patten turned out a 20,000 word book a week for over seventeen years, according to the dust jacket blurb on Mr. *Frank Merriwell*, 1941 Alliance.

Ca. 1910 Street & Smith, New Medal Library editions, (issued weekly and sold for fifteen cents), fragile books with pages that are usually quite brittle and browned. $20.00

1900 – 1930s David McKay, tan hardcover with black lettering. $15.00

Titles include:
Frank Merriwell's Schooldays
Frank Merriwell's Chums
Frank Merriwell's Foes
Frank Merriwell's Trip West
Frank Merriwell Down South
Frank Merriwell's Bravery
Frank Merriwell's Hunting Tour
Frank Merriwell at Yale
Frank Merriwell's Sports Afield
Frank Merriwell's Struggle
Frank Merriwell's First Job
Dick Merriwell's Promise
Dick Merriwell's Racket
Dick Merriwell's Dash

Frank Merriwell related titles:
Farewell, Frank Merriwell, Gerige Zuckerman, 1973 Dutton, hardcover: $20.00 with dust jacket
Mr. Frank Merriwell, Gilbert Patten, the original "Burt L. Standish," creator of Frank and Dick Merriwell, 1941 Alliance, hardcover, 305 pages, contains 27 stories of Frank as an adult. With dust jacket, which features a portrait surrounded by old book covers and illustrations: $50.00 with dust jacket

FRED FENTON SERIES, Allen Chapman (Stratemeyer pseudonym), ca. 1920s Cupples & Leon, small hardcover. ($30.00 with dust jacket) $15.00
Fred Fenton the Pitcher
Fred Fenton in the Line
Fred Fenton on the Crew
Fred Fenton on the Track
Fred Fenton: Marathon Runner

FREDDY CARR SERIES, Rev. Garrold, ca. 1910 Benziger Brothers, brown hardcover. $15.00
Boys of St. Batt's
Freddy Carr and His Friends
Freddy Carr's Adventures

FRENCH AND INDIAN WAR SERIES, Joseph Altsheler, North American frontier stories set in 1755 – 1763, ca. 1916 – 19 Appleton, hardcover with paste-on pictorial, 4 b/w plates. This popular series of adventure stories was re-issued in similar format several times. Probable first edition: $75.00 Later

printings: $20.00
Hunter of the Hills
Shadow of the North
Rulers of the Lake
Masters of the Peaks
Lords of the Wild
Sun of Quebec

FRIENDLY TERRACE SERIES, Harriet Lummis Smith, Page, also Burt, hardcover. $15.00
Girls of Friendly Terrace, 1912
Peggy Raymond's Vacation, 1913, illustrated by John Goss
Peggy Raymond's School Days, 1916, illustrated by Weston Taylor
Friendly Terrace Quartet, 1920

FRONTIER SERIES see PIONEER BOYS

FRONTIER GIRLS SERIES, Alice Curtis, 1929 – 37 Penn, hardcover with paste-on-pictorial, illustrators include R. Pallen Coleman ($60.00 with dust jacket) $30.00
Titles include:
Frontier Girl of Virginia, 1929
Frontier Girl of Massachusetts, 1930
Frontier Girl of Chesapeake Bay, 1934
Frontier Girl of Pennsylvania, 1942

FUDGE AND SHEILA see SHEILA AND FUDGE

FURY SERIES, Albert Miller, ca. 1960 Holt, TV series tie-in, boy-and-horse stories. Holt editions priced individually.
Grosset, pictorial hardcover: $20.00
Fury, Stallion of Broken Wheel Ranch, 1959, first edition, illustrations by James Schucker. ($40.00 with dust jacket) $15.00
Fury and the Mustangs, 1960, illustrations by Sam Savitt. ($20.00 with dust jacket) $10.00
Fury and the White Mare, 1962, illustrations by Ezra Jack Keats. ($25.00 with dust jacket) $15.00

Fury, other editions:
Fury, 1964 Silver Dollar Book, pictorial oversize hardcover, abridged story, illustrated by Everett Raymond Kinstler. $15.00
Fury, 1957, Little Golden Book, color illustrated hardcover. $10.00
Fury Takes the Jump, 1958, Little Golden Book, color illustrated hardcover. $10.00
Fury, Stallion of Broken Wheel Ranch, Famous Horse of Television, 1959 Winston, hardcover. ($40.00 with dust jacket) $15.00
Fury and the Mustangs, Authorized TV Edition, 1960 Holt, hardcover. ($25.00 with dust jacket) $10.00
Fury and the White Mare, 1962 Holt, hardcover, 189 pages. ($25.00 with dust jacket) $10.00

G

G-MEN SERIES, William Engle, Grosset & Dunlap, hardcover, pictorial endpapers. First Edition: $85.00 with dust jacket, later printings: ($35.00 with dust jacket) $15.00
G-Men Smash the Professor's Gang, 1939
G-Men in Jeopardy, 1938
G-Men Trap the Spy Ring, 1939

GARIS FAMILY: Series by Howard Garis, Lilian Garis, son Roger Garis, and daughter Cleo Fausta Garis. The four wrote over a thousand books, according to Roger Garis, so many that even he was not sure of all the titles, series, and pseudonyms. Many of their series were written for Stratemeyer. The Garises wrote complete series or several books in a series, wrote under their own names, and also wrote under pseudonyms. The following are some of the series to which each Garis contributed:
Howard: (in addition to his famous Uncle Wiggily stories) Daddy Stories, Dick and Janet Cherry series, Buddy series
Lilian: Girl Scout, Bobbsey Twins, Nancy Brandon, Motor Girls, Melody Lane mysteries, Barbara Hale, A Girl Called Ted, Two Girls, the Gloria books, Connie Loring, Judy Jordan, the Joan books
Roger: Outboard Boys, Buffalo Hunter series (updated rewrites of an 1890s series owned by Stratemeyer), X Bar X Boys
Cleo: mystery books including Missing at Marshlands, Mystery of Jockey Hollow (ca. 1934 Arden Blake mysteries), and Orchard Secret.

GARIS, LILIAN, BOOKS, Lilian Garis (also see Garis family) wrote numerous books for the Stratemeyer Syndicate under Stratemeyer pseudonyms. She also wrote series under her own name. And she did a number of two title books, possibly trial runs for longer series. These were often re-issued as part of other girls' series or as individual titles. Following are some of these books.
Ca. 1920s Whitman editions: $15.00
Ca. 1930s Grosset & Dunlap, advertised as "Lilian Garis Books for Girls." The Barbara Hale, Nancy Brandon, and Judy Jordan titles were listed as "Mystery Stories," hardcover editions: ($35.00 with dust jacket) $15.00
Garis books, Barbara Hale Series
Barbara Hale
Barbara Hale's Mystery Friend
Garis books, Cleo Series
Cleo's Misty Rainbow
Cleo's Conquest
Garis books, Connie Loring Series
Connie Loring
Connie Loring's Gypsy Friend

Garis books, Gloria Series
Gloria: A Girl and Her Dad
Gloria at Boarding School
Garis books, Judy Jordan Series
Judy Jordan
Judy Jordan's Discovery
Garis books, Nancy Brandon Series
Nancy Brandon
Nancy Brandon's Mystery
Garis books, Sally Series, illustrations by Thelma Gooch
Sally for Short
Sally Found Out
Garis books, Ted Series
Girl Called Ted
Ted and Tony

GARRY GRAYSON SERIES, Elmer Dawson, ca.1926 – 1932 Grosset, green hardcover, frontispiece by Walter Rogers, advertised as "Good clean football at its best and in addition, up-to-the-minute stories of school rivalries and boy life." Later reprints by Whitman. ($25.00 with dust jacket) $10.00
Garry Grayson's Hill Street Eleven
Garry Grayson at Lenox High
Garry Grayson's Football Rivals
Garry Grayson Showing His Speed
Garry Grayson at Stanley Prep
Garry Grayson's Winning Kick
Garry Grayson Hitting the Line
Garry Grayson's Winning Touchdown
Garry Grayson's Double Signals
Garry Grayson's Forward Pass

GIANT GOLDEN BOOKS, ca. 1940s – 50s Simon Schuster, 10¼ x 13 inches size, picture books with bright colored paper-over-board covers, full-color illustrations. $35.00
Titles include:
Animal Stories, George Duplaix, illustrated by Feodor Rojankovsky
Farm Stories, Kathryn and Byron Jackson, 1946, 76 pages, illustrations by Gustaf Tenggren
Tenggren's Cowboys and Indians, Kathryn and Byron Jackson, 1948, 96 pages, illustrations by Gustaf Tenggren
Golden Mother Goose, illustrated by Alice and Martin Provensen
Golden Dictionary, Ellen Walpole, illustrated by Gertrude Elliott
Golden Encyclopedia, Dorothy Bennett, illustrated by Cornelius DeWitt
Golden Bible, illustrated by Feodor Rojankovsky
Tenggren's Story Book, illustrations by Gustaf Tenggren
Walt Disney's Uncle Remus Stories
Walt Disney's Surprise Package
Captain Kangaroo, 1959

GIMLET, W.E. Johns, University of London Press or Brockhampton Press. Capt. Corrington King, better known as Gimlet, leads his crack commando squad through a series of thrilling WWII adventures. Like Johns' popular Biggles books, this series went through a number of reprintings and changes in publishers.

1940s London Press editions: (with dust jacket, RARE) $10.00. 1950s Brockhampton editions: ($25.00 with dust jacket) $10.00

King of the Commandos, 1943
Gimlet Goes Again, 1944
Gimlet Comes Home, 1946
Gimlet Mops Up, 1947
Gimlet's Oriental Quest, 1948
Gimlet Lends A Hand, 1949
Gimlet Bores In, 1950
Gimlet Off the Map, 1951
Gimlet Gets an Answer, 1952
Gimlet Takes a Job, 1954

GINNIE FELLOWS SERIES, Catherine Woolley, Morrow, hardcover, illustrated by Ursula Koering or Don Almquist. ($25.00 with dust jacket) $15.00

Ginnie and Geneva, 1948
Ginnie Joins In, 1951
Ginnie and the New Girl, 1954
Ginnie and the Mystery House, 1957
Ginnie and the Mystery Doll, 1960
Ginnie and her Juniors, 1963
Ginnie and the Cooking Contest, 1966
Ginnie and the Wedding Bells, 1967
Ginnie and the Mystery Cat, 1969
Ginnie and the Mystery Light, 1973

GINNY GORDON SERIES, Julie Campbell, 1948 – 50s

Whitman, hardcover, illustrated endpapers, b/w illustrations by Margaret Wesley. ($15.00 with dust jacket) $10.00

Later reprints in glossy hardcover with wraparound illustration, 2-color illustrations. $8.00

Ginny Gordon and the Disappearing Floor
Ginny Gordon and the Missing Heirloom
Ginny Gordon and the Disappearing Candlesticks
Ginny Gordon and the Mystery at the Old Barn
Ginny Gordon and the Broadcast Mystery
Ginny Gordon and the Lending Library

GIRL AVIATOR SERIES, Margaret Burnham, 1911 – 1912 Hurst, illustrated cloth hardcover, frontispiece, air adventures of Peggy and Jess. ($25.00 with dust jacket) $15.00

Reprint editions Donahue: ($20.00 with dust jacket) $10.00

Girl Aviators and the Phantom Airship
Girl Aviators on Golden Wings
Girl Aviators' Sky Cruise
Girl Aviators' Motor Butterfly

GIRL SCOUT SERIES, Katherine Galt, 1921 Saalfield, hardcover. ($35.00 with dust jacket) $15.00

Girl Scouts at Home
Girl Scouts Rally
Girl Scouts' Triumph

GIRL SCOUT SERIES, Lilian Garis, ca. 1920s Cupples & Leon, small size, cloth cover, illustrated, advertised as "The highest ideals of girlhood as advocated by the foremost organizations of America form the background for these stories and while unobtrusive, there is a message in every volume." $15.00

Girl Scout Pioneers
Girl Scouts at Bellaire
Girl Scouts at Sea Crest
Girl Scouts at Camp Comalong
Girl Scouts at Rocky Ledge

GIRL SCOUTS SERIES, Edith Lavell, 1922 – 25 Burt, 10 books, brown hardcover with printed illustration and gilt lettering. ($35.00 with dust jacket) $20.00

Girl Scouts at Miss Allen's School
Girl Scouts at Camp
Girl Scouts' Good Turn
Girl Scouts' Canoe Trip
Girl Scouts' Rivals
Girl Scouts' on the Ranch
Girl Scouts' Vacation Adventures
Girl Scouts' Motoring Trip
Girl Scouts' Captain
Girl Scouts' Director

GIRL SCOUT SERIES, Margaret Vandercook, 1914 – 23 Winston, brown pictorial hardcover, b/w frontispiece, 5 books $20.00
Girl Scouts of the Eagle's Wing
Girl Scouts in Beechwood Forest
Girl Scouts of the Round Table
Girl Scouts and the Open Road
Girl Scouts in Mystery Valley

GIRL SCOUT MYSTERY SERIES, Virginia Fairfax, 1933 – 36 Burt, hardcover. $10.00
Secret of Camp Pioneer
Curious Quest
Secret of Halliday House
Trail of the Gypsy Eight

GIRL SCOUTS SERIES, Lillian Elizabeth Roy, ca. 1915 Grosset, advertised as "The heroines of these pleasant stories are Girl Scouts and woven through the adventures and fun you will find the principles of Scouting carried out." $35.00
Girl Scouts at Dandelion Camp
Girl Scouts in the Adirondacks
Girl Scouts in the Rockies
Girl Scouts in Arizona and New Mexico
Girl Scouts in the Redwoods
Girl Scouts in the Magic City
Woodcraft Girls at Camp
Woodcraft Girls in the City
Woodcraft Girls Camping in Maine
Little Woodcrafter's Book
Little Woodcrafter's Fun on the Farm

GIRL SCOUTS SERIES, Mildred Wirt, cal 1950 Cupples & Leon, hardcover. ($30.00 with dust jacket) $10.00
Girl Scouts at Penguin Pass
Girl Scouts at Singing Sands
Girl Scouts at Mystery Mansion

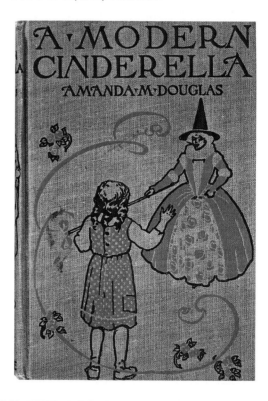

GIRLS' ELITE BOOKS, ca. 1912 Donohue, small, impressed cover illustration, b/w frontispiece, reprints of short novels. (Colorful dust jacket doubles price.) $10.00
Titles include:
Bee and the Butterfly, Lucy Foster Madison
Dixie School Girl, Gabrielle E. Jackson
Girls of Mount Morris, Amanda Douglas
Hope's Messenger, Gabrielle E. Jackson
Little Aunt, Marion Ames Taggart
Modern Cinderella, Amanda Douglas

GIRLS MYSTERY SERIES, Harriet Pyne Grove, ca. 1928 Saalfield, hardcover, titles crossover with other

girls' series. ($15.00 with dust jacket) $10.00
Titles include:
Secret of Steeple Rocks
S. P. Mystery
Strange Likeness

GIRLS OF CENTRAL HIGH SERIES, Gertrude Morrison, 1914 – 21 Grosset, reprints by World, Saalfield, Goldsmith. ($20.00 with dust jacket) $10.00
Girls of Central High
Girls of Central High at Basketball
Girls of Central High on the Stage
Girls of Central High on Track and Field
Girls of Central High on Lake Luna
Girls of Central High in Camp
Girls of Central High Aiding the Red Cross

GLAD BOOKS (Pollyanna) SERIES, Porter, Smith, Chalmers, 1913 – 49 Page Publications, hardcover with paste-on-pictorial, 6 b/w plates: $50.00
Grosset & Dunlap reprint, hardcover, illustrated endpapers: ($20.00 with dust jacket) $10.00
Eleanor Porter titles:
Pollyanna
Pollyanna Grows Up
Harriet Lummis Smith titles:
Pollyanna of the Orange Blossoms
Pollyanna's Jewel
Pollyanna's Debt of Honor
Pollyanna's Western Adventure
Elizabeth Borten titles:
Pollyanna in Hollywood
Pollyanna's Castle in Mexico
Pollyanna's Door to Happiness
Pollyanna's Golden Horseshoe
Margaret Piper Chalmers titles:
Pollyanna's Protegee

Pollyanna at Six Star Ranch
Virginia May Moffit title:
Pollyanna of Magic Valley

GLEN HAZARD SERIES, Mariston Chapman, Appleton-Century, Grosset & Dunlap, red hardcovers, illustrations, stories set in a small town in the mountains. ($20.00 with dust jacket) $10.00
Wildcat Ridge, 1932
Glen Hazard, 1933
Timber Trail, 1933
Eagle Cliff, 1934
Marsh Island Mystery, 1936
Rogues on Red Hill, 1937
Girls of Glen Hazard, 1937
Mystery of the Broken Key, 1938
Clue of the Faded Dress, 1938
Flood in Glen Hazard, 1939
Mystery of the Missing Car, 1939
Glen Hazard Cowboys, 1940
Mill Creek Mystery, 1940
Gulf Coast Treasure, 1941
Mountain Mystery, 1941
Mystery on the Mississippi, 1942
Trail Beyond the Rockies, 1943
Secret of Wildcat Cave, 1944
Treasure Hunters, 1945

GLENLOCH GIRLS SERIES, Grace May Remick, ca. 1909 – 12 Penn, hardcover with paste-on-pictorial, b/w plates by Ada Williamson, Ruth Shirley, and her friends, Charlotte, Betty, and Dorothy, share adventures with school pals. $25.00
Glenloch Girls
Glenloch Girls' Club
Glenloch Girls in the West
Glenloch Girls Abroad

GLORIA SERIES see GARIS

GO-AHEAD BOYS SERIES, Ross Kay, Barse and Hopkins, Goldsmith, hardcover. ($25.00 with dust jacket) $10.00
Go-Ahead Boys on Smuggler's Island, 1916
Go-Ahead Boys and the Treasure Cave, 1916
Go-Ahead Boys and the Mysterious Old House, 1916
Go-Ahead Boys in the Island Camp, 1916
Go-Ahead Boys and the Racing Motorboat, 1916
Go-Ahead Boys and Simon's Mine, 1917

GOLDEN BOYS SERIES, Levi P. Wyman, ca. 1920s Burt, impressed illustration on cover, b/w frontispiece. ($25.00 with dust jacket) $15.00
Golden Boys and their New Electric Cell
Golden Boys at the Fortress
Golden Boys in the Maine Woods
Golden Boys with the Lumber Jacks
Golden Boys on the River Drive
Golden Boys Rescued by Radio

Golden Boys along the River Allagash
Golden Boys at the Haunted Camp
Golden Boys Save the Chamberlin Dam
Golden Boys on the Trail

GOLDEN HOUR BOOKS, ca. 1902 Crowell, impressed illustration on hardcover, gilt lettering on spine, b/w frontispiece, decorated title page, reprints of earlier novels as well as new titles. $25.00
Little Dusky Hero, Harriet Comstock
Caxton Club, Amos Wells
Child and the Tree, Bessie Ulrich
Daisies and Diggleses, Evelyn Raymond
How the Twins Captured a Hessian, James Otis
I Can School, Eva Madden
Master Frisky, Clarence Hawkes
Miss De Peyster's Boy, Etheldred Barry
Molly, Barbara Yechton
Wonder Ship, Sophie Swett
Whispering Tongues, Homer Greene

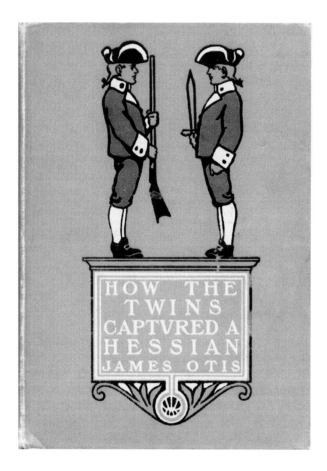

GOLDEN HOURS LIBRARY, 1967 Little Golden Books, reprints of 12 Little Golden Books boxed in a cardboard box that resembles a mantel clock. The books are 24 page size, and for this printing are identified by a picture of the clock on the lower corner of the cover. Complete set with box in good condition: $50.00. Individual books: $3.00 each

GOLDEN STALLION SERIES, Rutherford Montgomery, Little Brown, some titles reissued by Grosset & Dunlap as part of the FAMOUS HORSE STORIES. British editions issued by Hodder or White Lion.
Little Brown first edition: ($35.00 with dust jacket) $10.00
Little Brown later editions: ($25.00 with dust jacket) $10.00
Grosset & Dunlap hardcovers: ($15.00 with dust jacket) $10.00
Capture of the Golden Stallion, 1951
Golden Stallion's Revenge, 1953
Golden Stallion to the Rescue, 1954
Golden Stallion's Victory, 1956
Golden Stallion and the Wolf Dog, 1958
Golden Stallion's Adventure at Redstone, 1959
Golden Stallion and the Mysterious Feud, 1967
Golden Stallion, related titles:
Golden Stallion, 1962 Grosset, Montgomery (abridgement), illustrated by Al Brule. $12.00

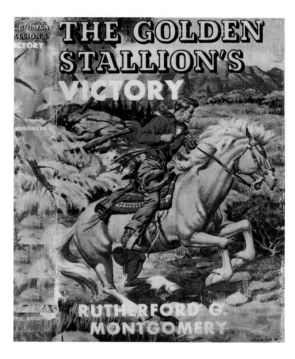

GOLDEN WEST BOYS SERIES, William S. Hart, ca. 1920 Houghton, illustrated cloth-over-board cover. ($45.00 with dust jacket) $10.00
Injun and Whitey
Injun and Whitey to the Rescue
Injun and Whitey Strike Out for Themselves

GOOD HOUSEKEEPING'S BEST BOOKS, Pauline Evans, 1957 Good Housekeeping Publications, hardcover, b/w illustrations. ($15.00 with dust jacket) $10.00
Titles include:
Good Housekeeping's Best Book of Adventure Stories
Good Housekeeping's Best Book of Animal Stories
Good Housekeeping's Best Book of Fun and Nonsense

Good Housekeeping's Best Book of Nature Stories

GRACE HARLOWE SERIES, Jessie Graham Flower, printed illustration on hardcover, advertised as the "college girls series."
Altemus editions: ($40.00 with dust jacket) $20.00
Saalfield editions: $15.00
Grace Harlowe High School Girls Series *ca.* 1915
Grace Harlowe's Plebe Year at High School
Grace Harlowe's Sophomore Year at High School
Grace Harlowe's Junior Year at High School
Grace Harlowe's Senior Year at High School
Grace Harlowe College Girl Series, ca. 1915 – 25
Grace Harlowe's First Year at Overton College
Grace Harlowe's Second Year at Overton College
Grace Harlowe's Third Year at Overton College
Grace Harlowe's Fourth Year at Overton College
Grace Harlowe's Return to Overton College
Grace Harlowe's Problem
Grace Harlowe's Golden Summer
Grace Harlowe Overland Riders Series, ca.1920
On the Old Apache Trail
On the Great American Desert
Among the Kentucky Mountaineers
In the Great North Woods
In the High Sierras
In the Yellowstone National Park
In the Black Hills
At Circle O Ranch
Among the Border Guerrillas
On the Lost River Trail
Grace Harlowe Overseas Series, ca. 1920s Altemus
Grace Harlowe Overseas
Grace Harlowe with the Red Cross in France
Grace Harlowe with the Marines at Chateau Thierry
Grace Harlowe with the U. S. Troops in the Argonne
Grace Harlowe with the Yankee Shock Boys at St.

Quentin
Grace Harlowe with the American Army on the Rhine

GRACE MAY NORTH BOOKS FOR GIRLS, Grace May North, ca. 1920s Saalfield and Burt, cloth-over-board cover. ($20.00 with dust jacket) $10.00
Meg of Mystery Mountain
Rilla of The Lighthouse
Nan of The Gypsies
Sisters

GRAFTON SCHOOL SERIES, Ralph Henry Barbour, Appleton, hardcover, 4 plates, sport stories, especially collectible for the three well-known artists who did the illustrations. Same-as-cover dust jackets. ($45.00 with dust jacket) $20.00
Rivals for the Team, 1916, illustrations by Charles Relyea
Winning His Game, 1917, illustrations by Walter Louderback
Hitting the Line, 1917, illustrations by Norman Rockwell

GRAPER GIRLS SERIES, Elizabeth Corbett, ca. 1940 Appleton, hardcover, b/w illustrations by Ruth King. $15.00
Graper Girls
Beth and Ernestine Graper
Growing Up with the Grapers
Graper Girls Go to College

GRAMMAR SCHOOL BOYS SERIES see DICK PRESCOTT

GRANDPA'S LITTLE GIRLS SERIES, Alice Curtis, 1907 – 10 Penn, printed picture of girls on the hardcover, 4 b/w plates by Wuanita Smith, 200+ pages. $35.00
Grandpa's Little Girls
Grandpa's Little Girls and their Friends
Grandpa's Little Girls at School
Grandpa's Little Girls' House-boat Party
Grandpa's Little Girls Grown Up

GREAT ACE SERIES, Noel Sainsbury, Cupples & Leon, hardcover with printed illustration of biplane, illustrated endpapers and frontispiece, adventures of Billy Smith. ($30.00 in dust jacket) $10.00
Billy Smith, Exploring Ace, or By Airplane to New Guinea, 1928 (first published by McBride)
Billy Smith, Exploring Ace, or By Airplane to New Guinea, 1928
Billy Smith, Secret Service Ace, or Airplane Adventures in Arabia, 1932
Billy Smith, Mystery Ace, or Airplane Discoveries in South America, 1932
Billy Smith, Trail Eater Ace, or Into the Wilds of Northern Alaska by Airplane, 1933
Billy Smith, Shanghaied Ace, or Malay Pirates and Solomon Island Cannibals, 1934

GREAT AMERICAN INDUSTRIES SERIES, Hugh Weir, Wilde, hardcover, paste-on-pictorial, frontispiece. $20.00
With the Flag at Panama, 1911
Young Shipper of the Great Lakes, 1912
Cinders, the Young Apprentice of the Steel Mill, 1914
Young Wheat Scout, 1915
Young Telephone Operator, or Winning with the Wire, 1917

GREAT BRAIN SERIES, John D. Fitzgerald, 1970s Dial, hardcover, b/w illustrations by Mercer Mayer.
First editions: ($35.00 with dust jacket) $15.00
Later printings: ($20.00 with dust jacket) $10.00
Great Brain, 1967
More Adventures of the Great Brain, 1969
Me and My Little Brain, 1972
Great Brain at the Academy, 1972
Great Brain Reforms, 1973
Return of the Great Brain, 1974
Great Brain Does It Again, 1975
Great Brain Is Back, 1995

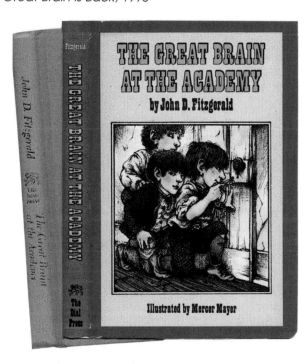

GREAT INDIAN CHIEFS SERIES, Everett G. Tomlinson, Appleton, red hardcover, gilt lettering, paste-on-pictorial. $20.00
Titles include:
Trail of Black Hawk, 1915
Trail of the Mohawk Chief, 1916
Trail of Tecumseh, 1917

GREAT McGONIGGLE SERIES, Scott Corbett, 1975 – 80 Little, Brown, hardcover, easy-to-read books, b/w illustrations by Bill Ogden. ($15.00 with dust jacket) $10.00
Great McGoniggle's Gray Ghost

Great McGoniggle's Key Play
Great McGoniggle Rides Shotgun
Great McGoniggle Switches Pitches

GREAT WEST SERIES, Edward Legrand Sabin, 1916 – 1919 Thomas Y. Crowell, pictorial hardcover, 4 plates, 300+ pages. $30.00
Boy Settler, or Terry in the New West
Great Pike's Peak Rush, or Terry in the New Gold Fields
On the Overland Stage, or Terry as a King Whip Cub
Opening the Iron Trail, or Terry as a "U Pay" Man

GREEN KNOWE SERIES, L. M. Boston, Harcourt or Atheneum, American editions, and Faber, UK editions, hardcover, illustrated by Peter Boston. This series was based on the author's own house.
Early UK editions: ($50.00 with dust jacket) $15.00
Early American editions: ($30.00 with dust jacket) $15.00
Children of Green Knowe, 1955
Treasure of Green Knowe, 1958 (British title: *Chimneys of Green Knowe*)
River at Green Knowe, 1959
Stranger at Green Knowe, 1961
Enemy at Green Knowe, 1964
Guardians of the House, 1974
Stones of Green Knowe, 1976
Green Knowe, related book:
Memory in a House, 1973 Bodley Head, non-fiction hardcover relating author's experience restoring her house. RARE

GREYCLIFF GIRLS SERIES, Harriet Grove, 1923 – 25 Burt, 8 books. ($20.00 with dust jacket) $10.00
Cathalina at Greycliff
Girls of Greycliff
Greycliff Wings
Greycliff Girls in Camp
Greycliff Heroine
Greycliff Girls in Georgia
Greycliff Girls Ranching
Greycliff Girls' Great Adventure

GRIDIRON SERIES, Harold Sherman, 1926 – 1930 Grosset & Dunlap, school football stories. ($45.00 with dust jacket) $15.00
Fight 'em, Big Three
One Minute to Play (novelization of the photoplay by Byron Morgan, one edition of this title was illustrated with photographs from film)
Touchdown!
Block That Kick!
Hold That Line!
Number 44 and Other Football Stories
Goal to Go!
Crashing Through
Other authors:
Under the Goal Posts, Dooley

Jimmy Makes the Varsity, Eddie Brooks, 1928

H

HADLEY CHILDREN MYSTERY SERIES, Dorothy Clewes, Collins, UK, Coward, US, hardcover. ($20.00 with dust jacket) $10.00
Mystery of the Scarlet Daffodil, 1953
Mystery of the Blue Admiral, 1954
Mystery of the Jade-Green Cadillac, 1958
Mystery of the Lost Tower Treasure, 1960
Mystery of the Singing Strings, 1961
Mystery of the Midnight Smugglers, 1964

HAL AND ROGER HUNT SERIES, Willard Price, Jonathan Cape, London, hardcover, color frontispiece, illustrations by Pat Marriot, early printing: ($50.00 with dust jacket) $20.00
John Day edition, map endpapers, illustrations by Peter Burchard: ($45.00 with dust jacket) $15.00
Amazon Adventure, 1949
South Sea Adventure, 1952
Underwater Adventure, 1954
Volcano Adventure, 1956
Whale Adventure, 1960
African Adventure, 1963
Elephant Adventure, 1964
Safari Adventure, 1966
Lion Adventure, 1967
Gorilla Adventure, 1969
Diving Adventure, 1970
Cannibal Adventure, 1972
Tiger Adventure, 1980
Arctic Adventure, 1983

HAL KEEN SERIES, Hugh Lloyd, 1931 – 34 Grosset,

orange hardcover, illustrations by Bert Salg. ($40.00 with dust jacket) $10.00
Hermit of Gordon's Creek
Kidnapped in the Jungle
Copperhead Trail Mystery
Smuggler's Secret
Mysterious Arab
Lonesome Swamp Mystery
Clue at Skeleton Rocks
Doom of Stark House
Lost Mine of the Amazon
Mystery at Dark Star Ranch

HANNAH SERIES, Mindy Skolsky, Harper, pictorial hardcover, illustrated by Karen Ann Weinhaus. ($20.00 with dust jacket) $10.00
Whistling Teakettle and Other Stories about Hannah, 1977
Carnival and Kopeck and More about Hannah, 1979
Hannah Is a Palindrome, 1980
Hannah and the Best Father on Route 9W, 1982

HAPPY HOLLISTERS SERIES, pseudonym Jerry West, (most titles credited to Andrew Sevenson, a partner in the Stratemeyer Syndicate), 1953 – 1970 Garden City or Doubleday, 33 books. Published in three formats: trade edition hardcover with dust jacket (price listed on dust jacket), trade hardcover with picture cover, and book club edition with dust jacket (dust jacket has no price; this format used for all 33 titles), two-color illustrations throughout by Helen Hamilton.
Hardcover: ($15.00 with dust jacket) $10.00
Pictorial cover: $10.00.
Note individual price for last titles in series.
Happy Hollisters, 1953
Happy Hollisters on a River Trip, 1953
Happy Hollisters at Sea Gull Beach, 1953

Happy Hollisters and the Indian Treasure, 1953
Happy Hollisters at Mystery Mountain, 1954
Happy Hollisters at Snowflake Camp, 1954
Happy Hollisters and the Trading Post Mystery, 1954
Happy Hollisters at Circus Isl and, 1955
Happy Hollisters and the Secret Fort, 1955
Happy Hollisters and the Merry-Go Round Mystery, 1955
Happy Hollisters at Pony Hill Farm, 1956
Happy Hollisters and the Old Clipper Ship, 1956
Happy Hollisters at Lizard Cove, 1957
Happy Hollisters and the Scarecrow Mystery, 1959
Happy Hollisters the Castle Rock Mystery, 1963
Happy Hollisters the Cuckoo ClockMystery, 1963
Happy Hollisters the Swiss Echo Mystery, 1963
Happy Hollisters the Sea Turtle Mystery, 1964
Happy Hollisters the Punch and Judy Mystery, 1964
Happy Hollisters the Whistle-Pig Mystery, 1964
Happy Hollisters the Ghost Horse Mystery, 1965
Happy Hollisters the Mystery of the Golden Witch, 1966
Happy Hollisters the Mystery of the Mexican Idol, 1967
Happy Hollisters and the Monster Mystery, 1969 ($25.00 with dust jacket)
Happy Hollisters and the Mystery of the Midnight Trolls, 1970 ($75.00 with dust jacket)

HARDY BOYS SERIES, Franklin W. Dixon (pseudonym for Stratemeyer Syndicate authors), Grosset & Dunlap, 124 volumes published between 1927 – 1994. Canadian Leslie McFarlane wrote many titles in the series between 1927 and 1947 (see Bibliography). Starting in 1959, the Stratemeyer Syndicate began revising all books published earlier. In 1979, Simon and Schuster bought out the Stratemeyer Syndicate and published new Hardy Boys titles under the "Wanderer Books" imprint. Grosset & Dunlap retained publication rights to older titles. Like other Grosset & Dunlap series, first editions are not marked, and dating books can be tricky. Most collectors identify "firsts" as books that do not list past their own title on the title list. Numerous reprints keep later editions' prices low, but prices on early editions, especially those with good dust jackets, continue to rise.

Hardy Boys, 1927 – 1932, first three books (Tower, House, and Secret) released in 1927 with red cloth imprinted with a black shield, blank endpapers, and dustjackets with white spine. Probable firsts: ($50.00 with dust jacket) $25.00. Early editions ($25.00 with dust jacket) $15.00

Tower Treasure
House on the Cliff
Secret of the Old Mill
Missing Chums
Hunting for Hidden Gold
Shore Road Mystery
Secret of the Caves
Mystery of Cabin Island
Great Airport Mystery
What Happened at Midnight
While the Clock Ticked

Hardy Boys, 1932 – 1941, blank endpapers are replaced with brown or orange endpapers showing one of the Hardys peering across a river with a pair of binoculars. Brown cloth binding, dust jackets switch from white spine to yellow spine in 1934 (volumes 1–12 still reprinted with white spine into 1940s). Editions printed during WWII (1943 – 48) use thinner paper and pages tend to brown. Probable firsts: (with dust jacket $35.00), $15.00; other editions (with dust jacket, $25.00), $15.00

Footprints Under the Window
Mark on the Door
Hidden Harbor Mystery
Sinister Sign Post
Figure in Hiding
Secret Warning
Twisted Claw
Disappearing Floor
Mystery of the Flying Express
Clue of the Broken Blade
Flickering Torch Mystery
Melted Coins
Short-Wave Mystery

Hardy Boys, 1945 – 1950, wrap-around scene on dust jackets, brown cloth cover, new cover art created for many of the older titles. Probable firsts: (with dust jacket $30.00), $15.00

Secret Panel
Phantom Freighter
Secret of Skull Mountain
Sign of the Crooked Arrow

Secret of Lost Tunnel
Wailing Siren Mystery

Hardy Boys, new titles, 1951 – 1962, brown cloth replaced by "tweed" cloth on hardcover. In 1958, the series drops the orange endpapers and uses a brown multi-image endpaper. Probable firsts: ($25.00 with dust jacket) $10.00 Later editions: ($20.00 with dust jacket) $10.00

Secret of Wildcat Swamp, 1952
Crisscross Shadow, 1953
Yellow Feather Mystery, 1954
Hooded Hawk Mystery, 1954
Clue in The Embers, 1955
Secret of Pirates' Hill, 1956
Ghost of Skeleton Rock, 1957
Mystery at Devil's Paw, 1959
Mystery of the Chinese Junk, 1960
Mystery of the Desert Giant, 1961

Hardy Boys, new titles, 1961 – 1979, format changes to pictorial hardcover editions. Endpapers switch to a multi-image on white background. Probable first editions: $20.00, later editions: $10.00

Clue of the Screeching Owl, 1962
Viking Symbol Mystery, 1963
Mystery of the Aztec Warrior, 1964
Haunted Fort, 1965
Mystery of the Spiral Bridge, 1966
Secret Agent on Flight 101, 1967
Mystery of the Whale Tattoo, 1968
Arctic Patrol Mystery, 1969
Bombay Boomerang, 1970
Danger on the Vampire Trail, 1971
Masked Monkey, 1972
Shattered Helmet, 1973
Clue of the Hissing Serpent, 1974
Mysterious Caravan, 1975
Witch-Master's Key, 1976
Jungle Pyramid, 1977
Mystery of the Firebird Rocket, 1978
Sting of the Scorpion, 1979
Night of the Werewolf, 1979
Mystery of the Samurai Sword, 1979

Hardy Boys, revised titles, 1959 – 1975. Titles originally published before 1959 are revised or completely rewritten. Copyright shows date of original story and date of revision. Text is shortened to 20 chapters, pictorial cover format used for books published after 1962. Hardcover with dust jacket: $15.00 Plain hardcover or pictorial hardcover: $10.00

Hardy Boys, related books:

Hardy Boys Detective Handbook, 1959 Grosset & Dunlap, hardcover, written "...in consultation with Captain D. A. Spina." ($25.00 with dust jacket) $15.00

Hardy Boys Detective Handbook, 1972 Grosset & Dunlap, a revised edition states "in consultation with William F. Flynn." $15.00

Hardy Boys and Nancy Drew Meet Dracula, 1978 Grosset & Dunlap, softcover only, tie-in to late 1970s television series. $10.00

Walt Disney's the Hardy Boys Coloring Book, 1957 Whitman, with drawings based on the Mickey Mouse Club productions. $20.00

Hardy Boys Clues to Color, 1978 Treasure Books, oversize color book, cover illustration similar to the 1970s pictorial covers. $15.00

HARKAWAY SERIES see JACK HARKAWAY

HARPER I Can Read BOOKS, 1960s Harper and Row, paper-over-board illustrated hardcover, limited vocabulary, color illustrations throughout. Harper hired some very fine illustrators, which makes many of these simple reader books highly collectible. Numerous individual titles were published under the I Can Read designation. The I Can Read Books also included some special categories. Unless specifically marked with another price, their prices fall in the following range:

Hardcover with dust jacket, $25.00
Illustrated hardcover without dust jacket: $15.00
HARPER I Can Read books include the following categories and titles:

Harper Early I Can Read
Come and Have Fun, Edith Hurd, illustrated by Clement Hurd
Albert the Albatross, Syd Hoff
Cat and Dog, Else Holmelund Minarik, illustrated by Fritz Siebel
What Have I Got?, Mike McClintock, illustrated by Leonard Kessler

Harper Mysteries I Can Read
Big Max, Kin Platt, illustrated by Robert Lopshire
Binky Brothers, Detectives, James Lawrence, illustrated by Leonard Kessler
Case of the Dumb Bells, Crosby Bonsall
Homework Caper, Joan M. Lexau, illustrated by Syd Hoff
Rooftop Mystery, Joan Lexau, illustrated by Syd Hoff
Strange Disappearance of Arthur Cluck, Nathaniel Benchley, 1967, illustrated by Arnold Lobel

Harper Science I Can Read
Greg's Microscope, Millicent Selsam, illustrated by Arnold Lobel
Penguins Are Coming!, R. L. Penney, 1969, illustrated by Tom Eaton
Plenty of Fish, Millicent Selsam, illustrated by Erik Blegvad
Red Tag Comes Back, Fred Phleger, illustrated by Arnold Lobel
Seeds and More Seeds, Millicent Selsam, illustrated by Tomi Ungerer
Tony's Birds, Millicent Selsam, illustrated by Kurt Werth

Harper Sports I Can Read
Here Comes the Strikeout, Leonard Kessler
Kick, Pass, and Run, Leonard Kessler
Last One In Is a Rotten Egg, Leonard Kessler

HARRIET THE SPY SERIES, Louise Fitzhugh, Harper, hardcover, later editions: ($20.00 with dust jacket) $10.00

Harriet the Spy, 1964 Harper, first edition: $100.00 with dust jacket

Long Secret, 1965 Harper, first edition: $60.00 with dust jacket

Sport, 1979 Delacorte, first edition: $85.00 with dust jacket by Robert Kinyon

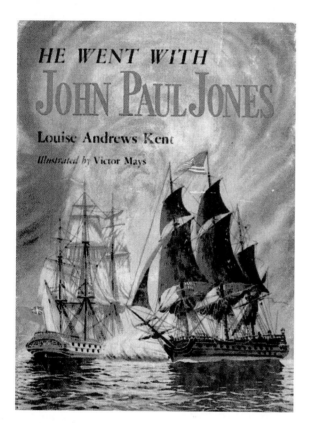

HE WENT WITH SERIES, Louise Andrews Kent, ca. 1950s, Houghton Mifflin, plain hardcover, b/w drawings, approximately 160 pages, wraparound illustration on dust jacket. ($25.00 with dust jacket) $10.00

He Went with Marco Polo
He Went with Christopher Columbus
He Went with Vasco Da Gama
He Went with Magellan
He Went with John Paul Jones

HEADLINE BOOKS FOR GIRLS, ca. 1930s Grosset, hardcover. ($15.00 with dust jacket) $10.00
Headline Divine Corners Stories, Faith Baldwin
Babs
Judy
Myra
Mary Lou
Headline Mysteries
Blue Junk, Priscilla Holton
At Midnight, Louise Platt Hauck
Nobody's Joan, Helen Berger

Stolen Blueprints, Ruth Grosby
Headline Historical Books, Lucy Foster Madison
Maid of Salem Towne
Daughter of the Union
Headline Career Books, Helen Diehl Olds
Barbara Benton, Editor
Joan of the Journal
Headline Western Books
Sidesaddle Ranch, Ann Spence Warner
Gold is Where You Find It, Ann Spence Warner
Days of Gold, Ann Spence Warner
Scarum, Marie de Nervaud

HEARTS SERIES, Emily Kimbrough, Dodd, Mead, hardcover. This started out as a single title memory of a trip to Europe with her friend, Cornelia Otis Skinner. The story was so funny and so popular Kimbrough continued the tales of her adventures. Skinner was a Broadway star, and writer Kimbrough worked as a magazine editior, then freelance writer.

Our Hearts Were Young and Gay, written with Cornelia Otis Skinner, 1942, teenage friends in the 1920s take their first trip abroad, b/w illustrations by Alajalov. First edition with dust jacket: $50.00 Later printings: ($20.00 with dust jacket) $10.00

We Followed Our Hearts to Hollywood, 1943, the pair are asked to help with the film production of their bestseller, illustrated by Helen E. Hokinson. ($25.00 with dust jacket) $10.00

How Dear to My Heart, 1944, tales of Emily's small town childhood in Muncie, Indiana, illustrated by Helen Hokinson. ($25.00 with dust jacket) $10.00

Innocents from Indiana, eleven-year-old Emily moves from Muncie to Chicago. ($25.00 with dust jacket) $10.00

Through Charlie's Door, 1952 Harper & Brothers, Emily's first job at Marshall Fields, b/w illustrations by Alice Harvey. ($25.00 with dust jacket) $10.00

HEIDI BOOKS, Johanna Spyri. The original novel inspired numerous editions, many illustrated by well-known artists, including a Windemere series edition with color plates by Maginal Wright Enright (see WINDEMERE). Shortened versions were featured in picture books for younger children. A very young Shirley Temple starred as Heidi in a film adaptation (see SHIRLEY TEMPLE). Two sequels by another author continued Heidi's story. A sampling of the many editions include:

Heidi (1. Her Years of Wandering and Learning & 2. How She Used What She Learned : Stories for Children and Those Who Love Children), translation by Louise Brooks, Cupples, Upham & Company, Boston, 1886, gray-green hardcover with a pine branch design, 668 pages, two volumes in one, second American edition, a collector's hard-to-find copy. $700.00

Heidi, 1901 edition Burt, decorated hardcover, unidentified illustrations. $45.00

Heidi, 1922 edition David McKay, pictorial cover, color plates by Jessie Willcox Smith, first thus: $100.00

Heidi, 1954 Little Golden Books, small pictorial hardcover, 28 pages, illustrated by Corinne Malvern. $5.00

Heidi Grows Up, Charles Tritten, 1938 Grosset & Dunlap, a sequel written by a translator of the original book, color frontispiece and b/w illustrations by Jean Coquillot, early printing: ($25.00 with dust jacket) $10.00

Heidi's Children, 1939 edition Grosset & Dunlap, hardcover, color and b/w illustations by Pelagie Doane. ($35.00 with dust jacket) $10.00

Heidi's Children, 1964 edition Collins, London, oversize, hardcover, Pelagie Doane illustrations. ($25.00 with dust jacket) $10.00

Heidi, related books:

Heidi, 1954 Little Golden Books, hardcover, foil spine, color illustrations by Corinne Malvern. $10.00

HELEN GRANT SERIES, Amanda Douglas (1831 – 1916), 1903 – 11 Lothrop, 9 titles, illustration on hardcover, Helen's life through college, illustrated by Amy Brooks and others. $15.00
Titles include:
Helen Grant at Aldred House
Helen Grant in College
Helen Grant, Senior
Helen Grant, Teacher
Helen Grant, Graduate
Helen Grant's Harvest Year

HENLEY SCHOOLBOY SERIES, Frank Channon, 1910 – 1913 Little, Brown, red hardcover with paste-on-pictorial, 4 plates. $20.00
American Boy at Henley
Jackson and His Henley Friends
Henley's American Captain
Henley on the Battleline

HENRY HUGGINS SERIES also see RAMONA SERIES, Beverly Cleary, Morrow, hardcover, b/w illustrations by Louis Darling.
Except as noted, first edition with dust jacket: $55.00
Later printings: ($20.00 with dust jacket) $10.00
Henry Huggins, 1950
Henry and Beezus, 1952, first edition with dust jacket: $75.00
Henry and Ribsy, 1954
Henry and the Paper Route, 1957
Henry and the Clubhouse, 1962
Ribsy, 1964

HENRY REED SERIES, Keith Robertson, Viking, hardcover, b/w illustrations by Robert McClosky. First editions: ($35.00 with dust jacket) $15.00
Later editions: ($15.00 with dust jacket) $10.00
Henry Reed, Inc., 1958
Henry Reed's Journey, 1963
Henry Reed's Babysitting Service, 1966
Henry Reed's Big Show, 1970
Henry Reed's Think Tank, 1986

HENTY BOOKS, G. A. Henty, historical and military adventure novels for boys, 1871 – 1902. Like his American counterpart Horatio Alger, Henty was enormously popular with young Victorians on both sides of the Atlantic. His primary publisher, Blackie & Son, estimated that more than 150,000 copies of his books were sold each year during the later half of the 19th century. Although not originally issued as a series, the Blackie/Scribner books were published in a uniform format. Both novels and magazine pieces were later collected into various boys series and school reader formats.

Henty, 1832 – 1903, served in the Crimean War and later worked as a war correspondent from 1865 to 1876. He wrote a number of adult novels, usually "three deckers" (three volumes), as well as collections based on his newspaper work. His first juvenile appeared in 1872, and he also served as an editor for boy's magazines. Today, collectors seek early editions with their highly decorated covers. Firsts are difficult to identify because his publishers rarely identified reprints. Entire books have been devoted to sorting out the many variants (see Bibliography).

Henty books, Blackie/Scribner original editions, (advertised as "The Famous Henty Books" by the 1890s): Early editions had cover illustrations printed on colored cloth-covered boards with gilt decoration on front and spine. All titles listed below were first published in England by Blackie & Son. In the US, they were originally imported by Scribner & Welford or by Charles Scribner's Sons (referred to as Scribner in this listing). By the 1890s, Scribner was printing their own editions, still in the same format as the Blackie editions. Late printings of both publishers dropped the gilt decoration. By the 1920s, Scribner used paste-on illustrations and same-as-cover dust jackets. Illustrated with black-and-white illustrations, some books also included maps of battlefields or territory covered by the adventure. Reprints done by various publishers, including Donahue and A.L. Burt.

Henty prices, Blackie, 1880s Blackie first editions: $300.00; 1890s Blackie first editions: $150.00; 1900s Blackie first editions: $100.00; later editions with gilt and fully illustrated: $100.00; plain editions (no gilt): $20.00.

Henty prices, Scribner, Scribner & Welford first American editions or 1880s Scribner imported editions with Blackie also listed on copyright page: $250.00; 1880s Scribner first American editions: $150.00; 1890s – 1900s Scribner first American editions: $100.00; later editions with gilt and illustrations: $75.00; later editions with plain or paste-on covers: $20.00 ($40.00 with dust jacket).

Henty prices, reprints: Donahue editions: $20.00. Hurst editions: $15.00. A.L. Burt editions: $10.00 ($30.00 with dust jacket), other publishers with well-decorated covers: $20.00 ($10.00 with plain covers; $30.00 with dust jackets).

Henty titles (dates given are the copyright dates of the first editions):

At Agincourt, 1897 Blackie (1896 Scribners), Wal Paget 12 illustrations.

At the Point of Bayonet, 1902 Blackie (1901 Scribners) Wal Paget 12 illustrations.

Beric the Briton, 1892 Blackie (1891 Scribners), W. Parkinson 12 illustrations.

Bonnie Prince Charlie, 1888 Blackie, Gordon Browne 12 illustrations.

Both Sides the Border, 1899 Blackie (1898 Scribner), Ralph Peacock 12 illustrations.

Bravest of the Brave, 1887 Blackie (Scribner & Welford), 8 illustrations by H.M. Paget.

By Conduct and Courage, 1905 Blackie (1904 Scribner), illustrated by William Rainey.

By England's Aid, 1891 Blackie, 10 full page illustrations by Alfred Pearse.

By Pike and Dyke, 1890 Blackie (Scribner & Welford), 10 full-page illustrations by Maynard Brown.

By Right of Conquest, 1891 Blackie, 10 full-page illustrations by W.S. Stacey.

By Sheer Pluck, 1884 Blackie, 8 full-page illustrations by Gordon Browne.

Captain Bayley's Heir, 1889 Blackie (Scribner & Welford), 12 full-page illustrations by H.M. Paget

Cat of Bubastes, 1889 Blackie, 8 full-page illustrations by J.R. Weguelin.

Chapter of Adventures, 1891 Blackie (Scribner & Welford), 8 full-page illustrations by W.H. Overend

Condemned as a Nihilist, 1893 Blackie (1892 Scribner), 12 full-page illustrations by Wal Paget.

Dash for Khartoum, 1892 Blackie (1891 Scribner), 10 illustrations by Joseph Nash.

Dragon and the Raven, 1886 Blackie (Scribner & Welford), 8 full-page illustrations by C.J. Staniland.

Facing Death, 1882 Blackie (A number of variants appear of first edition and book may not have been issued until 1883. See Dartt, listed in Bibliography, for full description), 8 full-page illustrations by Gordon Browne.

Final Reckoning, 1887 Blackie (Scribner & Welford), 8 full-page illustrations by W. B. Wollen.

For Name and Fame, 1886 Blackie, 8 full-page illustrations by Gordon Browne.

For the Temple, 1888 Blackie (Scribner & Welford), illustrated by Solomon J. Solomon.

Held Fast for England, 1892 Blackie (1891 Scribner), illustrated by Gordon Browne.

In Freedom's Cause, 1885 Blackie (Scribner & Welford), illustrated by Gordon Browne.

In Greek Waters, 1893 Blackie (1892 Scribner), 12 illustrations by W.S. Stacey and map.

In the Heart of the Rockies, 1895 Blackie (1894 Scribner), eight illustrations by G. Hindley.

In the Irish Brigade, 1901 Blackie (1900 Scribner), 12

illustrations by Charles M. Sheldon.

In the Reign of Terror, 1888 Blackie (Scribner & Welford), 8 illustrations by J. Schonberg.

Jacobite Exile, 1894 Blackie (1893 Scribner), 8 illustrations by Paul Hardy and map.

Knight of the White Cross, 1896 Blackie (1895 Scribner), 12 illustrations by Ralph Peacock "and A Plan" (Blackie edition also has a full-page portrait of Henty).

Lion of St. Mark, 1889 Blackie (Scribner), 10 illustrations by Gordon Browne.

Lion of the North, 1886 Blackie (Scribner), 12 illustrations by John Schonberg.

Maori And Settler, 1891 Blackie (Scribner & Welford), 8 full-page illustrations by Alfred Pearse and map.

March on London, 1898 Blackie (1897 Scribner), 8 illustrations by W. H. Margetson.

No Surrender!, 1900 Blackie (1899 Scribner), 8 illustrations by Stanley L Wood.

One of the 28th, 1890 Blackie (Scribner & Welford), 8 full-page illustrations by W.H. Overend and maps.

On the Irrawaddy, 1897 Blackie (1896 Scribner), 8 full-page illustrations by W. H. Overend.

Orange and Green, 1888 Blackie (Scribner), 8 full-page illustrations by Gordon Browne.

Out with Garibaldi, 1901 Blackie (1900 Scribner), 8 illustrations by W. Rainey.

Redskin and Cowboy, 1892 Blackie (1891 Scribner), 12 illustrations by Alfred Pearse.

Roving Commission, 1900 Blackie (1899 Scribner), 12 illustrations by William Rainey.

Saint Bartholomew's Eve, 1894 Blackie (1893 Scribner) 12 illustrations by H.J. Draper and map.

St. George for England, 1885 Blackie (Scribner), 8 full-page illustrations by Gordon Browne.

Soldier's Daughter, 1906 Blackie, cloth-covered boards with stamped on illustrations of Afridi warrior carrying sword and shield and illustration of heroine dressed as boy on spine, no gilt, collection of three Henty stories including "Nita: A Tom-Boy Solider." Illustrated by Frances Ewan.

Sturdy and Strong, 1888 Blackie (Scribner), 4 full-page illustrations by Robert Fowler.

Tales of Daring and Danger, 1890 Blackie (Scribner & Welford), collection of short stories.

Through Russian Snows, 1896 Blackie (1895 Scribner), 8 illustrations by W.H. Overend and maps.

Through the Fray, 1886 Blackie (Scribner & Welford), 12 full-page illustrations by H.M. Paget

Through the Sikh War, 1894 Blackie (1893 Scribner), 12 illustrations by Hal Hurst and map.

Through Three Campaigns, 1904 Blackie (1903 Scribner), illustrated by Wal Paget.

Tiger of Mysore, 1896 Blackie (1895 Scribner), illustrations and map.

To Herat and Cabul, 1902 Blackie (1901 Scribner) 8 illustrations by Charles Sheldon and map.

Treasure of the Incas, 1903 Blackie (1902 Scribner), 8 illustrations by Wal Paget and map.

True to the Old Flag, 1885 Blackie (Scribner), 12 illustrations by Gordon Browne.

Under Drake's Flag, 1883 Blackie (Scribner), 12 full-page illustrations by Gordone Browne.

Under Wellington's Command, 1899 Blackie (1898 Scribner), 12 illustrations by Wal Paget.

When London Burned, 1895 Blackie (1894 Scribner), 12 illustrations by J. Finnemore.

With Buller in Natal, 1901 Blackie (1900 Scribner), 10 illustrations by W. Rainey.

With Clive in India, 1884 Blackie (Scribner & Welford), 12 full-page illustrations by Gordon Browne

With Frederick the Great, 1898 Blackie (1897 Scribner), 12 illustrations by Wal Paget

With Kitchener in the Soudan, 1903 Blackie (1902 Scribner), 10 illustrations by W. Rainey and maps

With Lee in Virginia, 1890 Blackie (Scribner), illustrated by Gordon Browne.

With Moore at Carunna, 1898 Blackie (1897 Scribner), 12 illustrations by Wal Paget and map.

With Roberts to Pretoria, 1902 Blackie (1901 Scribner), 12 illustrations by Wiliam Rainey.

With the British Legion, 1903 Blackie (1902 Scribner), 10 full-page illustrations by Wal Paget.

With Wolfe in Canada, 1887 Blackie (Scribner & Welford), 12 full-page illustrations by Gordon Browne.

Won by the Sword, 1900 Blackie (1899 Scribner), 12 illustrations by Charles Sheldon and plans.

Wulf the Saxon, 1895 Blackie (1894 Scribner), 12 illustrations by Ralph Peacock.

Yarns on the Beach: A Bundle of Tales, 1886 Blackie (Scribner & Welford), two full-page illustrations by J.J. Proctor.

Young Carthaginian, 1887 Blackie (Scribner & Welford), 12 full-page illustrations by C.J. Staniland.

Henty, Griffith & Farran editions, 1871 to 1883, earliest publisher of Henty's boy books, these titles are similar in format to Blackie books. Cloth with printed illustrations and gilt decorations on cover and spine. Later editions issued by Blackie, Hurst, Copp Clarke and others. First editions RARE; early editions with gilt decorations: $200.00; later editions with no gilt: $30.00; other publishers' later editions: $15.00.

Friends Though Divided, 1883, illustrated with frontispeace.

In Times of Peril, 1881 (first published in US by Dutton), illustrated with frontispeace, gilt-edged pages. Dutton First American Edition RARE.

Out on the Pampas or the Young Settlers: A Tale for Boys, 1871, illustrated by J.B. Zewecker. Henty's first book for boys, the characters were named after and modeled upon his four children: Charles Gerald, Hubert, Maud, and Ethel.

Young Buglers, 1880, 8 illustrations by John Proctor and 11 plans of battles.

Young Franc-Tireurs, 1872, Illustrations by R.T. Landells.

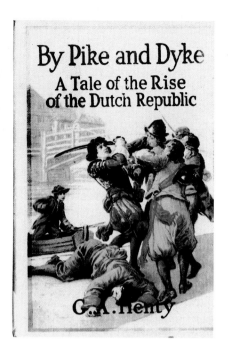

Scribner editions, ca. 1890, 1901, 1923

Henty, magazine annuals which reprinted Henty stories:

Nister's Holiday Annual, ca. 1902 – 1909, full pictorial paper-covered boards, Henty's short stories appeared in various volumes. $50.00 each

Union Jack, ca 1880 – 1883 Sampson Low, embossed cloth-covered boards with decorations and gilt, annuals of a boy's magazine edited by Henty and containing many Henty stories as well as Henty's Editor's Box which contained such offers as: "to any lad who shall obtain twelve new subscribers, I will send a copy of my Seaside Maidens bound in cloth, and to any who may get three new subscribers, I will send my photograph, with a line expressive of my thanks..." RARE

Henty, non-, title using the Henty name but not Henty:

Malcom the Waterboy, by D.T. Henty (credited to Edward Stratemeyer by Dartt, see Bibliography), part of Mershon's Boys' Own Series, also published by Stitt Publishing and others. RARE

HERBERT SERIES, Hazel Wilson, Knopf, pictorial hardcover, illustrated endpapers, b/w illustrations by John Barron. $15.00

Herbert, 1950

Herbert Again, 1951

More Fun with Herbert, 1954

Herbert's Homework, 1960

Herbert's Space Trip, 1965

Herbert's Stilts, 1972

HICKORY RIDGE BOY SCOUTS SERIES, Capt. Alan Douglas, ca. 1910 – 1920 New York Book Co., hardcover with paste-on-pictorial in colors, frontispiece, illustration by E. Caswell, reissued by Donohue in the Victory Boy Scouts Series. ($45.00 with dust jacket) $20.00

Campfires of the Wolf Patrol

Hickory Ridge Boy Scouts' Woodcraft, or How a Patrol Leader Made Good Hickory Ridge Boy Scouts' Pathfinder, or, Missing Tenderfoot

Hickory Ridge Boy Scouts' Fast Nine, or Challenge from Fairfield

Hickory Ridge Boy Scouts' Great Hike, or Pride of the Khaki Troop

Hickory Ridge Boy Scouts' Endurance Test, or How Clear Grit Won the Day

Hickory Ridge Boy Scouts Under Canvas, or Hunt for the Carteret Ghost

Hickory Ridge Boy Scouts Stormbound, or Vacation Among the Snow Drifts

Hickory Ridge Boy Scouts Afloat, or Adventures on Watery Trails

Hickory Ridge Boy Scouts' Tenderfoot Squad, or Camping at Raccoon Lodge

HIGH SCHOOL BOYS SERIES see DICK PRESCOTT

HIGHWOOD SERIES, Ralph Henry Barbour, 1928 – 1929 Appleton, hardcover, illustrated by F. Wagner, school sports. $20.00

Hunt Holds the Center
Lovell Leads Off
Grantham Gets On

HILDA OF GREYCOT SERIES, Mrs. Pemberton Ginther, ca. 1922 – 25 Penn Publishing, hardcover, illustrated by author. $20.00
Hilda of Greycot, 1923
Hilda of Landis and Company, 1924
Hilda of the Green Smock, 1925
Hilda of the Three Star Ranch, 1926

HILDEGARDE-MARGARET SERIES, Laura Richards, ca. 1890s Estes & Lauriat, Boston, small, decorated hardcover, 350+ pages, full page tipped-in illustrations, first edition: $100.00
Later Estes printings, frontispiece only: $25.00
Ca. 1915 editions Grosset, cloth-over-board cover, about 275 pages, no illustrations. $15.00
Queen Hildegarde
Hildegarde's Holiday
Hildegarde's Home
Hildegarde's Harvest
Hildegarde's Neighbors
Three Margarets
Margaret Montfort
Peggy
Rita
Fernley House
Merryweathers

HILL TOP BOYS SERIES, Cyril Burleigh, ca. 1915 Goldsmith, 1917 World, small, 122 pages, b/w illustrated endpapers. ($10.00 with dust jacket) $5.00
Hill Top Boys
Hill Top Boys in Camp

Hill Top Boys on Lost Island
Hill Top Boys on the River
Hill Top Boys Doing Their Bit

HILLSFIELD SERIES, Ralph Henry Barbour, 1931 – 1934 Appleton, hardcover. Like most Barbour books, reappear in several formats. Good printings of Neill illustrations can increase price. ($30.00 with dust jacket) $15.00
Fumbled Pass
Hero of the Camp
Cub Battery
Goal to Go
Beaton Runs the Mile
Southworth Scores

HILTON SERIES, Ralph Henry Barbour, 1899-1901 Appleton, hardcover, more school sports from this prolific writer, 6 b/w plates plus maps. $45.00
Halfback, 1899
For the Honor of the School, 1900
Captain of the Crew, 1901

HISTORICAL SERIES, by James Johonnot, 1887 Appleton, small size, brown board cover with black print illustration, b/w illustrations. $20.00
Grandfather Stories
Stories of Heroic Deeds
Stories of Our Country
Stories of Other Lands
Stories of Olden Times
Ten Great Events in History
How Nations Grow and Decay

HOCKEY SERIES, Harold Sherman, 1929 – 1931 Grosset & Dunlap, red hardcover, frontispiece, school ice hockey novels, also included in larger series of sports novels. ($25.00 with dust jacket) $10.00
Flashing Steel, 1929
Flying Heels, 1930
Slashing Sticks, 1931

HOME RUN SERIES, Harold Sherman, 1928-1932 Grosset & Dunlap, hardcover with baseball diamond design, illustrated endpapers, reappear in other formats in other sports series. ($25.00 with dust jacket) $10.00
Bases Full
Hit by Pitcher
Safe
Hit and Run
Batter Up
Double Play

HONEY BUNCH AND NORMAN SERIES, Helen Louise Thorndyke, pseudonym, (Stratemeyer Syndicate series, many by Josephine Lawrence, or Mildred Wirt Benson) ca. 1920 – on Grosset & Dunlap, 30+ books, hardcover with paste-on-pictorial, b/w plates, illustrators include Walter S. Rogers, Marie Schubert, Corinne Dillon, advertised as "pleasing series of stories for little girls from four to eight years old." Early printings: ($80.00 with dust jacket) $40.00

Ca. 1957 this series became the Honey Bunch and Norman series, featuring Honey Bunch Morton and her friend, Norman Clark, who appeared in earlier titles and were very popular with readers. Reprints of earlier titles (sometimes titles were altered) are included with new titles in the later series.

Plain hardcover: ($35.00 with dust jacket) $15.00

Pictorial paper-over-board cover: $20.00

Honey Bunch titles:

Honey Bunch: Just a Little Girl, 1923
Honey Bunch: Her First Visit to the City, 1923
Honey Bunch: Her First Days on the Farm, 1923
Honey Bunch: Her First Visit to the Seashore, 1924
Honey Bunch: Her First Little Garden, 1924
Honey Bunch: Her First Days in Camp, 1925
Honey Bunch: Her First Auto Tour, 1926
Honey Bunch: Her First Trip to the Ocean, 1927
Honey Bunch: Her First Trip West, 1928
Honey Bunch: Her First Summer on an Island, 1929
Honey Bunch: Her First Trip on the Great Lakes, 1930
Honey Bunch: Her First Trip in an Airplane, 1931
Honey Bunch: Her First Visit to the Zoo, 1932
Honey Bunch: Her First Big Adventure, 1933
Honey Bunch: Her First Big Parade, 1934
Honey Bunch: Her First Little Mystery, 1935
Honey Bunch: Her First Little Circus, 1936
Honey Bunch: Her First Little Treasure Hunt, 1937
Honey Bunch: Her First Little Club, 1938
Honey Bunch: Her First Trip in a Trailer, 1939
Honey Bunch: Her First Trip to a Big Fair, 1940
Honey Bunch: Her First Twin Playmates, 1941
Honey Bunch: Her First Costume Party, 1943
Honey Bunch: Her First Trip on a House Boat, 1945
Honey Bunch: Her First Winter at Snowtop, 1946
Honey Bunch: Her First Trip to the Big Woods, 1947
Honey Bunch: Her First Little Pet Show, 1948
Honey Bunch: Her First Trip to a Light House, 1949
Honey Bunch: Her First Visit to a Pony Ranch, 1950
Honey Bunch: Her First Tour of Toy Town, 1951
Honey Bunch: Her First Visit to Puppy Land, 1952
Honey Bunch: Her First Visit to Reindeer Farm, 1953

Honey Bunch and Norman titles:

Honey Bunch and Norman Ride with the Sky Mailman, 1954
Honey Bunch and Norman Visit Beaver Lodge, 1955
Honey Bunch and Norman, 1957, official beginning of the new series
Honey Bunch and Norman on Light House Island, 1957 (re-titled 1949 book)
Honey Bunch and Norman Tour Toy Town, 1957 (re-titled 1951 book)
Honey Bunch and Norman Play Detective at Niagara Falls, 1957

Honey Bunch and Norman Ride with the Sky Mailman, 1958, re-issue of 1954 book
Honey Bunch and Norman Visit Beaver Lodge, 1958, re-issue of 1955 book
Honey Bunch and Norman Visit Reindeer Farm, 1958 (re-titled 1953 book)
Honey Bunch and Norman in the Castle of Magic, 1959
Honey Bunch and Norman Solve the Pine Cone Mystery, 1960
Honey Bunch and Norman and the Paper Lantern Mystery, 1961
Honey Bunch and Norman and the Painted Pony, 1962
Honey Bunch and Norman and the Walnut Tree Mystery, 1963

HOPALONG CASSIDY SERIES, Clarence Mulford, (ca. 1910 McClurg) ca. 1950s Grosset & Dunlap, hardcover. ($30.00 with dust jacket) $10.00

Hopalong Cassidy
Coming of Hopalong Cassidy
Hopalong Cassidy Sees Red
Hopalong Cassidy's Private War
Hopalong Cassidy's Rustler Round-Up

Hopalong Cassidy, related titles:

Hopalong Cassidy and the Bar 20 Cowboys, Mulford, 1952 Little Golden Books, small hardcover, foil spine, color illustrations by Sahula-Dycke. $15.00

HORACE HIGBY SERIES, William Heuman, Dodd, Mead, hardcover, b/w illustrations by William Moyers. ($25.00 with dust jacket) $15.00
Horace Higby and the Scientific Pitch, 1968
Horace Higby and the Field Goal Formula, 1969
Horace Higby and the Gentle Fullback, 1970
Horace Higby, Coxswain of the Crew, 1971

HORATIO ALGER'S BOOKS see ALGER

"HOW-TO-DO-IT" SERIES, ca. 1920s edition Donahue, advertised as "printed from new plates and bound in cloth, profusely illustrated." $15.00
Carpentry for Boys
Electricity for Boys
Practical Mechanics for Boys

HUGO AND JOSEPHINE TRILOGY, Maria Gripe, illustrated by Harald Gripe, award-winning series about a charcoal maker's son and a minister's daughter, story set in Sweden.
Hugo and Josephine, 1969 Delacorte Press, first American edition. ($40.00 with dust jacket) $15.00
Josephine, 1970 Delacorte Press, first edition. ($30.00 with dust jacket) $15.00
Hugo, 1970 Delacorte Press, first edition. ($30.00 with dust jacket) $15.00

HUNNIWELL BOYS SERIES, Levi Wyman, ca. 1929 Burt, hardcover, several editions, frontispiece picture repeated on dust jacket. ($20.00 with dust jacket) $10.00
Hunniwell Boys in the Air
Hunniwell Boys' Victory
Hunniwell Boys in the Secret Service
Hunniwell Boys and the Platinum Mystery
Hunniwell Boys' Longest Flight
Hunniwell Boys in the Gobi Desert
Hunniwell Boys in the Caribbean
Hunniwell Boys' Non-Stop Flight Around the World

———— I ————

IKE AND MAMA SERIES, Carol Snyder, Coward, McCann, small hardcover, 45+ pages, b/w illustrations by Charles Robinson, funny stories of a New York boy in the early 1900s. ($20.00 with dust jacket) $10.00
Ike and Mama and the Once-a-Year Suit, 1978
Ike and Mama and the Block Wedding, 1979
Ike and Mama and the Once-in-a-Lifetime Movie, 1981
Ike and Mama and Trouble at School, 1983

INDIAN STORIES, Dietrich Lange, 1912 – 1931 Lothrop, Lee and Shepard, pictorial hardcover, 6 b/w plates, historical novels. ($35.00 with dust jacket) $15.00
On the Trail of the Sioux, 1912
Silver Island of the Chippewa, 1913
Lost in the Fur Country, 1914
In the Great Wild North, 1915
Lure of the Black Hills, 1916
Lure of the Mississippi, 1917
Silver Cache of the Pawnees, 1918
Shawnee's Warning, 1919
Threat of Sitting Bull, 1920
Raid of the Ottawa, 1921
Mohawk Ranger, 1922
Iroquois Scout, 1923
Sioux Runner, 1924
Golden Rock of the Chippewa, 1925
Boast of the Seminole, 1930
On the Fur Trail, 1931

INDIAN STORIES FOR BOYS, H.L. Risteen, ca. 1950

Cupples & Leon, hardcover. ($25.00 with dust jackets by Chris Richard Schaare) $15.00
Titles include:
Chippewa Captive
Indian Silver
Tomahawk Trail
Black Hawk's Warpath
Redskin Raiders

INJUN AND WHITEY see GOLDEN WEST

INSPECTOR TEARLE MYSTERIES, Scott Corbett, Little, Brown, hardcover, humorous mysteries at an easy reading level. Early printings: ($25.00 with dust jacket) $10.00
Case of the Gone Goose, 1966
Case of the Fugitive Firebug, 1969
Case of the Ticklish Tooth, 1974
Case of the Silver Skull, 1974
Case of the Burgled Blessing Box, 1975

ISABEL CARLETON SERIES, Margaret Ashmun, ca. 1915 Macmillan, cloth-over-board cover with paste-on-pictorial and gilt lettering, 3 b/w plates. Early editions: ($65.00 with dust jacket) $15.00
Isabel Carleton's Year
Heart of Isabel Carleton
Isabel Carleton's Friends
Isabel Carleton in the West
Isabel Carleton at Home

Illustrated by Emily A. McCully

ISABELLE SERIES, Constance Greene, Viking, hardcover, b/w illustrations by Emily A. McCully. ($20.00 with dust jacket) $10.00
Isabelle the Itch, 1973

Isabelle Shows Her Stuff, 1984
Isabelle and Little Orphan Frannie, 1988

ISLAND STALLION SERIES see BLACK STALLION SERIES

IVY HALL SERIES, Ruth Alberta Brown, ca. 1911 Saalfield, hardcover, illustrations by Alfred Russell. ($20.00 with dust jacket) $10.00
Tabitha at Ivy Hall
Tabitha's Glory
Tabitha's Vacation

J

JACK SERIES, George Bird Grinnell, 1899 – 1913 Stokes, pictorial hardcover, numerous b/w illustrations by Edward Demming. First edition: $200.00 with dust jacket. Other early editions: ($60.00 with dust jacket) $20.00
Jack, the Young Ranchman, or A Boy's Adventures in the Rockies
Jack Among the Indians, or A Boy's Summer on the Buffalo Plains
Jack in the Rockies, or A Boy's Adventures with a Pack
Jack, the Young Canoeman, or An Eastern Boy's Voyage in a Chinook Canoe
Jack, the Young Trapper, or An Eastern Boy's Fur Hunting in the Rocky Mountains
Jack, the Young Explorer, or A Boy's Experiences in the Unknown Northwest
Jack, the Young Cowboy, or An Eastern Boy's Experiences on a Western Roundup

JACK HARKAWAY SERIES, Bracebridge Hemying, undated ca. 1904 – 1910 Federal, or Allison, or Donohue, as well as Street and Smith's Round the World Series, paste-on-pictorial cover with impressed color decorations, as well as several other formats. The Harkaway stories appeared in several magazines and were published in book form in various combinations and editions, and are also bound under different titles, but always include the Harkaway name. (Some editions included dust jacket, which adds $10.00 to the price) $15.00
Jack Harkaway's School Days
Jack Harkaway After School Days
Jack Harkaway's Adventures Afloat and Ashore
Jack Harkaway at Oxford, 1
Jack Harkaway at Oxford, 2
Jack Harkaway Among the Brigand, 1
Jack Harkaway Among the Brigands, 2
Jack Harkaway and his Son's Adventures Round the World
Jack Harkaway's Adventures in America and Cuba
Jack Harkaway and His Son's Adventures in China
Jack Harkaway and His Son's Adventures in Greece, 1
Jack Harkaway and His Son's Adventures in Greece, 2

Jack Harkaway and His Son's Adventures in Australia
Adventures of Young Jack Harkaway and His Boy Tinker
Jack Harkaway's Boy Tinker Among the Turks

JACK HAZARD SERIES, J. T. Trowbridge, 1850s – 70s Osgood, hardcover, b/w illustrations: $50.00
1890s Porter and Coats edition: $25.00
Jack Hazard and His Fortunes
The Young Surveyor
Fast Friends
Doing His Best
A Chance for Himself
Lawrence's Adventures

JACK HEATON SERIES, Archie Frederick Collins, Stokes, printed illustration oncloth-over-board cover, about 250 pages, six b/w plate illustrations by Charles Cartwright. $15.00
Jack Heaton, Wireless Operator, 1919
Jack Heaton, Oil Prospector, 1920
Jack Heaton, Gold Seeker, 1921

JACK LIGHTFOOT SERIES, Maxwell Stevens, adventure books for boys, ca. 1910 Street & Smith, New Medal Library reprints: $20.00
Titles include:
Jack Lightfoot's Crack Nine
Jack Lightfoot Trapped
Jack Lightfoot's Rival
Jack Lightfoot in Camp
Jack Lightfoot's Canoe Trip
Jack Lightfoot's Hoodoo
Jack Lightfoot's Blind
Jack Lightfoot's Capture
Jack Lightfoot's Head Work
Jack Lightfoot's Wisdom

JACK LORIMER SERIES, Winn Standish, ca. 1906 Page, pictorial cloth-over-board cover, "high school stories for boys." $25.00
A. L. Burt reprints: ($20.00 with dust jacket) $12.00
Captain Jack Lorimer
Jack Lorimer's Champions
Jack Lorimer's Holidays
Jack Lorimer's Substitute
Jack Lorimer, Freshman

JACK RACE SERIES, Harry Hale, 1915 Hearst, pictorial hardcover, frontispiece. $25.00
Jack Race at Boarding School, or Leader of Merrivale Academy
Jack Race's Baseball Nine, or Winning the Junior League Pennant
Jack Race Speed King, or A Trip across the Continent
Jack Race Air Scout, or Adventures in a War Aeroplane
Jack Race on a Ranch, or Triumphs of a Tenderfoot

JACK RALSTON SERIES, also listed as SKY DETECTIVE SERIES, Ambrose Newcomb, 1930 edition Goldsmith. ($20.00 with dust jacket) $10.00
Eagles of the Sky
Sky Detectives
Wings over the Rockies
Sky Pilot's Great Chase
Trackers of the Fog Pack

JACK RANGER SERIES, Clarence Young (Stratemeyer Syndicate pseudonym), ca. 1910s Cupples & Leon, red hardcover, eight b/w plates by Charles Nuttell. ($40.00 with dust jacket) $15.00
Jack Ranger's School Days
Jack Ranger's Western Trip
Jack Ranger's School Victories
Jack Ranger's Ocean Cruise
Jack Ranger's Gun Club
Jack Ranger's Treasure Box

JACK WINTERS SERIES see AMERICAN BOYS SPORTS

JAKE AND JODY MYSTERY SERIES, Elizabeth Levy, Simon & Schuster, hardcover, young teen detectives solve funny mysteries. First edition: ($25.00 with dust jacket) $10.00
Case of the Wild River Ride, 1978
Case of the Frightened Rock Star, 1980
Case of the Counterfeit Race Horse, 1981
Case of the Fired Up Gang, 1981
Case of the Gobbling Squash, 1988
Case of the Mind Reading Mommies, 1989
Case of the Tattletale Heart, 1990
Case of the Dummy with Cold Eyes, 1991

JANE ALLEN COLLEGE SERIES, Edith Bancroft, ca. 1920 Cupples & Leon, advertised as "a series recognized as an authoritative account of the life of a college girl," hardcover with paste-on-illustration, b/w illustrations. ($50.00 with dust jacket) $20.00

1940s Saalfield reprints, plain hardcover: ($20.00 with dust jacket) $10.00

Jane Allen of the Sub Team
Jane Allen: Right Guard
Jane Allen: Center
Jane Allen: Junior

JANE STUART SERIES, Grace Remick, ca. 1913 Penn, hardcover with paste-on-illustration, illustrated by Ada Williamson, 370+ pages, 4 titles. $30.00

Jane Stuart, Twin
Jane Stuart at Rivercroft
Jane Stuart's Chum
Jane Stuart, Comrade

JANET LENNON see LENNON SISTERS

JEANNE SERIES, Alice Ross Colver, ca. 1920s Penn, hardcover. $25.00

Jeanne
Jeanne's House Party
Jeanne's Happy Year
Jeanne at Rainbow Lodge

JANICE DAY SERIES (originally published as the DO SOMETHING SERIES), Helen Beecher Long (Stratemeyer Series), ca. 1915 Sully, reprints by Goldsmith; Grosset; Saalfield; hardcover, humorous mysteries involving a teenage heroine. ($25.00 with dust jacket) $10.00

Janice Day at Poketown
Testing of Janice Day
How Janice Day Won

Mission of Janice Day
Janice Day, the Young Homemaker

JEAN CRAIG SERIES, Kay Lyttleton, World Publishing, hardcover. ($25.00 with dust jacket) $10.00
Pictorial hardcover: $15.00
Jean Craig in New York, 1948
Jean Craig, Nurse, 1949
Jean Craig, Graduate Nurse, 1950
Jean Craig Grows Up, 1952

JEAN MARY SERIES, Ella Dolbear Lee, ca. 1930 World, hardcover, about 250 pages. ($25.00 with dust jacket) $10.00
Jean Mary's Adventures
Jean Mary's Summer Mystery
Jean Mary in Virginia
Jean Mary's Romance
Jean Mary Solving a Mystery

JEFF WHITE SERIES, Lew Dietz, Little Brown, hardcover, illustrated by Kuhn and Moyers. ($35.00 with dust jacket) $15.00
Jeff White, Young Guide, 1951
Jeff White, Young Lumberjack, 1952
Jeff White, Forest Fire Fighter, 1954

JENNINGS SERIES, Anthony Malcolm Buckeridge, 1950 – 1977 Collins, hardcover, 22 titles. This English series began as radio plays in 1948, telling the adventures of Jennings and his friend, Darbishire, at the Linbury Court School. In the 1990s, Collins issued two final titles: *Jennings Again!* and *That's Jennings*. Like the Billy Bunter or William Brown books, prices in England tend to be higher than in the USA. First edition: $40.00 with dust jacket. Later printings: ($25.00 with dust jacket) $10.00

Jennings Goes to School, 1950
Jennings Follows a Clue, 1951
Jennings' Little Hut, 1951
Jennings and Darbishire, 1952
Jennings' Diary, 1953
According to Jennings, 1954
Our Friend Jennings, 1955
Thanks to Jennings, 1957
Take Jennings, for Instance, 1958
Jennings, as Usual, 1959
Trouble with Jennings, 1960
Just Like Jennings, 1961
Leave It to Jennings, 1963
Jennings, of Course!, 1964
Especially Jennings!, 1965
Bookfull of Jennings, 1966
Jennings Abounding, 1967
Jennings in Particular, 1968
Trust Jennings! 1969
Jennings Report, 1970
Typically Jennings!, 1971
Speaking of Jennings!, 1973
Jennings at Large, 1977

JERRY FORD WONDER SERIES, Fenworth Moore (Stratemeyer Syndicate pseudonym), ca. 1930s Cupples & Leon, red hardcover, frontispiece, illustrations by Russell Tandy. ($40.00 with dust jacket) $15.00

Wrecked on Cannibal Island
Lost in the Caves of Gold
Castaway in the Land of Snow
Prisoners on the Pirate Ship
Thrilling Stories for Boys, 1937, large volume containing the above four novels.

JERRY FOSTER SERIES, Elmer Ellsworth Ferris, Doubleday, brown hardcover, b/w plates. ($20.00 with dust jacket) $10.00

Jerry of Seven Mile Creek, 1938
Jerry at the Academy, 1940
Jerry Foster, Salesman, 1942

JERRY HICKS SERIES, William Heyliger, 1920s Grosset & Dunlap, green hardcover, four b/w plates by Bert Salg. ($100.00 with dust jacket) $25.00

Yours Truly, Jerry Hicks
Jerry Hicks, Ghost Hunter
Jerry Hicks and His Gang
Jerry Hicks, Explorer

JERRY JAKE SERIES, May Justus, 1942 – 1945 Albert Whitman, hardcover with paste-on-pictorial, decorated endpapers, illustrations by Christine Chisholm. ($35.00 with dust jacket) $20.00

Stepalong and Jerry Jake
Jerry Jake Carries On

Hurrah for Jerry Jake

JERRY TODD SERIES, Leo Edwards, 1923 – 38 Grosset, red hardcover, illustrated or map endpapers, 4 b/w plate illustrations by Bert Salg, through *Buffalo Bill Bathtub.* Advertised as "Detective stories for boys! Jerry Todd and his trusty pals solve many a baffling mystery in their home town." First editions with dust jacket are priced to $100.00 Later editions: ($40.00 with dust jacket) $20.00

Jerry Todd and the Whispering Mummy
Jerry Todd and the Rose-Colored Cat
Jerry Todd and the Oak Island Treasure
Jerry Todd and the Waltzing Hen
Jerry Todd and the Talking Frog
Jerry Todd and the Purring Egg
Jerry Todd and the Whispering Cave
Jerry Todd and the Pirate
Jerry Todd and the Bob-Tailed Elephant
Jerry Todd and the Editor-In-Grief
Jerry Todd and the Caveman
Jerry Todd and the Flying Flapdoodle
Jerry Todd and the Buffalo Bill Bathtub
Jerry Todd and the Up-The-Ladder Club, illustrated by Myrtle Sheldon
Jerry Todd and the Poodle Parlor, illustrated by Myrtle Sheldon
Jerry Todd and the Cuckoo Camp, illustrated by Herman Bachrach

JACK WINTERS SERIES see AMERICAN BOYS SPORTS SERIES

JIM FOREST SERIES, John and Nancy Rambeau, 1959

Harr Wagner, pictorial hardcover, color illustrations. $20.00

Jim Forest and Ranger Don
Jim Forest and the Mystery Hunter
Jim Forest and Lone Wolf Gulch
Jim Forest and the Bandits
Jim Forest and the Flood
Jim Forest and the Phantom Crater
Jim Forest and the Ghost Town
Jim Forest and Dead Man's Peak
Jim Forest and Lightning

JIM MASON SERIES, Elmer Russell Gregor, Appleton, red hardcover, frontispiece. ($25.00 with dust jacket) $15.00
Jim Mason, Backwoodsman, 1923
Jim Mason, Scout, 1923
Captain Jim Mason, 1924
Mason and His Rangers, 1926
Three Wilderness Scouts, 1930

JIM SPURLING SERIES, Albert Tolman, 1918 – 1927 Harper, pictorial hardcover, frontispiece and b/w plates. Hard-to-find. $50.00
Jim Spurling, Fisherman, or Making Good, illustrated by Bert Salg.
Jim Spurling, Millman
Jim Spurling, Leader, or Ocean Camp
Jim Spurling, Trawler, or Fishing with Cap'n Tom

JIMMIE DRURY SERIES, David O'Hara, 1938 – 1941 Grosset & Dunlap, orange hardcover, illustrated endpapers and frontispiece, mysteries. ($35.00 with dust jacket) $15.00
Jimmie Drury: Candid Camera Detective
What the Dark Room Revealed
Caught by the Camera
By Bursting Flash Bulbs

JIMMY KIRKLAND SERIES, Hugh Fullerton, 1915 Winston, baseball stories by a newspaper sports writer, pictorial hardcover, 4 b/w plates by Charles Paxson Gray. $25.00
Jimmy Kirkland of the Shasta Boys Team
Jimmy Kirkland of the Cascade College Team
Jimmy Kirkland and the Plot for a Pennant

JOAN FOSTER SERIES, Alice Mary Colver, Dodd Mead, hardcover. ($40.00 with dust jacket) $15.00
Joan Foster, Freshman, 1942
Joan Foster, Sophomore, 1948
Joan Foster, Junior, 1950
Joan Foster, Senior, 1950
Joan Foster in Europe, 1951
Joan Foster, Bride, 1952

JOE STRONG SERIES, Vance Barnum (Stratemeyer Syndicate pseudonym), 1917 Sully, light hardcover, frontispiece. ($35.00 with dust jacket) $15.00
1940s edition Whitman, hardcover, no illustrations. ($20.00 with dust jacket) $10.00
Joe Strong, the Boy Wizard, or Mysteries of Magic Exposed
Joe Strong on the Trapeze, or Daring Feats of a Young Circus Performer
Joe Strong, Boy Fish, or Marvelous Doings in the Big Tank
Joe Strong on the High Wire, or Motorcycle Perils of the Air
Joe Strong and his Wings of Steel, or Young Acrobat in the Clouds
Joe Strong and his Box of Mystery, or Ten Thousand Dollar Trick
Joe Strong, Boy Fire Eater, or Most Dangerous Performance on Record

JOEY SERIES, Robert Martin, ca. 1950s Thomas Nelson, London, red hardcover, b/w illustrations by T. R. Freeman. ($20.00 with dust jacket) $10.00
Joey and the Helicopter
Joey and the Magic Pony
Joey and the Square of Gold
Joey and the Squib
Joey and the River Pirates
Joey and the Master Plan
Joey and the Mail Robbers

JOLLY GOOD SERIES, Mary P. Wells Smith (1840 – 1930), ca. 1870s – 90s Roberts, 8 books with titles such as *Jolly Good Times at School: Also, Some*

Times Not Quite So Jolly. Small decorated hardcover, 275+ pages, frontispiece. Early editions by Roberts: $35.00
Jolly Good Times at Hackmatack, 1891 Roberts
Jolly Good Times Today, 1894 Roberts
Jolly Good Summer, 1895 Roberts
Jolly Good Times at School, 1925 edition, illustrations by Helen Mason Grose. $25.00
Jolly Good Times, A Child-life on a Farm, 1927 edition, illustrations by Helen Mason Grose. $25.00

JORDAN SERIES, Janet Lambert, 1945 – 1950s Dutton, first edition: $150.00 with dust jacket
Grosset reprint: ($40.00 with dust jacket) $25.00
Just Jennifer
Friday's Child
Confusion – By Cupid
Dream for Susan
Love Taps Gently
Myself and I
Stars Hang High
Wedding Bells
Bright Tomorrow

JOSHUA COBB SERIES, Margaret Hodges, Farrar, hardcover. ($25.00 with dust jacket) $10.00
Hatching of Joshua Cobb, 1967, illustrated by W. T. Mars
Making of Joshua Cobb, 1971, illustrated by Richard Cuffari
Freewheeling of Joshua Cobb, 1974, illustrated by Richard Cuffari

JOURNEYS THROUGH BOOKLAND SET, Charles Sylvester, ca. 1910 Bellows-Reeve, hardcover, b/w illustrations, 10 volumes, collections of children's literature. $15.00 each

JOYCE PAYTON SERIES, Dorothy Whitehill, ca. 1930s Grosset & Dunlap, hardcover. ($25.00 with dust jacket) $10.00
Joy and Gypsy Joe
Joy and Pam
Joy and Her Chums
Joy and Pam at Brookside
Joy and Pam A-sailing
Joy and Pam as Seniors

JUDY BOLTON MYSTERY SERIES, Margaret Sutton, ca. 1930s Grosset Dunlap, cover and endpaper illustrations by Pelagie Doane. Girl sleuth solves crimes with the aid of friends. Collectors of girl sleuths consider Judy one of the brightest and most believable. Sutton confined Judy to a small town setting and realistic crimes.
Pelagie Doane's high fashion dust jackets (first title, 1932, through Musical Tree, 1948) are another plus. Originally the books contained four plates, but after 1939 there is only a frontispiece. Some of the war year prints, ca. late 1940s, dropped the frontispiece. Titles from 1964 on (*Hidden Clue*) were issued in illustrated hardcover without a dust jacket.
1930s titles, early printings: ($75.00 with Doane dust jacket) $15.00
1940s titles, early printings: ($50.00 with Doane dust jacket) $15.00
1948 – 1956, early printings: ($35.00 with dust jacket) $15.00
1957 – 1963, early printings: ($75.00 with dust jacket) $15.00
Picture cover reprints: $25.00
1964 – 1968 titles were published in picture cover only, hard-to-find, see titles for price.
Vanishing Shadow, 1932
Haunted Attic, 1932
Invisible Chimes, 1932
Seven Strange Clues, 1932
Ghost Parade, 1933
Yellow Phantom, 1933
Mystic Ball, 1934
Voice in the Suitcase, 1935
Mysterious Half Cat, 1936
Riddle of the Double Ring, 1937
Unfinished House, 1938
Midnight Visitor, 1939
Name on the Bracelet, 1940
Clue in the Patchwork Quilt, 1941
Mark on the Mirror, 1942
Secret of the Barred Window, 1943
Rainbow Riddle, 1946
Living Portrait, 1947
Secret of the Musical Tree, 1948

Warning on the Window, 1949
Clue of the Stone Lantern, 1950
Spirit of Fog Island, 1951
Black Cat's Clue, 1952
Forbidden Chest, 1953
Haunted Road, 1954
Clue in the Ruined Castle, 1955
Trail of the Green Doll, 1956
Haunted Fountain, 1957
Clue of the Broken Wing, 1958
Phantom Friend, 1959
Discovery at Dragon's Mouth, 1960
Whispered Watchword, 1961
Secret Quest, 1962
Puzzle in the Pond, 1963
Hidden Clue, 1964, hard-to-find, $100.00
Pledge of the Twin Knights, 1965, hard-to-find, $100.00
Search for the Glowing Hand, 1966, hard-to-find, $120.00
Secret of the Sand Castle, 1967, hard-to-find, $200.00

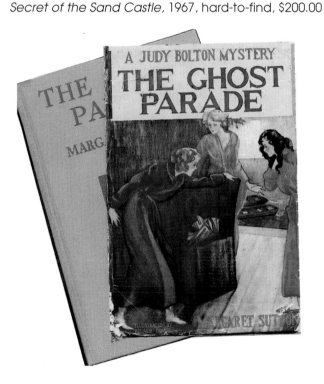

JULIA REDFERN SERIES, Eleanor Cameron, Dutton, hardcover, full page b/w illustrations by Gail Owens. Irrepressible Julia plunges from one disaster to another, in a series that moves backwards in time. ($30.00 with dust jacket) $10.00
Room Made of Windows
Julia and the Hand of God
That Julia Redfern
Julia's Magic
Private World of Julia Redfern

JUSTICE SERIES, Virginia Hamilton, Greenwillow, hardcover. ($20.00 with dust jacket) $10.00
Justice and Her Brothers, 1979
Dustland, 1980

Gathering, 1981

JUST WILLIAM see WILLIAM BROWN

K

KATHY MARTIN, NURSE, SERIES, Josephine James, ca. 1960s Golden Press, yellow spine, illustrated hardcover. $15.00
Cap for Kathy
Junior Nurse
Senior Nurse
Patient in 202
Assignment in Alaska
Private Duty Nurse
Search for an Island
Sierra Adventure
Courage in Crisis
Off-Duty Nurse
Affair of the Heart
Peace Corps Nurse
African Adventure

KATIE JOHN SERIES, Mary Calhoun, Harper, hardcover, illustrations by Paul Frame. ($25.00 with dust jacket) $10.00
Katie John, 1960
Depend on Katie John, 1961
Honestly, Katie John, 1963
Katie John and Heathcliff, 1980

KATIE ROSE SERIES, Lenora Mattingly Weber, Crowell, hardcover.
First edition: ($150.00 with dust jacket) $50.00
Don't Call Me Katie Rose, 1964
Winds of March, 1965
New and Different Summer, 1966
I Met a Boy I Used to Know, 1967

Angel in Heavy Shoes, 1968, dust jacket by Muriel Wood

KATRINKA SERIES, Helen Haskell, 1915 – 39 Dutton, 5 books. ($50.00 with dust jacket) $15.00
Titles include:
Katrinka, the Story of a Russian Child, 1915
Katrinka Grows Up, 1932, illustrated by Ilse Bischoff
Peter, Katrinka's Brother, 1933, illustrated by Theodore Nadejen

KATY DID SERIES, Susan Coolidge (Sarah Woolsey), ca. 1860s, five titles, first editions are RARE
Little Brown ca. 1930 edition, with paste-on-pictorial and six color plates by Ralph Coleman: $35.00
What Katy Did, 1872
What Katy Did Next, 1886
What Katy Did at School, 1873

KAY TRACEY MYSTERY SERIES, Frances Judd (pseudonym of Stratemeyer Syndicate), 1934 – 42 Cupples & Leon, yellow hardcover, frontispiece. Dust jacket features a design of an open book and a black bar under the title with the words "Kay Tracey Mystery Stories." ($40.00 with dust jacket) $15.00
Later editions: ($20.00 with dust jacket) $10.00
1950s edition Doubleday, with revised order of titles, wraparound illustration on dust jacket: ($25.00 with dust jacket) $10.00
Titles in order originally issued by Cupples & Leon:
Secret of the Red Scarf, 1934
Strange Echo, 1934
Mystery of the Swaying Curtains, 1935
Shadow on the Door, 1935

Six Fingered Glove Mystery, 1936
Green Cameo Mystery, 1936
Secret at the Windmill, 1937
Beneath the Crimson Brier Bush, 1937
Message in the Sand Dunes, 1938
Murmuring Portrait, 1938
When the Key Turned, 1939
In the Sunken Garen, 1939
Forbidden Tower, 1940
Sacred Feather, 1940
Lone Footprint, 1941
Double Disguise, 1941
Mansion of Secrets, 1942
Mysterious Neighbors, 1942

KEN SERIES, Basil William Miller, 1941 – 1957, Western and adventure stories with Christian elements. Early dust jackets were illustrated with a different picture for each book. Later jackets were uniform in design. ($10.00 with dust jackets) $5.00
Ken Rides the Range, 1941
Ken Bails Out, 1942
Ken Captures a Foreign Agent, 1943
Ken's Mercy Flight to Australia, 1944
Ken in Alaska, 1944
Ken Saddles Up, 1945
Ken South of the Border, 1947
Ken on the Argentine Pampas, 1947
Ken on the Navajo Trail, 1948
Ken Follows the Chuck Wagon, 1950
Ken Hits the Cowboy Trail, 1951
Ken, Range Detective, 1952
Ken and the Cattle Thieves, 1953
Ken, Range Hero, 1954
Ken and the Navajo Treasure Map, 1955
Ken on the Anchor D Ranch, 1956
Ken and the Lost Indian Treasure, 1957

KEN HOLT MYSTERY SERIES, Bruce Campbell (pseudonym of Samuel and Beryl Epstein), 1949 – 1963 Grosset & Dunlap, hardcover, 18 titles. Each came with a white dust jacket with different color illustration for each book. Spine shows head of Ken Holt in a shield-shaped panel. Uncredited illustrations. Illustrated endpapers signed James M. Will or Wills. Firsts, listing to self: Prices vary widely by dealer, but generally, a first in a good dust jacket can be found in the $50.00 to $100.00 range.
Later editions: ($30.00 with dust jacket) $15.00
Pictorial hardcover editions: $20.00
Secret of Skeleton Island, 1949
Riddle of the Stone Elephant, 1949
Black Thumb Mystery, 1950
Clue of the Marked Claw, 1950
Clue of the Coiled Cobra, 1951
Secret of Hangman's Inn, 1951
Mystery of the Iron Box, 1952
Clue of the Phantom Car, 1953

Mystery of the Galloping Horse, 1954
Mystery of the Green Flame, 1955
Mystery of the Grinning Tiger, 1956
Mystery of the Vanishing Magician, 1956
Mystery of the Shattered Glass, 1958
Mystery of the Invisible Enemy, 1959
Mystery of Gallows Cliff, 1960
Clue of the Silver Scorpion, 1961
Mystery of the Plumed Serpent, 1962
Mystery of the Sultan's Scimitar, 1963

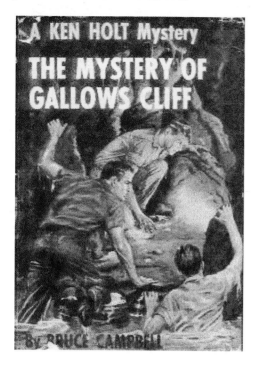

KEN MCLAUGHLIN see FLICKA

KENT BARSTOW ADVENTURE SERIES, Rutherford Montgomery, 1958 – 1964 Duell, Sloan and Pearce, 7 books, cloth hardcover. Cold war adventures featuring Barstow, a young U.S. Air Force officer. ($15.00 with dust jacket) $10.00
Kent Barstow, Special Agent, 1958
Missile Away!, 1959
Mission Intruder, 1960
Kent Barstow, Space Man, 1961
Kent Barstow and the Commando Flight, 1963
Kent Barstow Aboard the Dyna Soar, 1964
Kent Barstow on a B-70 Mission, 1964

KHAKI BOYS SERIES, Capt. Gordon Bates, ca. 1920 Cupples & Leon, small size, cloth cover, illustrations by Hastings. $10.00
Khaki Boys at Camp Sterling
Khaki Boys on the Way
Khaki Boys at the Front
Khaki Boys Over the Top
Khaki Boys Fighting to Win
Khaki Boys Along the Rhine

KHAKI GIRLS SERIES, Edna Brooks, Cupples & Leon, small size, cloth cover, illustrations. $15.00
Khaki Girls Behind the Lines, 1918
Khaki Girls of the Motor Corps, 1918
Khaki Girls at Windsor Barracks, 1919
Khaki Girls in Victory, 1920

KID FROM TOMKINVILLE SERIES, John R. Tunis, Morrow, hardcover, baseball stories. First edition: ($50.00 with dust jacket) $20.00
Reprints: ($15.00 with dust jacket) $10.00
Kid from Tomkinville, 1940
Keystone Kids, 1943
Rookie of the Year, 1944
Kid Comes Back, 1946

KIM ALDRICH MYSTERY SERIES, Jinny McDonnell, ca. 1970 Whitman, pictorial hardcover. $15.00
Miscalculated Risk, 1972
Silent Partner, 1972
Long Shot, 1974
Deep Six, 1974

KNOCKABOUT CLUB SERIES, ca. 1890s Estes, color illustrated paper-over-board cover, illustrated endpapers, b/w illustrations. $30.00
Knockabouts in the Woods, C. A. Stephens
Knockabouts Alongshore, Stephens
Knockabouts in the Tropics, Stephens
Knockabouts in the Everglades, F. A. Ober
Knockabouts in the Antilles, Ober

KOKO SERIES, Basil William Miller, 1947 – 1956 Zondervan, hardcover, 7 titles. Books tell the story of Kris Cory and his sled dog Koko. ($15.00 with dust jacket) $10.00
Koko, King of the Arctic Trail, 1947
Koko of the Airways, 1948
Koko and the Eskimo Doctor, 1949
Koko and the Timber Thieves, 1951
Koko and the Fur Thieves, 1953
Koko on the Yukon, 1954
Koko and the Mounties, 1956

---- **L** ----

LA ROCHELLE SERIES, Elinor Brent-Dyer, W.R. Chambers, UK, hardcover. Several early dust jackets illustrated by Percy Tarrant but re-issued later with dust jackets by Nina K. Brisley (see also CHALET SCHOOL and CHUDLEIGH HOLD). 1920s editions: RARE
1950s reprints: ($90.00 with dust jacket) $35.00
Gerry Goes to School, 1922, dust jacket by Nina K. Brisley
Head Girl's Difficulties, 1923
Maids of La Rochelle, 1924
Seven Scamps, 1927, dust jacket by Percy Tarrant
Heather Leaves School, 1929, dust jacket by Percy Tarrant
Janie of La Rochelle, 1932, dust jacket by Percy Tarrant
Janie Steps In, 1953

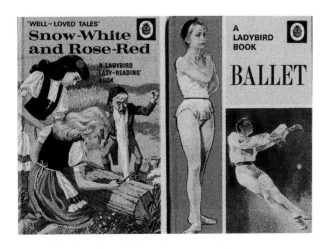

LADYBIRD BOOKS, Wills & Hepworth, UK, small illustrated hardcover.
Ladybird Books began as large size editions, 1916 Wills and Hepworth, Loughborough, UK. By the 1950s the expanded line included the small illustrated hardcovers remembered by most collectors. In the 1970s the line became part of the Pearson Group and a subsidiary of Penguin, and numerous new formats and sizes were introduced. Ladybird is the English term for the insect called ladybug in the US, and the little bug is featured in the cover design. The books were grouped by subject, include a wide range of titles and authors. Most of the books from the 1950s, 60s, 70s, resell in the collector market in the $5.00 to $20.00 range.

LAKEPORT SERIES, Edward Stratemeyer, ca. 1908 – 1912 Lothrop, Lee and Shepard, cloth-over-board cover, frontispiece illustration, illustrations. ($20.00 with dust jacket) $10.00
Gun Club Boys of Lakeport, or The Island Camp
Baseball Boys of Lakeport, or The Winning Run
Boat Club Boys of Lakeport, or Water Champions
Football Boys of Lakeport, or More Goals Than One
Automobile Boys of Lakeport, or A Run for Fun and Fame
Aircraft Boys of Lakeport, or Rivals of the Clouds

LAKEWOOD BOYS SERIES, Levi Wyman, 1920s Burt, pictorial hardcover, frontispiece. ($20.00 with dust jacket) $10.00
Lakewood Boys on the Lazy S
Lakewood Boys and the Lost Mine
Lakewood Boys in the Frozen North
Lakewood Boys and the Polo Ponies
Lakewood Boys in the South Sea Islands
Lakewood Boys in Montana
Lakewood Boys in the African Jungle

LAMBERT BOOKS, Janet Lambert wrote teen romances in the 1940s, 50s, and 60. Her popular novels usually became series, but in some cases, she only wrote one or two titles in a planned series. The longer series can be found under their series names: CAMPBELL, CANDY KANE, CINDA HOLLISTER, JORDAN, PATTY AND GINGER, PARRI MacDONALD, PENNY PARRISH (including the Tippy Parrish books). However, at various times all of her titles were reprinted in various formats, sometimes under the series name "Lambert Books," and those titles not included in series listings are listed here.
Lambert books featuring Christie Drayton:

Dutton first edition with dust jacket: $100.00
Grosset & Dunlap reprints: ($35.00 with dust jacket) $20.00
Where the Heart Is, 1948
Treasure Trouble, 1951
Lambert book featuring Sugar Bradley:
Sweet as Sugar, 1967 Dutton, listed on its dust jacket as the first in the Sugar Bradley series. This is the only Sugar Bradley title and is hard to find. The first edition hardcover shows the JL logo, for Janet Lambert, and lists Lambert's fifty titles under the heading "Lambert Books." This list includes all of the titles in the above named series plus the Christie Drayton and Sugar Bradley books. ($150.00 with dust jacket) $35.00

LAND OF THE FREE SERIES, Winston, hardcover, b/w illustrations. ($20.00 with dust jacket) $10.00
Titles include:
Colt of Destiny, Alida Milkus, 1950
Door to the North: Saga of 14th Century America, Coatsworth, 1951
Last Fort, Elizabeth Coatsworth, 1952
Runner in the Sun, McNickle, 1954
Sign of the Golden Fish, Gertrude Robinson, 1949
Sing in the Dark, Maude Thomas, 1954
Tidewater Valley, Jo Lundy, 1954

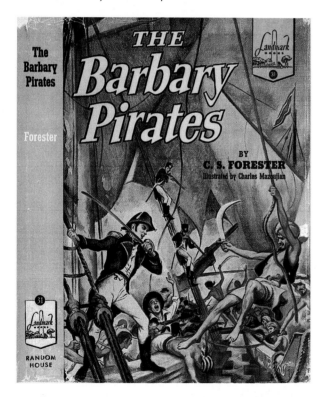

LANDMARK BOOKS, circa 1950s – 1960s Random House, hardcover, b/w or b/w/color illustrations, a series of non-fiction books written about various historical events, biographies, and special interest topics. Books by well-known authors or unusual topics may command slightly higher prices.

($20.00 with dust jacket) $8.00
Titles include:
Barbary Pirates, C. S. Forester, 1953
Betsy Ross and the Flag, Jane Mayer, 1952
Chief of the Cossacks, Harold Lamb, 1959
Daniel Boone: The Opening of the Wilderness, John Mason Brown, 1952, illustrated by Lee J. Ames
Early Days of Automobiles, Elizabeth Janeway, 1956, illustrated by Bertha Depper
Ethan Allen and the Green Mountain Boys, Slater Brown, 1956, illustrated by William C. Moyers
Erie Canal, Samuel Hopkins Adams, 1953, illustrated by Leonard Vosburgh
F.B.I., Quentin Reynolds, 1954, illustrated with photographs
Guadalcanal Diary, Richard Tregaskis, 1955 illustrated with photographs
Genghis Khan and the Mongol Horde, Harold Lamb, 1954
Hawaii Gem of the Pacific, Oscar Lewis, 1954
Lawrence of America, Alistair MacLean, 1962
Mr. Bell Invents the Telephone, Katherine B. Shippen 1952, illustrated by Richard Floethe
Our Independence and the Constitution, Dorothy Canfield Fisher, 1950, illustrated by Robert Doremus
Paul Revere and the Minute Men, Dorothy Canfield Fisher, 1950, illustrated by Norman Price
Peter Stusyvesant of Old New York, Crouse, 1954
Pony Express, Samuel Adams, 1950
Rise and Fall of Adolf Hitler, William L. Shirer, 1961, illustrated with photographs
Royal Canadian Mounted Police, Richard L. Neuberger, 1953. illustrated by Lee J. Ames.
Santa Fe Trail, Samuel Adams,1951
Slave Who Freed Haiti: The Story of Toussaint Louverture, Scherman, 1954
Swamp Fox of the Revolution, Stewart Holbrook, 1959, illustrated by Ernest Richardson
Story of Albert Schweitzer, Anita Daniel, 1957
Story of the U.S. Marines, George P. Hunt, 1951, illustrated by Charles J. Mazoujian
Story of the U.S. Air Force, Loomis, 1959
Trappers and Traders of the Far West, James Daugherty, 1952, illustrated by author
Wild Bill Hickok, Stewart H. Holbrook, 1952, illustrated by Ernest Richardson
Winter at Valley Forge, F. Van Wyck Mason, 1953
Wright Brothers: Pioneers of American Aviation, Quentin Reynolds, 1950, illustrated by Jacob Landau

LANKY LAWSON SERIES, Harry Roe (Stratemeyer Syndicate pseudonym), 1929 – 1930 Barse, green hardcover, frontispiece, three illustrations by David Randolph. $15.00
Grosset and Dunlap editions: ($25.00 with dust jacket) $10.00
Lanky Lawson, the Boy from Nowhere

Lanky Lawson with the One-Ring Circus
Lanky Lawson and His Trained Zebra

LANSING SPORTS SERIES, Hawley Williams (William Heyliger), 1912 – 1917 Appleton, illustration on hardcover, four plates by George Avison, hard-to-find, early editions: $200.00 to $300.00

Quarterback Reckless
Batter Up
Five Yards to Go
Winning Hit
Johnson of Lansing
Fair Play
Straight Ahead

LARRY DEXTER SERIES, (labeled NEWSPAPER SERIES on cover), Howard Garis, 1907 – 1915 Grosset & Dunlap, hardcover, b/w plates. ($40.00 with dust jacket) $20.00

From Office Boy to Reporter
Larry Dexter, Young Reporter
Larry Dexter in Belgium

LASSIE THE DOG BOOKS, movies, TV series, picture books, and a variety of novels by other writers were inspired by Eric Knight's original novel about a boy and his collie, *Lassie Come Home*. A sample of the later novels follows the listing of the original story.

Lassie Come Home, 1940 John Winston, Philadelphia and Toronto, hardcover, first American edition, illustrated by Marguerite Kirmse: ($50.00 with dust jacket) $15.00

Lassie Come Home, 1940 Grosset and Dunlap Famous Dog Stories Series edition, hardcover, early printing: $25.00 with dust jacket

Lassie Come Home, 1941 Cassell, hardcover, early edition, illustrated by Marguerite Kirmse: ($30.00 with dust jacket) $15.00

Lassie novels, other authors, Whitman, color illustrated hardcover, TV series tie-in: $10.00
Titles include:
Lassie, Forbidden Valley, Schroeder, 1959
Lassie, Treasure Hunter, Harry Timmins, 1960
Lassie and the Mystery at Blackberry Bog, Snow
Lassie and the Secret of the Summer, Snow, 1958
Lassie: The Wild Mountain Trail, Edmonds, 1966
Lassie and the Cub Scout, Michelson, 1966
Lassie, the Mystery of the Bristlecone Pine, Frazee, 1967
Lassie, Adventure In Alaska, Elrick, 1967
Lassie and the Firefighters, Michelson, 1968
Lassie, Secret of the Smelters' Cave, Frazee, 1968
Lassie Lost in the Snow, Steve Frazee, 1969
Lassie, Tell-a-Tale Books, Whitman, small pictorial hardcover. $10.00
Lassie and the Kittens, Grant, 1956
Lassie Finds a Friend, 1960
Hooray for Lassie, Borden, 1964

Lassie and the Cub Scout, Michelson, 1966
Lassie and the Busy Morning, Lewis, 1973
Lassie, Big Little Books, Whitman: $10.00
Lassie and the Shabby Sheik, Elrick, 1968
Lassie, Little Golden Books, color illustrated small hardcover: $8.00
Lassie Shows the Way, 1956
Lassie and the Daring Rescue, 1956
Lassie and Her Day in the Sun, 1958
Lassie and the Lost Explorer, 1958
Lassie and the Big Clean-up Day, 1972
Lassie, coloring book:
Lassie Coloring Book, 1958 Whitman, featuring the boy and dog from the TV series, two versions, one with an artist-drawn cover, one with a photo cover. $15.00

LAVELL MYSTERY SERIES, Edith Lavell, ca. 1920s Saalfield, hardcover. ($20.00 with dust jacket) $10.00
Mystery of the Secret Band
Mystery of the Fires
Mystery at Dark Cedar

LAWRENCEVILLE SCHOOL SERIES, Owen Johnson. These popular novels were also serialized in magazines and used for PBS TV productions. Ca. 1909 – 1922 Dodd, Mead, hardcover, ten b/w plates: $100.00

Ca. 1909 – 1922 Little, Brown reprint, hardcover, ten b/w plates: $50.00

Ca. 1910 – 1922 Baker & Taylor edition, first thus, pictorial hardcover, halftone frontispiece and plates by Frederic R. Gruger: (RARE with dust jacket) $100.00

1920s – 1930s Little, Brown editions, red pictorial hardcover, also in plain hardcover, also in gilt stamped black leather cover, b/w plates or photos: $25.00

Burt editions, pictorial hardcover, plates: $25.00

1930s edition Grosset, hardcover: ($25.00 with dust jacket) $10.00

Eternal Boy (Baker & Taylor title: *Prodigious Hickey*)
Hummingbird
Varmint: A Lawrenceville Story
Tennessee Shad
Skippy Bedelle
Related book:
Stover at Yale, 1912 Stokes, hardcover. $30.00
Lawrenceville Stories, 1967 Simon & Schuster, hardcover, collection of three of the novels, introduction by Cleveland Amory, original illustrations. ($25.00 with dust jacket) $10.00

LEAVE IT TO BEAVER SERIES, Beverly Cleary, Berkeley, 3 books based on the popular TV series. Published in paperbacks only: $10.00
Leave it to Beaver, 1960
Beaver and Wally, 1961
Here's Beaver!, 1961
Leave it to Beaver, Little Golden Book:
Leave it to Beaver, Lawrence Alson, 1959, small color illustrated hardcover, foil spine, 24 pages, color illustrations by Mel Crawford. $15.00
Leave it to Beaver, related title:
Leave It to Beaver, a Book to Color, 1958 Saalfield, oversize, cover illustration of TV series boys, coloring book b/w pages. $15.00

LEFTY LOCKE see BIG LEAGUE

LEND-A-HAND BOYS SERIES, St. George Rathborne, 1931 editions Goldsmith, hardcover. Same dust jacket design for all books. ($25.00 with dust jacket) $10.00
Lend-a-hand Boys of Carthage, or Waking Up the Home Town
Lend-a-hand Boys' Sanitary Squad, or When the Fever Came to Blairstown
Lend-a-hand Boys' Teamwork, or Putting Their Shoulders to the Wheel
Lend-a-hand Boys as Wild Game Protectors, or Little Four-footed Brother in the Fur Coat

LENSKI see LOIS LENSKI

LENNON SISTERS SERIES, ca. 1960s Whitman, pictorial hardcover. $20.00
Titles include:
Lennon Siters and the Secret of Holiday Island, Doris Schroeder
Janet Lennon and Adventure at Two Rivers, Barlow Meyers
Janet Lennon at Camp Calamity, Barlow Meyers
Janet Lennon and the Angels, Barlow Meyers

LET'S GO SERIES, Harriet Huntington.
Let's Go Outdoors, 1939 Doubleday, picture book with photo endpapers and full-page photo illustrations by Preston Duncan. ($20.00 with dust jacket) $15.00
Let's Go to the Desert, 1941 Doubleday, picture book, illustrated with photographs. $15.00
Let's Go to the Seashore, 1949 Doubleday, square picture book, illustrated with full-page photographs. $15.00

LET'S MAKE BELIEVE SERIES, Lilian Garis, ca. 1920s Donohue, advertised as "large clear type on superior quality paper, frontispiece and jacket printed in full colors." $20.00
Let's Make Believe We're Keeping House
Let's Play Circus
Let's Make Believe We're Soldiers

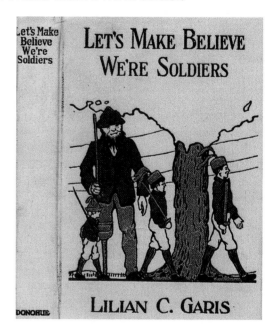

LET'S PLAY SERIES, Edith Lowe, 1939 Whitman, small, color illustrations by Ruth Newton. $25.00
Let's Play Fireman
Let's Play Postman
Let's Play Store

LETTY SERIES, Helen Griffith, 1910 – 18 Penn, hardcover, 7 titles. ($20.00 with dust jacket) $15.00
Titles include:
Letty's Good Luck
Letty and the Twins
Letty at the Conservatory
Letty and Miss Grey
Letty Grey, Heiress

LIBRARY OF PIONEERING AND WOODCRAFT, Ernest Thompson Seton, 1930 Doubleday, 6 volume set, hardcover, illustrated, matching set: $150.00. Individual titles: $20.00

Later editions: $70.00 for complete set, $10.00 per book
Rolf in the Woods
Wild Animal Ways
Two Little Savages
Book of Woodcraft and Indian Lore
Woodland Tales
Wild Animals at Home

LINCOLN HIGH SCHOOL SERIES, Joseph Gollomb, Macmillan, gilt imprinted black cover, 4 b/w illustrations: $20.00
Later reprints: ($20.00 with dust jacket) $10.00
Tuning in at Lincoln High School, 1925
That Year at Lincoln High, 1934
Working Through Lincoln High School, 1936

LINDA CARLTON SERIES, Edith Lavell, ca. 1930s Saalfield, hardcover. ($20.00 with dust jacket) $10.00
Linda Carlton, Air Pilot
Linda Carlton's Ocean Flight
Linda Carlton's Island Adventure

LINDA CRAIG SERIES, Ann Sheldon (Stratemeyer Syndicate pseudonym), 1960s Doubleday, pictorial hardcover, decorated endpapers. $15.00
Linda Craig and the Palomino Mystery
Linda Craig and the Clue on the Desert Trail
Linda Craig and the Secret of Rancho Del Sol
Linda Craig and the Mystery of Horseshoe Canyon
Linda Craig and the Mystery in Mexico
Linda Craig and the Ghost Town Treasure

LINDA LANE SERIES, Josephine Lawrence, ca. 1920s Barse & Hopkins, cloth-over-board cover, b/w illustrations. ($20.00 with dust jacket) $10.00

Linda Lane
Linda Lane Helps Out
Linda Lane's Plan
Linda Lane Experiments

LINDA SERIES, Nancy Dudley, Coward-McCann, hardcover, three-color illustrations by Sofia. ($20.00 with dust jacket) $10.00
Linda Goes to the Hospital, 1953
Linda Travels Alone, 1955
Linda Goes to a TV Studio, 1957
Linda Goes on a Cruise, 1958

LINDENDALE SERIES, Daniel Wise, c. late 1800s $15.00

LINGER-NOTS SERIES, Agnes Miller, Cupples & Leon, small size, impressed cover illustration, b/w frontispiece ($25.00 with dust jacket) $15.00
Linger-Nots and the Mystery House, 1923
Linger-Nots and the Valley Feud, 1923
Linger Nots and Their Golden Quest, 1923
Linger-Nots and the Whispering Charm, 1925

LITTLE BLACK, Walter Farley see BLACK STALLION SERIES

LITTLE BOOKS see LOIS LENSKI

LITTLE COLONEL SERIES, Annie Fellow Johnston, 1894 – 1914 Page, 17 books, beige hardcover with printed color illustration, b/w plates. First edition (list-to-self on title or advertising page): $50.00 Later printings: $25.00
Little Colonel

Little Colonel's House Party
Little Colonel's Holidays
Little Colonel's Hero
Little Colonel at Boarding School
Little Colonel in Arizona
Little Colonel's Christmas Vacation
Little Colonel: Maid of Honor
Little Colonel's Knight Comes Riding
Mary Ware: The Little Colonel's Chum
Mary Ware in Texas
Mary Ware's Promised Land
Little Colonel Good Time Book
Little Colonel Stories, 1919, b/w plates, 192 pages
Little Colonel Stories, Second Series, 1931 illustrated by Harold Cue

Little Colonel, related titles, Johnston, published by Page:

Story of the Red Cross as told to the Little Colonel, illustrated by John Goss, 1918, an excerpted story from Little *Colonel's Hero*, hardcover with oval paste-on-illustration. $65.00

Land of the Little Colonel, reminiscence and autobiography, illustrated from original photographs, 1929 Page, pictorial cover with gilt in slipcase. $90.00

LITTLE COUSIN see OUR LITTLE COUSIN

LITTLE FEATHER SERIES, Bernard Alvin Palmer, Zondervan, hardcover. ($12.00 with dust jacket) $5.00
Little Feather at Big Bear Lake, 1944
Little Feather Goes Hunting, 1946
Little Feather Rides Herd, 1947
Little Feather and the Mystery Mine, 1948
Little Feather at Tonka Bay, 1950
Little Feather and the Secret Package, 1951

Little Feather and the River of Grass, 1953

LITTLE GIRL SERIES, Amanda Douglas, 1896 – 1909 Dodd, hardcover, each novel about a girl in a different historical or geographic location. $30.00
Little Girl in Old New York, 1896
Little Girl in Old Boston, 1898
Little Girl in Old Philadelphia, 1899
Little Girl in Old Washington, 1900
Little Girl in Old New Orleans, 1901
Little Girl in Old Detroit, 1902
Little Girl in Old St. Louis, 1903
Little Girl in Old Chicago, 1904
Little Girl in Old Quebec 1906
Little Girl in Old San Francisco, 1905
Little Girl in Old Baltimore, 1907
Little Girl in Old Salem, 1908
Little Girl in Old Pittsburg, 1909

LITTLE GOLDEN BOOKS, various authors/illustrators, 1942 on, Western Publishing, (publisher listed as Western, Simon and Schuster, or Golden Press), 600+ titles through 1973. Western had sold more than a billion copies of Little Golden Books by the 1950s. Collectors seek first editions, editions with unusual gimmicks (see LITTLE GOLDEN, Band Aids) or books illustrated by name illustrators. First editions were marked with an "A" — often printed on the lower right corner of the last page, slightly hidden under binding. Price printed on book, or the color of the spine, or the design on the back cover, can also help identify books. Original prices were: 25 cents (1942 – 1962), 29 cents (1962 – 1968), 39 cents (1968 – 1974), 40 cents (1974 – 1977). Early 1940s titles were 42 pages long. By the 1950s, the length was cut to 28 pages and then to 24 pages. The numbering system does not indicate the chronological order of a book in a series, as many earlier titles were replaced with new titles using the same number in the 1960s and 1970s. For example, #315 was used for *Legend of Wyatt Earp* (1958) and *Sesame Street: the Together Book*, (1971). The authors of this price guide highly recommend *Collecting Little Golden Books* by Steve Santi for complete bibliographical information. Prices given below are average prices for single titles.

Little Golden Books, general titles, 1950 – 1969, "antique gold" foil spine hardcover with leaves and flower pattern.
1950s first editions, $15.00
1960s first editions, $12.00
Later editions: nonfiction titles such as *Airplanes*, #373: $5.00; popular comic strip characters, such as Bugs Bunny, #72, $8.00.
Popular illustrators Garth Williams and Eloise Wilkin, first editions, $20.00, later editions $10.00. Titles that command higher than normal prices

generally feature popular TV shows, themes, or artwork.

Little Golden Books, general titles, 1969 – 1975, "gold" foil spine hardcover with animal pattern. First editions, $8.00, later printings, $4.00. Higher prices for popular comic characters or illustrators.

Little Golden Books, 1948 – 1960s, cloth covers. A number of other cover materials were used for Little Golden Books besides the standard slick paper-over-board hardcover. Some titles were released in "special bound in cloth editions" (ca. 1948), "Duro-Tuff" two color covers (ca. 1950), and Goldencraft library or school editions (1950s – 1960s). Goldencraft also manufactured a stiff cardboard cover with a fabric spine. $5.00 to $10.00 range

Little Golden Books, Giant, 1957 – 1959, various authors and illustrators, series numbers 5001 - 5027. 56 pages, original cover price 50 cents. Cover states "A Giant Little Golden Book." Books were often a collection of stories or reprints of earlier titles.

Individual titles: $10.00

Walt Disney titles: $20.00.

Some exceptions:

My Christmas Treasury, 1957, illustrated by Lowell Hess, 72 pages, $20.00

Adventures of Lassie, 1958, three complete stories, $15.00

Hans Christian Anderson's Fairy Tales, 1958, 72 pages, $20.00

Captain Kangaroo, 1959, "three books in one!", $15.00

Cub Scouts, 1959, Bruce Brian, illustrated by Mel Crawford, $20.00

Mother Goose Rhymes, 1959, illustrated by Feodor Rojankovsky, $30.00

My Pets, 1959, Patsy Scarry, illustrated by Eloise Wilkin, $30.00

Nursery Tales, 1959, illustrated by Richard Scarry, 72 pages, $20.00

This World of Ours, 1959, J.W. Watson, illustrated by Eloise Wilkin, $30.00

Little Golden Books, Disney, 1948 – 1978, 148 titles including Mickey Mouse Club titles. Gold foil spine (except for Mickey Mouse Club). Series numbers begin with "D" — revised editions printed after 1985 begin with "105-." First editions should have "A" printed on lower right corner of inside back page (position of A moves or can be hidden by binding).

1950s first editions: $15.00

1960s first editions: $12.00

1970s first editions: $10.00

Other editions, $5.00.

Some titles are more difficult to find and command higher than normal prices.

Little Golden Books, Mickey Mouse Club, 1954 – 1957, red foil spine with Disney cartoon characters,

club emblem printed on cover. Numbered as part of Little Golden Disney series. First editions: $12.00

Later printings: $6.00

Popular characters, movies or TV shows may command higher prices.

Little Golden Books, Ding Dong School, ca. 1959 – 1960. Golden Press, 8 titles. Reprints of the earlier Rand McNally titles done as part of the standard Little Golden Book format, 24 pages. Gold foil spines, pictorial covers state "Golden Press" or "A Little Golden Book." $10.00

Little Golden Books, First Golden Learning Library, 1965, Jane Werner Watson, 16 volumes. Illustrations by William Dugan. Different color foil spines, full color illustrations, same format as Little Golden Books. Sample titles: Book of B or First Book of S.

Price for complete 16 volume set in boxed carrying case: $175.00

Complete set without carrying case, $100.00

Individual titles, $5.00

Little Golden Books, Eager Reader Series, 1974 – 1975, boxed set of 8 volumes. Solid gold spine, large type, cover copy reads "a book you can read by yourself." Boxed set, $35.00. Individual titles, $2.00

Little Golden Books, Novelty, with novelty toys, paper dolls, or commercial products, 1950s – 1960s. Several Little Golden titles were issued with toys such as paper dolls or novelty products attached. Prices shown are for books with products still attached. (If the product is missing, the price is usually in the under $5.00 range.)

Little Benny Wanted a Pony, 1950, illustrated by Richard Scarry, with a "real MASK" intact, $25.00

Happy Birthday, 1952, illustrated by Retta Worcester, 42 pages with party favors, original cover price 35 cents, $20.00

Fun With Decals, 1952, illustrated by Corinne Malvern, #139 with decals, $30.00

Tex and His Toys, 1952, illustrated by Corinne Malvern, #129 with Texel Cellophane Tape, $50.00

Christmas Manger, 1953, 28 pages, #176 with cut-out Nativity scene, $25.00

Little Golden Paper Dolls, 1951, 28 pages, #113 with paper dolls, $35.00

Little Golden Paper Dolls, later printing, 24 pages, series #280, with paper dolls, $25.00

Paper Doll Wedding, 1954, #193 (also issued as an Activity book) with paper dolls, $35.00

How to Tell Time, 1957, cover has Gruen "watch" with movable hands, $25.00

How to Tell Time, later printings, cover "watch" missing Gruen name, with movable hands, $20.00

Betsy McCall, 1965, #559, with Betsy paper doll, $30.00

Little Golden Books, Jig-Saw Puzzles, ca. 1949 – 1950, various authors and illustrators. On top of cover, tag line may state "A LITTLE GOLDEN BOOK plus a real JIG-SAW PUZZLE."

Book with intact puzzle in back cover, $45.00

Book without puzzle, $10.00

Jolly Barnyard, 1950, illustrated by Tibor Gergely, 42 pages, #67

Katie the Kitten, 1949, illustrated by Alice and Martin Provenson, 28 pages #75

Baby's House, 1950, illustrated by Mary Blair, 28 pages #80

Duck and His Friends, 1950, illustrated by Richard Scarry, 28 pages, #81

Pets for Peter, 1950, illustrated by Battaglia, 28 pages, #82

Brave Cowboy Bill, 1950, illustrated by Richard Scarry, 42 pages, #93

Jerry At School, 1950, illustrated by Corinne Malvern, 42 pages, #94

When I Grow Up, 1950, illustrated by Corrine Malvern, 42 pages, #96

Little Golden ABC, 1951, illustrated Cornelius De Witt, 28 pages, #101

Ukelele and Her New Doll, 1951, illustrated by Campbell Grant, 28 pages, #102

Little Golden Books, Activity Books, 1955 – 1963, 50 titles, hardcovers. The activities books used series numbers A1 through A52 (not to be confused with the "A" indicating edition). Books featured paper dolls, stamps, wheels, or paints in cover. General prices: stamp books with stamps, $15.00; wheel books with wheel, $10.00; paper doll books with paper dolls, $35.00. Books with activities missing, $5.00.

Unusual titles, hard-to-find:

Animal Paintbook (with three paints in cover), 1955, Hans Helweg, illustrated by author, $45.00

Cinderella (with paper dolls), 1960, illustrated by Gordon Laite, $45.00

Clown Coloring Book, 1955, illustrations by Art Seiden, with crayon box, $45.00

Gordon's Jet Flight (with paper model jet), Naomi Glasson, illustrated by Mel Crawford, $50.00

Hansel and Gretel (with paper dolls), 1961, illustrated by Judy and Barry Martin, $40.00

Little Red Riding Hood (with paper dolls), 1959, Sharon Kostner, $40.00

Mickey Mouse Club Stamp Book (with stamps), Kathleen Daly, illustrated by Julius Svendsen, $50.00

My Little Golden Calendar (double page calendar), 1961, Richard Scarry, $30.00

Story of Baby Jesus Stamps (with stamps), 1957, J.W. Watson, illustrated by Eloise Wilkin, $45.00

Trim the Christmas Tree (#A15 with tree punch-out), 1957, Elsa Nast, illustrated by Doris Henderson, $35.00

Trucks (with two paper model trucks), 1955, Kathryn Jackson, illustrated by Ray Quigley, $50.00

Little Golden Books, Band-Aid Books, 1950 – 1979, Helen Gaspard (Dr. Dan) or Kathryn Jackson (Nurse Nancy), illustrated by Corrine Malvern. Hardcovers were issued with Johnson and Johnson Band-Aids inserted. Pre-1960 books with Band-Aids: RARE.

Pre-1960, without Band-Aids: $20.00

Later printings, without Band-Aids: $10.00

Doctor Dan the Bandage Man, 1950, series #111, 42 pages, with six Band-Aids.

Doctor Dan the Bandage Man, 1957, series #295, 24 pages, with six "stars 'n strips" Band-Aids.

Doctor Dan the Bandage Man, later reprint, series #312-07 (1970s reprint), with "two real" Band-Aids.

Doctor Dan at the Circus, 1960, by Pauline Wilkins, illustrated by Katherine Sampson, series #399, 24 pages with circus patterned Band-Aids.

Nurse Nancy, 1952, series #154 with six Band-Aids "in three shapes."

Nurse Nancy, 1959, series #346 with Band-Aids.

Nurse Nancy, 1962, series #473 with "Stars 'n Strips" Band-Aids.

Little Golden Books, Record Sets, ca. 1948 – 1970s. A variety of records with book formats were issued for Little Golden Books. "Little Golden Records" (1948/1950) were issued as single records pressed in yellow plastic. Prices are higher for popular characters or known narrators such as actor Danny Kaye. $35.00

Record Sets, 1956, black record accompanied by regular Little Golden Book book, series number begins with C. $30.00

Golden Story Book and Record Album, ca. 1960s, 33⅓ long playing record with 24 page soft cover book, series numbers begin with GST. $20.00

Read and Hear, ca. 1960s, 45 rpm record inserted into front cover of book. Series numbers 151 through 176. $20.00

Disneyland Record, ca. 1970s, 33⅓ rpm record inserted into back cover. Series numbers 201 through 255. $20.00

LITTLE HOUSE SERIES, Laura Ingalls Wilder, Harper Brothers, cloth hardcover with a small single-color illustration printed on the cloth, color decoration endpapers, b/w illustrations by Helen Sewell. Some of the books had color frontispieces, some had two color illustrations. This classic series is a fictionalized biography based on the author's childhood. The length, vocabulary, and plot complication increases throughout the books as Laura grows from the four-year-old in *Little House in the Big Woods* to a young wife in *These Happy Golden Years*. (The books were sold with a plain protective tissue overwrap, which adds about $15.00 to the value.) Early printings: $75.00

E. M. Hale edition: $40.00
Little House in the Big Woods, 1932
Farmer Boy, 1933
Little House on the Prairie, 1935
On the Banks of Plum Creek, 1937
On the Shores of Silver Lake, 1939
Long Winter, 1940
Little Town on the Prairie, 1941
These Happy Golden Years, 1943

Little House Series, same text with new b/w illustrations by Garth Williams, 1953 editions Harper, hardcover. Williams travelled to many of the story locations and filled his illustrations with authentic historical detail.

First edition thus: ($50.00 with dust jacket) $15.00
Later printings: ($20.00 with dust jacket) $10.00
Little House in the Big Woods
Little House on The Prairie
Farmer Boy
On The Banks of Plum Creek
By The Shores of Silver Lake
Long Winter
Little Town on the Prairie
These Happy Golden Years
First Four Years

Little House, related books:

On The Way Home, 1962 Harper & Row, Laura's diary of the family move from South Dakota to Missouri, 1894, with explanations by her daughter, Rose Wilder Lane, small illustrated hardcover, illustrated with b/w photographs. $20.00

West From Home, 1974 Harper & Row, letters from Laura to Almanzo on her trip to San Francisco, 1915, edited by Roger MacBride, hardcover, photo illustrations. First edition with dust jacket: $30.00

Little House, related books, Roger MacBride:

MacBride was a friend of Laura's daughter, Rose Wilder Lane, and wrote several stories about the Wilder family.

On the Other Side of the Hill, 1995 Harper Collins, hardcover, b/w illustrations. ($20.00 with dust jacket) $10.00

In the Land of the Big Red Apple, 1995 Harper Collins, hardcover, b/w illustrations. ($20.00 with dust jacket) $10.00

Little Town in the Ozarks, 1996 Harper Collins, hardcover, b/w illustrations. ($20.00 with dust

jacket) $10.00

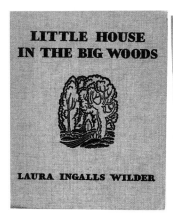

Sewell cover, Williams dust jacket

LITTLE INDIAN SERIES, David Cory, 1922 Saalfield, pictorial paper-over-board cover, frontispiece by Lee Haynes. $10.00
Little Indian
White Feather
Star Boy
1930s Grosset editions, color print illustration on cover, illustrated endpapers, b/w illustrations. ($25.00 with dust jacket) $20.00
Little Indian
White Otter
Red Feather (new title for *White Feather*)
Star Maiden
Lone Star
Raven Wing

LITTLE LEAGUE SERIES, Curtis Kent Bishop, 1953 – 1968 Steck Co. or Lippincott, hardcover, 13 titles. Steck Co. (Austin, TX) published titles 1 – 5, Lippincott published titles 6–13. ($20.00 with dust jacket) $10.00
Larry of the Little League, 1953
Larry Leads Off, 1954
Larry Comes Home, 1955
Little League, 1956
Little League Way, 1957
Lank of the Little League, 1958
Little League Heroes, 1960
Little League Double Play, 1962
Little League Amigo, 1964
Little League Stepson, 1965
Little League Visitor, 1966
Little League Victory, 1967
Little League Brother, 1968

LITTLE LUCIA SERIES, Mabel Louise Robinson, ca. 1922 – 1923 Dutton, hardcover with gilt, b/w full page illustrations by Mary Sherwood Wright, 4 titles. $20.00
Little Lucia

Little Lucia's Island Camp
Little Lucia's School
Little Lucia and Her Puppy

LITTLE MAID SERIES, Alice Curtis, 1913 – 37 Penn, hardcover with paste-on-pictorial, b/w illustrations, 24 titles. $30.00
1950s Knopf reprints: ($30.00 with dust jacket) $15.00
Typical titles:
Little Maid of Bunker Hill
Little Maid of Narrangansett Bay
Little Maid of Monmouth
Little Maid of Provincetown
Little Maid of Fort Pitt
Little Maid of Old Philadelphia
Little Maid of Old Connecticut
Little Maid of Massachusetts Colony
Little Maid of New Hampshire
Little Maid of Quebec
Little Maid of Old New York
Little Maid of Mohawk Valley
Little Maid of Old Maine
Little Maid of Boston
Little Maid of Virginia
Little Maid of Maryland

LITTLE MISS WEEZY SERIES, Penn Shirley, 1886 – 89 Lothrop, Lee & Shepard, pictorial or impressed cloth hardcover, b/w illustrations. First edition: $35.00
Little Miss Weezy, 1886
Little Miss Weezy's Brother, 1888
Little Miss Weezy's Sister, 1890

LITTLE ORPHAN ANNIE BOOKS, Harold Gray, ca. 1930s Cupples & Leon hardback numbered volumes, 84+ pages of Chicago Tribune comics per book. $60.00
Little Orphan Annie, 1926
Little Orphan Annie in the Circus, 1927
Little Orphan Annie Bucking the World, 1929
Little Orphan Annie Shipwrecked, 1931
Little Orphan Annie and Uncle Dan, 1933
Little Orphan Annie, related books:
Little Orphan Annie and the $1,000,000 Formula, 1936 Whitman Big Little Book, cardboard covers,b/w illustrations. $55.00
Little Orphan Annie in the Movies, 1941 Whitman Big Little Book, cardboard covers, b/w illustrations. $55.00
Little Orphan Annie with the Circus, 1941 Whitman Big Little Book, cardboard covers, b/w illustrations. $35.00
Little Orphan Annie and the Haunted Mansion, 1941 Whitman Better Little Book, cardboard covers, 425 pages, a Flip It book. $40.00
Arf! The Life and Hard Times of Little Orphan Annie: 1935 – 1945, 1970 Arlington House, hardcover, collection of daily strips. ($40.00 with dust jacket) $20.00

LITTLE PEOPLE EVERYWHERE SERIES, Etta McDonald and Julia Dalrymple, 1909 – 16 Little Brown, paste-on-pictorial hardcover, illustrated with b/w photos, 14 books. $20.00
Rafael in Italy
Ume San in Japan
Marta in Holland
Donald in Scotland
Gerda in Sweden
Boris in Russia
Josefa in Spain
Manuel in Mexico
Betty in Canada
Collette in France

LITTLE PRINCESS SERIES, Aileen Higgins, 1909 Penn Publishing, hardcover, illustrated by Ada Williamson, 5 titles. $20.00
Little Princess of the Stars and Stripes
Little Princess of the Patio
Little Princess of the Pines
Little Princess of the Ranch
Little Princess of the Tonopah

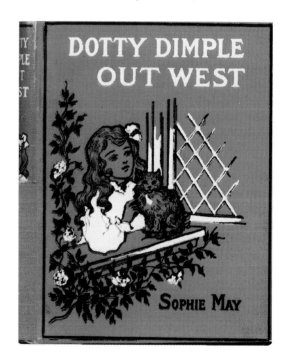

LITTLE PRUDY SERIES, Sophie May, 1863 – 65 Lee & Shepard, hardcover. $25.00
Ca. 1920s Cupples & Leon edition, small hardcover, illustrations. $15.00
Little Prudy
Little Prudy's Sister Susy
Little Prudy's Captain Horace
Little Prudy's Cousin Grace
Little Prudy's Story Book
Little Prudy's Dotty Dimple
Little Prudy's Children Series, Sophie May, 1915 editions, Lothrop, Lee & Shepard, small hardcover with

printed or impressed design, b/w illustrations. $20.00

Wee Lucy
Jimmy Boy
Kyzie Dunlee
Wee Lucy's Secret
Jimmy, Lucy and All
Lucy in Fairyland

Little Prudy's Flyaway Series, Sophie May, 1870 – 73 Lee & Shepard, hardcover, b/w illustrations. $25.00

Little Folks Astray
Prudy Keeping House
Aunt Madge's Story
Little Grandmother
Little Grandfather
Miss Thistledown

Little Prudy's Dotty Dimple books, Sophie May, ca. 1860s Lee & Shepard, blue hardcover, b/w engraving illustrations: $75.00

Ca. 1900 edition Lothrop, Lee, and Shepard, small brown hardcover with gilt illustration, b/w illustrations. $30.00

Ca. 1910 – 1930 edition, small red hardcover with impressed illustration in white and black, b/w illustrations. ($25.00 with matching dust jacket) $15.00

Little Prudy's Dotty Dimple
Dotty Dimple at her Grandmother's
Dotty Dimple at Home
Dotty Dimple Out West
Dotty Dimple at Play
Dotty Dimple at School
Dotty Dimple's Flyaway

LITTLE RED HOUSE SERIES, Amanda Douglas, 1912 – 16 Lothrop, Lee & Shepard, decorated hardcover, illustrated by Louise Wyman. $25.00

Children in the Little Old Red House
Red House Children at Grafton
Red House Children Growing Up
Red House Children's Vacation
Red House Children Year
Little Red House in the Hollow, 1918 Jacobs

LITTLE RUNAWAYS SERIES, Alice Curtis, 1906 – 14 Penn Publishing, paste-on-pictorial hardcover, illustrations by Wuanita Smith, 4 titles: $15.00; 1930s editions illustrated by Ruth Rollins: $15.00

Little Runaways, 1906
Little Runaways at Home
Little Runaways and Mother, 1913
Little Runaways at Orchard House, 1914

LITTLE WASHINGTONS SERIES, Lillian Elizabeth Roy, ca. 1920 Grosset, advertised as "This Series presents early American history in a manner that impresses the young readers. George and Martha Washington Parke, two young descendants of the famous General, follow in play exactly the life of

the great American." Color illustrated endpapers, b/w illustrations. $20.00

Little Washingtons
Little Washingtons' Relatives
Little Washingtons' Travels
Little Washingtons at School
Little Washingtons' Holidays
Little Washingtons: Farmers

LITTLE WOMEN SERIES, Louisa May Alcott. The continuing tales of the March family, favorites from the first edition, these books have been reprinted continually in various formats and illustrated by numerous illustrators.

Some early printings of Alcott's series:

Little Women, 1871 Roberts Brothers, Boston, cloth hardcover with gilt lettering, advertising pages, b/w illustrations: $700.00

Little Women, 1926 John C. Winston edition, hardcover with paste-on-pictorial, illustrated endpapers, 4 color plates plus b/w illustrations by Clara Burd. $40.00

Little Women, 1935 Whitman, Big Little Book, b/w movie photo illustrations featuring Katherine Hepburn and Joan Bennett. $35.00

Aunt Jo's Scrap-Bag, 1872 Roberts Brothers, early edition in green hardcover, 215 pages, illustrated. $125.00

Eight Cousins, 1875 Roberts Brothers, dark blue hardcover with gilt, 291 pages, frontispiece with tissue, advertising pages. Early edition: $100.00

Jo's Boys, and How They Turned Out, ca. 1886 Roberts Brothers, Boston, cloth hardcover with gilt lettering, early printing: $150.00

Little Women, Orchard House Edition, ca. 1936 Little, Brown, advertised as "The complete story of the

Little Women is told in *Little Women, Little Men,* and *Jo's Boys*....The Orchard House edition has been published to answer the need for an attractive, popular-priced, uniform edition of all three books." Hardcover with endpaper photograph of Alcott home, Orchard House, at Concord, Massachusetts. ($35.00 with dust jacket) $25.00

Little Women, Illustrated Junior Library Editions, ca. 1949 Grosset & Dunlap, hardcover, 10 color plates plus b/w illustrations: ($25.00 with dust jacket) $10.00

LOG CABIN see ELLIS

LOIS LENSKI LITTLE BOOKS SERIES, written and illustrated by Lenski, Oxford, illustrated cloth-over-board hardcover, square shape, b/w/contrasting color illustrations, illustrated endpapers, easy readers. $45.00
With cloth-over-board plain cover: $20.00
Little Auto, 1934
Little Sail Boat, 1937
Little Airplane, 1938
Little Farm, 1942
Little Fire Engine, 1946

LONE HUNTER SERIES, Donald Emmet Worcester, 1956 – 1959 Oxford or Walck, hardcover, b/w and two-color illustrations by Harper Johnson. ($15.00 with dust jacket) $10.00
Lone Hunter's Gray Pony, 1956

Lone Hunter and the Cheyennes, 1957
Lone Hunter's First Buffalo Hunt, 1958
Lone Hunter and the Wild Horses, 1959

LONE RANGER SERIES, Fran Striker, Grosset & Dunlap, brown, tan or gray hardcover with red lettering, pictorial endpapers, frontispiece, novels based on the radio and comic strip stories. Early edition with dust jacket: $50.00
Later edition: ($25.00 with dust jacket) $10.00
Sampson Low, UK, edition: ($25.00 with dust jacket) $10.00
Whitman pictorial paper-over-cardboard: $20.00
Lone Ranger, 1937
Lone Ranger and the Mystery Ranch, 1938
Lone Ranger and the Gold Robbery, 1939
Lone Ranger and the Outlaw Stronghold, 1939
Lone Ranger and Tonto, 1940
Lone Ranger at the Haunted Gulch, 1941
Lone Ranger Traps the Smuggler, 1941
Lone Ranger Rides Again, 1943
Lone Ranger Rides North, 1946
Lone Ranger and the Silver Bullet, 1948
Lone Ranger on Powder Horn Trail, 1949
Lone Ranger In Wild Horse Canyon, 1950
Lone Ranger and the War Horse, 1951
Lone Ranger West of Maverick Pass, 1951
Lone Ranger on Gunsight Mesa, 1952
Lone Ranger and the Bitter Spring Feud, 1953
Lone Ranger and the Code of the West, 1954
Lone Ranger: Trouble on the Santa Fe, 1955
Lone Ranger on Red Butte Trail, 1956

Lone Ranger and the Outlaw Stronghold, 1959 Sampson, UK

Lone Ranger, Little Golden Books, small illustrated hardcovers, 24 pages, $12.00

Lone Ranger, 1956, Steffi Fletcher, illustrated by Joseph Dreany

Lone Ranger and Tonto, 1957, Charles Verral, illustrated by Edwin Schmidt

Lone Ranger and the Talking Pony, 1958, Emily Brown, illustrated by Frank Bolle

Lone Ranger, other books:

Lone Ranger and the War Horse, 1951 Whitman Authorized edition, hardcover, color illustrations by Joseph Dreany. $15.00

Lone Ranger Annual, 1952 World, London, hardcover, cartoon strips, 93 pages. $15.00

Lone Ranger Adventure Stories, adapted by Arthur Groom for the Warner film, 1957 Western, oversize pictorial hardcover, 77 pages, photo illustrations. $30.00

Lone Ranger and the Desert Storm, Revena, 1957 Whitman Tell-a-Tale book. $10.00

Lone Ranger and the Ghost Horse, Alice Sankey, 1957 Whitman, small hardcover, illustrated by Bob Totten. $15.00

Lone Ranger, paperbacks:

Striker titles published by Pinnacle, ca. 1970s: $10.00

Lone Ranger, coloring books, prices are for clean, uncolored books: *Hi-Yo Silver!,* the Lone Ranger Paint Book, 1938 Whitman, illustrated by Ted Horn. $50.00

Lone Ranger Coloring Book, 1951 Whitman. $35.00

Lone Ranger Coloring Book, 1953 Whitman. $30.00

Tonto Coloring Book, 1957 Whitman. $35.00

LONG TRAIL BOYS, Dale Wilkins, 1923 – 1928 Winston, hardcover with illustration, 250+ pages, frontispiece. $15.00

Long Trail Boys at Sweet Water, or Mystery of the White Shadow

Long Trail Boys and the Gray Cloaks, or Mystery of the Night Riders

Long Trail Boys and the Scarlet Sign

Long Trail Boys and the Vanishing Rider

Long Trail Boys and the Mystery of the Fingerprints

Long Trail Boys and the Mystery of the Unknown Messenger

LOST TREASURE SERIES, ca. 1940s Saalfield, hardcover, reprints of three of the books in the Adventure & Mystery Series For Girls, Burt Publishing.

($20.00 with wraparound illustration dust jacket) $10.00

Phantom Town, Carol Norton

Phantom Town Yacht, Carol Norton

Finding the Lost Treasure, Helen M. Persons

LOUIE MAUDE SERIES, Helen Sherman Griffith, 1924 Penn, small hardcover, 4 titles. $25.00

Louie Maude, 1924

Louie Maude and the Caravan, 1925

Louie Maude and the Mary Ann, 1927

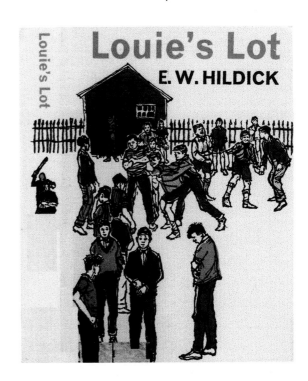

LOUIE'S LOT SERIES, E. W. Hildick, David White and Doubleday, hardcover, illustrated by Iris Scheitzer. ($25.00 with dust jacket) $10.00

Louie's Lot, 1968

Louie's Snowstorm, 1974

Louie's S.O.S., 1978

Louie's Ransom, 1978

LUCILE see CAMPFIRE GIRLS, LUCILE SERIES

LUCKY SERIES, Elmer Sherwood, ca. 1916 – 1922 Whitman, hardcover with paste-on-pictorial, color frontispiece plus plates by Neill O'Keefe. $25.00

Whitman, plain hardcover edition: ($25.00 with dust jacket) $10.00

Whitman TED MARSH editions, changing the titles by replacing "Lucky" with "Ted Marsh" (example: Ted Marsh, the Boy Scout), pictorial paper-over-board covers, no dust jackets, illustrations by Neill O'Keefe: $15.00

Lucky, the Boy Scout
Lucky and His Friend Steve
Lucky, the Young Volunteer
Lucky Finds a Friend
Lucky on an Important Mission
Lucky, the Young Soldier
Lucky, the Young Navy Man
Lucky, the Young Gentleman
Lucky and His Travels

LUCKY TERRELL SERIES, Canfield Cook, ca. 1943 Grosset, hardcover, illustrated endpapers. frontispiece. ($20.00 with dust jacket) $10.00

Spitfire Pilot
Sky Attack
Secret Mission
Lost Squadron
Springboard to Tokyo
Wings Over Japan
Flying Jet
Flying Wing

LUCRETIA ANN SERIES, Ruth Gipson, 1930s Caxton Printers, Ltd, Caldwell, ID, hardcover, illustrated by Agnes Kay. $20.00

Lucretia Ann on the Sagebrush Plains
Randall Lucretia Ann on the Oregon Trail
Lucretia Ann in the Golden West

LUCY SERIES, Jacob Abbot, see COUSIN LUCY

LUCY SERIES, Lucy Sypher, Atheneum, hardcover. ($30.00 with dust jacket) $10.00

Edge of Nowhere, 1972
Cousins and Circuses, 1974
Spell of the Northern Lights, 1975
Turnabout Year, 1976

LUCY GORDON SERIES, Aline Havard, Penn, hardcover. $15.00

Captain Lucy and Lieutenant Bob, 1918
Captain Lucy in France, 1919
Captain Lucy's Flying Ace, 1920
Captain Lucy in the Home Sector, 1921

LUDELL SERIES, Brenda Wilkinson, Harper, hardcover. ($25.00 with dust jacket) $10.00

Ludell, 1975
Ludell and Willie, 1977

Ludell's New York Time, 1980

—— **M** ——

MADELINE SERIES, Ludwig Bemelmans, oversize picture books with color illustrated hardcovers and endpapers, and color illustrations throughout by author. The first book was published in 1939, and first editions are hard-to-find. The series is constantly reprinted, usually in full size reproductions of the originals, including same-as-cover dust jackets. Price varies with publisher and date. Later editions: ($20.00 with dust jacket) $10.00

Madeline, 1939 Simon & Schuster, 46 pages, first American edition with dust jacket: $300.00

Madeline's Rescue, 1953 Viking, first American edition with dust jacket: $400.00

Madeline and the Bad Hat, 1957 Viking, first American edition with dust jacket: $400.00

Madeline and the Gypsies, 1959 Andre Deutsch, first UK edition with dust jacket: $75.00

Madeline in London, 1961 Viking, first US edition, and 1962 Andre Deutsch, first UK edition with dust jacket: $75.00

Madeline's Christmas, (first published as a special Christmas insert, 1956 *McCall's* magazine) 1985 Viking, first edition with dust jacket: $50.00

Related books:
Madeline, 1954 Little Golden Book $15.00

MADGE MORTON SERIES, Amy Chalmers, ca. 1930s Altemus, hardcover with paste-on-pictorial: $20.00

Saalfield reprints: ($15.00 with dust jacket) $10.00
Madge Morton – Captain of the Merry Maid
Madge Morton's Secret
Madge Morton's Trust
Madge Morton's Victory

MADGE STERLING SERIES, Ann Wirt, 1932 Goldsmith, hardcover. ($15.00 with dust jacket) $10.00
Missing Formula
Deserted Yacht
Secret of the Sundial

MAGGIE MARMELSTEIN SERIES, Marjorie Sharmat, Harper, hardcover, illustrations by Ben Schecter, schoolgirl's misadventures. ($15.00 with dust jacket) $10.00
Getting Something on Maggie Marmelstein, 1971
Maggie Marmelstein for President, 1975
Mysteriously Yours, Maggie Marmelstein, 1982

MAGGIE MUGGINS BOOKS, Mary Grannan, stories from a children's program broadcast weekly on CBC in Canada, Pennington Press, hardcover. ($15.00 with dust jacket) $10.00
Maggie Muggins Bedtime Stories, 1959, b/w/orange illustrations by Lonnie Stern
More Maggie Muggins, 1959, illustrations by Bernard Zalusky
Maggie Muggins and Her Animal Friends, 1959, illustrations by Bernard Zalusky
Maggie Muggins and Her Animal Friends, 1959, illustrated by Bernard Zalusky
Maggie Muggins Bedtime Stories, 1959, b/w/orange illustrations
More Maggie Muggins, 1959, illustrations by Bernard Zalusky
Maggie Muggins, Thomas Allen Publishers, Toronto:
Maggie Muggins and the Cottontail, 1960, first edition, hardcover, illustrated by Pat Patience. ($30.00 with dust jacket)
Maggie Muggins and Mr. McGarrity, 1960, first edition, hardcover, illustrated by Pat Patience. ($30.00 with dust jacket)

MAGGIE ROSS SERIES, Joan Lingard, Nelson, hardcover. ($20.00 with dust jacket) $10.00
Clearance, 1974
Resettling, 1975
Pilgrimage, 1976

MAGNUS SERIES, Hans Peterson, 1960s, translated by Marianne Turner for Pantheon, or Madeleine Hamilton for Viking, first American edition, hardcover, illustrated by Ilon Wikland. First edition with dust jacket: $50.00
Later editions: ($25.00 with dust jacket) $15.00
Magnus and the Squirrel
Magnus and the Wagon Horse
Magnus in the Harbor
Magnus in Danger
Magnus and the Ship's Mascot

MAIDA SERIES, Inez Irwin, 1909 – 49 Grosset, hardcover, frontispiece. ($20.00 with dust jacket) $10.00
Maida's Little Shop
Maida's Little House
Maida's Little School
Maida's Little Island
Maida's Little Camp
Maida's Little Village
Maida's Little Houseboat
Maida's Little Theatre

MAIL PILOT SERIES, Lewis Theiss, Wilde, gray hardcover with photo illustrations, see PEE WEE DEWIRE overlapping characters. ($50.00 with dust jacket) $20.00
Flying the U. S. Mail to South America, or How Pan American Airships Carry on in Sun and Storm Above the Rolling Caribbean, 1934
Mail Pilot of the Caribbean, or The Adventures of Gin-

ger Hale Above the Southern Seas, 1935
Flying Explorer, or How a Mail Pilot Penetrated The Basin of the Amazon, 1936
From Coast to Coast with the U. S. Mail, 1936
Flood Mappers Afloat, or How Ginger Hale and the Scouts of the Bald Eagle Patrol Surveyed the Watershed, 1937
Wings Over the Andes, 1939

MALORY TOWERS SERIES, Enid Blyton, ca. 1945 Metheun, small hardcover, b/w illustrations by Stanley Lloyd, map and illustration of the school and grounds on the endpapers. It's off to boarding school for young Darrell Rivers. Early printings: ($40.00 with dust jacket) $15.00
First Term at Malory Towers
Second Form at Malory Towers
Third Year at Malory Towers
Upper Fourth at Malory Towers
In the Fifth at Malory Towers
Last Term at Malory Towers

MARCO SERIES, John T. Foster, Dodd Mead, hardcover, b/w illustrations by Lorence Bjoklund. Boys' mystery series set in New Orleans.($15.00 with dust jacket) $10.00
Weekly Reader editions, $10.00
Marco and the Tiger, 1967
Marco and the Sleuth Hound, 1969
Marco and that Curious Cat, 1970

MARCY RHODES SERIES, Rosamund du Jardin (1902 – 1963), 1950s Lippincott, hardcover. See also TOBY HEYDON and PAM AND PENNY. ($35.00 with dust jacket) $15.00
Wait for Marcy, 1950
Marcy Catches Up, 1952
Man for Marcy, 1954
Senior Prom, 1957

MARGARET MONTFORT SERIES, (also called FERNLEY HOUSE SERIES) Laura Richards, 1897 – 1901 Dana Estes, Boston, hardcover with b/w plate illustrations by Etheldred Barry, 5 titles. $20.00
1930s L. C. Page reprints: ($30.00 with dust jacket) $10.00
Titles include:
Margaret Montfort
Fernley House

MARJORIE SERIES, Lorna Hill, 1948 – 1962, hardcover, first editions had various publishers (dates and publishers noted below). Titles later were reissued by Thomas Nelson. See also DANCING PEELS, PATIENCE, SADLER WELLS, and VICARAGE CHILDREN. ($20.00 with dust jackets) $10.00
Marjorie and Co, 1948, Art & Educational
Stolen Holiday, 1948, Art & Educational
Border Peel, 1950, Art & Educational
Castle in Northumbria, 1953 Burke
No Medals For Guy, 1962 Thomas Nelson

MARJORIE SERIES, Alice Curtis, 1905 – 1913 Penn $15.00

MARJORIE SERIES, Carolyn Wells, 1905 – 12 Grosset, 6 titles, advertised as "happiest books that have ever been written especially for her majesty, the American girl." $20.00
Marjorie's Vacation
Marjorie's Busy Days

Marjorie's New Friend
Marjorie in Command
Marjorie's MayTime
Marjorie at Seacote

MARJORIE SERIES, Mrs. Geo. Paull, 1900 – 04 Jacobs, illustration on hardcover, 3 titles. $20.00

MARJORIE DEAN SERIES, Pauline Lester, ca. 1917 A. L. Burt, cloth-over-board cover with impressed illustration. ($25.00 with dust jacket) $15.00
Marjorie Dean, High School Freshman
Marjorie Dean, High School Sophomore
Marjorie Dean, High School Junior
Marjorie Dean, High School Senior
Marjorie Dean, College Freshman
Marjorie Dean, College Sophomore
Marjorie Dean, College Junior
Marjorie Dean, College Senior
Marjorie Dean, Post-Graduate
Marjorie Dean, Marvelous Manager
Marjorie Dean's Romance
Marjorie Dean Macy

MARK MALLORY see WESTPOINT

MARK TIDD SERIES, Clarence Kelland, 1913 – 1928 Harper and Brothers, pictorial hardcover, illustrated endpapers in some, b/w illustrations. In each book the protagonist explains, "My name is Marcus Aurelius Fortunatus Tidd. My f-f-friends call me Mark Tidd." Early printing: ($125.00 with dust jacket) $65.00
Grosset, orange hardcover, pictorial endpapers, frontispiece. ($75.00 with dust jacket) $30.00
Mark Tidd
Mark Tidd in the Backwoods
Mark Tidd in Business
Mark Tidd's Citadel
Mark Tidd, Editor
Mark Tidd, Manufacturer
Mark Tidd in Italy
Mark Tidd in Egypt
Mark Tidd in Sicily

MARLOWE BOOKS FOR GIRLS, Amy Bell Marlowe (Stratemeyer Syndicate pseudonym), ca. 1914 Grosset, advertised as "thoroughly up-to-date and wholly American in scene and action." ($35.00 with dust jacket) $15.00
Oldest of Four
Girls at Hillcrest Farm
Little Miss Nobody
Girl from Sunset Ranch
Wyn's Camping Days, 1914, illustrated by W. Rogers
Frances of the Ranges
Girls of Rivercliff School
When Oriole Came to Harbor Light
When Oriole Traveled Westward

When Oriole Went to Boarding School

MARLOWS SERIES, Antonia Forest, 1948 – 1976, Faber and Faber, 8 titles. Although the author never meant to write a series, new accounts of the eight Marlow children appeared regularly. Hardcovers in good condition are hard-to-find for most of the series. Prices in England tend to be double that of American prices.
First editions with dust jackets: $80.00
Later editions: ($35.00 with dust jackets) $20.00
Autumn Term, 1948
Marlows and the Traitor, 1953
Falconer's Lure: Story of a Summer Holiday, 1957
End of Term, 1959
Peter's Room, 1961
Thuggery Affair, 1965
Ready-Made Family, 1967
Cricket Term, 1974
Attic Term, 1976
Marlows, related books:
Player's Boy, 1970, Faber, hardcover, first with dust jacket, $50.00; later editions: ($25.00 with dust jackets) $10.00
Players and the Rebels, 1971, Faber, hardcover, first with dust jacket, $50.00; later editions: ($25.00 with dust jackets) $10.00

MARTHA SLAWSON, Julie Lippmann, ca. 1912 Holt, Rinehart & Winston, hardcover, three titles.
Grosset & Dunlap reprints: $15.00
Titles include:
Martha-By-The-Day
Martha and Cupid

MARY AND JERRY DENTON MYSTERY SERIES, Francis Hunt (Stratemeyer Syndicate pseudonym), 1935 Grosset, hardcover, b/w illustrations by Margaret Ayer. ($25.00 with dust jackets) $10.00
Messenger Dog's Secret
Mystery of the Toy Bank
Story the Parrot Told
Secret of the Missing Clown
Mystery of the Crooked Tree

MARY FRANCES SERIES, Jane Eayer Fryer, Winston, cloth-over-board cover with paste-on-pictorial, illustrated endpapers, color illustrations throughout.
Mary Frances Garden Book, or Adventures Among the Garden People, 1916, color illustrations by William Zwirner. Early editions with dust jacket: $200.00 Without dust jacket: $100.00
Mary Frances Housekeeper Book, or Adventures Among the Doll People, 250 pages. Difficult to find. Early editions with dust jacket: $250.00 Without dust jacket: $150.00
Mary Frances Sewing Book, 1913 Winston, color illustrations by Jane Allen Boyer. Early editions with

dust jacket: $200.00 Without dust jacket: $100.00

Mary Frances Cook Book, or Adventures Among the Kitchen People, 170 pages, illustrations by Margaret Hayes and Jane Allen Boyer. Early editions with dust jacket: $200.00 Without dust jacket: $100.00

Mary Frances First Aid Book, 1916, color frontispiece, blue type, blue/red line drawings by Jane Allen Boyer, hard to find. Early editions with dust jacket: $300.00 Without dust jacket: $200.00

Mary Frances Storybook, 1921, illustrated by Edwin Prittie Early editions with dust jacket: $100.00 Without dust jacket: $50.00

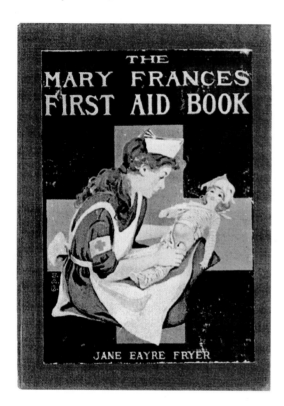

MARY JANE SERIES, Clara Judson, 1918 – 39 Barse, hardcover. $15.00

Ca. 1930s reprints, Grosset & Dunlap, hardcover. ($25.00 with dust jacket) $15.00

Mary Jane, Her Book
Mary Jane, Her Visit
Mary Jane, Kindergarten
Mary Jane, Down South
Mary Jane, City Home
Mary Jane, in New England
Mary Jane, Country Home
Mary Jane, at School
Mary Jane, in Canada
Mary Jane, Summer Fun
Mary Jane, Winter Sports
Mary Jane, Vacation
Mary Jane, in England
Mary Jane, in Scotland
Mary Jane, in France
Mary Jane, in Switzerland
Mary Jane, in Italy

MARY LEE SERIES, Anna Merrill, ca. 1920 Whitman, small, color illustration on cover, illustrated end-papers, b/w illustrations. $15.00

Mary Lee's Friend
Mary Lee at Washington
Mary Lee, the Red Cross Girl
Mary Lee, the Campfire Girl

MARY LOU SERIES, Edith Lavell, 1935 Burt, hardcover: ($25.00 with dust jacket) $15.00

Saalfield reprints: ($15.00 with dust jacket) $10.00

Mystery of the Fires
Mystery of the Secret Band
Mystery at Dark Cedars

MARY LOUISE SERIES, Edith Van Dyne (pseudonym of L. Frank Baum who began the series. Titles after 1919 were written by Emma Sampson), 1916 – 22 Reilly, hardcover. $25.00

Mary Louise
Mary Louise and the Liberty Girls
Mary Louise Stands the Test
Mary Louise at Dorfield
Mary Louise Adopts a Soldier
Mary Louise in the Country
Mary Louise Solves a Mystery

MARY ROSE SERIES, Mary Mabel Wirries, ca. 1920s Benziger, hardcover. $15.00

Titles include:
Mary Rose at Boarding School, 1924
Mary Rose, Graduate, 1926
Mary Rose at Rose Gables, 1928
Mary Rose in Friendville, 1930
Mary Rose's Sister Bess, 1932

MARY ROSE AND JO-BETH MYSTERY SERIES, Eth Clifford, Houghton, funny adventures of two young sisters who stumble into mysterious situations. ($20.00 with dust jacket) $10.00

Help! I'm a Prisoner in the Library, 1979
Dastardly Murder of Dirty Pete, 1981
Just Tell Me When We're Dead, 1983
Scared Silly, 1988

MAXIE SERIES, Elsie Bell Gardner, 1932 – 39 Cupples & Leon, hardcover. ($40.00 with dust jacket) $20.00

Maxie, an Adorable Girl, ca. 1932
Maxie in Venezuela, ca. 1932
Maxie Searching for Her Parents, ca. 1932
Maxie at Brinksome Hall, ca. 1934
Maxie and Her Adventures in Spain, ca. 1936
Maxie in the Jungle, ca. 1937
Maxie and the Golden Bird, ca. 1939

McGONIGGLE SERIES see GREAT McGONIGGLE

McGURK MYSTERY SERIES, E. Hildick, 1973 – 1990 Macmillian or Grosset & Dunlap, hardcover, 20 titles in series about eleven-year-old McGurk and his McGurk Detective Organization. After first title the b/w illustrations are by Lisl Weil through *Slingshot Sniper* then by Kathy Parkinson. ($15.00 with dust jackets) $10.00

Weekly Reader editions: $10.00.
Nose Knows, 1973, illustrated by Unada Gliewe
Deadline for McGurk, 1975, illustrated by Lisl Weil
Case of the Condemned Cat, 1975
Case of the Nervous Newsboy, 1976
Great Rabbit Rip-off, 1977
Case of the Invisible Dog, 1977
Case of the Secret Scribbler, 1978
Case of the Phantom Frog, 1979
Case of the Treetop Treasure, 1980
Case of the Snowbound Spy, 1980
Case of the Bashful Bank Robber, 1981
Case of the Four Flying Fingers, 1981
Case of the Felon's Fiddle, 1982
McGurk Gets Good and Mad, 1982
Case of the Slingshot Sniper, 1983
Case of the Vanishing Ventriloquist, 1985, illustrated by Kathy Parkinson
Case of the Muttering Mummy, 1986
Case of the Wandering Weathervanes, 1988
Case of the Purloined Parrot, 1990
Case of the Dragon in Distress, 1991
Case of the Weeping Witch, 1992
Case of the Desperate Drummer, 1993
Case of the Fantastic Footprints, 1994

MEADOWBROOK GIRLS SERIES, Janet Aldridge, 1913 Altemus, 6 titles, hardcover. $10.00
Meadowbrook Girls Under Canvas
Meadowbrook Girls Across Country
Meadowbrook Girls Afloat
Meadowbrook Girls in the Hills
Meadowbrook Girls by the Sea
Meadowbrook Girls on the Tennis Courts

MEG SERIES, Holly Beth Walker, Whitman, pictorial hardcover, illustrated endpapers, illustrated by Cliff Schule. $15.00
Meg and the Disappearing Diamonds, 1967
Meg: Secret of the Witch's Stairway
Meg: The Treasure Nobody Saw, 1970
Meg: Mystery in Williamsburg, 1972

MEG OF HERON'S NECK SERIES, Elizabeth Ladd, Morrow, hardcover, b/w illustrations by Mary Stevens, adventures on a island in Maine. ($25.00 with dust jacket) $10.00
Meg of Heron's Neck, 1961
Mystery for Meg, 1962
Meg's Mysterious Island, 1963
Meg and Melissa, 1964
Trouble on Heron's Neck, 1966
Treasure on Heron's Neck, 1967

MEL MARTIN BASEBALL SERIES, John Cooper (Stratemeyer Syndicate pseudonym), 1947 – 1953 Cupples & Leon, hardcover, 6 titles. Baseball-related mystery stories. Reprints by Garden City or Books Inc.
Cupples & Leon editions: $30.00 with dust jackets
Later reprints: ($15.00 with dust jacket) $10.00
Mystery at the Ball Park, 1947
Southpaw's Secret, 1947
Phantom Homer, 1952
First Base Jinx, 1952
Fighting Shortstop, 1953
College League Mystery, 1953

MELENDY FAMILY SERIES, Elizabeth Enright, Holt, Rinehart, hardcover, illustrated by author. Early edition: ($100.00 with dust jacket) $50.00
Saturdays, 1941
Four Story Mistake, 1942
Then There Were Five, 1944
Spiderweb for Two, 1951

MELINDA SERIES, Doris Gates, Viking, hardcover, novels about a 12-year-old and her horse. ($40.00 with dust jacket) $10.00
Morgan for Melinda, 1980
Horse for Melinda, 1981
Filly for Melinda, 1984

MELODY LANE MYSTERY SERIES, Lilian Garis, ca. 1930s Grosset & Dunlap ($25.00 with dust jacket) $15.00

Ghost of Melody Lane
Forbidden Trail
Tower Secret
Wild Warning
Terror at Moaning Cliff
Drogon of the Hills
Mystery of Stingyman's Alley
Secret of the Kashmir Shawl

MERCER BOYS SERIES, Capwell Wyckoff, World, plain hardcover. ($25.00 with dust jacket) $10.00
1940s World reprints "Falcon" books, small glossy pictorial hardcover: $15.00
Mercer Boys' Cruise in the Lassie, 1929
Mercer Boys at Woodcrest, 1929
Mercer Boys on a Treasure Hunt, 1929
Mercer Boys' Mystery Case, 1929
Mercer Boys on the Beach Patrol, 1929
Mercer Boys in Summer Camp, 1929
Mercer Boys as First Classmen, 1930
Mercer Boys and the Indian Gold, 1932
Mercer Boys with the Air Cadets, 1932
Mercer Boys and the Steamboat Riddle, 1933

MERRIWEATHER GIRLS SERIES, Lizette Edholm, 1932 Goldsmith, hardcover. ($20.00 with dust jacket) $10.00
Merriweather Girls on Camper's Trail
Merriweather Girls and the Mystery of the Queen's Fan
Merriweather Girls in Quest of Treasure
Merriweather Girls at Good Old Rock Hill

MERRIWELL see FRANK MERRIWELL

MERRY LYNN SERIES, Harriet Pyne Grove, ca. 1915 Burt, hardcover, illustrated, "for girls 12 to 17 years." ($20.00 with dust jacket) $10.00
Merilyn Enters Beechwold
Merilyn at Camp Meenahga
Merilyn Tests Loyalty
Merilyn's New Adventure
Merilyn Forrester, Co-Ed
"Merry Lynn" Mine

MERRYVALE BOYS SERIES, Alice Hale Burnett, 1916 New York Book, paste-on- pictorial on hardcover, 4 plates by Charles Lester. $15.00
Circus Day at Merryvale
Father Brown's Indian Tale
Picnic Day at Merryvale
Christmas Holidays at Merryvale
Merryvale Boys on the Farm
Halloween at Merryvale

MERRYVALE GIRLS SERIES, Alice Burnett, New York Book, paste-on-pictorial on hardcover, 4 plates by Charles Lester. $15.00
Beth's Garden Party, 1916
Day at the Country Fair, 1916
Geraldine's Birthday Surprise, 1916
Mary Entertains the Sewing Club, 1916
Merryvale Girls in the Country, 1917
Merryvale Girls at the Seaside, 1919

MEXICAN MYSTERY STORIES FOR GIRLS, Helen Randolph, 1936 Burt, reprints by Saalfield using original dust jacket art. ($20.00 with dust jacket) $10.00
Crossed Trails in Mexico
Mystery of Carlitos
Secret of Casa Grande

MEXICAN WAR SERIES, Capt. Ralph Bonehill (Stratemeyer pseudonym, Edward Stratemeyer named in later reprints), Dana Estes; Lothrop, Lee and Shepard; pictorial hardcover, frontispiece. $30.00
For the Liberty of Texas, 1900
With Taylor on the Rio Grande, 1901
Under Scott in Mexico, 1902

MICHAEL AND MARY SERIES, Malcolm Saville, 1950s John Murry, London, hardcover, illustrated by Lunt Roberts. $15.00

MILDRED SERIES, Martha Finley, ca. 1870 – 90 Routledge, also ca. 1915 Dodd Mead, illustrated cloth-over-board cover, companion series to ELSIE SERIES. $25.00
1920s Burt reprints, colored cloth hardcover with printed design. Dust jacket uses same design of flower and vine edging, but is white with red printing. ($35.00 with dust jacket) $15.00
Mildred Keith
Mildred at Roselands
Mildred and Elsie
Mildred at Home
Mildred's Married Life
Mildred's Boys And Girls
Mildred's New Daughter

MILL CREEK IRREGULARS SERIES, August Derleth, first eight titles published by Duell Sloan and Pearce, hardcover. ($35.00 with dust jackets) $12.00

Moon Tenders, 1958
Mill Creek Irregulars, Special Detectives, 1959
Pinkertons Ride Again, 1960
Ghost of Black Hawk Island, 1961
Tent Show Summer, 1963
Irregulars Strike Again, 1964
House by the River, 1965
Watcher on the Heights, 1966
Prince Goes West, 1968 Meredith Press
Three Straw Men, 1968 Candlelight Press

MILLERS SERIES, Alberta Constant, Crowell, hardcover. First edition with dust jacket: $40.00, later printings: ($20.00 with dust jackets) $10.00
Those Miller Girls, 1965
Motoring Millers, 1969
Does Anybody Care About Lou Emma Miller?, 1979

MILLERS SERIES, Clara Dillingham Pierson, ca. 1905 Dutton, illustrated cloth-over-board cover, b/w plates. $20.00
Millers at Pencroft
Three Little Millers
Millers and Their Playmates
Millers and Their New Home

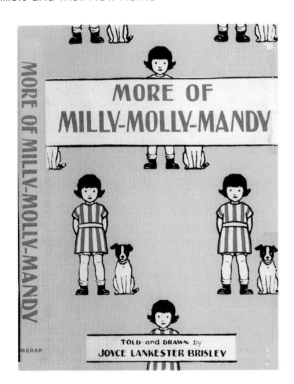

MILLY-MOLLY-MANDY SERIES, Joyce Lankester Brisley, author-artist, studied art in London and, with her two artist sisters, had paintings hung at the Royal Academy. She wrote and illustrated many single titles, as well as this popular series.
Harrap, London, small hardcover with color frontispiece and b/w illustrations by author, early editions: ($70.00 with dust jacket) $40.00
McKay and Australian reprints: ($30.00 with dust jacket) $15.00
Milly-Molly-Mandy Stories, 1928
More of Milly-Molly-Mandy, 1929
Further Doings of Milly-Molly-Mandy, 1932
Milly-Molly-Mandy Again, 1948
Milly-Molly-Mandy & Co., 1955
Milly-Molly-Mandy and Billy Blunt, 1967

MIMI HAMMOND SERIES, Anne Pence Davis, ca. 1935 Goldsmith, hardcover, three titles. ($20.00 with dust jacket) $10.00

MINUTE BOYS SERIES, first two titles by Edward Stratemeyer, then continued by James Otis, 1898 – 1912 Estes; Page; pictorial hardcover, b/w plates. $25.00
Minute Boys of Lexington
Minute Boys of Bunker Hill
Minute Boys of the Green Mountains
Minute Boys of the Mohawk Valley
Minute Boys of the Wyoming Valley
Minute Boys of South Carolina
Minute Boys of Long Island
Minute Boys of New York City
Minute Boys of Boston
Minute Boys of Philadelphia
Minute Boys of York Town

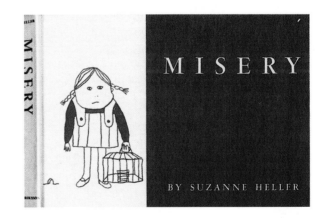

MISERY SERIES, Suzanne Heller
Misery, 1964 Paul Eriksson, small oblong hardcover, blue/white print and illustrations, illustrations by author. ($25.00 with dust jacket) $10.00
Misery Loves Company, 1962 Eriksson, small oblong hardcover, illustrated by author. ($20.00 with dust jacket) $10.00
More Misery, 1965 Eriksson, hardcover, illustrated by author. ($20.00 with dust jacket) $10.00

MISHMASH SERIES, Molly Cone, 1962 – 80s Houghton, hardcover, b/w illustrations by Leonard Shortall, dust jackets have wraparound illustrations.
($25.00 with dust jacket) $10.00
Mishmash
Mishmash and the Substitute Teacher
Mishmash and the Sauerkraut Mystery

Mishmash and the Venus Flytrap
Mishmash and Uncle Looey
Mishmash and the Robot
Mishmash and the Big Fat Problem

MISS MINERVA SERIES, was created by Frances Boyd Calhoun (1867 – 1909, b. Va.), who wrote the first title, but died the year of its publication. Emma Speed Sampson continued the series through the 1920s. Reilly & Lee, red hardcover with black lettering and illustration, b/w drawings thoughout. Illustrator for the Sampson titles was Wiliam Donahey, twelve titles plus a cookbook. Early printings: ($50.00 with dust jacket) $25.00
Titles include:
Miss Minerva and William Green Hill, 1909, illustrated by Angus MacDonall
Billy and the Major
Miss Minerva's Baby
Miss Minerva and the Old Plantation
Miss Minerva Broadcasts Billy
Miss Minerva's Scallywags
Miss Minerva Goin' Places
Miss Minerva's Mystery

MISS PAT SERIES, Pemberton Ginther, 1915 – 17 Winston, pictorial hardcover, decorated endpapers, frontispiece by author. 11 titles. ($35.00 with dust jacket) $15.00
Titles include:
Miss Pat at School
Miss Pat at Artemis Lodge
Miss Pat in Buenos Ayres
Miss Pat and Company Limited

Miss Pat and Her Sisters
Miss Pat in the Old World
Miss Pat's Great Idea

MISTER PENNY SERIES, Marie Hall Ets
Mister Penny, 1935 edition Viking, pictorial oversize oblong hardcover boards with cloth spine, b/w illustrations by author. Early editions: ($50.00 with dust jacket) $30.00
Mister Penny's Race Horse, 1956 Viking, first edition, hardcover, illustrated endpapers, illustrations by author. ($35.00 with dust jacket) $15.00
Mister Penny's Circus, 1961 Viking, first edition, hardcover, illustrations by author. ($40.00 with dust jacket) $20.00

MISTY THE HORSE SERIES, Marguerite Henry, Rand McNally and Macmillan, hardcover, color and b/w illustrations by Wesley Dennis, early edition prices shown with titles.
Reprints and book club editions with illustrations by Don Bolognese: ($20.00 with dust jacket) $10.00
Collins reprints: $15.00
Misty of Chincoteague, 1947, first edition, hard-to-find, early editions: ($65.00 with dust jacket) $15.00
Sea Star, 1949, first edition, hard-to-find, early editions: ($45.00 with dust jacket) $20.00
Stormy, Misty's Foal, 1963, first edition: ($50.00 with dust jacket) $20.00
Misty's Twilight, 1992, first edition: ($25.00 with dust jacket) $15.00
Misty, related book:
Pictorial Life Story of Misty, 1976 Rand McNally, pictorial hardcover, b/w and color photos and Wesley Dennis illustrations, a "true story" of the pony that inspired the original Misty book. First edition: $60.00

MOFFAT SERIES, Eleanor Estes, Bodley Head, London: Harcourt edition, hardcover, b/w illustrations by Louis Slobodkin, early printings: ($35.00 with dust jacket) $15.00
Moffats, 1941
Middle Moffat, 1942
Rufus M, 1943
Moffat Museum, 1983

MOLLY SERIES, Miriam Chaikin, Harper, hardcover, illustrations by Richard Egielski, stories set in the 1930s. ($20.00 with dust jacket) $10.00
I Should Worry, I Should Care, 1979
Finders Weepers, 1980
Getting Even, 1982
Lower! Higher! You're a Liar!, 1984
Friends Forever, 1988

MOLLY BROWN SERIES, Nell Speed, 1912 – 21 Hurst, decorated hardcover, four half-tone illustrations

by Charles Wrenn, early printing: $25.00
Hurst and Burt later printings, usually with frontispiece
only: $15.00
Molly Brown's Freshman Days
Molly Brown's Sophomore Days
Molly Brown's Junior Days
Molly Brown's Senior Days
Molly Brown's Post Graduate Days
Molly Brown's Orchard Home
Molly Brown of Kentucky
Molly Brown's College Friends

MOTION PICTURE CHUMS SERIES, Victor Appleton
(Stratemeyer Syndicate pseudonym), 1913 Gros-
set, small size, illustrations, also see MOVING PIC-
TURE BOYS. Stories of three boys who buy a movie
theatre. $15.00
*Motion Picture Chums' First Venture, or Opening a
Photo Playhouse in Fairlands*
*Motion Picture Chums at Seaside Park, or The Rival
Photo Theatres of the Boardwalk*
*Motion Picture Chums on Broadway, or The Mystery
of the Missing Cash Box*
*Motion Picture Chums' Outdoor Exhibition, or The Film
that Solved a Mystery*
*Motion Picture Chums' New Idea, or The First Educa-
tional Photo Playhouse*
*Motion Picture Chums at the Fair, or The Greatest Film
Ever Exhibited*
*Motion Picture Chums' War Spectacle, or The Film
that Won the Prize*

MOTION PICTURE COMRADES SERIES, Elmer Barnes,
1917 New York Book, pictorial hardcover, fron-
tispiece by Lester. ($50.00 with dust jacket) $20.00
Saalfield edition, see MOVING PICTURE COMRADES.
($20.00 with dust jacket) $10.00
*Motion Picture Comrades' Great Venture, or On the
Road with the Big Round-Top*
*Motion Picture Comrades in African Jungles, or Cam-
era Boys in Wild Animal Land*
*Motion Picture Comrades Along the Orinoco, or Fac-
ing Perils in the Tropics*
*Motion Picture Comrades Aboard a Submarine, or
Searching for Treasure Under the Sea*
*Motion Picture Comrades Producing a Success, or
Featuring a Sensation*

MOTOR BOAT CLUB SERIES, Irving Hancock, 1909 –
1912 Altemus, hardcover with printed illustration,
b/w frontispiece. ($40.00 with dust jacket) $15.00
*Motor Boat Club of the Kennebec, or Secret of Smug-
gler's Island*
*Motor Boat Club at Nantucket, or Mystery of the Dun-
stan Heir*
*Motor Boat Club off Long Island, or Daring Game at
Racing Speed*
*Motor Boat Club and the Wireless, or Dot, Dash and
Dare Cruise*

*Motor Boat Club in Florida, or Laying the Ghost of Alli-
gator Swamp*
*Motor Boat Club at the Golden Gate, or A Thrilling
Capture in the Great Fog*
*Motor Boat Club on the Great Lakes, or Flying Dutch-
man of the Big Fresh Water*

MOTOR BOAT BOYS SERIES, Louis Arundel, 1912 –
1915 Donohue, hardcover with "Motor Boat
Boys" in white lettering on front and spine, picto-
rial endpapers, frontispiece. ($30.00 with dust
jacket) $15.00
Motor Boat Boys' Mississippi Cruise, or Dash for Dixie
*Motor Boat Boys on the St Lawrence, or Solving the
Mystery of the Thousand Islands*
*Motor Boat Boys on the Great Lakes, or Exploring the
Mystic Island of Mackinac*
*Motor Boat Boys Down the Coast, or Through Storm
and Stress to Florida*
*Motor Boat Boys Among the Florida Keys, or Struggle
for Leadership*
*Motor Boat Boys' River Chase, or Six Chums Afloat
and Ashore*
*Motor Boat Boys Down the Danube, or Four Chums
Abroad*

MOTOR BOYS SERIES, Clarence Young (Stratemeyer
Syndicate pseudonym), ca. 1906 – 1920s Cupples
& Leon, hardcover with printed illustration, four
b/w plates. Early editions: ($75.00 with dust jack-
et) $20.00
Motor Boys
Motor Boys Overland
Motor Boys in Mexico
Motor Boys Across the Plains
Motor Boys Afloat
Motor Boys on the Atlantic
Motor Boys in Strange Waters
Motor Boys in on the Pacific
Motor Boys in the Clouds

Motor Boys over the Rockies
Motor Boys over the Ocean
Motor Boys on the Wing
Motor Boys after a Fortune
Motor Boys on the Border
Motor Boys under the Sea
Motor Boys on Road and River
Motor Boys at Boxwood Hall
Motor Boys on a Ranch
Motor Boys in the Army
Motor Boys on the Firing Line
Motor Boys Bound for Home
Motor Boys on Thunder Mountain

Motor Boys, Second Series, by Clarence Young, ca. 1920 Cupples & Leon, pictorial hardcover, frontispiece. Early editions: ($75.00 with dust jacket) $20.00

Ned, Bob and Jerry at Boxwood Hall
Ned, Bob and Jerry on the Ranch
Ned, Bob and Jerry in the Army
Ned, Bob and Jerry on the Firing Line
Ned, Bob and Jerry Bound for Home

MOTOR CYCLE CHUMS SERIES, Lieut. Howard Payson, 1912 Hurst, pictorial hardcover, four plates by Charles Wrenn, first edition: $100.00
Later editions: $40.00
Motor Cycle Chums Around the World
Motor Cycle Chums of the Northwest Patrol
Motor Cycle Chums in the Goldfields
Motor Cycle Chums Whirlwind Tour
Motor Cycle Chums South of the Equator
Motor Cycle Chums Through Historic America

MOTOR GIRLS SERIES, Margaret Penrose (Stratemeyer Syndicate pseudonym), ca. 1920s Cupples & Leon, small size, cloth covers, illustrations, advertised as "No one is better equipped to furnish these tales than Mrs. Penrose who, besides being an able writer, is an expert automobilist." ($40.00 with dust jacket) $15.00
Goldsmith reprint: ($20.00 with dust jacket) $10.00
Motor Girls
Motor Girls on a Tour
Motor Girls at Lookout Reach
Motor Girls through New England
Motor Girls on Cedar Lake
Motor Girls on the Coast
Motor Girls on Crystal Bay
Motor Girls on Waters Blue
Motor Girls at Camp Surprise
Motor Girls in the Mountains

MOTOR MAIDS SERIES, Katherine Stokes, ca. 1911 – 12 Donohue, blue cloth-over-board cover with impressed illustration, illustrations by Charles Wrenn, four travelers, a chaperone, and a little red car, tour the world. ($30.00 with dust jacket) $15.00

Donohue, pictorial beige hardcover: $20.00
Hurst edition with pictorial boards has same-design dust jacket. ($30.00 with dust jacket) $15.00
Motor Maids Across the Continent
Motor Maids' School Days
Motor Maids at Sunrise Camp
Motor Maids by Rose, Shamrock and Thistle
Motor Maids by Palm and Pine
Motor Maids In Fair Japan

MOTOR POWER SERIES see BOB STEELE

MOTOR RANGERS SERIES, Marvin West, 1911 – 14 Hurst, illustrated cloth-over-board cover, illustrations by Charles Wrenn. ($50.00 with dust jacket) $20.00
Lost Mine
Through the Sierras
On Blue Water
Cloud Cruiser
Wireless Station
Touring for the Trophy

MOTORCYCLE CHUMS SERIES, Andrew Carey Lincoln, 1912 – 1914 Donohue, khaki pictorial hardcover, pictorial endpapers, frontispiece by C. H. Lawrence. First edition: ($200.00 with dust jacket) $60.00
Later editions other colors on covers, plain endpapers: $30.00
Motorcycle Chums in New England, or Mt. Holyoke Adventure
Motorcycle Chums in the Land of the Sky, or Thrilling Adventures on the Carolina Border
Motorcycle Chums on the Santa Fe Trail, or Key to the Indian Treasure Cave

Motorcycle Chums in Yellowstone Park, or Lending a Helping Hand
Motorcycle Chums in the Adirondacks, or Search for the Lost Pacemaker
Motorcycle Chums Stormbound, or Strange Adventures of a Road Chase

MOUNTAIN BOYS see PHIL BRADLEY

MOUNTAIN PONY SERIES, Henry V. Larom, 1946 – 1950 Whittsley, hardcover: ($30.00 with dust jacket) $15.00
Grosset & Dunlap, hardcover (as part of FAMOUS HORSES SERIES). ($15.00 with dust jacket) $10.00
Paperbacks issued by Scholastic or Tab. $15.00
Mountain Pony: A Story of the Wyoming Rockies, 1946
Mountain Pony and the Pinto Colt, 1947
Mountain Pony and the Rodeo Mystery, 1949
Mountain Pony and the Elkhorn Mystery, 1950

MOVING PICTURE BOYS SERIES, Victor Appleton (Stratemeyer Syndicate pseudonym), ca. 1913 – 1920s Grosset, see MOTION PICTURE CHUMS, continuing stories of three chums, using the stories from the CHUMS series for the last five titles. ($35.00 with dust jacket) $15.00
Moving Picture Boys
Moving Picture Boys in the West
Moving Picture Boys on the Coast
Moving Picture Boys in the Jungle
Moving Picture Boys in Earthquake Land
Moving Picture Boys and the Flood
Moving Picture Boys at Panama
Moving Picture Boys Under the Sea
Moving Picture Boys on the War Front
Moving Picture Boys on French Battlefields
Moving Picture Boys' First Showhouse
Moving Picture Boys at Seaside Park
Moving Picture Boys on Broadway
Moving Picture Boys' Outdoor Exhibition
Moving Picture Boys' New Idea

MOVING PICTURE COMRADES SERIES, Elmer Tracy Barnes (Stratemeyer Syndicate pseudonym), 1917 Saalfield (first published as MOTION PICTURE COMRADES, New York Book Company). Tan or red hardcover, frontispiece. ($20.00 with dust jacket) $10.00
Moving Picture Comrades' Great Venture, or On the Road with the Big Round-Top
Moving Picture Comrades in African Jungles, or Camera Boys in Wild Animal Land
Moving Picture Comrades Along the Orinoco, or Facing Perils in the Tropics
Moving Picture Comrades Aboard a Submarine, or Searching for Treasure Under the Sea
Moving Picture Comrades Producing a Success, or Featuring a Sensation

MOVING PICTURE GIRLS SERIES, Laura Lee Hope (Stratemeyer Syndicate pseudonym), 1914 Grosset, or World, small hardcover, b/w illustrations, stories of young actresses. ($25.00 with dust jacket) $15.00
Goldsmith reprints: ($15.00 with dust jacket) $10.00
Moving Picture Girls
Moving Picture Girls at Oak Farm
Moving Picture Girls Snowbound
Moving Picture Girls under the Palms
Moving Picture Girls at Rocky Ranch
Moving Picture Girls at Sea
Moving Picture Girls in War Plays

MR. TWIDDLE SERIES, Enid Blyton, Newnes, ca. 1950s George Newnes, London, hardcover, illustrated by Hilda McGavin. ($35.00 with dust jacket) $15.00
Dean & Son Ltd., hardcover, b/w illustrations, 1960s reprints: ($25.00 with dust jacket) $15.00
Dean & Son Ltd., pictorial glazed boards, b/w illustrations, 1960s reprints: $15.00
Hello, Mr. Twiddle!
Well, Really, Mr. Twiddle!
Don't Be Silly, Mr. Twiddle!

MRS. COVERLET SERIES, Mary Nash, Little, Brown, hardcover, humorous stories about an absent housekeeper and take-charge children, b/w illustrations by Garrett Price. ($20.00 with dust jacket) $10.00
While Mrs. Coverlet Was Away, 1958
Mrs. Coverlet's Magicians, 1961
Mrs. Coverlet's Detectives, 1965

MRS. PIGGLE-WIGGLE SERIES, Betty MacDonald, Lippincott, small, hardcover, about 220 pages, b/w illustrations. Perennial favorite, this series has been reprinted often. 1950s printings: ($40.00 with dust jacket) $15.00

Mrs. Piggle-Wiggle, 1947, hardcover, b/w illustrations by Hilary Knight. First edition with dust jacket: $200.00

Mrs. Piggle-Wiggle's Magic, (1949) 1957 edition with b/w illustrations by Hilary Knight. First edition with dust jacket: $200.00

Mrs. Piggle-Wiggle's Farm, 1954, green hardcover, b/w illustrations by Maurice Sendak. First edition in dust jacket: $300.00

Hello, Mrs. Piggle-Wiggle, 1957, b/w illustrations by Hilary Knight. First edition with dust jacket: $150.00

MUSEUM SERIES, Francis Rolt-Wheeler, 1916 – 1927 Lothrop, Lee and Shepard, paste-on-pictorial hardcover, illustrations and photographs. ($25.00 with dust jacket) $15.00

Monster Hunters
Polar Hunters
Aztec Hunters
Wreck Hunters
Sahara Hunters
Sea Hunters
Hunters of the Ocean Depths
News Hunters
Tusk Hunters

MUSKET BOYS SERIES, George Warren, ca. 1910 Cupples & Leon, pictorial hardcover, eight plates. Later editions has frontispiece only, illustrations by Charles Nuttall. $20.00

Goldsmith editions, plain hardcover, no illustrations:

($15.00 with dust jacket) $10.00

Musket Boys of Old Boston, or The First Blow for Liberty

Musket Boys Under Washington, or The Tories of Old New York

Musket Boys on the Delaware, or A Stirring Victory at Trenton

MYSTERY AND ADVENTURE SERIES, Hugh McAlister (James Andrew Braden), 1930 Saalfield, red hardcover, frontispiece. Two of the titles appear in the AIR ADVENTURE SERIES. Several titles were also re-issued in two-in-one and three-in-one volumes, and possibly in other formats. ($25.00 with dust jacket) $10.00

Mystery at Roaring Brook Farm: The Story of a Boy Attaining Success in Agriculture

Flaming River: The Story of an Intrepid Boy Who Developed a Petroleum Field

Conqueror of the High Road: A Story of a Boy's Persistence in the Field of Automobile Development

Stand By: The Story of a Boy's Achievement in Radio

Viking of the Sky: A Story of a Boy Who Gained Success in Aeronautics

Flight of the Silver Ship: Around the World Aboard a Giant Dirigible

Steve Holworth of the Oldham Works: The Story of a Boy Who Chose a Career in the Rubber Industry

Sea Gold: The Story of a Boy Who Mastered Deep Sea Diving

MYSTERY BOYS SERIES, A. Van Buren Powell, ca. 1930 Burt, and World Publishing, illustrated cover and illustrated endpapers, 280+ pages. ($20.00 with dust jacket) $15.00

Mystery Boys and the Inca Gold
Mystery Boys and Captain Kidd's Message
Mystery Boys and the Secret of the Golden Sun
Mystery Boys and the Chinese Jewels
Mystery Boys and the Hindu Treasure

MYSTERY HUNTERS SERIES, Capwell Wyckoff, 1934 – 1936 Burt, dark green hardcover with yellow lettering, pictorial endpapers, frontispiece: ($40.00 with dust jacket) $15.00

Saalfield edition, dark blue hardcover, frontispiece. ($15.00 with dust jacket) $10.00

Mystery Hunters at the Haunted Lodge
Mystery Hunters at Lakeside Camp
Mystery Hunters at Old Frontier
Mystery Hunters on Special Detail

MYSTERY SERIES, Christine Govan and Emmy West, 1957 Sterling Publishing, hardcover, book jacket illustration by Frederick Chapman. ($20.00 with dust jacket) $10.00

Mystery at Moccasin Bend
Mystery at the Shuttered Hotel
Mystery at the Mountain Face

Mystery at Shingle Rock
Mystery at the Indian Hide-Out

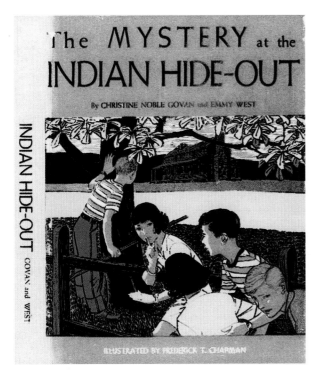

MYSTERY SERIES BOOKS, ca. 1930s McLoughlin Publishing, hardcover, reprints by Milton Bradley. ($20.00 with dust jacket) $10.00
Face in the Mist, Homer Hurlbut
Secret of Lost River, Howard Garis
Mystery of the Brass Bound Box, Howard Garis
Face in the Dismal Cavern, Howard Garis

MYSTERY STORIES FOR BOYS SERIES, Roy Snell, 1920-1939 Reilly and Lee, hardcover, frontispiece by Garrett Price. ($40.00 with dust jacket) $10.00
Triple Spies
Lost in the Air
Panther Eye
Crimson Flash
White Fire
Black Schooner
Hidden Trail
Firebug
Red Lure
Forbidden Cargoes
Johnny Longbow
Rope of Gold
Arrow of Fire
Gray Shadow
Riddle of the Storm
Galloping Ghost
Whispers at Dawn
Mystery Wings
Red Dynamite
Seal of Secrecy
Shadow Passes

Sign of the Green Arrow

MYSTERY STORIES FOR GIRLS BOOKS, ca. 1936 Cupples & Leon, various authors, hardcover. ($75.00 with dust jacket) $15.00
Titles include:
Clue at Crooked Lane, Mildred A. Wirt
Hollow Wall Mystery, Mildred A. Wirt
Shadow Stone, Mildred A. Wirt
Wooden Shoe Mystery, Mildred A. Wirt
Through the Moon-Gate Door, Mildred A. Wirt
Secret Stair, Pemberton Ginther
Thirteenth Spoon, Pemberton Ginther

N

NAN SHERWOOD SERIES, Annie Rowe Carr (Stratemeyer Syndicate pseudonym), 1916 – 1937 Saalfield, also Goldsmith; World; hardcover, frontispiece illustration. ($30.00 with dust jacket) $10.00
Nan Sherwood at Pine Camp, 1916
Nan Sherwood at Lakeview Hall, 1917
Nan Sherwood's Winter Holidays, 1918
Nan Sherwood at Rose Ranch, 1919
Nan Sherwood at Palm Beach, 1921
Nan Sherwood's Summer Holidays, 1922
Nan Sherwood on the Mexican Border, 1937 (World only)

NANCY BRANDON SERIES see GARIS

NANCY DREW SERIES, Carolyn Keene, pseudonym, 1930 – 1979 Grosset & Dunlap, (Edward Stratemeyer syndicated books. Early plot outlines by Stratemeyer, plot outlines after 1930 were created by his daughter Harriet S. Adams.) Girl sleuth lives with her widowed father, who is an attorney, and a motherly housekeeper, and drives around in her own car (see Penny Nichols series and Penny Parker series).
Nancy Drew Scrapbook, Karen Plunkett Powell, states that the first seven books and several later books were written by Mildred Wirt Benson, others were written by Walter Karig, Harriet Adams, Margaret Sherf Beebe, Iris Vinton, possibly Lilian Garis, and other writers, all working from Stratemeyer or Adams outlines. 1930 – 1950 b/w illustrations and color dust jackets by Russell Tandy.
Later illustrators include Bill Gillies and Rudy Nappi. Gillies began a new series of dust jackets in the 1950s and Rudy Nappi did new dust jacket designs in the 1960s. Books issued from 1950 – 1953 had only a frontispiece illustration, books printed after 1954 had 6 black-and-white illustrations.
In 1962, Grosset dropped the hardcover format with dust jacket and began issuing all titles in the yellow spine picture-cover hardcovers. In 1979, Simon & Schuster began publishing new Drew

titles under their Minstrel or Wanderer imprints. As with Hardy Boys, collectors identify "firsts" as books that do not list beyond their own title in the book or dust jacket advertisements for the series.

Nancy Drew, 1930 – 1950

Blue hardcover with dust jackets, first editions: usually can be found in the $60.00 to $100.00 range, though books in very good condition can go much higher.

Later edition blue hardcovers with dust jacket: $40.00

Secret of the Old Clock, 1930
Hidden Staircase, 1930
Bungalow Mystery, 1930
Mystery of Lilac Inn, 1930
Secret of Shadow Ranch, 1931
Secret of Red Gate Farm, 1931
Clue in the Diary, 1932
Nancy's Mysterious Letter, 1932
Sign of the Twisted Candles, 1933
Password to Larkspur Lane, 1933
Clue of the Broken Locket, 1934
Message in the Hollow Oak, 1935
Mystery of the Ivory Charm, 1936
Whispering Statue, 1937
Haunted Bridge, 1937
Clue of the Tapping Heels, 1939
Mystery of the Brass Bound Trunk, 1940
Mystery at the Moss Covered Mansion, 1941
Quest of the Missing Map, 1942
Clue in the Jewel Box, 1943
Secret in the Old Attic, 1944
Clue in the Crumbling Wall, 1945
Mystery of the Tolling Bell, 1946
Clue in the Old Album, 1947
Ghost of Blackwood Hall, 1948
Clue of the Leaning Chimney, 1949

Nancy Drew, 1950 to 1962, new titles published by Grosset & Dunlap after 1950, unrevised versions (24 or 25 chapters).

1950 – 1953 blue hardcover, frontispiece illustration: ($35.00 with dust jacket) $20.00

1952 – 1962 blue tweed hardcover, 6 illustrations: ($35.00 with dust jacket) $20.00

Yellow spine pictorial hardcovers (beginning 1962) : under $10.00 (Probable first editions: $15.00)

Secret of the Wooden Lady, 1950
Clue of the Black Keys, 1951
Mystery at the Ski Jump, 1952
Clue of the Velvet Mask, 1953
Ringmaster's Secret, 1953
Scarlet Slipper Mystery, 1954
Witch Tree Symbol, 1955
Hidden Mystery, 1956
Haunted Showboat, 1957
Secret of the Golden Pavilion, 1959
Clue in the Old Stagecoach, 1960
Mystery of the Fire Dragon, 1961
Clue of the Dancing Puppet, 1962
Moonstone Castle Mystery, 1963

Clue of the Whistling Bagpipes, 1964
Phantom of Pine Hill, 1965
Mystery of the 99 Steps, 1966
Clue in the Crossword Cipher, 1967
Spider Sapphire Mystery, 1968
Invisible Intruder, 1969
Mysterious Mannequin, 1970
Crooked Bannister, 1971
Secret of Mirror Bay, 1972
Double Jinx Mystery, 1973
Mystery of the Glowing Eye, 1974
Secret of the Forgotten City, 1975
Sky Phantom, 1976
Strange Message in the Parchment, 1977
Mystery of Crocodile Island, 1978
Thirteenth Pearl, 1979

Nancy Drew, revised titles, 1959 – 1961, tweed hardcover, text shortened to 20 chapters. ($20.00 with dust jacket) $10.00

Secret of the Old Clock, 1959 (1930)
Hidden Staircase, 1959 (1930)
Bungalow Mystery, 1960 (1930)
Mystery at Lilac Inn, 1961 (1930)
Secret of Red Gate Farm, 1961 (1931)

Nancy Drew, unrevised titles, 1962 – 1977, yellow pictorial hardcovers. Text length generally 24 to 25 chapters, copyright date shown is original publication date (i.e. text written before 1960s). $15.00

Nancy Drew, revised titles, 1962 – 1977, yellow pictorial hardcovers. Cover art usually by Rudy Nappi. Text shortened to 20 chapters. List below shows original publication date in parentheses. $6.00

Secret of the Old Clock, 1959 (1930)
Hidden Staircase, 1959 (1930)
Bungalow Mystery, 1960 (1930)
Mystery at Lilac Inn, 1961 (1930)
Secret of Red Gate Farm, 1961 (1931)
Clue in the Diary, 1962 (1932)
Secret of Shadow Ranch, 1965 (1930)
Clue of the Broken Locket, 1965 (1934)
Password to Larkspur Lane, 1966 (1932)
Ghost of Blackwood Hall, 1967 (1948)
Clue of the Leaning Chimney, 1967 (1949)
Secret of the Wooden Lady, 1967 (1950)
Nancy's Mysterious Letter, 1968 (1932)
Sign of the Twisted Candles, 1968 (1932)
Clue of the Black Keys, 1968 (1951)
Mystery at the Ski Jump, 1968 (1952)
Clue of the Tapping Heels, 1969 (1939)
Quest of the Missing Map, 1969 (1942)
Clue of the Velvet Mask, 1969 (1953)
Whispering Statue, 1970 (1937)
Secret in the Old Attic, 1970 (1944)
Mystery of the Moss-Covered Mansion, 1971 (1941)
Message in the Hollow Oak, 1972 (1935)
Haunted Bridge, 1972 (1937)
Clue in the Jewel Box, 1972 (1943)
Clue in the Crumbling Wall, 1973 (1945)
Mystery of the Tolling Bell, 1973 (1946)

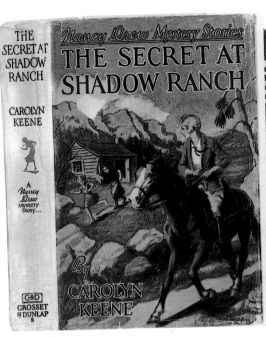

Covers by Tandy, Gillies, Nappi

Mystery of the Ivory Charm, 1974 (1936)
Ringmaster's Secret, 1974 (1953)
Scarlet Slipper Mystery, 1974 (1954)
Witch Tree Symbol, 1975 (1955)
Hidden Window Mystery, 1975 (1956)
Mystery of the Brass-Bound Trunk, 1976 (1940)
Clue in the Old Album, 1977 (1947)

Nancy Drew, related titles:

Nancy Drew, British editions, ca. 1960s Sampson Loew, hardcovers. ($25.00 with dust jackets) $10.00

Nancy Drew, British editions, ca. 1970 – 1990s Collins, color illustrated hardcovers, b/w frontispiece. $10.00

Nancy Drew Cookbook: Clues to Good Cooking, 1973 Grosset & Dunlap, yellow illustrated hardcover, red endpapers. First printing (1973 on copyright page, no other dates) $40.00 Later printings, white endpapers: $20.00.

Nancy Drew Cameo Editions, 1959 – 60 Grosset & Dunlap, book club hardcovers with "cameo locket" picture of Nancy on endpapers, color dust jackets by Polly Bolian, 9 illustrations per volume. ($30.00 with dust jacket) $10.00

Nancy Drew Double Editions, ca. 1970s Grosset & Dunlap, lavender spine pictorial hardcover, each volume contains two revised (post – 1959) versions of Nancy Drew novels. $10.00.

Nancy Drew Triple Editions, ca. late 1960s or early 1970s Grosset & Dunlap, pictorial hardcover, each volume contains three revised (post-1959) versions of Nancy Drew novels. $10.00.

Picture Book Nancy Drew, 1977 Grosset & Dunlap, 2 titles, oversized pictorial hardcover, 62 pages, illustrated, easier vocabulary for younger readers. $15.00

Mystery of the Lost Dogs
Secret of the Twin Puppets

NANCY KIMBALL SERIES, Carli Laklan, Doubleday, hardcover. ($25.00 with dust jacket) $10.00

Nurse's Aide, 1962
Nurse in Training, 1965
Second-Year Nurse, 1967

NANCY PEMBROKE SERIES, Margaret Van Epps, 1930 World (also reprinted by Burt), hardcover, about 250 pages. ($25.00 with dust jacket) $10.00

Nancy Pembroke, College Maid
Nancy Pembroke's Vacation in Canada
Nancy Pembroke, Sophomore at Roxford
Nancy Pembroke in New Orleans
Nancy Pembroke, Junior

NAT RIDLEY, Nat Ridley, Jr. (pseudonym), ca. 1926 Garden City Publishing, hardcover. The Nat Ridley character appeared in magazine and dime novel editions also. $30.00

Crime on the Limited, or Nat Ridley in the Follies
Guilty or Not Guilty? or Nat Ridley's Great Race Track Case
In the Nick of Time, or Nat Ridley Saving a Life
Scream in the Dark, or Nat Ridley's Crimson Clue
Tracked to the West, or Nat Ridley at the Magnet Mine

NATHALIE SERIES, Anna Chapin Ray, ca. 1905 Little, Brown, cloth hardcover with print illustration and gilt lettering, color frontispiece and b/w plates by Alice Barber Stephens. $30.00

Nathalie's Chum
Ursula's Freshman
Nathalie's Sister

NATURE MYSTERY SERIES, Mary Adrian, 1956 – 1971 Hastings House, 10 titles, various illustrators. ($20.00 with dust jacket) $10.00
Uranium Mystery, 1956
Fox Hollow Mystery, 1959
Rare Stamp Mystery, 1960
Mystery of the Night Explorers, 1962
Skin Diving Mystery, 1964
Mystery of the Dinosaur Bones, 1965
Indian Horse Mystery, 1966
Kite Mystery, 1968
Lightship Mystery, 1969
Ghost Town Mystery, 1971

NAVY BOYS SERIES, William Chipman, Frederick Ober, James Otis, 1898 – 1904 Burt editions, pictorial hardcover, frontispiece, originally published as individual novels by the three authors under various titles, then re-titled to form a series on a theme of navy adventures for boys. Some of these novels may be found in other series. ($35.00 with dust jacket) $10.00
Navy Boys in New York Bay
Navy Boys in Defense of Liberty
Navy Boys on Long Island Sound
Navy Boys at the Siege of Havana
Navy Boys with Grant at Vicksburg
Navy Boys Cruise with John Paul Jones
Navy Boys on Lake Ontario
Navy Boys' Cruise to the Bahamas

Navy Boys in the Track of the Enemy
Navy Boys' Daring Capture
Navy Boys' Cruise with Columbus

NAVY BOYS SERIES, Halsey Davidson, 1918 – 1920 Sully, gray pictorial hardcover, frontispiece by R. G. Herbert, World War I stories for boys. $30.00
Navy Boys After the Submarines, or Protecting the Giant Convoy
Navy Boys Chasing a Sea Raider, or Landing a Million Dollar Prize
Navy Boys Behind the Big Guns, or Sinking the German U-Boats
Navy Boys to the Rescue, or Answering the Wireless Call for Help
Navy Boys at the Big Surrender, or Rounding Up the German Fleet
Navy Boys on Special Service, or Guarding the Floating Treasury

NED, BOB, AND JERRY see MOTOR BOYS

NEW TOM SWIFT JR. ADVENTURES SERIES see TOM SWIFT

NEWBERY AWARD BOOKS, this award is for writing and content. Started in 1922, the Newbery Award is presented annually by the American Library Association to an author for an outstanding juvenile book. The book is in print before the award is given. Therefore, some people collect the first printing of the winning titles before they were winners, and other collectors look for editions displaying the Newbery Award emblem on the dust jacket. Prices vary widely.
If a book was by a little known writer, the first edition may have had a small printing and will therefore

command a larger price.

After the award is named, the winning book usually has a large printing and even early editions are available to collectors at a modest price: ($25.00 or less with dust jacket) $15.00

Exceptions are works of authors who then went on to much greater fame, and the large early printings still don't meet collector demand. Into this category often fall works of author-illustrators, such as Lois Lenski.

Other exceptions are books that are part of a popular series and have a cross-over demand from collectors.

Story of Mankind, Hendrik Willem van Loon, 1922
Voyages of Dr. Dolittle, Hugh Lofting, 1923
Dark Frigate, Charles Boardman Hawes, 1924
Tales from Silver Lands, Charles J. Finger, 1925
Shen of the Sea, Arthur Chrisman, 1926
Smoky, the Cowhorse, Will James, 1927
Gay-Neck, Dhan Gopal Mukerji, 1928
Trumpeter of Krakow, Eric Kelly, 1929
Hitty, Her First Hundred Years, Rachel Field, 1930
Cat Who Went to Heaven, Elizabeth Coatsworth, 1931
Waterless Mountain, Laura Adams Armer, 1932
Young Fu of the Upper Yangtze, Elizabeth Lewis, 1933
Invincible Louisa, Cornelia Meigs, 1934
Dobry, Monica Shannon, 1935
Caddie Woodlawn, Carol Ryrie Brink,1936
Roller Skates, Ruth Sawyer, 1937
White Stag, Kate Seredy, 1938
Thimble Summer, Elizabeth Enright, 1939
Daniel Boone, James Daugherty, 1940
Call It Courage, Armstrong Sperry, 1941
Matchlock Gun, Walter Edmonds, 1942
Adam of the Road, Elizabeth Janet Gray, 1943
Johnny Tremain, Esther Forbes, 1944
Rabbit Hill, Robert Lawson, 1945
Strawberry Girl, Lois Lenski, 1946
Miss Hickory, Carolyn Bailey, 1947
Twenty-One Balloons, William Pene du Bois, 1948
King of the Wind, Marguerite Henry, 1949
Door in the Wall, Marguerite de Angeli, 1950
Amos Fortune, Free Man, Elizabeth Yates, 1951
Ginger Pye, Eleanor Estes, 1952
Secret of the Andes, Ann Nolan Clark, 1953
And Now Miguel, Joseph Krumgold, 1954
Wheel of the School, Meindert DeJong, 1955
Carry On, Mr. Bowditch, Jean Lee Latham, 1956
Miracles on Maple Hill, Virginia Sorensen, 1957
Rifles for Watie, Harold Keith, 1958
Witch of Blackbird Pond, Elizabeth George Speare, 1959
Onion John, Joseph Krumgold, 1960
Island of the Blue Dolphins, Scott O'Dell, 1961
Bronze Bow, Elizabeth George Speare, 1962
Wrinkle in Time, Madeleine L'Engle
It's Like This, Cat, Emily Neville, 1964
Shadow of the Bull, Maia Wojciechowska, 1965

I, Juan de Pareja, Elizabeth de Trevinor, 1966
Up a Road Slowly, Irene Hunt, 1967
From the Mixed up Files of Mrs. Basil E. Frankweiler, E. L. Konigsburg, 1968
High King, Lloyd Alexander, 1969
Sounder, William H. Armstrong, 1970
Summer of the Swans, Betsy Byars, 1971
Mrs. Frisby and the Rats of Nimh, Robert O'Brien, 1972
Julie of the Wolves, Jean Craighead George, 1973
Slave Dancer, Paula Fox, 1974
M. C. Higgins, the Great, Virginia Hamilton, 1975
Grey King, Susan Cooper, 1976
Roll of Thunder, Hear My Cry, Mildred Taylor, 1977
Bridge to Terabithia, Katherine Paterson, 1978
Westing Game, Ellen Raskin, 1979
Gathering of Days, Joan W. Blos, 1980
Jacob I Have Loved, Katherine Paterson, 1981
Visit to William Blake's Inn, Nancy Willard, 1982
Dicey's Song, Cynthia Voigt, 1983
Dear Mr. Henshaw, Beverly Cleary, 1984
Hero and the Crown, Robin McKinley, 1985
Sarah, Plain and Tall, Patricia MacLachlan, 1986
Whipping Boy, Sid Fleischman, 1987
Lincoln, a Photobiography, Russell Freedman, 1988
Joyful Noise: Poems for Two Voices, Paul Fleischman, 1989
Number the Stars, Lois Lowry, 1990
Maniac Magee, Jerry Spinelli, 1991
Shiloh, Phyllis Naylor, 1992
Missing May, Cynthia Rylant, 1993
Giver, Lois Lowry, 1994
Walk Two Moons, Sharon Creech, 1995
Midwife's Apprentice, Karen Cushman, 1996
View from Saturday, E. L. Konigsburg, 1997

NEWSPAPER SERIES see LARRY DEXTER

NICK CARTER was a fictitious detective, probably created by John Coryell. The Nick Carter stories first appeared in Street & Smith magazines in the 1890s, written by Coryell and several other writers using the Nick Carter pseudonym, and then were reprinted and expanded in numerous paperback formats. The pseudonym was later used by the Stratemeyer Syndicate, and at various times stories were collected or reprinted in a number of series, some in hardcover. *Stratemeyer Pseudonyms and Series Books*, Deidre Johnson, 1982 Greenwood Press, does an excellent job of sorting out these titles.

Following are a few of the early undated Whitman editions, ca. 1920 – 1930s, cardboard or thin hardcover. ($30.00 with dust jacket) $15.00

Man Who Stole Millions
Stolen Race Horse
Stolen Pay Train
Secret Agents in Brazil
Triple Crime
Gideon Drexel's Millions

Nick Carter, modern collection:
Nick Carter, Detective: Six Astonishing Adventures, 1963 Macmillan, hardcover, compiled by Robert Clurman. ($20.00 with dust jacket) $10.00

NOEL AND HENRY SERIES, Josephine Pullein-Thompson, 1946-1957 Collins, hardcover, 5 titles, English "pony" series. ($15.00 with dust jacket) $10.00
Six Ponies, 1946
Pony Club Team, 1950
Radney Riding Club, 1951
One Day Event, 1954
Pony Club Camp, 1957

NOISY VILLAGE SERIES, Astrid Lindgren, Viking, hardcover, b/w illustrations by Ilon Wikland. First edition with dust jacket: $50.00 Later printings: ($25.00 with dust jacket) $15.00
Children of Noisy Village, 1962
Happy Times in Noisy Village, 1963
Christmas in Noisy Village, 1964
Springtime in Noisy Village, 1966

NORA AND TEDDY, Hurwitz see RUSSELL

NORMAN CARVER see TWO LIVE BOYS

NORTH POLE SERIES, Edwin James Houston (1847 – 1914), 1907 Winston, green pictorial hardcover, four plates by Louis Dougherty, map, 370+ pages. Hard-to-find. $60.00
Search for the North Pole
Discovery of the North Pole
Cast Away at the North Pole

NORTH STAR BOOKS, 1950 Houghton Mifflin, hardcover. ($20.00 with dust jacket) $10.00
Titles include:
Gold in California, Paul I. Wellman
Sailing the Seven Seas, Mary Ellen Chase
Thoreau of Walden Pond, Sterling North
Ticonderoga: Story of a Fort, Bruce Lancaster

NORTHBANK SPORTS SERIES, Ralph Henry Barbour,

1921 – 1922 Appleton, pictorial hardcover, frontispiece, school sports by the most prolific author in that category, and some of these titles may appear in other series.
Early editions: $35.00
Three Base Benson
Kick Formation
Coxswain of the Eight

NORTHWEST SERIES, LeRoy W. Snell (except as noted), ca. 1930s Cupples & Leon, cloth-on-board cover, illustrated endpaper, frontispiece, Canadian Royal Mounted Police novels for boys. Some of these titles also appear in Reilly's Radio-Phone Boys Series. ($25.00 with dust jacket) $10.00
Lead Disk
Shadow Patrol
Wolf Cry
Spell of the North
Challenge of the Yukon
Phantom of the Rivers
Sergeant Dick, author Rowe
Carcajou
Danger Trails North, author Bennett

NURSES THREE SERIES, Jean Kirby, Whitman, color illustrated hardcover, adventures of the three Scott sisters. $10.00
Kelly Scott: A Career for Kelly, 1963
Penny Scott: First Assignment, 1963
Tracy Scott: A Very Special Girl, 1963
Kelly Scott: On Call for Trouble, 1964
Penny Scott: Danger Island, 1964
Tracy Scott: Tracy's Little People, 1965
Penny Scott: Olympic Duty, 1965
Nurses Three, related books:
There are two paper doll books of the Scott sisters, ca. 1964 and 1965.

——— ○ ———

O'KEEFE FAMILY see AUSTINS

OAKDALE ACADEMY SERIES, Morgan Scott, 1911 – 1913 Hurst, impressed illustration on hardcover, four b/w plates by Martin Lewis, 300+ pages. $30.00
Burt edition, hardcover. ($40.00 with dust jacket) $15.00
Ben Stone at Oakdale
Boys of Oakdale Academy
Rival Pitchers of Oakdale
Oakdale Boys In Camp
Great Oakdale Mystery
New Boys at Oakdale

OBADIAH SERIES, Brinton Turkle, ca. 1970s Dutton,

oblong hardcover, color illustrations by author. First edition with dust jacket: $75.00 Later printings and book club edition: ($35.00 with dust jacket) $20.00

Thy Friend, Obadiah
Obadiah the Bold
Adventures of Obadiah
Rachel and Obadiah

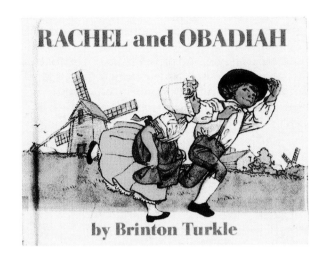

OCEAN WIRELESS BOYS SERIES, Capt. Wilbur Lawton, 1914–1917 Hurst, pictorial hardcover, frontispiece and plates, more exciting radio-adventure stories for boys. $20.00

Ocean Wireless Boys on the Atlantic
Ocean Wireless Boys and the Lost Liner
Ocean Wireless Boys of the Iceberg Patrol
Ocean Wireless Boys and the Naval Code
Ocean Wireless Boys on the Pacific
Ocean Wireless Boys on Warswept Seas

OLD DEERFIELD SERIES, Mary Smith, 1904 – 1909 Little, Brown, gray pictorial hardcover with red letters, four to six plates, some by Bridgman, American colonies novels for boys. ($20.00 with dust jacket) $10.00

Boy Captive of Old Deerfield
Boy Captive in Canada
Boys of the Border
Boys and Girls of Seventy-Seven

OLD GLORY SERIES, Edward Stratemeyer, ca. 1900 Lee & Shepard, illustrated hardcover, b/w illustrations by A. B. Shute, also re-issued in editions with somewhat altered titles. $25.00

Under Dewey at Manila, or The War Fortunes of a Castaway
Young Volunteer in Cuba, or Fighting for the Single Star
Fighting in Cuban Waters, or Under Schley on the Brooklyn
Under Otis in the Philippines, or A Young Officer in the Tropics

Campaign of the Jungle, or Under Lawton Through Luzon
Under MacArthur in Luzon, or Last Battles in the Philippines

OLD SQUIRE'S FARM SERIES, Charles Asbury Stephens, 1912 – 1914 Mason, gray hardcover with gilt lettering, plates. $20.00

When Life was Young at the Old Farm
Haps and Mishaps at the Old Farm
Great Year of Our Lives at the Old Squire's
Busy Year at the Old Squire's

OLD YELLER SERIES, Fred Gipson, Harper, hardcover, dog stories.
Early editions: ($25.00 with dust jacket) $10.00
Old Yeller, 1956
Savage Sam, 1962
Little Arliss, 1978

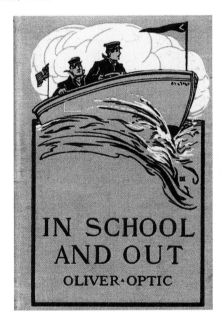

OLIVER OPTIC SERIES (William T. Adams, 1822 – 1897), Adams was a prolific writer of adventure novels for young readers. His numerous titles cross-over in series and appear under other series names. His series dealing with Civil War themes are his most popular.

Early editions with Civil War themes, gilt-decorated or gilt lettered hardcovers, generally sell in the $35.00 to $50.00 range.

Early editions with non-Civil War themes, gilt-decorated or gilt lettered hardcovers, generally sell in the $20.00 to $40.00 range.

Post-1900 editions: $15.00

Boat Club, or Bunkers of Rippleton, 1855, may have been the first Optic title for children, printed as an individual title, but in later editions it was included in various series.

Oliver Optic Series: All-Over-the-World

Millionaire at Sixteen, or Cruise of the Guardian-

Mother, 1892

Up and Down the Nile, or Young Adventurers in Africa, 1894

Young Navigators, or Foreign Cruise of the Maud, 1893

Pacific Shores, or Adventures in Eastern Seas, 1898

Oliver Optic Series: American Boy

Little by Little, or Cruise of the Flyaway

Young Knight Errant, or Cruising in the West Indies

Oliver Optic Series: Army and Navy, 1860s – 1890s Lee and Shepard, brown cloth-over-board cover with gilt, Civil War novels.

Yankee Middy

Young Lieutenant, 1865

Oliver Optic Series: Blue and Gray, ca. 1880s Lee & Shepard, blue and gray cloth-over-board cover with gilt, small, b/w illustrations, Civil War novels.

At the Front

Fighting for the Right, 1892

Taken by the Enemy

On the Blockade, 1890

Within the Enemy's Lines, 1889

Lieutenant at Eighteen, 1895

An Undivided Union (last book in series, completed by Edward Stratemeyer, hard-to-find, double price), 1899

Oliver Optic Series: Goldwing Club, 1880s Lee & Shepard, pictorial hardcover, small, 340+ pages.

Titles include:

All Adrift, 1883

Oliver Optic Series: Great Western, ca. 1870s

Going South, or Yachting on the Atlantic Coast

Lake Breezes, or Cruise of the Sylvania

Going West, or Perils of a Poor Boy, 1875

Going South, or Yachting on the Atlantic Coast, 1879

Oliver Optic Series: Lake Shore, ca. 1870s Lee & Shepard, cloth-over-board cover, small, b/w illustrations.

Bear and Forbear

Brake Up, or Young Peacemakers

Lightning Express, or Rival Academies

Through by Daylight, or Young Engineer of the Lake Shore Railroad

On Time, or Young Captain

Oliver Optic Series: Sailor Boy, undated Donohue, color illustrated cloth-over-board cover.

Titles include:

Sailor Boy, or Jack Somers in the Navy

Oliver Optic Series: Soldier Boy, Donohue or A. L. Burt, decorated hardcover.

Fighting Joe, Soldier Boy

Fighting Joe, Fortunes of a Staff Officer

Tom Somers in the Army

Oliver Optic Series: Starry Flag

Freaks of Fortune, or Half Round the World

Make or Break, or Rich Man's Daughter

Oliver Optic Series: Upward and Onward, ca. 1860s

Field and Forest, or Fortunes of a Farmer

Plane and Plank, or Mishaps of a Mechanic

Poor and Proud, or Fortunes of Katy Redburn

Oliver Optic Series: Yacht Club, ca. 1870s, blue cloth-over-board cover with gold lettering and sailing vessel decoration, small, b/w illustrations. Titles include:

Little Bobtail

Oliver Optic Series: Young America Abroad, 1870s – 1890s Lee & Shepard, cloth-over-board cover with gilt lettering and ship, frontispiece illustration, 300+ pages.

Dikes and Ditches, Young America in Holland and Belgium

Cross and Crescent, Young America in Turkey and Greece

Down the Rhine, Young America in Germany

Outward Bound, Young America Afloat

Palace or Cottage, Young America in France and Switzerland

Red Cross, or Young America in England and Wales

Sunny Shores, Young America in Italy and Austria

Northern Lands, or Young America in Russia and Prussia

Oliver Optic Series, ca. 1910 Hurst, reprints of a number of titles with no theme, gray cloth-over-board cover with impressed boat design, frontispiece illustration of William T. Adams and his signature, 250+ pages.

All Aboard

Boat Club

Brave Old Salt

Do Something

Fighting Joe

Haste and Waste

Hope and Have

In School and Out

Little by Little

Little Merchant

Now or Never

Outward Bound

Poor and Proud

Proud and Lazy

Rich and Humble

Sailor Boy

Soldier Boy

Try Again

Watch and Wait

Work and Win

Yankee Middy

Young Lieutenant

OLLIE'S TEAM SERIES, C. Philbrook, Hastings House, hardcover. ($20.00 with dust jacket) $10.00

Ollie's Team and the Baseball Computer, 1967

Ollie's Team and the Football Computer, 1968

Ollie's Team and the Basketball Computer, 1969

Ollie's Team Plays Baseball, 1970

Ollie, the Backward Forward, 1971

Ollie's Team and the Alley Cats, 1971

Ollie's Team and the 200 Pound Problem, 1972

Ollie's Team and the Million Dollar Mistake, 1973

ONE END STREET SERIES, Eve Garnett, ca. 1940s Vanguard, hardcover, bw drawings by author. First edition with dust jacket: $100.00 Later printings: ($30.00 with dust jacket) $15.00
Family from One End Street
Further Adventures of Family from One End Street
Holiday at Dewdrop Inn

ORIOLE PUTNAM SERIES, Amy Bell Marlowe, 1920s Grosset, three titles which were part of the Marlow Books for Girls. ($30.00 with dust jacket) $15.00

ORPHELINES SERIES, Natalie Savage Carlson, Harper, oversize, illustrated hardcover, charming b/w illustrations by Fermin Rocker or Garth Williams. Girls in a French orphanage create their own family through a number of funny adventures. First edition: ($30.00 with dust jacket) $15.00
Happy Orpheline, 1957
Brother for the Orphelines, 1959
Pet for the Orphelines, 1962
Orphelines in the Enchanted Castle, 1964
Grandmother for the Orphelines, 1964

OUR BOYS SERIES, Capt. William Perry, 1918 – 1919 Saalfield, hardcover, frontispiece by Clare Angell, World War I novels for boys. $20.00
Our Jackies with the Fleet
Our Pilots in the Air
Our Sammies in the Trenches

OUR LITTLE COUSIN SERIES, Mary Hazelton Wade, Elizabeth MacDonald, Isaac Headland, Blanche McManus, H. Lee Pike, Edward Butler, Mary Nixon-Roulet, Claire Coburn, ca. 1900 – 1905 Page, decorated hardcover, color illustrations. $25.00
Our Little African Cousin
Our Little Armenian Cousin
Our Little Brown Cousin
Our Little Canadian Cousin
Our Little Chinese Cousin
Our Little Cuban Cousin
Our Little Dutch Cousin
Our Little English Cousin
Our Little Eskimo Cousin
Our Little French Cousin
Our Little German Cousin
Our Little HawaiianCousin
Our Little Indian Cousin
Our Little Irish Cousin
Our Little Italian Cousin
Our Little Japanese Cousin
Our Little Jewish Cousin
Our Little Korean Cousin
Our Little Mexican Cousin
Our Little Norwegian Cousin
Our Little Panama Cousin
Our Little Philippine Cousin
Our Little Porto Rican Cousin
Our Little Russian Cousin
Our Little Scotch Cousin
Our Little Siamese Cousin
Our Little Spanish Cousin
Our Little Swedish Cousin
Our Little Swiss Cousin
Our Little Turkish Cousin

OUR LITTLE COUSIN SERIES, continuing the earlier series, Clara Winlow, 1911 – 25 Page, hardcover, illustrated. $15.00
Our Little Bohemian Cousin
Our Little Bulgarian Cousin
Our Little Carthaginian Cousin
Our Little Czecho-Slovak Cousin
Our Little Finnish Cousin
Our Little Jugoslav Cousin
Our Little Roumanian Cousin
Our Little Ukrainian Cousin

OUR LITTLE FRIENDS SERIES, Frances Carpenter, 1931 – 41 American Book, hardcover, 2-color illustrations. $15.00
Our Little Friends of China
Our Little Friends of Eskimo Land
Our Little Friends of the Arabian Desert
Our Little Friends of Norway
Our Little Friends of Switzerland

OUR YOUNG AEROPLANE SCOUTS SERIES, Horace

Porter, 1914 – 17 Burt, printed illustration on cloth-over-board cover, b/w frontispiece. ($35.00 with dust jacket) $15.00
Our Young Aeroplane Scouts in England
Our Young Aeroplane Scouts in Italy
Our Young Aeroplane Scouts in France and Belgium
Our Young Aeroplane Scouts in Germany
Our Young Aeroplane Scouts in Russia
Our Young Aeroplane Scouts in Turkey
Our Young Aeroplane Scouts in the Balkans

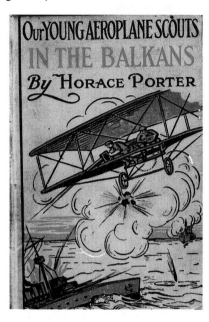

OUTBOARD BOYS SERIES, Roger Garis, 1933 – 34 Burt, cloth-over-board cover, frontispiece by Warre, mysteries for boys. ($50.00 with dust jacket) $10.00
Outboard Boys at Mystery Island, or Solving the secret of the Hidden Cove
Outboard Boys at Shadow Lake, or Solving the Secret of the Strange Monster
Outboard Boys at Pirate Beach, or Solving the Secret of the Houseboat
Outboard Boys at Shark River, or Solving the Secret of the Mystery Tower

OUTDOOR CHUMS SERIES, Captain Quincy Allen (Stratemeyer Syndicate pseudonym), ca. 1911 Grosset, illustrated tan cloth-over-board hardcover. $20.00
Goldsmith reprints: ($15.00 in dust jacket) $10.00
Outdoor Chums
Outdoor Chums on the Lake
Outdoor Chums in the Forest
Outdoor Chums on the Gulf
Outdoor Chums after a Big Game
Outdoor Chums on a House Boat
Outdoor Chums in the Big Woods
Outdoor Chums at Cabin Point

OUTDOOR GIRLS SERIES, Laura Lee Hope (Strate-meyer Syndicate pseudonym), 1913 – 33 Grosset, hardcover, b/w illustrations. ($30.00 with dust jacket) $10.00
Outdoor Girls at Deepdale
Outdoor Girls at Rainbow Lake
Outdoor Girls in a Motor Car
Outdoor Girls in a Winter Camp
Outdoor Girls in Florida
Outdoor Girls at Ocean View
Outdoor Girls on Pine Island
Outdoor Girls in Army Service
Outdoor Girls at Hostess House
Outdoor Girls at Bluff Point
Outdoor Girls at Wild Rose Lodge
Outdoor Girls in the Saddle
Outdoor Girls Around the Campfire
Outdoor Girls on Cape Cod
Outdoor Girls at Foaming Falls
Outdoor Girls Along the Coast
Outdoor Girls at Spring Hill Farm
Outdoor Girls at New Moon Ranch
Outdoor Girls on a Hike
Outdoor Girls on a Canoe Trip
Outdoor Girls at Cedar Ridge
Outdoor Girls in the Air
Outdoor Girls in Desert Valley

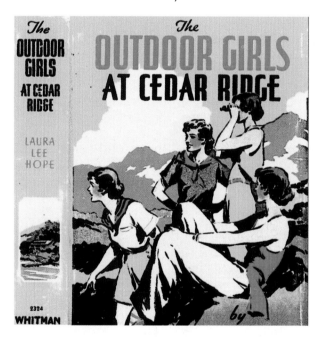

OVER THERE SERIES, Capt. George Ralphson, 1919 – 1920 Donohue, hardcover, frontispiece, World War I novels for boys. ($25.00 with dust jacket) $10.00
Over There with the Marines at Chateau Thierry
Over There with the Canadian at Vimy Ridge
Over There with the Doughboys at St. Mihiel
Over There with Pershing's Heroes at Cantigny
Over There with the Engineers at Cambrai
Over There with the Tanks in the Argonne Forest

OX SERIES, John Ney, Little, Brown or Lippincott, hardcover, misadventures of a rich kid. First edition: ($25.00 with dust jacket) $10.00
Ox, the Story of the Kid at the Top, 1970
Ox Goes North, 1973
Ox Under Pressure, 1976
Ox and the Prime-Time Kid, 1985

— P —

PAGE TWINS see TWINS, Dorothy Whitehill

PAM AND PENNY SERIES, Rosamund du Jardin (1902 – 1963), 1950s Lippincott, hardcover. See also MARCY RHODES and TOBY HEYDON. First edition with dust jacket: $150.00 Later editions: ($25.00 with dust jacket) $10.00
Double Date, 1952
Double Feature, 1953
Showboat Summer, 1955
Double Wedding, 1958

PAN-AMERICAN SERIES, Edward Stratemeyer, 1902 – 1911 Lee & Shepard; Lothrop, Lee and Shepard, pictorial hardcover, gilt lettering on spine, some Charles Nuttall illustrations. First edition, wide price variation from $35.00 to $100.00
Lost on the Orinoco, or American Boys in Venezuela
Young Volcano Explorers, or American Boys in the West Indies
Young Explorers of the Isthmus, or American Boys in Central America
Young Explorers of the Amazon, or American Boys in Brazil
Treasure Seekers of the Andes, or American Boys in Peru
Chased Across the Pampas, or American Boys in Argentina

PARRI MacDONALD SERIES, Janet Lambert, Dutton, hardcover. First edition: ($175.00 with dust jacket) $40.00
Introducing Parri, 1962

That's My Girl, 1964
Stagestruck Parri, 1966

PATIENCE SERIES, Lorna Hill, 1951 – 1955 Burke, hardcover. See also DANCING PEELS, MARJORIE, SADLER WELLS, and VICARAGE CHILDREN. ($25.00 with dust jacket) $10.00
They Called Her Patience, 1951
It Was All Through Patience, 1952
So Guy Came Too, 1954
Five Shilling Holiday, 1955

PATRICK PENNINGTON SERIES, Karen Peyton, Crowell, hardcover.
First edition: ($25.00 with dust jacket) $10.00
Pennington's Last Term, 1970
Pennington's Seventeenth Summer, 1970
Beethoven's Medal, 1971
Pennington's Heir, 1973
Marion's Angels, 1979

PATRIOT LAD SERIES, Russell Carter, Penn Publishing, green hardcover with paste-on-pictorial, 3 b/w plates, first five titles illustrated by Henry Pitz. ($20.00 with dust jacket) $10.00
Patriot Lad of Old Boston, 1923
Patriot Lad of Old Philadelphia, 1924
Patriot Lad of Old Salem, 1925
Patriot Lad of Old Trenton, 1926
Patriot Lad of Old Cape Cod, 1927
Patriot Lad of Old Long Island, 1928
Patriot Lad of Old Saratoga, 1929
Patriot Lad of Old Rhode Island, 1930
Patriot Lad of Old Maine, 1932
Patriot Lad of Old New Hampshire, 1933
Patriot Lad of Old Connecticut, 1935
Patriot Lad of Old West Point, 1936

PATSY CARROLL SERIES, Grace Gordon, ca. 1920 Cupples, small size, illustrated cloth cover, illustrations, advertised as "a series permeated with the vibrant atmosphere of the great outdoors" ($25.00 with dust jacket) $10.00
Patsy Carroll at Wilderness Lodge
Patsy Carroll under Southern Skies
Patsy Carroll in the Golden West
Patsy Carroll in Old New England

PATTY AND GINGER SERIES, Janet Lambert, 1950s Dutton, hardcover. Book Club edition: ($35.00 with dust jacket) $20.00
We're Going Steady, first edition: ($150.00 with dust jacket) $20.00
Boy Wanted, first edition: ($75.00 with dust jacket) $20.00
Spring Fever, first edition: ($75.00 with dust jacket) $20.00
Summer Madness, first edition: ($75.00 with dust jacket) $20.00

Extra Special, first edition: ($75.00 with dust jacket) $20.00

On Her Own, first edition: ($150.00 with dust jacket) $20.00

PATTY FAIRFIELD SERIES, Carolyn Wells, 1901 – 1919 Dodd, Mead, decorated hardcover, seventeen titles. $20.00
Grosset reprints: ($25.00 with dust jacket) $10.00
Patty Fairfield
Patty at Home
Patty in the City
Patty's Summer Days
Patty in Paris
Patty's Friends
Patty's Pleasure Trip
Patty's Success
Patty's Motor Car
Patty's Butterfly Days
Patty's Social Season
Patty's Suitors
Patty's Romance
Patty's Fortune
Patty Blossom
Patty Bride
Patty and Azalea

PATTY LOU SERIES, Basil Miller, 1942 – 50 Zondervaan, 9 titles. $10.00

PAUL AND PEGGY SERIES, Florence E. Scott, Hurst, hardcover. $20.00
Here and There with Paul and Peggy, 1914
Across the Continent with Paul and Peggy, 1915
Through Yellowstone with Paul and Peggy, 1916

PEACE GREENFIELD SERIES, Ruth Alberta Brown, ca. 1912 Saalfield, hardcover, b/w frontispiece by Corinne Bailey. ($25.00 with dust jacket) $10.00
At the Little Brown House
Lilac Lady
Heart of Gold

PECK'S BAD BOY SERIES, Hon. George W. Peck, ca. 1900 Thompson & Thomas, Chicago, American edition, impressed illustration on hardcover, b/w illustrations by D. S. Groesbeck and R. W. Taylor. $25.00
Peck's Bad Boy and His Pa
Peck's Uncle Ike
How Private Peck Put Down the Rebellion
Peck's Bad Boy Abroad
Grocery Man and Peck's Bad Boy

PEE WEE DEWIRE SERIES, Lewis Theiss, Wilde, hardcover, b/w illustrations, World War II adventures of Pee Wee Dewire and Colvin Criswell. See MAIL PILOT SERIES. First edition: ($50.00 to $100.00 with dust jacket) $20.00

Flying with the CAA: How Two of Uncle Sam's Youngest Airmen Saved a Great Defense Plant, 1941
Flying for Uncle Sam: A Story of Civilian Pilot Training, 1942
Flying with the Coastal Patrol, 1943

PEE WEE HARRIS SERIES, Percy Fitzhugh, 1922 – 1930 Grosset & Dunlap, hardcover, Fitzhugh's comic version of Boy Scout adventures, four b/w plates by Barbour. Early edition: ($40.00 with dust jacket) $10.00
Pee Wee Harris, 1922
Pee Wee Harris on the Trail, 1922
Pee Wee Harris in Camp, 1922
Pee Wee Harris in Luck, 1922
Pee Wee Harris Adrift, 1922
Pee Wee Harris, F O B Bridgeboro, 1923
Pee Wee Harris: Fixer, 1924
Pee Wee Harris as Good as His Word, 1925
Pee Wee Harris: Mayor for a Day, 1926
Pee Wee Harris and the Sunken Treasure, 1927
Pee Wee Harris on the Briny Deep, 1928
Pee Wee Harris in Darkest Africa, 1929
Pee Wee Harris Turns Detective, 1930

PEGGY LANE THEATER SERIES, Virginia Hughes, ca. 1960s Grosset & Dunlap, color illustrated hardcover, b/w illustrations by Sergio Leone. $10.00
Peggy Finds the Theater
Peggy Plays Off-Broadway
Peggy Goes Straw Hat
Peggy on the Road
Peggy Goes Hollywood
Peggy's London Debut
Peggy Plays Paris
Peggy's Roman Holiday

PEGGY LEE SERIES, Anna Andrews, Cupples & Leon, hardcover, stories set on a coffee plantation in Central America. ($25.00 with Russell Tandy dust jacket) $15.00
Peggy Lee of the Golden Thistle Plantation, 1931
Peggy Lee and the Mysterious Islands, 1931
Peggy Lee, Sophomore, 1932
Peggy Lee Stories for Girls, 1936

PEGGY RAYMOND see FRIENDLY TERRACE

PEGGY STEWART SERIES, Gabrielle E. Jackson, 1911 – 12 Macmillan, 1920 – 21 Putnam, hardcover. ($30.00 with dust jacket) $15.00
Peggy Stewart, 1911
Peggy Stewart at School, 1912
Peggy Stewart Navy Girl at Home, 1920
Peggy Stewart Navy Girl at School, 1921

PEMROSE LORRY SERIES, Isabel Hornibrook, 1921 – 1926 Little, Brown, illustrated by Nana Bickford.

($30.00 with dust jacket) $15.00
Pemrose Lorry, Camp Fire Girl
Pemrose Lorry, Radio Amateur
Pemrose Lorry, Sky Sailor
Pemrose Lorry, Torchbearer

PENELOPE SERIES, Kate Douglas Wiggin, ca. 1910 – 1915 Houghton Mifflin, hardcover, frontispiece. Also published by Gay & Bird, London, with Charles Brock illustrations. $30.00
Penelope's Experiences
Penelope's Irish Experiences
Penelope's Progress
Penelope's Postscripts

PENNY SERIES, A. Stephen Tring, 1950s Oxford, hardcover, illustrated by T. R. Freeman. ($20.00 with dust jacket) $15.00
Penny Dreadful, 1950
Penny Dramatic
Penny Puzzled, 1955
Penny Penitent, 1956
Penny in Italy, 1957
Penny and the Pageant, 1959
Penny Says Good-bye, 1961

PENNY MARSH SERIES see DODD MEAD CAREER

PENNY NICHOLS SERIES, Joan Clark (Mildred Wirt), Goldsmith, red cloth-over-board cover, Penny's dad runs the Nichols Detective Agency, and somehow Penny is constantly the center of a mystery. Penny is a cute blonde teenager who roars around in her own roadster and lives with her widowed father and motherly housekeeper. The author penned the majority of the early Nancy Drew books and also wrote the Penny Parker books. The three series are fun to compare. ($25.00 with dust jacket) $15.00
Penny Nichols Finds a Clue, 1936
Penny Nichols and the Black Imp, 1936
Penny Nichols and the Mystery of the Lost Key, 1936
Penny Nichols and the Knob Hill Mystery, 1939

PENNY PARKER MYSTERY SERIES, Mildred A. Wirt, 1940s Cupples and Leon, cloth-over-board cover, frontispiece illustration, dust jacket illustrated by K. S. Woerner. Blonde girl sleuth lives with her widowed father and kindly housekeeper, drives her own car (see Penny Nichols series and Nancy Drew series), but is much sassier and independent than Nichols or Drew. She is also an extremely careless driver. ($35.00 with dust jacket) $15.00
Tale of the Witch Doll, 1939
Vanishing Houseboat, 1939
Danger at the Drawbridge, 1940
Behind the Green Door, 1940
Clue of the Silken Ladder, 1941
Secret Pact, 1941
Clock Strikes Thirteen, 1942
Wishing Well, 1942
Saboteurs on the River, 1943
Ghost Beyond the Gate, 1943
Hoofbeats on the Turnpike, 1944
Voice from the Cave, 1944

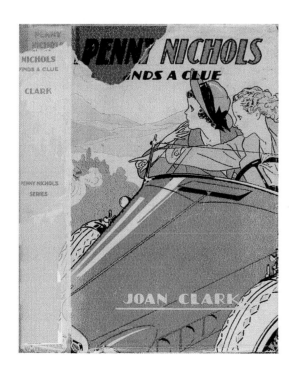

Guilt of the Brass Thieves, 1945
Signal in the Dark, 1946
Whispering Walls, 1946
Swamp Island, 1947
Cry at Midnight, 1947

PENNY PARRISH and TIPPY PARRISH SERIES, also see JORDAN BOOKS, Janet Lambert, 1940s Dutton, first edition hardcover: ($200.00 in dust jacket) $35.00
Grosset reprints. ($50.00 in dust jacket) $20.00
Star Spangled Summer, 1941
Dreams of Glory, 1942
Glory Be!, 1943
Up Goes the Curtain, 1946
Practically Perfect, 1947
Reluctant Heart, 1950
Miss Tippy, 1948
Little Miss Atlas, 1949
Miss America, 1951
Don't Cry, Little Girl, 1952
Rainbow After Rain, 1953, hard-to-find
Welcome Home, Mrs. Jordan, 1953, hard-to-find
Song in Their Hearts, 1956, hard-to-find

PENROD SERIES, Booth Tarkington, Doubleday, hardcover, re-issued continually, Gordon Grant drawings illustrate the first and last titles, illustrations by Worth Brehm in the second title. First editions with dust jacket priced from $50.00 to $200.00
Early editions and reprints: ($35.00 in dust jacket) $10.00
Penrod, 1914
Penrod and Sam, 1916
Penrod Jashber, 1929
Related book:

Penrod: His Complete Story, 1931 Doubleday, collection of the three novels, hardcover. ($50.00 in dust jacket) $15.00

PERRY PIERCE MYSTERY SERIES, Clinton Locke (Stratemeyer Syndicate pseudonym), 1931 – 1934 Altemus; Donohue; Goldsmith, hardcover, frontispiece and dust jacket illustrations by Russell Tandy. ($25.00 in dust jacket) $10.00
Who Closed the Door, or Perry Pierce and the Old Storehouse Mystery
Who Opened the Safe, or Perry Pierce and the Secret Cipher Mystery
Who Hid the Key, or Perry Pierce Tracing Counterfeit Money
Who Took the Papers, or Perry Pierce Gathering the Printed Clues

PETER AND POLLY SERIES, Rose Lucia, American Book Co., ca. 1918, print illustrated cloth-over-board cover, small, 175+ pages, two-color and b/w illustrations. $20.00
Peter and Polly in Summer
Peter and Polly in Winter
Peter and Polly in Spring
Peter and Polly in Auturm

PETER LOOMIS SERIES, Margaret Chalmers, 1914 – 25 Page, 6 titles. $10.00

PETER-PAN TWINS SERIES, Betty Kessler Lyman and Rhoda Chase, illustrator, 1923 – 28 Whitman, oversize color illustrated hardcover with red spine, 12 pages, color illustrations by Rhoda Chase. $35.00
Peter-Pan Twins Are Now in School

Playtime for the Peter-Pan Twins
Peter-Pan Twins Are Glad to Help
Peter Pan Twins Stay at Home
Peter-Pan Twins Return to School

PETER POTTS SERIES, Clifford Hicks, hardcover. ($20.00 in dust jacket) $10.00
Peter Potts, 1971 Dutton
Pop and Peter Potts, 1984 Holt
Peter Potts Book of World Records, 1987 Holt

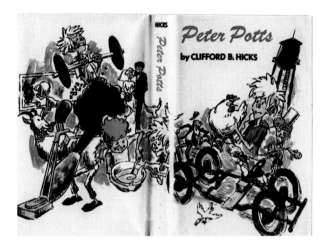

PETERSHAM SERIES, Maud and Miska Petersham, mid-1930s Winston, square or oblong cloth-over-board cover with paste-on-illustration, color illustrations throughout by authors. ($45.00 with dust jacket) $20.00
Story Book of Aircraft
Story Book of Clothes
Story Book of Coal
Story Book of Corn
Story Book of Cotton
Story Book of Food
Story Book of Gold
Story Book of Earth's Treasures
Story Book of Iron and Steel
Story Book of Oil
Story Book of Rayon
Story Book of Rice
Story Book of Sugar
Story Book of Things We Use
Story Book of Wheat

PHANTOM SERIES, Carol Norton, ca. 1930s Saalfield, hardcover. ($20.00 in dust jacket) $10.00
Phantom Town Mystery
Phantom Treasure
Black Box

PHIL BRADLEY SERIES, Silas Boone, 1915 – 1919 New York Book; Donohue, tan pictorial hardcover, frontispiece. ($35.00 in dust jacket) $15.00
Phil Bradley's Mountain Boys, or Birch Bark Lodge
Phil Bradley at the Wheel, or Mountain Boys' Mad

Auto Dash
Phil Bradley's Shooting Box, or Mountain Boys on Currituck Sound
Phil Bradley's Snowshoe Trail, or Mountain Boys in the Canadian Wilds
Phil Bradley's Winning Way
Phil Bradley's Big Exploit

PHILIP KENT SERIES, T. Truxton Hare, ca. 1915 Penn, color paste-on-illustration on cloth-over-board cover, 7 b/w plate illustrations by R. L. Boyer. $15.00
Philip Kent
Philip Kent in Lower School
Philip Kent in Upper School
Philip Kent of Malvern

PHILLIPS EXETER SERIES, Albertus Dudley, 1903 – 1913 Lee & Shepard, then Lothrop, Lee and Shepard, illustration printed on hardcover, plate illustrations by Charles Copeland, also photos, school sports stories. $35.00
Following the Ball
Making the Nine
In the Line
With Mask and Mitt
Great Year
Yale Cup
Full-Back Afloat
Pecks in Camp
Half-Miler

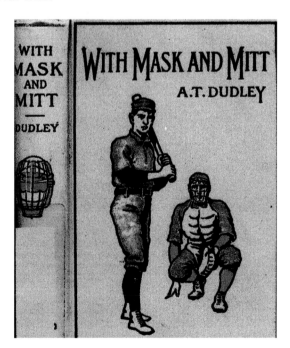

PIET POTTER SERIES, Robert Quackenbush, McGraw-Hill Weekly Reader edition, pictorial hardcover, illustrated by author, mysteries. $10.00
Piet Potter's First Case, 1980
Piet Potter Returns, 1980

Piet Potter to the Rescue, 1981
Piet Potter Strikes Again, 1981
Piet Potter on the Run, 1981
Piet Potter's Hot Clue, 1982

PIGEON CAMP SERIES, Martha James, Lothrop, Lee and Shepard, green hardcover with pictorial, six plates by J. W. Kennedy. $20.00
Jimmie Suter, 1906
Boys of Pigeon Camp, 1907
Hero of Pigeon Camp, 1908

PINCH OF FOUR CORNERS SERIES, Larry Callen, Little Brown, hardcover.   ($20.00 in dust jacket) $10.00
Pinch, 1975
Deadly Mandrake, 1978
Sorrow's Song, 1979
Muskrat War, 1980, dust jacket by Mel Williges

PIONEER BOYS SERIES, Harrison Adams, (Stratemeyer Syndicate pseudonym), 1912 – 1920s Page, hardcover, these titles were also included other series. $20.00
Pioneer Boys of the Ohio
Pioneer Boys on the Great Lakes
Pioneer Boys of the Mississippi
Pioneer Boys of the Missouri
Pioneer Boys of the Yellowstone
Pioneer Boys of the Columbia
Pioneer Boys of the Colorado
Pioneer Boys of Kansas

PIONEER SCOUT SERIES, Everett Tomlinson, Double-day, green hardcover, illustrated by various artists. (These books have also been included in other series.) $25.00
Titles include:
Scouting with Daniel Boone, 1914
Scouting with Kit Carson, 1916
Scouting with General Funston, 1917
Scouting with General Pershing, 1918

PIONEER SERIES, James Otis, 1912 – 1913 American Book Company, brown hardcover, b/w illustrations. $20.00
Hannah of Kentucky: A Story of the Wilderness Road
Benjamin of Ohio: A Story of the Settlement of Marietta
Seth of Colorado: A Story of the Settlement of Denver
Antoine of Oregon: A Story of the Oregon Trail
Martha of California: A Story of the California Trail
Philip of Texas: A Story of Sheep Raising in Texas

POLLY BREWSTER SERIES, Lillan Roy, 1922 – 32 Whitman, hardcover. ($25.00 in dust jacket) $15.00
Polly of Pebbly Pit
Polly and Eleanor
Polly in New York
Polly and Her Friends Abroad

Polly's Business Venture
Polly's Southern Cruise
Polly in South America
Polly in the Southwest
Polly in Alaska
Polly in the Orient
Polly in Egypt
Polly's New Friend
Polly and Carola
Polly and Carola at Ravenswood
Polly Learns to Fly

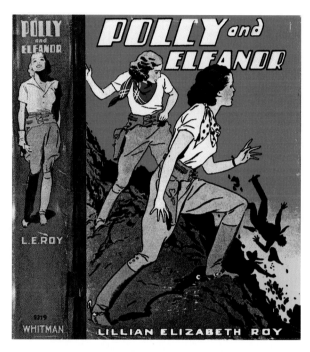

POLLY FRENCH SERIES, Francine Lewis (Helen Wells), ca. 1954 Whitman, laminated pictorial boards with wraparound illustration, small, illustrated endpapers, illustrations throughout by Nina Albright. $20.00
Polly French at Whitford High
Polly French Takes Charge
Polly and the Surprising Stranger

POLLY PRENTISS SERIES, Elizabeth Lincoln Gould, 1913 Penn, hardcover, illustrated by Ida Waugh. $15.00
Little Polly Prentiss
Polly Prentiss Goes A-visiting
Polly Prentiss Goes to School
Polly Prentiss Keeps a Promise

POLLY SERIES, Emma Dowd, 1912 – 21 Houghton, 5 titles, hardcover. $15.00
Polly of the Hospital Staff, 1912
Polly of Lady Gay Cottage, 1913
Polly and the Princess, 1917
When Polly was Eighteen, 1921

POLLY SERIES, Dorothy Whitehill, ca. 1920s Barse, cloth-over-board cover, b/w illustrations. ($20.00

with dust jacket) $10.00
Polly's First Year at Boarding School
Polly's Summer Vacation
Polly's Senior Year at Boarding School
Polly Sees the World at War
Polly and Lois
Polly and Bob
Polly's Reunion
Polly's Polly
Polly at Pixies' Haunt
Polly's House Party

POLLYANNA see GLAD Series

PONY RIDER BOYS SERIES, Frank Patchen, 1920s Saalfield; Altemus, illustrated cloth-over-board cover, b/w illustrations. ($25.00 with dust jacket) $15.00
Pony Rider Boys in the Rockies
Pony Rider Boys in Texas
Pony Rider Boys in Montana
Pony Rider Boys in the Ozarks
Pony Rider Boys in New Mexico
Pony Rider Boys in the Grand Canyon
Pony Rider Boys with the Texas Rangers
Pony Rider Boys on the Blue Ridge
Pony Rider Boys in New England
Pony Rider Boys in Louisiana
Pony Rider Boys in Alaska

POPPY OTT SERIES, Leo Edwards, ca. 1926 – 39 Grosset, advertised as "packed full of the side-splitting adventures which a group of 100% American boys share," first eight titles were illustrated by Bert Salg. ($40.00 with dust jacket) $15.00
Poppy Ott and the Stuttering Parrot
Poppy Ott's Seven League Stilts
Poppy Ott and the Galloping Snail
Poppy Ott's Pedigreed Pickles

Poppy Ott and the Freckled Goldfish
Poppy Ott and the Tittering Totem
Poppy Ott and the Prancing Pancake
Poppy Ott Hits the Trail
Poppy Ott & Co., Inferior Decorators, illustrated by Myrtle Sheldon
Poppy Ott Detective Stories: Monkey's Paw, 1938
Poppy Ott Detective Stories: Hidden Dwarf, 1939

POWER BOYS SERIES, Mel Lyle, Whitman, glossy pictorial hardcover, illustrated by Raymond Burns. $10.00
Mystery of the Flying Skeleton, 1964
Mystery of the Haunted Skyscraper, 1964
Mystery of the Double Kidnapping, 1965
Mystery of the Million Dollar Penny, 1965
Mystery of the Burning Ocean, 1965
Mystery of the Vanishing Lady, 1967

PRINCESS POLLY SERIES, Amy Brooks, (1914 Platt & Peck) undated A. L. Burt reprints, cloth-over-board cover with printed illustration, frontispiece. $15.00
Princess Polly
Princess Polly's Playmates
Princess Polly at School
Princess Polly by the Sea
Princess Polly at Play
Princess Polly's Gay Winter
Princess Polly at Cliffmore

PRUE AND RANDY SERIES, Amy Brooks, 1908 – 13 Lothrop, Lee & Shepard, hardcover with impressed illustration, b/w illustrations by

author. $20.00
Randy's Summer
Randy's Winter
Randy and Her Friends
Little Sister Prue
Prue at School
Prue's Playmates
Randy and Prue

PURPLE PENNANT SERIES, Ralph Henry Barbour, Appleton, hardcover with paste-on-pictorial and gilt lettering, 4 two-color plates by Norman Rockwell, popular with both Barbour and Rockwell collectors. $100.00
Lucky Seventh, 1915
Secret Play, 1915
Purple Pennant, 1916

PUTNAM HALL SERIES, Arthur M. Winfield (Edward Stratemeyer), 1901 – 1911 Mershon; Chatterton; Stitt; Grosset, advertised as "Companion Stories to the famous Rover Boys Series." Putnam Hall was the military academy that the Rover Boys attended. These stories feature different characters. Also, the titles vary somewhat, according to publisher.
With pre-1920 dust jacket: $30.00 to $50.00. Later printings: ($20.00 with dust jacket) $15.00
Grosset used the following titles:
Cadets of Putnam Hall
Rivals of Putnam Hall
Champions of Putnam Hall
Rebellion at Putnam Hall

Camping Out Days at Putnam Hall
Mystery of Putnam Hall

QUEEN HILDEGARDE SERIES see Hildegarde-Margaret Series

QUINNEBASSET SERIES, Sophie May, 1871-91, ca. 1891 boxed set Lee & Shepard, color illustrations.
Set of 6 in original box: $95.00
Individual books: $10.00
Our Helen
In Old Quinnebasset
Janet, A Poor Heiress
Asbury Twins
Doctor's Daughter
Joy Bells

QUIZ KIDS BOOKS, based on the popular radio series.
Quiz Kids Box of Questions and Answers, 1941 Saalfield, paper-over-cardboard box, color illustration from first title, contained four books, each with color illustrated paper cover, 20 pages with quizzes and b/w illustrations. The titles were *This Big World, Questions and Answers, Americas Question Book,* and *Yesterday, Today, Tomorrow.* Price of four books, with box in good condition: $60.00 Price of individual books: $10.00
Quiz Kids, related books:
Quiz Kids and the Crazy Question, ca. 1950s Whitman Authorized Editions, hardcover, illustrated endpapers, b/w illustrations, featuring the Quiz Kids in a

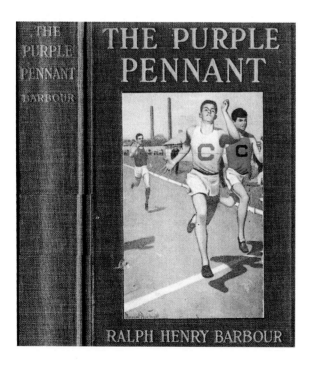

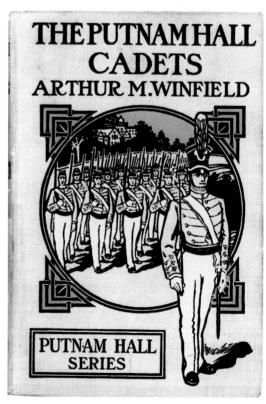

fictional adventure/mystery story. ($25.00 with dust jacket) $10.00

──────── **R** ────────

RACER BOYS SERIES, Clarence Young (Stratemeyer Syndicate pseudonym), 1912 – 1914 Cupples & Leon, brown or green hardcover with design, 4 b/w plates by Walter Rogers. $20.00
Racer Boys, or The Mystery of the Wreck
Racer Boys at Boarding School, or Striving for the Championship
Racer Boys to the Rescue, or Stirring Days in a Winter Camp
Racer Boys on the Prairies, or The Treasure of Golden Peak
Racer Boys on Guard, or The Rebellion at Riverview Hall
Racer Boys Forging Ahead, or The Rivals of the School League
Racer Boys, Frank and Andy series, Vance Barnum (Stratemeyer Syndicate pseudonym), 1921 Sully, reprinted by Whitman, hardcover, re-titled (and new psuedonym) books that were originally published as RACER BOYS. $15.00
Frank and Andy Afloat
Frank and Andy at Boarding School
Frank and Andy in a Winter Camp

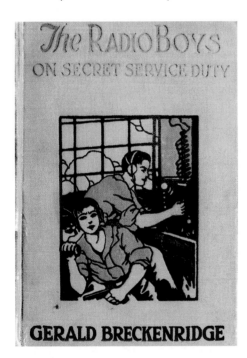

RADIO BOYS SERIES, Gerald Breckenridge, ca. 1920s A. L. Burt, hardcover with gilt lettering and stamped illustration, b/w frontispiece. ($25.00 with dust jacket) $10.00
Radio Boys on the Mexican Border
Radio Boys on Secret Service Duty
Radio Boys with the Revenue Guards

Radio Boys Search for the Incas' Treasure
Radio Boys Rescue the Lost Alaska Expedition
Radio Boys in Darkest Africa
Radio Boys Seek the Lost Atlantis
Radio Boys with the Border Patrol
Radio Boys as Soldiers of Fortune

RADIO BOYS SERIES, Allen Chapman (Stratemeyer Syndicate pseudonym), ca.1907 – 15 Grosset & Dunlap, radio set design on blue hardcover, frontispiece, advertised as "Fascinating radio adventures founded on fact and containing full details of radio work. Each volume has a foreword by Jack Binns, the well known radio expert." First edition (list to title) with dust jacket: $75.00
Later printings: ($40.00 with dust jacket) $15.00
Radio Boys First Wireless
Radio Boys at Ocean Point
Radio Boys at the Sending Station
Radio Boys at Mountain Pass
Radio Boys Trailing a Voice
Radio Boys with the Forest Rangers
Radio Boys with the Iceberg Patrol
Radio Boys with the Flood Fighters
Radio Boys on Signal Island
Radio Boys in Gold Valley
Radio Boys Aiding the Snowbound
Radio Boys on the Pacific
Radio Boys to the Rescue

RADIO BOYS SERIES, ca. 1920 Donohue, hardcover, frontispiece. Radio stories were so popular, Donohue put together this series using several authors. ($40.00 with dust jacket) $15.00
Radio Boys in the Secret Service, Frank Honeywell
Radio Boys on the Thousand Islands, Frank Honeywell
Radio Boys in the Flying Service, J. W. Duffield
Radio Boys Under the Sea, J. W. Duffield
Radio Boys Cronies, Wayne Whipple
Radio Boys Loyalty, Wayne Whipple

RADIO DETECTIVE SERIES, Hyatt Verrill, 1922 Appleton, red hardcover with paste-on-illustration, frontispiece by Richard Holberg. $30.00
Radio Detectives, 1922
Radio Detectives Under the Sea, 1922
Radio Detectives Southward Bound, 1922
Radio Detectives in the Jungle, 1922
Radio Detectives, related title:
Home Radio, How to Make and Use it, Verrill, 1924 Harper, hardcover, 105 pages. $30.00

RADIO GIRLS SERIES, Margaret Penrose (Stratemeyer Syndicate pseudonym), 1920s Cupples & Leon, hardcover, b/w illustrations by Thelma Gooch, later reprinted as part of Goldsmith's CAMPFIRE GIRLS series with title changes. Hard-to-find. $85.00
Radio Girls of Roselawn

Radio Girls on the Program
Radio Girls on Station Island
Radio Girls at Forest Lodge

RADIO PALS SERIES, Charles Ludwig, 1952 – 55 Van Kampen, pictorial hardcover, reprints by Zondervan. $20.00
Radio Pals Marooned
Radio Pals on Bar T Ranch
Radio Pals Fight the Flood
Radio Pals in the Hands of the Mau Mau
Radio Pals in the Flaming Forest

RADIO-PHONE BOYS STORIES, Roy Snell (James Craig), 1922 – 1928 Reilly and Lee, hardcover, frontispiece. Mysteries solved by Curly Carson and his friends using their radio skills. $15.00
Curly Carson Listens In
On the Yukon Trail
Desert Patrol
Sea-Going Tank
Flying Sub
Dark Treasure
Whispering Isles
Invisible Wall

RAILROAD SERIES, Allan Chapman, (Stratemeyer Syndicate pseudonym) ca. 1910 – 1930 Mershon, then Grosset; Chatterton-Peck, advertised as "Railroad stories are dear to the heart of every American boy. Ralph is determined to be a railroad man. He starts at the foot of the ladder but through manly pluck wins out."
Mershon and Chatterton editions, locomotive design printed on red hardcover, 4 b/w plates: $40.00
Grosset editions, light colored hardcover: ($45.00 with dust jacket) $15.00
Ralph in the Round House
Ralph in the Switch Tower
Ralph on the Engine
Ralph on the Overland Express
Ralph the Train Dispatcher
Ralph on the Army Train
Ralph on the Midnight Flyer
Ralph and the Missing Mail Pouch
Ralph on the Mountain Division
Ralph and the Train Wreckers
Ralph on the Railroad, 1933 Grosset, large volume contains the first four Ralph novels

RALPH OSBORN SERIES, Lt. Commander Edward Beach, ca. 1910 Wilde, green hardcover, black lettering, frontispiece and four plates by Frank Merrill. $20.00
Ralph Osborn, Midshipman at Annapolis
Midshipman Ralph Osborn at Sea
Ensign Ralph Osborn, His Trials and Triumphs in a Battleship's Engine Room
Lieutenant Ralph Osborn Aboard a Destroyer

RAMBLER CLUB SERIES, W. Crispin Sheppard, Penn Publishing, pictorial gray hardcover, b/w frontispiece and illustrations by author. First edition: $50.00 Later printings: $20.00
Rambler Club Afloat, 1909
Rambler Club's Winter Camp, 1910
Rambler Club in the Mountains, 1910
Rambler Club on Circle T Ranch, 1911
Rambler Club Among the Lumberjacks, 1911
Rambler Club's Gold Mine, 1912
Rambler Club's Aeroplane, 1912
Rambler Club's Houseboat, 1912
Rambler Club's Motor Car, 1913
Rambler Club's Ball Nine, 1913
Rambler Club with the Northwest Mounted, 1914
Rambler Club's Football Team, 1914
Rambler Club's Motor Yacht, 1915
Rambler Club on the Texas Border, 1915
Rambler Club in Panama, 1916

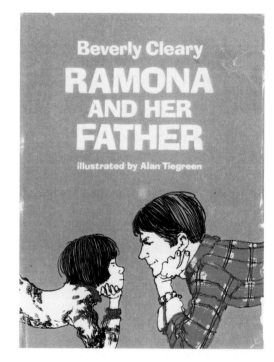

RAMONA QUIMBY SERIES, also see HENRY HUGGINS SERIES, Beverly Cleary, Morrow, hardcover, b/w illustrations. First editions with dust jackets, through *Ramona the Brave*: $60.00
First editions with dust jackets, from *Ramona and Her Father on*: $35.00 Later editions: ($20.00 with dust jacket) $15.00
Beezus and Ramona, 1955, b/w illustrations by Louis Darling
Ramona the Pest, 1968, b/w illustrations by Louis Darling
Ramona the Brave, 1975, b/w illustrations by Louis Darling
Ramona and Her Father, 1975, b/w illustrations by Alan Tiegreen
Ramona and Her Mother, 1979, b/w illustrations by

Alan Tiegreen
Ramona Quimby, Age 8, 1981, b/w illustrations by Alan Tiegreen
Ramona Forever, 1984, b/w illustrations by Alan Tiegreen

RANCH AND RANGE SERIES, St. George Rathborne, published by Street and Smith; Federal; David McKay, hardcover, 4 b/w plates, all three publishers used the same illustrations. $20.00
Sunset Ranch, 1901
Chums of the Prairie, 1902
Young Range Riders, 1902

RANCH GIRLS SERIES, Margaret Vandercook, 1911 – 24 Winston, hardcover, b/w illustrations. ($25.00 with dust jacket) $15.00
Ranch Girls at Rainbow Lodge
Ranch Girls' Pot of Gold
Ranch Girls at Boarding School
Ranch Girls in Europe
Ranch Girls at Home Again
Ranch Girls and Their Great Adventure
Ranch Girls and Their Heart's Desire
Ranch Girls and the Silver Arrow
Ranch Girls and the Mystery of the Three Roads

RANDOLPH SERIES, Helen Randolph, 1936 Saalfield, hardcover. ($20.00 with dust jacket) $10.00
Secret of Casa Grande
Mystery of Carlitos
Crossed Trails in Mexico

RANDY SERIES see PRUE

RANDY STARR see SKY FLYERS

RANGE AND GRANGE HUSTLERS SERIES, Frank Gee Patchin, Altemus, pictorial on beige hardcover, 4 b/w plates. $15.00
Range and Grange Hustlers on the Ranch, or The Boy Shepherds of the Great Divide, 1912
Range and Grange Hustlers' Greatest Roundup, or Pitting Their Wits Against a Packer's Combine, 1912
Range and Grange Hustlers on the Plains, or Following the Steam Plows Across the Prairies, 1913
Range and Grange Hustlers at Chicago, or The Conspiracy of the Wheat Pit, 1913

RANGER BOYS SERIES, Claude H. La Belle, ca. 1920 Burt, illustrated cloth-over-board cover, frontispiece illustration. advertised as "adventures of three boys with the forest rangers in the State of Maine." ($20.00 with dust jacket) $10.00
Ranger Boys to the Rescue
Ranger Boys Find the Hermit
Ranger Boys and the Border Smugglers
Ranger Boys Outwit the Timber Thieves

Ranger Boys and Their Reward

RAY DECKER SERIES, Richard Graber, Harper and Row, blue hardcover with gilt lettering, novels set in the late 1930s, small town Minnesota. ($20.00 with dust jacket) $10.00
Little Breathing Room, 1978
Pay Your Respects, 1979
Black Cow Summer, 1980

RAYMOND BENSON see TWO LIVE BOYS

READ-AND-SING BOOKS, written and illustrated by Lois Lenski, Walck, small oblong hardcover, two-color illustrations, music arrangements by Clyde Robert Bulla. ($40.00 with dust jacket) $25.00
At Our House
I Went for a Walk
When I Grow Up

REAL BOOKS, 1950s – 60s Garden City, hardcover, illustrated. ($15.00 with dust jacket) $10.00
Numerous titles, including:
Real Book about Pets, Bates
Real Book about Treasure Hunting, Burton
Real Book about Amazing Animals, Dickinson
Real Book of Great American Journeys
Real Book about Trains, Cole
Real Book about Farms, Howard
Real Book about Horses, Sherman
Real Book about Airplanes, Whitehorse
Real Book about the Texas Rangers, Allen
Real Book About Spies, Epstein
Real Book about Stars, Goodwin
Real Book about Space Travel, Goodwin
Real Book about Sports, Bonner
Real Book about Baseball, Hopkins
Real Book about Pirates, Epstein
Real Book About Buffalo Bill, Regli
Real Book About Alaska, Williams

REAL LIFE STORIES, Whitman, pictorial hardcover.

$10.00

Titles include:

Nurses Who Led the Way, DeLeeuw, 1961

Heroes in Blue And Gray, Alter, 1965

Great War, Stories of World War I, Jablonski, 1965

REBECCA SERIES, Kate Douglas Wiggin. This popular series was reprinted often, and copies are easy to find. Reprints: ($20.00 with dust jacket) $10.00

Rebecca of Sunnybrook Farm, 1903 Riverside, cloth hardcover, color plate illustrations. $75.00

Rebecca of Sunnybrook Farm, 1931 edition Riverside, color paste-on-pictorial on cloth cover, color plates and b/w illustrations by Helen Mason Grose. $20.00

More About Rebecca, 1907 edition Grosset & Dunlap, hardcover. $25.00

New Chronicles of Rebecca, 1907 Houghton, b/w paste-on-pictorial on cover, b/w illustrations by F. C. Yohn. $35.00

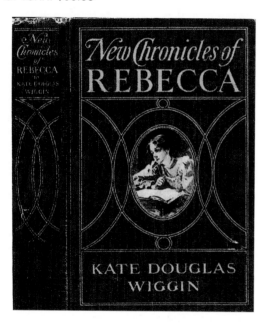

RECREATION SERIES, Edward Robins, 1912 George W Jacobs, hardcover. ($50.00 with dust jacket) $20.00

Boys in Early Virginia

Chasing an Iron Horse

With Thomas in Tennessee

With Washington in Braddock's Campaign

RED CROSS SERIES, Margaret Vandercook, 1916 – 20 Winston, hardcover, frontispiece. ($25.00 with dust jacket) $15.00

Red Cross Girls in the British Trenches

Red Cross Girls on the French Firing Line

Red Cross Girls in Belgium

Red Cross Girls with the Russian Army

Red Cross Girls with the Italian Army

Red Cross Girls with the Stars and Stripes

Red Cross Girls Afloat with the Flag

Red Cross Girls with Pershing to Victory

Red Cross Girls with the U. S. Marines

Red Cross Girls in the National Capital

RED PLUME SERIES, Edward Williams, ca. 1925 Harper and Brothers, hardcover, 4 b/w plates by Stinemetz. $30.00

Red Plume

Red Plume Returns

Red Plume with the Royal Northwest Mounted

RED RANDALL SERIES, Sidney Bowen, ca. 1940s Grosset, hardcover, illustrated endpapers, frontispiece, illustrations by Ralph Smith, WW2 adventures. ($30.00 with dust jacket) $15.00

Red Randall at Pearl Harbor

Red Randall on Active Duty

Red Randall over Tokyo

Red Randall at Midway

Red Randall on New Guinea

Red Randall in the Aleutians

Red Randall in Burma

Red Randall's One Man War

RED RYDER SERIES, various authors, stories based on the newspaper comic strip by Fred Harman, books published by Whitman, hardcover. ($35.00 with dust jacket) $15.00

Big Little Books, ca. 1940s – 50s: $35.00

Whitman, glossy illustrated hardcover: $15.00

Titles include:

Red Ryder and the Secret of Wolf Canyon, ca. 1941, Stevens

Red Ryder and the Mystery of Whispering Walls, 1941, Russell Winterbotham

Red Ryder and the Adventure at Chimmney Rock, 1946, Lawrence Keating

Red Ryder and the Secret of the Lucky Mine, ca. 1947

Carl Smith
Red Ryder and the Riddle of Roaring Range, 1951
Red Ryder and the Gun-smoke Gold, 1954
Red Ryder, related material:
When You Comin' Back, Red Ryder? A play in two
    acts, by Mark Medoff, 1974 Dramatists Play Ser-
    vice, NY: $15.00
Red Ryder comics, ca. 1940s Dell: $10.00

REED CONROY SERIES, Alan Gregg, 1940 – 1948 Dou-
    bleday, blue hardcover with gilt lettering, pictori-
    al endpapers. ($60.00 with dust jacket) $20.00
Winged Mystery
Hidden Wings Mystery
Skywinder Mystery
Mystery of the King Turtle
Mystery in the Blue
Mystery of Batty Ridge
Mystery of Flight 24
Flying Wing Mystery

REGIONAL SERIES see AMERICAN REGIONAL

RENFREW SERIES, Laurie Erskine, 1922 – 1941 Apple-
    ton, hardcover, color frontispiece. ($40.00 with
    dust jacket) $15.00
Grosset & Dunlap editions, red hardcover, map end-
    papers, frontispiece. ($30.00 with dust jacket)
    $10.00
Renfrew of the Royal Mounted
Renfrew Rides Again
Renfrew Rides the Sky
Renfrew Rides North
Renfrew's Long Trail
Renfrew Rides the Range
Renfrew in the Valley of the Vanished Men
Renfrew Flies Again

REVOLUTIONARY SERIES see MUSKET BOYS

REX LEE AIR SERIES, Thomson Burtis, 1928 – 1932 Gros-
    set & Dunlap, khaki hardcover, frontispiece.
    ($25.00 with dust jacket) $10.00
Gypsy Flyer
On the Border Patrol
Ranger of the Sky
Sky Trailer
Ace of the Air Mail
Night Flyer
Mysterious Flight
Rough Rider of the Air
Aerial Acrobat
Trailing Air Bandits
Flying Detective

REX KINGDON SERIES, Gordon Braddock, ca. 1915
    Burt and Hurst, hardcover, illustrated, "high school
    stories of outdoor sports." ($20.00 with dust jack-
    et) $10.00

Rex Kingdon of Ridgewood High
Rex Kingdon in the North Woods
Rex Kingdon at Walcott Hall
Rex Kingdon Behind the Bat
Rex Kingdon on Storm Island

RICK AND RUDDY SERIES, Howard Garis, 1920s Milton
    Bradley, tan hardcover, 4 b/w plates by Milo Win-
    ter, adventures of Rick and his dog, Ruddy.
    ($35.00 with dust jacket) $15.00
Rick and Ruddy
Rick and Ruddy in Camp
Rick and Ruddy Afloat
Rick and Ruddy Out West
Rick and Ruddy on the Trail
1930s editions McLoughlin, 256 pages, wraparound
    color illustration on cover boards, b/w fron-
    tispiece, same books with new titles. $30.00
McLoughlin titles:
Mystery of the Brass Bound Box
Swept from the Storm
Face in the Dismal Cavern
Secret of Lost River
On the Showman's Trail

RICK BRANT SCIENCE-ADVENTURE SERIES (or RICK
    BRANT ELECTRONIC ADVENTURE SERIES), John L.
    Blaine (pseudonym for Harold Goodwin or Peter
    Harkins), 1947-1968 Grosset & Dunlap, 23 titles.
    "Rick Brant Electronic Adventure Series" and
    "Rick Brant Science-Adventure Stories" both used
    by Grosset & Dunlap as series name. "Electronic
    Adventure" name was the earlier, but many
    books use both series designations in different

places in the jacket or hardcover text. "Electronic Adventure" was dropped soon after the picture cover format was introduced. First editions were not identified by publisher who kept the same copyright date for all. Most collectors label the first two titles as probable first editions if the title listings do not exceed books published that year.

Rick Brant, 1947 – 1960 tweed hardcovers, illustrated endpapers, b/w frontispiece. $10.00
With dust jacket that lists to self: $40.00
With later dust jacket: $20.00
Pictorial hardcover: $10.00
Rocket's Shadow, 1947 (probable first jacket lists to Lost City)
Lost City, 1947
Sea Gold, 1947
100 Fathoms Under, 1947
Whispering Box Mystery, 1948
Phantom Shark, 1949
Smuggler's Reef, 1950
Caves of Fear, 1951
Stairway to Danger, 1952
Golden Skull, 1954
Wailing Octopus, 1956
Electronic Mind Reader, 1957
Scarlet Lake Mystery, 1958
Pirates of Shan, 1958
Rick Brant, 1960 – 1962, hardcover, series titles list-to-self probable firsts: $50.00 Later printings: $20.00
Blue Ghost Mystery, 1960
Egyptian Cat Mystery, 1961
Flaming Mountain, 1962
Rick Brant, 1963 – 1968, pictorial hardcover, no dust jackets issued, series titles probable firsts list-to-self. (For some titles, only one or two printings were done). Probable firsts: $55.00 Later printings $35.00
Flying Stingaree, 1963
Ruby Ray Mystery, 1964
Veiled Raiders, 1965
Rocket Jumper, 1966, hard-to-find, $125.00
Deadly Dutchman, 1967, hard-to-find, $125.00
Danger Below, 1968
Rick Brant, related titles:
Rick Brant's Science Projects, 1960 Grosset & Dunlap, non-fiction, hard-to-find. $700.00 with dust jacket
Deadly Dutchman, Mystery & Adventure, 1986 reprint, pictorial endpapers with map of world showing locales of Rick Brant's adventures. Hard-to-find: $75.00
Magic Talisman, 1989 Manuscript Press, manuscript written for, but never published by Grosset & Dunlap. Map of Spindrift Island on endpapers. Limited edition of 500 copies. RARE

RIDDLE CLUB SERIES, Alice Hardy (Stratemeyer Syndicate pseudonym), ca. 1920s Grosset, 6 books, advertised as "full of adventures and doings of six

youngsters, but as added attraction, each book is filled with a lot of the best riddles you ever heard," illustrated by Walter Rogers. $15.00
Riddle Club at Home
Riddle Club in Camp
Riddle Club Through the Holidays
Riddle Club at Sunrise Beach
Riddle Club at Shadybrook
Riddle Club at Rocky Falls

RIDERS, HO! SERIES, Rutherford Montgomery, 1942 – 1946 McKay, hardcover, color frontispiece by Wittmack. ($25.00 with dust jacket) $10.00
Sea Raiders, Ho!
Thunderboats, Ho!
Rough Riders, Ho!

RIN TIN TIN SERIES, based on the movie and TV dog stories, several publishers.
Hardcover with dust jacket: $20.00
Pictorial hardcover: $15.00
Titles include:
Rin Tin Tin and Rusty, Monica Hill, 1955 Simon and Schuster
Rin Tin Tin and the Lost Indian, Monica Hill, illustrated by Hamilton Greene, 1956 Simon and Schuster
Rin Tin Tin, One of the Family, Frank Kearns, Whitman
Rin Tin Tin's Rinty; Julie Tatham, 1954 Whitman
Rin Tin Tin, related books:
Rin-Tin-Tin book of Dog Care, photographed and edited by Robert and Gwenn Broadman, 1958 Prentice-Hall. ($20.00 with dust jacket) $10.00
Rin Tin Tin Story, James English, 1949 Dodd, Mead, photo illustrations. First edition: ($50.00 with dust jacket) $20.00

RIVAL CAMPERS SERIES, Ruel Smith, 1905 – 1907 Page, hardcover with printed illustration, 4 or 6 b/w plates by A. B. Shute. ($40.00 with dust jacket) $15.00
Rival Campers, or Adventures of Henry Burns
Rival Campers Afloat, or Prize Yacht "Viking"
Rival Campers Ashore, or Mystery of the Red Mill
Rival Campers Among the Oyster Pirates, or Jack Harvey's Adventures

RIVER MOTOR-BOAT SERIES, Harry Gordon, 1913 – 1915 Burt, hardcover, frontispiece. ($30.00 with dust jacket) $15.00
River Motor-Boat Boys on the Amazon, or Secret of Cloud Island
River Motor-Boat Boys on the Columbia, or Confession of a Photograph
River Motor-Boat Boys on the Colorado, or Clue in the Rocks
River Motor-Boat Boys on the Mississippi, or Trail to the Gulf
River Motor-Boat Boys on the St. Lawrence, or Lost Channel

River Motor-Boat Boys on the Ohio, or Three Blue Lights

River Motor-Boat Boys on the Yukon, or Lost Mine of Rainbow Bend

River Motor-Boat Boys on the Rio Grande, or In Defense of the "Rambler"

ROB RANGER SERIES, Lt. Lionel Lounsberry, 1903 Street and Smith, Federal, and David McKay editions, hardcover, frontispiece. $15.00

Rob Ranger's Mine, or Boy Who Got There

Rob Ranger the Young Ranchman, or Going It Alone at Lost River

Rob Ranger's Cowboy Days, or Young Hunter of the Big Horn

ROBIN HOOD SERIES, Paul Castleton, Cupples & Leon, hardcover, frontispiece. ($20.00 with dust jacket) $10.00

Thrilling Adventures of Robin Hood, 1940

Son of Robin Hood, 1941

Son of Robin Hood in Nottingham, 1942

ROBIN KANE SERIES, Eileen Hill, 1960s Whitman, wrap-around pictorial hardcover, b/w illustrations. $10.00

Mystery of the Blue Pelican, 1966

Mystery of the Phantom, 1966

Mystery of Glengary Castle, 1966

Mystery in the Clouds, 1971

ROCKSPUR SERIES, Gilbert Patten, ca. 1900 McKay, illustrated cloth-over-board cover, b/w plate illustrations. $20.00

Rockspur Nine

Rockspur Eleven

Rockspur Rivals

ROCKY MCCUNE SPORTS STORIES, Wilfred McCormick (see also BRONC BURNETT), 1955 – 65 David McKay or Duell Sloan. Early printings: ($100.00 with dust jacket) $40.00

Man on the Bench

Captive Coach

Bigger Game

Hot Corner

Five Yards to Glory

Proud Champions

Automatic Strike

Too Many Forwards

Double Steal

Play for One

Five Man Break

Home Run Harvest

Phantom Shortstop

Two-One-Two Attack

Long Pitcher

Wild on the Bases

ROGER BAXTER MYSTERY SERIES, Charles Strong or Martin Colt (pseudonyms of Samuel and Beryl Epstein, see KEN HOLT), ca. 1947 Messner, hardcover. $70.00

Stranger at the Inlet

Secret of Baldhead Mountain

Riddle of the Hidden Pesos

ROGER TEARLE SERIES, Scott Corbett, Little, Brown, 5 titles, hardcover, illustrations by Paul Frame. ($30.00 with dust jacket) $15.00

Case of the Gone Goose, 1966

Case of the Fugitive Firebug, 1969

Case of the Ticklish Tooth, 1971

Case of the Silver Skull, 1974

Case of the Burgled Blessing Box, 1975

ROLLO SERIES, Jacob Abbott (1803 – 1879), 28 titles, 1840s-1860s Reynolds and others, including J. Allen, Boston, first editions with cloth cover, gilt cover lettering, engraving illustrations, nursery tales (possibly based on author's son): $50.00 Later printings, including Ginn Co.: $20.00

Titles include:

Rollo Code of Morals

Rollo Learning to Talk

Rollo's Experiments

Rollo on the Atlantic

Rollo in Paris

Rollo on the Rhine

Rollo in Geneva

Rollo Learning to Read

Rollo at School

Rollo at Work

ROMANCE OF KNOWLEDGE BOOKS, ca. 1920s Little, Brown, hardcover with paste-on-illustration, about 300 pages, color plates plus b/w illustrations. $25.00

Young Folk's Book of the Heavens, Mary Proctor, 4 color plates

Young Folk's Book of Discovery, T. C. Bridges, 8 color plates

Young Folk's Book of Myths, Amy Cruse, 8 color plates

Young Folk's Book of Invention, T. C. Bridges, 4 color plates

Young Folk's Book of Other Lands, Dorothy Stuart, 4 color plates

Young Folk's Book of Epic Heroes, Amy Cruse, 8 color plates

ROMPER ROOM BOOKS, TV tie-in publications

Romper Room, Little Golden Books, ca. 1950s and 1960s, color illustrated hardcover with foil spine, color illustrations throughout. $10.00

Titles include:

Romper Room Do Bees: A Book of Manners, 1956, Nancy Claster, illustrated by Eleanor Dart

Romper Room Exercise Book, 1964, Nancy Claster, illustrated by Sergio Leone

Romper Room, Wonder Books, ca. 1950s and 1960s, small illustrated hardcover. $10.00

Titles include:

Romper Room Book of Finger Plays and *Action Rhymes,* 1955, June Pierce, illustrated by Ruth Wood

What Time Is It? A Romper Room Book, 1954, John Peter, illustrated by Joseph Zabinski, with "a practice clock on back cover"

Can You Guess? A Romper Room Book, 1953, Leonore Klein, illutrated by Ruth Wood

Romper Room Do Bee Book of Manners, 1960, Nancy Claster, illustrated by Art Seiden

Romper Room Safety Book, 1965, Nancy Claster, illustrated by Art Seiden

ROSALIE DARE SERIES, Amy Brooks, ca. 1920s Lothrop and Lee, small hardcover, b/w plates by author. $15.00

Titles include:

Rosalie Dare
Rosalie Dare's Test

ROSS GRANT SERIES, John Garland, 1915 – 1918 Penn, paste-on-pictorial hardcover, b/w plates, Wyoming adventures. $20.00

Ross Grant, Tenderfoot
Ross Grant, Gold Hunter
Ross Grant on the Trail
Ross Grant in Miner's Camp

ROUNDABOUT AMERICA SERIES, Lois Lenski, Lippincott, hardcover, b/w illustrations by Lenski, who did several series based on historical and geographic themes. First edition: ($125.00 with dust jacket) $25.00

Titles include:

We Live In The South, 1952
Peanuts for Billy Ben, 1952
We Live in the City, 1954
Berries in the Scoop, 1956
Little Sioux Girl, 1958
We Live in the Country, 1960

We Live in the Southwest, 1962
High-Rise Secret, 1966

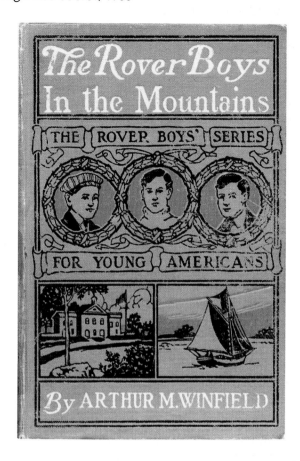

ROVER BOYS SERIES, Arthur M. Winfield (Edward Stratemeyer), 1899 – 1926 Stitt, also Grosset and Whitman reprints, cloth-over-board cover, b/w illustrations. Also, see PUTNAM HALL SERIES.

Pre-1920 printings: ($50.00 with dust jacket) $15.00
Later editions: ($30.00 with dust jacket) $15.00

Rover Boys: First Series: ca. 1899 – 1910

Rover Boys at School
Rover Boys on the Ocean
Rover Boys in the Jungle
Rover Boys out West
Rover Boys on the Great Lakes
Rover Boys in the Mountains
Rover Boys in Camp
Rover Boys on Land and Sea
Rover Boys on the River
Rover Boys on the Plains
Rover Boys in Southern Waters
Rover Boys on the Farm
Rover Boys on Treasure Isle
Rover Boys at College
Rover Boys Down East
Rover Boys in the Air
Rover Boys in New York
Rover Boys in Alaska
Rover Boys In Business
Rover Boys on a Tour

Rover Boys: Second Series: ca. 1919, the main characters in the second series are the children of the first series' characters.
Rover Boys at Colby Hall
Rover Boys on Snowshoe Island
Rover Boys under Canvas
Rover Boys on a Hunt
Rover Boys in the Land of Luck
Rover Boys at Big Horn Ranch
Rover Boys at Big Bear Lake
Rover Boys Shipwrecked
Rover Boys on Sunset Trail
Rover Boys Winning a Fortune

ROY BLAKELY SERIES, Percy Fitzhugh, ca. 1920s Grosset, hardcover, 4 b/w plates, Boy Scout adventures. ($25.00 with dust jacket) $15.00
Roy Blakeley
Roy Blakeley's Adventures in Camp
Roy Blakeley's Camp on Wheels
Roy Blakeley, Pathfinder
Roy Blakeley's Silver Fox Patrol
Roy Blakeley's Motor Caravan
Roy Blakeley, Lost, Strayed or Stolen
Roy Blakeley's Bee Line Hike
Roy Blakeley at the Haunted Camp
Roy Blakeley's Funny-Bone Hike
Roy Blakeley's Tangled Trail
Roy Blakeley on the Mohawk Trail
Roy Blakeley's Elastic Hike
Roy Blakeley's Roundabout Hike
Roy Blakeley's Happy-Go-Lucky Hike
Roy Blakeley's Go-As-You-Please Hike
Roy Blakeley's Wild Goose Chase
Roy Blakeley Up in the Air

ROY ROGERS SERIES, various authors, books feature the singing movie star and his wife, Dale Evans.
Roy Rogers, ca. 1950s Little Golden Books, small illustrated hardcover, foil spine, color illustrations. $20.00
Roy Rogers and the New Cowboy, 1953, Annie Bedford, illustrated by Mel Crawford
Roy Rogers and Cowboy Toby, 1954, Elizabeth Beecher, illustrated by Mel Crawford
Dale Evans and the Lost Goldmine, 1954, Monica Hill, illustrated by Mel Crawford
Roy Rogers and the Mountain Lion, 1955, Ann McGovern, illustrated by Mel Crawford
Dale Evans and the Coyote, 1956, Gladys Wyatt, illustrated by Joseph Dreany
Roy Rogers and the Indian Sign, 1956, Gladys Wyatt, illustrated Mel Crawford
Roy Rogers, other books:
Roy Rogers and the Ghost of Mystery Rancho, Walker Tompkins, 1950 Whitman, hardcover. $15.00
Roy Rogers and Dale Evans in River of Peril, Cole Fannin, 1957 Whitman, hardcover. ($15.00 with dust jacket) $10.00

Roy Rogers, coloring books, prices are for clean, uncolored books:
Roy Rogers Paint Book, 1944 Whitman, drawings by Betty Goodan. $45.00
Roy Rogers and Dale Evans Coloring Book, 1951 Whitman, cover features Roy, Dale, and Trigger, the horse, drawings by Peter Alvarado. $35.00
Roy Rogers' Double-R-Bar Ranch, 1955 Whitman, photo cover of Roy, Dale, and their dog. $35.00
Dale Evans Coloring Book, 1957 Whitman, cover illustration of Dale on her horse. $35.00

ROY STOVER MYSTERY STORIES, Phillip Bartlett (Stratemeyer Syndicate pseudonym), 1929 – 1934 Barse, hardcover, 4 b/w illustrations, hard-to-find. Grosset & Dunlap edition, orange hardcover, pictorial endpapers, frontispiece by John Foster. ($25.00 with dust jacket) $10.00
Lakeport Mystery
Mystery of the Snowbound Express
Cliff Island Mystery
Mystery of the Circle of Fire

RUBY AND RUTHY SERIES, Minnie E. Paull, ca. 1894 Dana Estes, Boston, brown hardcover with gilt, decorated endpapers, 8 b/w plates: $40.00
Ca. 1890s editions Page, cream-colored hardcover with stamped illustration: $25.00
Ca. 1920s Cupples and Leon editions, hardcover: $15.00
Ruby and Ruthy
Ruby's Ups and Downs
Ruby at School
Ruby's Vacation

RUPERT PIPER SERIES, Ethelyn Parkinson, Abingdon, hardcover. ($20.00 with dust jacket) $10.00
Terrible Troubles of Rupert Piper, 1963
Operation that Happened to Rupert Piper, 1966
Rupert Piper and Megan the Valuable Girl, 1972
Rupert Piper and the Dear, Dear Birds, 1976
Rupert Piper and the Boy Who Could Knit, 1979

RUSHTON BOYS SERIES, Spencer Davenport (Stratemeyer Syndicate pseudonym) possible other author names used on reprints, 1916 Hearst, reprints by Sully or Whitman, hardcover, b/w illustrations by Walter Rogers. $20.00
Rushton Boys at Rally Hall, or Great Days in School and Out
Rushton Boys in the Saddle, or Ghost of the Plains
Rushton Boys at Treasure Cove, or Missing Chest of Gold

RUSS FARRELL SERIES, Thomson Burtis, 1924 – 1929 Doubleday, red hardcover, b/w frontispiece, motion picture tie-in. ($50.00 with dust jacket) $15.00
Russ Farrell, Airman

Russ Farrell, Test Pilot
Russ Farrell, Circus Flyer
Russ Farrell, Border Patrolman
Russ Farrell Over Mexico

RUSSELL SERIES, Johanna Hurwitz, Morrow, tales of a five-year-old, which makes this a fun read-aloud series for small children. Russell and friends live in an apartment building in New York City. Hardcover, b/w illustrations by Lillian Hoban. ($15.00 with dust jacket) $10.00
Rip-roaring Russell, 1983
Russell and Elisa, 1989
Russell Rides Again, 1985
Russell Sprouts, 1987
Russell titles are still being added by Morrow, with paperback Puffin reprints, illustrations by Heather Maione.
Russell, related titles:
Busybody Nora, 1976
Nora and Mrs. Mind-Your-Own-Business, 1977
New Neighbors for Nora, 1979
Superduper Teddy, 1980

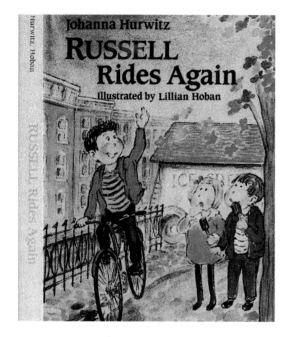

RUTH DARROW FLYING STORIES, Mildred Wirt, 1930 – 31 Barse, hardcover. (Wirt had a pilot's license.) $40.00
In the Air Derby
In the Fire Patrol
In the Yucatan
And the Coast Guard

RUTH FIELDING SERIES, Alice B. Emerson (Stratemeyer Syndicate pseudonym), 1913 – 1930s Cupples & Leon, printed illustration tan cover, frontispiece, mysteries for girls. Advertised as "Ruth Fielding was an orphan and came to live with her miserly uncle. Her adventures and travels make stories

that will hold the interest of every reader."
The hardcover design was changed once, updating Ruth's costume to a shorter skirt in 1929. There were four dust jacket designs, one done by the well-known illustrator Clara Burd. ($30.00 with dust jacket) $15.00
Ruth Fielding of the Red Mill
Ruth Fielding at Briarwood Hall
Ruth Fielding at Snow Camp
Ruth Fielding at Lighthouse Point
Ruth Fielding at Silver Ranch
Ruth Fielding on Cliff Island
Ruth Fielding at Sunrise Farm
Ruth Fielding and the Gypsies
Ruth Fielding in Moving Pictures
Ruth Fielding Down in Dixie
Ruth Fielding at College
Ruth Fielding in the Saddle
Ruth Fielding in the Red Cross
Ruth Fielding at the War Front
Ruth Fielding Homeward Bound
Ruth Fielding Down East
Ruth Fielding in the Great Northwest
Ruth Fielding on the St. Lawrence
Ruth Fielding Treasure Hunting
Ruth Fielding in the Far North
Ruth Fielding at Golden Pass
Ruth Fielding in Alaska
Ruth Fielding and her Great Scenario
Ruth Fielding at Cameron Hall
Ruth Fielding Clearing Her Name
Ruth Fielding in Talking Pictures
Ruth Fielding and Baby June
Ruth Fielding and Her Double
Ruth Fielding and Her Greatest Triumph
Ruth Fielding and Her Crowning Victory

S

SADDLE BOYS SERIES, Captain James Carson (Stratemeyer Syndicate pseudonym), ca. 1920s Cupples & Leon, gray hardcover, blue lettering, illustrations by W. S. Rogers. ($20.00 with dust jacket) $10.00

Saddle Boys of the Rockies
Saddle Boys in the Grand Canyon
Saddle Boys on the Plains
Saddle Boys at Circle Ranch
Saddle Boys on Mexican Trails

SADLER'S WELLS SERIES, Lorna Hill, 1950 – 1964 Evans (American editions published by Holt), 14 titles. Ballet series based on the school experiences of the author's daughter at Sadler's Wells, later called the Royal Ballet School, in London. See also MARJORIE, DANCING PEELS, PATIENCE, and VICARAGE CHILDREN.
First editions: $25.00 with dust jacket
Later editions: ($15.00 with dust jacket) $10.00
Dream of Sadler's Wells, 1950
Veronica at the Wells, 1951
Masquerade at the Wells, 1952
No Castanets at the Wells, 1953
Jane Leaves the Wells, 1953
Ella at the Wells, 1954
Return to the Wells, 1955
Rosanna Joins the Wells, 1956
Principal Role, 1957
Swan Feather, 1958
Dress-Rehearsal, 1959
Back-Stage, 1960
Vicki in Venice, 1962
Secret, 1964

SAFETY FIRST CLUB SERIES, William Nichols, Penn Publishing, blue hardcover, four or five plates. $15.00
Safety First Club, 1916
Safety First Club and the Flood, 1917
Safety First Club Fights Fire, 1923

SAILOR JACK SERIES, S. and J. Wasserman, ca. 1960 Benific Press, hardcover. $10.00
Sailor Jack and Bluebell's Dive
Sailor Jack Goes North
Sailor Jack and the Jet Plane
Sailor Jack and the Target Ship
Sailor Jack's New Friend
Sailor Jack And Homer Pots

SALLY SERIES see GARIS

SALLY SERIES, Dorita Fairlie Bruce (1885 – 1970), 1956 – 1961, 3 titles. Last series written by the famous author of the "Dimsie" books. ($25.00 with dust jacket) $10.00
Sally Scatterbrain, 1956
Sally Again, 1959
Sally's Summer Term, 1961

SALLY SMITH SERIES, Elizabeth Coatsworth, hardcover, Macmillan, b/w illustrations by Helen Sewell, adventures of an orphan in Colonial America: ($70.00 with dust jacket) $20.00

1960 reprints by Blackie, London, illustrated by Caroline Sharpe: ($20.00 with dust jacket) $10.00
Away Goes Sally, 1934
Five Bushel Farm, 1939
Fair American, 1940
White Horse, 1942
Wonderful Day, 1946

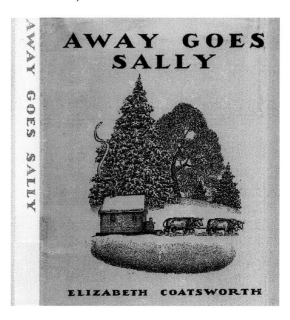

SAM STEELE SERIES see BOY FORTUNE HUNTERS

SAMPEY PLACE SERIES, Frances Fitzpatrick Wright, Abingdon Press, hardcover, illustrated endpapers, illustrated by Margaret Ayer. ($20.00 with dust jacket) $10.00
Secret of Old Sampey Place, 1946
Daybreak at Sampey Place, 1954
Surprise at Sampey Place, 1950

SANDSY SERIES, Gardner Hunting, Harper and Brothers, hardcover, four b/w plates. $15.00
Sandsy's Pal, 1915
Sandsy Himself, 1917
Sandsy Puts It Over, 1924

SANDY COVE, Alice Dalgliesh, Macmillan, hardcover, illustrated by Hildegard Woodward. ($75.00 with dust jacket) $40.00
Blue Teapot, Sandy Cove Stories, 1931
Relief's Rocker, a Story of Sandy Cove and the Sea, 1932
Roundabout; Another Sandy Cove Story, 1934

SANDY STEELE ADVENTURE SERIES, Roger Barlow, Simon & Schuster, 6 titles, hardcover. ($20.00 with dust jacket) $10.00
Black Treasure, 1959
Danger at Mormon Crossing, 1959
Stormy Voyage, 1959
Fire at Red Lake, 1959

Secret Mission to Alaska, 1959
Troubled Water, 1959

SASEK SERIES, Miroslav Sasek, 1959 – 74 Macmillan, oversize hardcover picture books, glossy illustrated cover, color illustrations throughout by author. The dust jackets have the same illustrations as the covers. ($40.00 with same-as-cover dust jacket) $25.00
This is Paris
This is London
This is Rome
This is New York
This is Edinburgh
This is Munich
This is Venice
This is San Francisco
This is Israel
This is Cape Canaveral, published in 1963, hard-to-find first edition, later editions of this title are renamed *This is Cape Kennedy.* ($75.00 with dust jacket) $45.00
This is Cape Kennedy, 1964
This is Ireland
This is Hong Kong
This is Greece
This is Texas
This is the United Nations
This is Australia
This is Historic Britain

SATURDAYS see MELENDY FAMILY

SCHOOL ATHLETIC SERIES, John Prescott Earl, Penn Publishing, green hardcover, frontispiece and b/w plates by Ralph Boyer. $40.00
On the School Team, 1908
School Team in Camp, 1909

Captain of the School Team, 1910
School Team on the Diamond, 1911

SCIENTIFIC AMERICAN BOY SERIES, Russell Bond, Munn; Scientific American Publishing, hardcover with paste-on-pictorial, illustrated with line drawings and photos. $45.00
Scientific American Boy, or The Camp at Willow Clump Island, 1905
Scientific American Boy at School, 1910
With the Men Who Do Things, 1913
Pick, Shovel and Pluck, 1914

SCOTT BURTON SERIES, Edward Cheyney, Appleton, illustrated cloth-over-board cover, four b/w plates. $15.00
Scott Burton, Forester, 1917
Scott Burton on the Range, 1920
Scott Burton and the Timber Thieves, 1922
Scott Burton, Logger, 1923
Scott Burton's Claim, 1926

SCOUT DRAKE SERIES, Isabel Hornibrook, Little, Brown, hardcover, four plates by Gallagher. ($40.00 with dust jacket) $20.00
Drake of Troop One, 1916
Scout Drake in War Time, 1918
Coxswain Drake of the Seascouts, 1920
Drake and the Adventurer's Cup, 1922

SCOUT PATROL BOYS SERIES, Jack Wright, 1933 World Syndicate Publishing, hardcover with silver lettering. ($15.00 with dust jacket) $10.00
Scout Patrol Boys at the Circle U Ranch
Scout Patrol Boys Exploring the Yucatan
Scout Patrol Boys and the Hunting Lodge Mystery
Scout Patrol Boys in the Frozen South

SCRANTON HIGH SERIES, Donald Ferguson, ca. 1919 World, Goldsmith, hardcover. ($15.00 with dust jacket) $10.00
Chums of Scranton High
Chums of Scranton High out for the Pennant
Chums of Scranton High on the Cinder Path
Chums of Scranton High at Ice Hockey

SCRIBNER CLASSICS, listed on dust jackets as "Scribner Jr. Classics" and "Scribner Illustrated Classics" with crossovers in titles to both series, Charles Scribner's Sons, NY, color paste-on-pictorial on cloth hardcover, color endpapers, color plate illustrations. First editions in this series are new editions of previously published books, some using illustrations from an earlier edition, some using new illustrations. The Scribner Illustrated Classics series was advertised as "books of rare beauty and tested literary quality, presented in handsome format and strikingly illustrated in color by such famous artists as N. C. Wyeth, Maxfield Parrish, Jessie Willcox Smith and others. ... They are to be found in two groups — the Popular Group, issued at a remarkably low price, and the Quality Group, published at a higher but still very reasonable price." The higher-priced books were printed on better quality paper and often contained 12 color plates. The lower-priced books usually contained 8 or less color plates.

Titles include:

Arabian Nights, edited by Wiggins and Smith, 1909, illustrator Maxfield Parrish. ($150.00 with dust jacket) $100.00

Black Arrow, R. L. Stevenson, 1916, illustrations by N. C. Wyeth. ($150.00 with dust jacket) $100.00

Boy's King Arthur, Sidney Lanier, 1947 edition, 9 color plates by N. C. Wyeth ($70.00 with dust jacket) $40.00

Drums, Boyd, illustrations by N. C. Wyeth. ($75.00 with dust jacket) $30.00

Hans Brinker, Mary Mapes Dodge, 1936, illustrator Geroge Wharton Edwards. ($40.00 with dust jacket) $25.00

Poems of Childhood, Eugene Field, ca. 1932, title page dated 1904 but on the reverse side, copyright dates for individual poems in the collection are dated up to 1922. This is oversize, 200 pages, printed on a lesser quality paper, and contains 8 color plates from the original 1904 Maxfield Parrish illustrated edition. ($100.00 with dust jacket) $55.00

Sampo, James Baldwin, illustrations by N. C. Wyeth. ($150.00 with dust jacket) $75.00

Treasure Island, R. L. Stevenson, 1911, illustrations by N. C. Wyeth. ($165.00 with dust jacket) $100.00

Westward Ho!, Charles Kingsley, 1940s edition, illustrations by N. C. Wyeth. ($65.00 with dust jacket) $40.00

Wind in the Willows, Kenneth Grahame, 1928, 12 color plate illustrations by Nancy Barnhart. ($65.00 with dust jacket) $40.00

Yearling, Marjorie Rawlings, (1938), 1946 edition, color illustrated endpapers, 12 color plates, illustrator N. C. Wyeth. ($65.00 with dust jacket) $40.00

SEA WOLF MYSTERY SERIES, Robert Wise, 1974 EMC Corporation, hardcover, illustrations by Paul Snyder. $10.00

Ghost Town Monster
Mystery of Tanglefoot Island
Mystery of Totem Pole Inlet
Treasure of Raven Hill

SECKATARY HAWKINS SERIES, Robert Schulkers, 1921 – 1930 Robert F. Schulkers, Publisher, hardcover, illustrations by Carl Williams. This is a series of newspaper humor stories about a boys' club who solves mysteries. The stories have appeared in several formats with individual collections printed as single titles by other publishers.

Schulkers, Publisher, first edition: $400.00 range
1950s reprints: ($25.00 with dust jacket) $10.00

Seckatary Hawkins in Cuba, 1921
Red Runners, 1922
Gray Ghost, 1926
Stormie, the Dog Stealer, 1925
Knights of the Square Table, 1926
Ching Toy, 1926
Chinese Coin, 1926
Yellow Y, 1926
Herman the Fiddler, 1930

SECRET CIRCLE MYSTERY SERIES, Arthur Hammond, editor, Little, Brown, hardcover, 6 titles, various authors, b/w illustrations. ($15.00 with dust jackets) $10.00

Mystery of Monster Lake, David Gammon, 1962
Riddle of the Haunted River, Lawrence Earl, 1962
Legend of the Devil's Lode, Robert Collins, 1962
Secret Tunnel Treasure, Arthur Hammond, 1962
Mystery of the Muffled Man, Max Braithwaite, 1962
Clue of the Dead Duck, Scott Young, 1962

SECRET SEVEN SERIES, Enid Blyton, ca. 1960s Brockhampton Press, hardcover. ($25.00 with dust jacket) $10.00

Secret Seven and the Mystery of the Empty House
Secret Seven and the Circus Adventure
Secret Seven and the Tree House Adventure
Secret Seven and the Railroad Mystery
Secret Seven Get Their Man
Secret Seven and the Case of the Stolen Car
Secret Seven and the Hidden Cave Adventure
Secret Seven and the Grim Secret
Secret Seven and the Missing Girl Mystery
Secret Seven and the Case of the Music Lover
Secret Seven and the Bonfire Adventure
Secret Seven and the Old Fort Adventure
Secret Seven and the Case of the Dog Lover
Secret Seven and the Case of the Old Horse

SHEILA AND FUDGE SERIES, Judy Blume, Dutton and Bradbury, hardcover. Numerous reprints of these popular stories, and fairly large first printings after the first title. ($20.00 with dust jacket) $10.00

Otherwise Known as Sheila the Great, 1972, first edition with dust jacket: $95.00
Tales of a Fourth Grade Nothing, 1972
Superfudge, 1980
Pain and the Great One, 1984
Fudge-a-Mania, 1990

SHELDON SIX SERIES, Grace May Remick, Penn, hardcover. $65.00

Titles include:
Sheldon Six, Anne, 1920
Sheldon Six, Rose, 1921, illustrated by Isabel M. Cale
Sheldon Six, Connie, 1923
Sheldon Six, Susan, 1924

SHERBURNE SERIES, Amanda Minnie Douglas, 1892 – 1907 Dodd, 12 titles, cloth-over-board hardcover. $10.00

Sherburne House, 1892
Lyndell Sherburne; A Sequel to Sherburne House, 1893
Sherburne Cousins, 1894
Sherburne Romance, 1895
Mistress of Sherburne, 1896
Children at Sherburne House, 1897
Sherburne Girls, 1898
Heir of Sherburne, 1899
Sherburne Inheritance, 1901
Sherburne Quest, 1902
Honor Sherburne, 1904
In the Sherburne Line, 1907

SHIP AND SHORE SERIES, Edward Stratemeyer, Merriam; Lee & Shepard; hardcover, frontispiece, b/w plates in early editions. ($20.00 with dust jacket) $10.00

Last Cruise of the Spitfire, or Luke Foster's Strange Voyage, 1894
Reuben Stone's Discovery, or The Young Miller of Torrent Bend, 1895
True to Himself, or Roger Strong's Struggle for Place, 1900

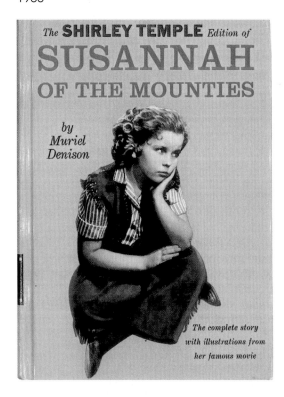

SHIRLEY TEMPLE EDITION BOOKS, ca. late 1930s – 40s Random House, hardcover with photo illustration of Shirley Temple in costume, interior b/w photo illustrations from movies based on these novels and starring Shirley Temple. ($35.00 with dust jacket) $15.00
1960s glossy illustrated hardcover reprints: $20.00

Heidi, Johanna Spyri
Littlest Rebel, Edward Peple
Rebecca of Sunnybrook Farm, Kate Douglas Wiggin
Susannah of the Mounties, Muriel Denison
Captain January, Laura E. Richards, and *Little Colonel* by Annie Fellows Johnston, 2 novels in one book

Shirley Temple related books:

Shirley Temple Treasury, 1959 Random House, hardcover, illustrated by Robert Patterson drawings and photographs from motion picutres featuring Shirley Temple. First edition: ($65.00 with dust jacket) $25.00

SHOES SERIES, Noel Streatfeild, Random House, hardcover, b/w illustrations. British series released under other titles.
First edition with dust jacket: $50.00
Later printings: ($25.00 with dust jacket) $15.00
American titles:

Ballet Shoes, 1937, illustrated by Richard Floethe
Circus Shoes, 1939, illustrated by Richard Floethe
Theatre Shoes, 1945, illustrated by Richard Floethe
Party Shoes, 1947, illustrated by Richard Floethe
Movie Shoes, 1949, illustrated by Susanne Suba
Skating Shoes, 1951, illustrated by Richard Floethe
Family Shoes, 1954, illustrated by Richard Floethe
Dancing Shoes, 1958, illustrated by Richard Floethe
New Shoes, 1960, illustrated by Vaike Low
Travelling Shoes, 1962, illustrated by Reisie Lonette
Tennis Shoes, 1977, illustrated by Richard Floethe

SIGNATURE BOOKS, 1950s Grosset & Dunlap, hardcover. ($15.00 with dust jacket) $10.00
Numerous titles including:

Story of Daniel Boone, Steele
Story of Marco Polo, Price
Story of Geronimo, Kjelgaard
Story of Crazy Horse, Meadowcroft
Story of Kit Carson, Collier NY
Story of Lafayette, Wilson
Story of Edith Cavell, Vinton
Story of Good Queen Bess, Malkus

SILAS SERIES, Cecil Bodker, Delacorte, hardcover, translated from Danish, story of a boy who runs away from the circus. ($20.00 with dust jacket) $10.00
Silas and the Black Mare, 1967
Silas and Ben Godik, 1978
Silas and Runaway Coach, 1978

SILVER CHIEF SERIES, Jack O'Brien, Winston, numerous reprints, a perennial favorite like *Lassie,* single titles were also added to other dog series. ($20.00 with dust jacket) $10.00
Silver Chief, Dog of the North, 1933
Silver Chief to the Rescue, 1937
Return of Silver Chief, 1943
Royal Red, 1951
Silver Chief's Revenge, 1954
Silver Chief, related title:
Silver Chief's Big Game Trail, Albert Miller, 1961 Holt

SILVER FOX FARM SERIES, James Otis, 1910 – 1913 Crowell, hardcover, eight b/w plates by Charles Copeland. ($25.00 with dust jacket) $10.00
Wireless Station at Silver Fox Farm
Aeroplane at Silver Fox Farm
Building an Airship at Silver Fox Farm
Airship Cruising from Silver Fox Farm

SILVER GATE SERIES, Penn Shirley, 1897 Lothrop Lee, hardcover, b/w illustrations. $10.00
Young Master Kirke
Merry Five
Happy Six

SILVER STAR SERIES, Basil Miller, 1946 – 1956 Zondervan, Christian series featuring the ranchers Kay and Kim and their horse Silver Star. Plastic coated hardbacks with pictorial covers: $10.00
Kay and Kim in Wild Horse Canyon, 1946
Silver Star in Rainbow Valley, 1948
Silver Star and the Black Raider, 1950
Silver Star and the Mustang Roundup, 1951
Silver Star and the Navajos, 1953
Silver Star on the Painted Desert, 1956

SIMON BLACK SERIES, Ivan Southall, 1950 – 1961, Angus & Robertson, 8 titles. Australian boys' series, compared by collectors to Tom Swift Jr. or Rick Brant. At least first three books originally issued on a lower grade post-WWII paper, and then reissued with better paper and dust jackets in the late 1950s and early 1960s. Abridged editions issued in laminated hardcover. Various illustrators including I. Maher, Wal Stackpool or Frank Norton.
Hardcover with dust jacket: $15.00
Laminated hardcover: $10.00
Meet Simon Black, 1950
Simon Black in Peril, 1951
Simon Black in Coastal Command, 1953
Simon Black in China, 1954
Simon Black and the Spacemen, 1955
Simon Black in the Antarctic, 1956
Simon Black Takes Over, 1959
Simon Black at Sea, 1961

SINBAD THE DOG SERIES, Kin Platt, Delacorte and Chilton, hardcover. ($20.00 with dust jacket) $10.00
Sinbad and Me, 1966
Mystery Witch Who Wouldn't, 1969
Ghost of Hellshire Street, 1980

SIX GIRLS SERIES, Marion Ames Taggart (1866 – 1945), 1906 – 12 Wilde, 7 titles. $20.00
Six Girls and Bob, 1906
Six Girls and the Tea Room, 1907
Six Girls Growing Older, 1908
Six Girls and the Seventh One, 1909
Betty Gaston the Seventh Girl, 1910
Six Girls and Betty, 1911
Six Girls Grown Up, 1912

SIX LITTLE BUNKERS SERIES, Laura Lee Hope (Stratemeyer Syndicate pseudonym), ca. 1918 – 1933 Grosset & Dunlap, tan hardcover with paste-on illustration, b/w plates by Emmet Owen or Walter

Rogers. $20.00

Six Little Bunkers at Grandma Bell's, 1918
Six Little Bunkers at Aunt Jo's
Six Little Bunkers at Cousin Tom's
Six Little Bunkers at Grandpa Ford's
Six Little Bunkers at Uncle Fred's
Six Little Bunkers at Captain Ben's, 1920
Six Little Bunkers at Cowboy Jack's
Six Little Bunkers at Mammy June's
Six Little Bunkers at Farmer Joel's
Six Little Bunkers at Miller Ned's
Six Little Bunkers at Indian John's, 1925
Six Little Bunkers at Happy Jim's
Six Little Bunkers at Skipper Bob's
Six Little Bunkers at Lighthouse Nell's, 1930
Six Little Bunkers, 1933 large volume containing four titles.

SKIPPY DARE MYSTERY SERIES, Hugh Lloyd, 1934 Grosset & Dunlap, red hardcover, black lettering with series title on cover, illustrated endpapers, frontispiece by Seymour Fogel. ($50.00 with dust jacket) $30.00
Among the River Pirates
Held for Ransom
Prisoners in Devil's Bog

SKIPPY SERIES, Percy Crosby
Skippy, a Novel, 1929 Putnam, black hardcover with gilt, b/w and color cartoon illustrations. ($75.00 with dust jacket) $45.00
Dear Sooky, 1929 Putnam, illustrated paper-over-board cover, 7 tipped in plates by author. ($75.00 with dust jacket) $45.00
Dear Sooky, undated Grosset edition ca. 1932, title shown on cover as Sooky, but on title plate and

copyright listing as *Dear Sooky*. Cloth-over-board cover with impressed illustration, 124 pages, 7 cartoon color plates mounted on plain pages, illustrations by author. ($40.00 with dust jacket) $25.00
Skippy Rambles, 1932 Putnam first edition, cloth-over-board cover, b/w illustrations and photos. ($75.00 with dust jacket) $45.00

Skippy, related book:
Skippy, Crayon and Coloring Book, 1931 McLoughlin Brothers, based on Percy Crosby drawings, contains color and b/w pictures, clean, uncolored book: $50.00

SKY BUDDIES SERIES, Edith Craine, 1930 World Syndicate Publishing, hardcover, frontispiece, reprints of other series. ($20.00 with dust jacket) $10.00
Air Mystery of Isle La Motte
Cap Rock Flyers
Sky Buddies Secret of Cuzco
Flying to Amy-Ran Fastness

SKY DETECTIVE SERIES see JACK RALSTON SERIES

SKY FLYERS, RANDY STARR SERIES, Eugene Martin (Stratemeyer Syndicate pseudonym), ca. 1930s Altemus, reprints by Saalfield, cloth-over-board cover, 200+ pages, b/w illustrations. ($20.00 with dust jacket) $10.00
Randy Starr After an Air Prize
Randy Starr Above Stormy Seas
Randy Starr Leading the Air Circus
Randy Starr Tracing the Air Spy

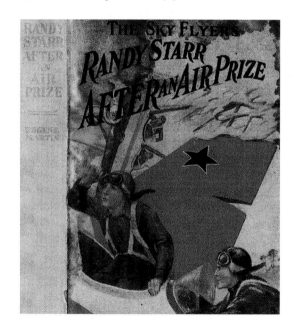

SKY SCOUT SERIES, see AIR MYSTERY SERIES, Van Buren Powell, 1932 Burt, orange hardcover, black lettering, frontispiece. ($30.00 with dust jacket) $10.00
Mystery Crash

Haunted Hanger
Vanishing Airliner
Ghost of Mystery Airport

SKYLARKING COMRADES SERIES, Delmore Marquith, ca. 1930 World Syndicate Publishing, blue hardcover, gilt lettering, paste-on-pictorial. ($35.00 with dust jacket) $15.00
Border-Line Mystery
Flying Buddies of Texas
Flying in Southern Wilderness
Emerald Temple Air Mystery

SLIM TYLER AIR SERIES, Richard Stone (Stratemeyer Syndicate pseudonym), ca. 1920s Cupples & Leon, red hardcover, frontispiece. ($50.00 with dust jacket) $20.00
Sky Riders of the Atlantic
Lost Over Greenland
Air Cargo of Gold
Adrift Over Hudson Bay
Airplane Mystery
Secret Sky Express
Aviation Stories for Boys, 1936, large volume containing first four books.

SMILER SERIES, Victor Canning, Heinemann, UK and Morrow, US, hardcover. ($15.00 with dust jacket) $10.00
Runaways, 1971
Flight of the Grey Goose, 1973
Painted Tent, 1974

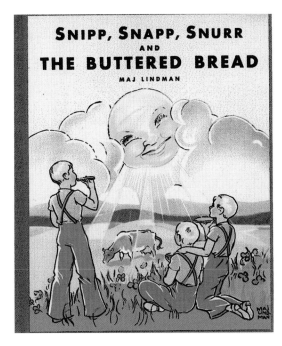

SNIPP, SNAPP, SNURR SERIES, written and illustrated by Maj Lindman, Whitman, oversize books with bright colored cover illustrations, color illustrations throughout.

First US oversize editions published in the 1930s and 1940s: ($150.00 with dust jacket) $80.00
8x10 reprints, ca. 1940s Whitman, cloth-over-board cover with paste-on-pictorial, color illustrations throughout: ($110.00 with same-as-cover dust jacket) $50.00
First US editions published in the 1950s: ($90.00 with dust jacket) $50.00
Titles include:
Snipp, Snapp, Snurr and the Red Shoes, 1932
Snipp, Snapp, Snurr and the Buttered Bread, 1934
Snipp, Snapp, Snurr and the Magic Horse, 1935
Snipp, Snapp, Snurr and the Gingerbread, 1936
Snipp, Snapp, Snurr and the Big Surprise, 1937
Snipp, Snapp, Snurr and the Yellow Sled, 1936
Snipp, Snapp, Snurr and the Big Farm, 1946
Snipp, Snapp, Snurr Learn to Swim, 1954
Snipp, Snapp, Snurr and the Reindeer, 1957
Snipp, Snapp, Snurr and the Seven Dogs, 1959

SOLDIERS OF FORTUNE SERIES, Edward Stratemeyer, Lothrop, Lee & Shepard, hardcover, eight plates by A. B. Shute. $20.00
On to Pekin, or Old Glory in China, 1900
Under the Mikado's Flag, or Young Soldiers of Fortune, 1904
At the Fall of Port Arthur, or A Young American in the Japanese Navy, 1905
With Togo for Japan, or Three Young Americans on Land and Sea, 1906

SOMEWHERE SERIES, Martha Trent, ca. 1918 Barse, hardcover, illustrations by Charles Wrenn, World War 1 stories. $40.00
Helen Carey: Somewhere in America
Lucia Rudini: Somewhere in Italy
Alice Blythe: Somewhere in England
Maricken de Bruin: Somewhere in Belgium
Phoebe Marshal: Somewhere in Canada
Valerie Duval: Somewhere in France

SON OF ROBIN HOOD SERIES see ROBIN HOOD

SOU'WESTER SERIES, Arthur Baldwin, Random House, oversize hardcover, sailing adventures of two young brothers, blue/w pictorial endpapers, b/w illustrations by Gordan Grant. Early printings: ($35.00 with dust jacket) $15.00
Sou'wester Sails, 1936
Sou'wester Goes North, 1938
Sou'wester Victorious, 1939
Sou'wester, related title:
Junior Skipper's Handbook, 1940, hardcover, illustrated by author. $10.00

SOUP AND ROB SERIES, Robert Peck, Knopf or Delacorte, hardcover, b/w illustrations by Charles Lilly, lighthearted tales of a Vermont childhood. Early printings: ($30.00 with dust jacket) $10.00

Soup, 1974
Soup and Me, 1975
Soup for President, 1978
Soup's Drum, 1980
Soup on Wheels, 1981
Soup in the Saddle, 1983
Soup's Goat, 1984
Soup on Ice, 1985
Soup on Fire, 1987
Soup's Uncle, 1988
Soup's Hoop, 1990
Soup in Love, 1992
Soup Ahoy, 1994
Soup 1776, 1995
Soup, related titles, paperback: $8.00
Little Soup's Birthday, 1991 Dell
Little Soup's Hayride, 1991 Dell

SOUTH TOWN SERIES, Lorenz Graham, Follett and Crowell, hardcover, dust jacket illustration by Ernie Crichlow. Early printings: ($30.00 with dust jacket) $10.00
South Town, 1958
North Town, 1965
Whose Town?, 1969
Return to South Town, 1976

SPEEDWELL BOYS SERIES, Roy Rockwood (Stratemeyer Syndicate pseudonym), ca. 1915 Cupples & Leon, light hardcover with printed illustration, logo on spine, frontispiece by W. S. Rogers. $15.00
Speedwell Boys on Motor Cycles
Speedwell Boys and Their Racing Auto
Speedwell Boys and Their Power Launch
Speedwell Boys in a Submarine
Speedwell Boys and Their Ice Racer

SPORT STORIES FOR BOYS BOOKS, Harold M. Sherman, ca. 1930s Grosset & Dunlap, hardcover. ($25.00 with dust jacket) $15.00
Batter Up!
Double Play
Bases Full!
Hit by Pitcher

Safe!
Hit and Run
Mayfield's Fighting Five
Get 'Em, Mayfield!
Shoot that Ball!
Flashing Steel
Flying Heels
Slashing Sticks
Number 44

SPOTLIGHT CLUB MYSTERIES, Florence Heide, Whitman, hardcover, illustrated by Seymour Fleishman, early printings: $25.00
Weekly Reader edition: $10.00
Mystery of the Silver Tag, 1972
Mystery of the Missing Suitcase, 1972
Hidden Box Mystery, 1973
Mystery of the MacAdoo Zoo, 1973
Mystery of the Melting Snowman, 1974
Mystery of the Whispering Voice, 1974
Mystery of the Bewitched Bookmobile, 1975
Mystery of the Lonely Lantern, 1976
Mystery of the Keyhole Carnival, 1977
Mystery of the Southport Cinema, 1978
Mystery of the Forgotten Island, 1979
Mystery of the Mummy's Mask, 1979
Mystery of the Midnight Message, 1982
Mystery of the Vanishing Visitor, 1983
Mystery of Danger Road, 1983

SPRINGBOARD SPORTS SERIES, Alex B. Allen, Whitman, 4 titles, pictorial hardcovers, various artists. $10.00.
No Place for Baseball, 1973

Fifth Down, 1974
Danger on Broken Arrow Trail, 1974
Tennis Menace, 1975

SPY SERIES, Anne Emery, ca. 1965 Rand McNally, hardcover, map endpapers, b/w illustrations, historical novels with teenage heroes. ($20.00 with dust jacket) $10.00
Spy in Old West Point, illustrations by Lorence F. Bjorklund
Spy in Old Detroit, illustrations by H. B. Vestal
Spy in Old New Orleans, illustrations by Emil Weiss
Spy in Old Philadelphia, illustrations by H. B. Vestal
Spy in Williamsburg, illustrations by Manning de V. Lee
Spy, related book:
Drumbeats in Williamsburg, continues the adventures of the young hero of the Williamsburg *Spy* novel, illustrations by Manning de V. Lee

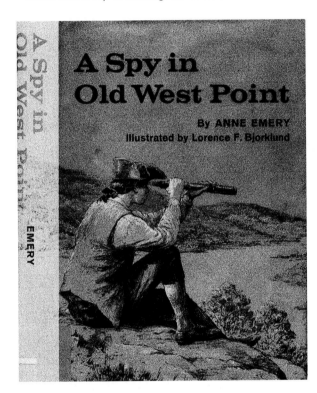

SQUARE DOLLAR BOYS SERIES, Irving Hancock, 1912 Altemus, tan hardcover with red lettering, four plates. $20.00
Square Dollar Boys Wake Up
Square Dollar Boys Smash the Ring
Square Dollar Boys Still Hunt

ST. CLARE SERIES, Enid Blyton, ca. 1940s Methuen, small hardcover, b/w illustrations. ($30.00 with dust jacket) $10.00
Twins at St. Clare's
O'Sullivan Twins
Summer Term at St. Clare's
Second Form at St. Clare's
Claudine at St. Clare's

Fifth Formers of St. Clare's

ST. DUNSTAN SERIES, Warren Eldred, Lothrop, Lee & Shepard, red hardcover with paste-on-pictorial, gold lettering, b/w plates. $35.00
Crimson Ramblers, 1910
Camp St. Dunstan, 1911
Classroom and Campus, 1912
St. Dunstan Boy Scouts, 1913

ST. LAWRENCE RIVER SERIES, Everett Tomlinson, Lothrop, Lee & Shepard, hardcover, gilt lettering, eight b/w plates by A. B. Shute. $45.00
Camping on the St. Lawrence, 1899
House-Boat on the St. Lawrence, 1900
Cruising on the St. Lawrence, 1902

ST. MARY'S SERIES, William Heyliger, 1911 – 1915 Appleton, tan hardcover with impressed illustration, b/w plates, school sports. Hard-to-find, priced from $75.00 up
Bartley, Freshman Pitcher
Bucking the Line
Captain of the Nine
Strike Three
Off Side
Against Odds

 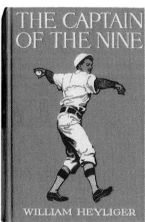

ST. NICHOLAS see ANNUALS

ST. TIMOTHY'S SERIES, Arthur Stanwood Pier, several editions and reprints.
1930s edition Scribner, first title only, hardcover: ($25.00 with dust jacket) $15.00 Houghton, hardcover, 4 b/w plates, early printings: $25.00
Grosset and Stokes editions, hardcover, 4 b/w plates: ($30.00 with dust jacket) $15.00
Boys of St. Timothy's, 1904
Harding of St. Timothy's, 1906
New Boy, 1908
Crashaw Brothers, 1910
Jester of St. Timothy's, 1911
Grannis of the Fifth, 1914
Son Decides, 1918

Dormitory Days, 1919
David Ives, 1922
Friends and Rivals, 1925
Boy from the West, 1930

STACY BELFORD SERIES, Lenora Mattingly Weber, Crowell, hardcover, another teen romance series (what else with these titles?) by this popular writer. First edition with dust jacket by Robert Levering: $200.00 and up
How Long Is Always?, 1970
Hello, My Love, Goodbye, 1971
Sometimes a Stranger, 1972

STEELEY SERIES, W.E. Johns, George Newnes. Adventure/mystery series by the popular author of the BIGGLES books. Written for an older audience than Biggles, Steeley is an embittered WWI flying ace who helps Scotland Yard solve crimes. 1930s original Newnes hardcover editions: RARE. 1950s Latimer House reprints: ($100.00 with dustjacket) $40.00
Sky High, 1936
Steeley Flies Again, 1936
Murder by Air, 1937
Murder at Castle Deeping, 1938
Wings of Romance, 1939
Related title:
Sinister Service, 1942 Oxford University Press, revised version of the Steeley magazine story "Nazi in New Forest" with the hero's name changed to Lance Lovells. Hardcover ($100.00 with dust jacket) $40.00

STEP-UP SERIES, DeKay, White, and other authors, ca. 1960s Random House, hardcover, illustrations, map or illustrated endpapers. ($15.00 with dust jacket) $10.00
Titles include:
Meet John F. Kennedy, 1965
Meet Andrew Jackson, 1967
Meet Theodore Roosevelt, 1967
Meet Christopher Columbus, 1968

STEVE CANYON ADVENTURE SERIES, Milton Caniff, Grosset & Dunlap, hardcover, uncredited illustrations copy Caniff's newspaper strip style. ($35.00 with dust jacket) $10.00
Steve Canyon: Operation Convoy, 1959
Steve Canyon: Operation Snowflower, 1959
Steve Canyon: Operation Foo Ling, 1959
Steve Canyon: Operation Eel Island, 1959
Steve Canyon, related books:
Milton Caniff's Steve Canyon, 1959 Little Golden Books, hardcover. $20.00

STEVE KNIGHT FLYING SERIES, Ted Copp, Grosset & Dunlap, orange hardcover with black lettering and airplane illustration, frontispiece. ($35.00 with dust jacket) $15.00
Devil's Hand, 1941
Bridge of Bombers, 1941
Phantom Fleet, 1942

STONEMASON SERIES, Alan Garner, Collins, UK, and World, US, hardcover, saga of a stonemason's family. ($20.00 with dust jacket) $10.00
Stone Book, 1976
Granny Reardon, 1977
Aimer Gate, 1979
Tom Fobbie's Day, 1979

STORIES OF THE TRIANGULAR LEAGUE SERIES, Albertus Dudley, ca. 1910 Lothrop, Lee & Shepard, illustration printed on hardcover, plate illustrations by Charles Copeland, school sports stories. $25.00
School Four
At the Home-Plate
Unofficial Prefect

"STORY BOOK OF" SERIES see PETERSHAM SERIES

STORY HOUR READERS, Ida Coe and Alice Christie, ca. 1914 American Book Company, hardcover, about 22 pages, illustrations by Maginal Enwright. $40.00

STRATEMEYER POPULAR SERIES, Edward Stratemeyer, ca. 1890s Lothrop, Lee and Shepard, hardcover, frontispiece, some have additional b/w plates. Although later printings advertise themselves as "bound in gold and colors," they actually lack gilt. This is a put-together series of stories of boys pursuing first jobs or careers, and other titles were added to later editions by Grosset. Early editions: $30.00, Grosset & Dunlap reprints: $15.00

Last Cruise of the Spitfire
Richard Dare's Venture
Oliver Bright's Search
Reuben Stone's Discovery
Young Auctioneer
Bound to be an Electrician
Shorthand Tom, the Reporter
Fighting for His Own
To Alaska for Gold
True to Himself
Joe, the Surveyor
Two Young Lumbermen
Larry, the Wanderer

STRATEMEYER SYNDICATE was started by Edward Stratemeyer (b. New Jersey, 1862 – 1930) who wrote the Rover Boys series under the pseudonym Arthur M. Winfield. Stratemeyer created series ideas and plot outlines, then hired writers at a flat fee per book, using pseudonyms. His freelance writers often wrote under several names, and the same pseudonym was often used by several writers. Syndicate pseudonyms include Alice Emerson, Laura Lee Hope, Margaret Penrose, Carolyn Keene, Victor Appleton, Mabel Hawley, Frances Judd.

Stratemeyer's daughter, Harriet Stratemeyer Adams, headed the firm after her father's death in 1930, and for several years was assisted by her sister, Edna Stratemeyer Squier.

SUBMARINE BOYS SERIES, Victor Durham, ca. 1910 Altemus, and Saalfield, cloth-over-board cover, frontispiece illustration, several formats. $10.00
Submarine Boys' Trial Trip
Submarine Boys and the Middies
Submarine Boys and the Spies
Submarine Boys for the Flag
Submarine Boys' Lightning Cruise
Submarine Boys on Duty
Submarine Boys' Secret Mission

SUBMARINE CHUMS SERIES, Sherwood Dowling, 1914 – 1915 Appleton, hardcover, frontispiece by Varian, boys build their own submarine. $20.00
Cruise of the Gray Whale
Gray Whale Warship
Gray Whale Flagship
Gray Whale Derelict

SUE BARTON SERIES, Helen Boylston, hardcover. Little, Brown, cloth hardcover, color frontispiece. (First editions: $100.00 with dust jacket) $30.00
Bodley Head editions: ($50.00 with dust jacket) $20.00
Sue Barton, Student Nurse, 1936
Sue Barton, Senior Nurse, 1937
Sue Barton, Visiting Nurse, 1938
Sue Barton, Rural Nurse, 1939, dust jacket by Major Felten
Sue Barton, Superintendent of Nurses, 1940
Sue Barton, Neighborhood Nurse, 1949
Sue Barton, Staff Nurse, 1952

SUGAR CREEK GANG SERIES (or "New Sugar Creek Gang" series), Paul Hutchens, Eerdsman Publishers, then Von Kampen after 1947, hardcover, 28 titles, Christian adventure/mystery series. Von Kampen picked up the series in 1947 after Hutchens left Eerdsman. Same characters con-

tinue through books. ($15.00 with dust jacket) $10.00
Sugar Creek Gang, a Story for Boys, 1940
We Killed a Bear, 1940
Further Adventures of the Sugar Creek Gang, 1940
Sugar Creek Gang Goes Camping, 1941
Sugar Creek Gang in Chicago, 1941
Sugar Creek Gang in School, 1942
Mystery at Sugar Creek, 1943
Sugar Creek Gang Flies to Cuba, 1944
One Stormy Day at Sugar Creek, 1946
New Sugar Creek Mystery, 1946
Shenanigans at Sugar Creek, 1947
Sugar Creek Gang Goes North, 1947
Adventure in an Indian Cemetery, 1947
Sugar Creek Gang Digs for Treasure, 1948
Northwoods Manhunt, 1948
Haunted House at Sugar Creek, 1949
Lost in a Sugar Creek Blizzard, 1950
Sugar Creek Gang on the Mexican Border, 1950
Green Tent Mystery at Sugar Creek, 1950
10,000 Minutes at Sugar Creek, 1952
Trap Line at Sugar Creek, 1953
Blue Cow at Sugar Creek, 1953
Watermelon Mystery at Sugar Creek, 1955
Sugar Creek Gang at Snow Goose Lodge, 1957
Old Stranger's Secret at Sugar Creek, 1957
Sugar Creek Gang Goes Western, 1957
Wild Horse Canyon Mystery, 1959
Howling Dog in Sugar Creek Swamp, 1968

SUMMER VACATION SERIES, Mary Smith, Little, Brown, red hardcover, gold lettering, b/w plates. $15.00
Four on a Farm, 1911
Two in a Bungalow, 1914
Three in a Camp, 1916
Five in a Ford, 1918

SUMMER TRILOGY, Robert Lipsyte, Harper, hardcover. ($20.00 with dust jacket) $10.00
One Fat Summer, 1977
Summer Rules, 1981
Summerboy, 1982

SUNNY BOY SERIES, Ramy Allison White (Stratemeyer Syndicate pseudonym), ca. 1920s Barse, cloth-over-board cover, b/w illustrations. ($20.00 with dust jacket) $10.00
Sunny Boy in the Country
Sunny Boy at the Seashore
Sunny Boy in the Big City
Sunny Boy in School and Out
Sunny Boy and His Playmates
Sunny Boy and His Games
Sunny Boy in the Far West
Sunny Boy on the Ocean
Sunny Boy with the Circus
Sunny Boy and His Big Dog
Sunny Boy in the Snow

Sunny Boy at Willow Farm
Sunny Boy and His Cave
Sunny Boy at Rainbow Lake

SUSANNAH SERIES, Muriel Denison, this popular series was reprinted in a variety of formats (see SHIRLEY TEMPLE).
1930s – 1940s Dodd, Mead edition, hardcover, illustrated endpapers, b/w illustrations by Marguerite Bryan: ($40.00 with dust jacket) $15.00
Susannah of the Mounties, 1936
Susannah of the Yukon, 1936
Susannah at Boarding School, 1938
Susannah Rides Again, 1940

SUSANNAH AND LUCY MYSTERIES, Patricia Elmore, Dutton, hardcover, b/w illustrations by Joel Schick. First edition: ($30.00 with dust jacket) $15.00
Susannah and the Blue House Mystery, 1980
Susannah and the Poison Green Halloween, 1982
Susannah and the Purple Mongoose Mystery, 1992

SWALLOWS AND AMAZONS SERIES, Arthur Ransome, (1884 – 1967)
Camping and sailing adventures of the Walker family and their catboat, Swallow, and the Blackett girls, these popular books were reprinted in various formats.
Hardcover, early printings: ($60.00 with dust jacket) $20.00
1940s and 1950s reprints: ($40.00 with dust jacket) $15.00
Swallows and Amazons, 1931 edition Cape, illustra-

tions by Clifford Webb. First edition with dust jacket: RARE

Swallows and Amazons, 1931 edition Lippincott, illustrations by Helene Carter. First edition with dust jacket: RARE.

Swallowdale, 1932, Lippincott, illustrations by Helene Carter. First edition: RARE.

Peter Duck, 1932 Cape, author illustrations, color map endpapers. First edition with dust jacket: RARE

Winter Holiday, 1934 edition Lippincott, illustrations by Helene Carter. First edition with dust jacket: RARE

Coot Club, 1934 Cape, green hardcover with gilt, pictorial endpapers, line drawings. First edition: ($500.00 with dust jacket) $50.00

Pigeon Post, 1937 Cape, illustrations by Mary Shepard. First edition: ($400.00 with dust jacket) $50.00

We Didn't Mean to Go to Sea, 1937 Cape, illustrations by author. First edition: ($300.00 with dust jacket) $50.00

Secret Water, 1939 Cape, green hardcover with gilt lettering, map endpapers, illustrations. First edition: ($300.00 with dust jacket) $50.00

Big Six, 1940 Cape, illustrations by author. First edition: ($300.00 with dust jacket) $50.00

Missee Lee, 1941 Cape, b/w illustrations by author. First edition: ($250.00 with dust jacket) $50.00

Picts and the Martyrs, 1943 Cape, green hardcover with gilt, map endpapers, illustrations by author. First edition: ($175.00 with dust jacket) $40.00

Great Northern?, 1947 Cape, green hardcover with gilt, illustrations by author. First edition: ($100.00 with dust jacket) $40.00

T

T. HAVILAND HICKS SERIES, J. R. Elderdice, 1915 – 1916 Appleton, hardcover, b/w plates, T. Haviland and his banjo go to college. $20.00

T. Haviland Hicks, Freshman
T. Haviland Hicks, Sophomore
T. Haviland Hicks, Junior
T. Haviland Hicks, Senior

TAMMY SERIES, Elizabeth Baker, Houghton Mifflin, hardcover, Illustrated by Beth Krush. ($30.00 with dust jacket) $15.00

Tammy Camps Out, 1958
Tammy Climbs Pyramid Mountain, 1962
Tammy Goes Canoeing, 1966
Tammy Camps in the Rocky Mountains, 1970

TED AND NINA SERIES, Marguerite DeAngeli, Doubleday, small, illustrated endpapers, color illustrations by author. ($75.00 with dust jacket) $50.00

Ted and Nina Go to the Grocery Store, 1935
Ted and Nina Have a Happy Rainy Day, 1936
Summer Day with Ted and Nina, 1940

Ted and Nina Story Book, 1965

TED JONES SERIES, Frank Glines Patchin (1861 – 1925), 1928 Altemus, hardcover. $20.00

Ted Jones, Fortune Hunter
Ted Jones at Desperation Island
Ted Jones under Sealed Orders
Ted Jones' Weeks of Terror

TED MARSH SERIES see LUCKY SERIES

TED SCOTT SERIES, Franklin Dixon (Stratemeyer Syndicate pseudonym), 1927 – 1943 Grosset & Dunlap, red or tan hardcover, illustrated endpapers, illustrations by Walter Rogers, J. Clemens Gretta, and others. The series can also be found with altered titles and sequence, and some proposed titles may have been dropped. ($25.00 with dust jacket) $20.00

Ted Scott, Over the Ocean to Paris, 1927
Ted Scott, Rescued in the Clouds, 1927
Ted Scott, Over the Rockies with the Air Mail, 1927
Ted Scott, First Stop, Honolulu
Ted Scott, Search for the Lost Flyers, 1928
Ted Scott, South of the Rio Grande
Ted Scott's Hop to Australia, or Across the Pacific, 1928
Ted Scott, Lone Eagle of the Border, 1929
Ted Scott Flying Against Time, 1929
Ted Scott, Over the Jungle Trails, 1929
Ted Scott, Lost at the South Pole, 1929
Ted Scott, Through the Air to Alaska, 1929
Ted Scott, Flying to the Rescue, 1930
Ted Scott, Danger Trails of the Sky, 1931
Ted Scott, Following the Sun Shadow, 1932
Ted Scott, Battling the Wind, 1933

Ted Scott, Brushing the Mountain Top, 1934
Ted Scott, Castaways of the Stratosphere, 1935
Ted Scott, Hunting the Sky Spies, 1941
Ted Scott, Pursuit Patrol, 1943

TED WILFORD MYSTERIES, Norvin Pallas, 1951 – 1967 Ives Washburn, 15 titles, hardcover. ($15.00 with dust jacket) $10.00
Secret of Thunder Mountain, 1951
Locked Safe Mystery, 1954
Star Reporter Mystery, 1955
Singing Tree Mystery, 1956
Empty House Mystery, 1957
Counterfeit Mystery, 1958
Stolen Plans Mystery, 1959
Scarecrow Mystery, 1960
Big Cat Mystery, 1961
Missing Witness Mystery, 1962
Baseball Mystery, 1963
Mystery of Rainbow Gulch, 1964
Abandoned Mine Mystery, 1965
S. S. Shamrock Mystery, 1966
Greenhouse Mystery, 1967

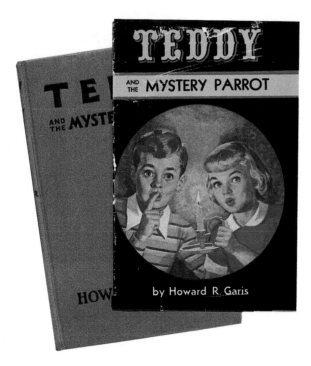

TEDDY SERIES, Howard Garis, Cupples & Leon, red hardcover, black lettering, frontispiece. ($20.00 with dust jacket) $10.00
Teddy and the Mystery Dog, 1936
Teddy and the Mystery Monkey, 1936
Teddy and the Mystery Cat, 1937
Teddy and the Mystery Parrot, 1938
Teddy and the Mystery Pony, 1939
Teddy and the Mystery Deer, 1940
Teddy and the Mystery Goat, 1941

TEEN-AGE LIBRARY BOOKS, ca. 1948 Grosset, hardcover, about 250 pages, b/w illustrations throughout. Each book is a collection of short stories on the title subject. ($15.00 with dust jacket) $5.00
Titles include:
Teen-Age Adventure Stories
Teen-Age Aviation Stories
Teen-Age Baseball Stories
Teen-Age Boy Scout Stories
Teen-Age Companion Stories
Teen-Age Football Stories
Teen-Age Historical Stories
Teen-Age Mystery Stories
Teen-Age Outdoor Stories
Teen-Age Sea Stories
Teen-Age Sports Stories
Teen-Age Stories of Action
Teen-Age Stories of the West
Teen-Age Treasure Chest of Sports Stories

TELEVISION RELATED BOOKS see WHITMAN TV, also LEAVE IT TO BEAVER, WALTONS.

TEXAN SERIES, Joseph Altsheler, 1912 – 1913 Appleton, hardcover, frontispiece and three plates, Texas-Mexican War. First edition with dust jacket: $200.00
1950s reprints: ($30.00 with dust jacket) $15.00
Texan Star
Texan Scouts
Texan Triumph

THEY CAME FROM SERIES, Clara Ingram Judson, ca. 1940s Houghton Mifflin, hardcover, b/w illustrations. ($30.00 with dust jacket) $10.00
They Came from Sweden
They Came from France

They Came from Scotland
They Came from Dalmatia, Petar's Treasure
They Came from Ireland, Michael's Victory
They Came from Bohemia, The Lost Violin
They Came from China, The Green Ginger Jar

THIS IS see SASEK

THREE BOYS SERIES, Nan Hayden Agle and/or Ellen Janet Wilson (Cameron), 1951 – 1968 Scribners, hardcover, illustrated endpapers, illustrations by Marian Honigman. Heroes are the triplets Abercrombie, Benjamin, and Christopher. ($15.00 with dust jacket) $10.00
Three Boys and a Lighthouse, 1951
Three Boys and the Remarkable Cow, 1952
Three Boys and a Tugboat, 1953
Three Boys and a Mine, 1954
Three Boys and a Train, 1956
Three Boys and a Helicopter, 1958
Three Boys and Space, 1962
Three Boys and H2O, 1968

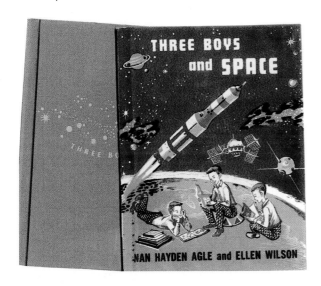

THREE INVESTIGATORS see ALFRED HITCHCOCK AND THE THREE INVESTIGATORS.

THREE JAYS SERIES, Pat Smythe, 1958 – 1961 Cassell, 6 titles, hardcover. ($15.00 with dust jacket) $10.00
Jacqueline Rides for a Fall, 1957
Three Jays Against the Clock, 1958
Three Jays on Holiday, 1958
Three Jays Go to Town, 1959
Three Jays Over the Border, 1960
Three Jays Go to Rome, 1960
Three Jays Lend a Hand, 1961

THRILLING NAVAL STORIES SERIES, T. T. Jeans, R. N., ca. 1920 Blackie and Son, impressed illustration on cover, b/w plate illustrations. $15.00
Naval Venture
Gunboat and Gun-runner

John Graham, Sub-Lieutenant, R. N.
On Foreign Service
Ford of H.M.S. Vigilant
Mr. Midshipman Glover

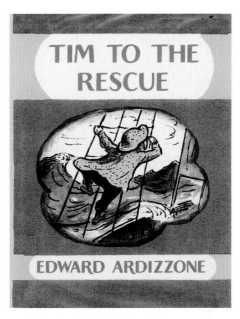

TIM AND LUCY SERIES, Edward Ardizzone, oversize hardcover, color illustrations by author, Oxford Press, London, first edition: $50.00 to $100.00 with dust jacket
Later editions and reprints: ($25.00 with dust jacket) $15.00
Little Tim and the Brave Sea Captain, 1936, firsts are hard-to-find
Tim and Lucy Go to Sea, 1938
Tim to the Rescue, 1949
Tim and Charlotte, 1951
Tim in Danger, 1953
Tim All Alone, 1956
Tim's Friend Towser, 1962
Tim and Ginger, 1965
Tim to the Lighthouse, 1968
Tim's Last Voyage, 1972
Ship's Cook Ginger, 1977

TIM MURPHY, REPORTER, SERIES, Graham Dean, 1931 – 1934 Goldsmith, hardcover. ($25.00 with dust jacket) $10.00
Daring Wings
Sky Trails
Circle Four Patrol
Treasure Hunt of the S – 18

TIMBER TRAIL RIDERS SERIES, Michael Murray, 1960s Whitman, glossy pictorial hardcover. $10.00
Mysterious Dude
Luck of Black Diamond
Texas Tenderfoot – A Dave Talbot Story
Long Trail North

TIPPY PARRISH see PENNY PARRISH

TISH STERLING SERIES, Norma Johnston, Atheneum, hardcover, journals of a teenager in the Bronx. Early edition with dust jacket: $50.00 Later editions: ($20.00 with dust jacket) $10.00
Keeping Days, 1973
Glory in the Flower, 1974, dust jacket by Velma Ilsley
Mustard Seed of Magic, 1977
Nice Girl Like You, 1980
Myself and I, 1981

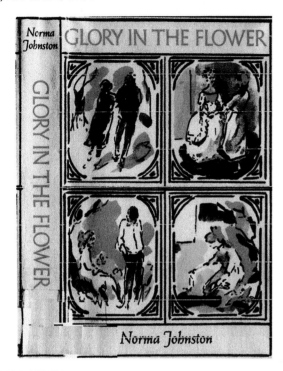

TOBY SERIES, Robbie Branscum, Doubleday, hardcover, orphan growing up in rural Arkansas. ($20.00 with dust jacket) $10.00
Toby, Granny and George, 1976
Toby Alone, 1979
Toby and Johnny Joe, 1979

TOBY HEYDON SERIES, Rosamund du Jardin, Lippincott, hardcover. First edition with dust jacket: $85.00 up
Later printings: ($20.00 with dust jacket) $10.00
Practically Seventeen, 1949
Class Ring, 1951
Boy Trouble, 1953
Real Thing, 1956
Wedding in the Family, 1958
One of the Crowd, 1961

TOD HALE SERIES, Ralph Henry Barbour, 1926 – 1929 Dodd, Mead, brown hardcover with paste-on-pictorial, four plates by Leslie Crump, school sports, of course. $25.00
Grosset edition, hardcover, frontispiece. ($20.00 with dust jacket) $10.00

Tod Hale with the Crew
Tod Hale at Camp
Tod Hale on the Scrub
Tod Hale on the Nine

TOD MORAN SERIES, Howard Pease, Doubleday, hardcover, pictorial or map endpapers, reissued in several variations. ($20.00 with dust jacket) $10.00
Tod Moran: The Tattooed Man, 1926
Tod Moran: The Jinx Ship, 1927
Tod Moran: Shanghai Passage, 1929
Tod Moran: The Ship Without a Crew, 1934
Tod Moran: Wind In the Rigging, 1935
Tod Moran: Hurricane Weather, 1936
Tod Moran: Foghorns, 1937
Tod Moran: Highroad to Adventure, 1939
Tod Moran: The Black Tanker, 1941
Tod Moran: Night Boat, 1942
Tod Moran: Heart of Danger, 1946
Tod Moran: Captain of the Araby, 1953
Tod Moran: Mystery on Telegraph Hill, 1961

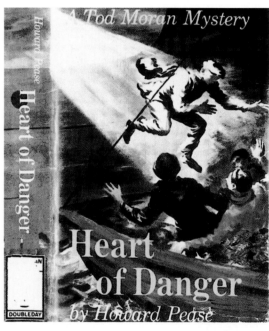

TOLLIVER ADVENTURE SERIES, Alan Stone (Stratemeyer Syndicate pseudonym), 1967 World, pictorial hardcover. $20.00
Tollivers and the Mystery of the Lost Pony
Tollivers and the Mystery of Pirate Island
Tollivers and the Mystery of the Old Jalopy

TOM FAIRFIELD SERIES, Allen Chapman (Stratemeyer Syndicate pseudonym), ca. 1915 Cupples & Leon, blue hardcover with printed red/blue illustration, b/w frontispiece. ($20.00 with dust jacket) $10.00
Tom Fairfield's School Days
Tom Fairfield at Sea
Tom Fairfield in Camp

Tom Fairfield's Pluck and Luck
Tom Fairfield's Hunting Trip

TOM HUNTNER SPORTS SERIES, Ken Anderson, ca. 1945 Zondervan, hardcover. ($20.00 with dust jacket) $10.00
Tom Huntner, Sophomore Forward
Tom Huntner, Sophomore Pitcher
Tom Huntner, Sophomore Halfback

TOM QUEST SERIES, Fran Striker, Grosset & Dunlap, tweed hardcover, pictorial endpapers, frontispiece. First edition: $40.00 with dust jacket
Later Grosset printings: ($25.00 with dust jacket) $10.00
Clover Books, McLoughlin Bros. glossy illustrated hardcover: $15.00
Sign of the Spiral, 1947
Telltale Scar, 1947
Clue of the Cypress Stump, 1948
Secret of the Lost Mesa, 1949
Hidden Stone Mystery, 1950
Secret of Thunder Mountain, 1952
Inca Luck Piece, 1955
Mystery of the Timber Giant, 1955

TOM SAWYER SERIES, Mark Twain (Samuel Clemens, 1835 – 1910), these American classics are reprinted regularly by a variety of publishers and in various formats and are easily available. Tom's adventures begin in Hannibal, Missouri, a small river town where Twain once lived, and include Tom's best friends, Becky Thatcher and Huckleberry Finn.

Ca. 1930s Winston reprints, hardcover with paste-on pictorial and gilt trim, b/w illustrations: $15.00
Grosset & Dunlap illustrated glossy hardcover editions: $15.00
Sample listing of early editions and values:
Adventures of Tom Sawyer, 1876 Roman, RARE
Adventures of Tom Sawyer, ca. 1930s Harper & Bros., black hardcover with paste-on-pictorial, color frontispiece, 15 b/w plates by Worth Brehm. ($45.00 with dust jacket) $30.00
Adventures of Tom Sawyer, 1930 Random House, oversize, brown leather spine, illustrated hardcover, gilt lettering, illustrated endpapers, illustrated by Donald McKay, limited edition of 2000 sold in slipcase. $35.00
Adventures of Tom Sawyer, 1931 Winston, decorated hardcover with paste-on-pictorial and gilt trim, b/w illustrations by Peter Hurd. $20.00
Adventures of Huckleberry Finn, 1885 Webster, pictorial green hardcover, illustrated by Edward Kemble. RARE
Adventures of Huckleberry Finn, ca. 1940 Harper & Bros., paste-on-pictorial hardcover, b/w plates by Worth Brehm. ($45.00 with dust jacket) $30.00
Tom Sawyer Abroad: Tom Sawyer, Detective and Other Stories, ca. 1894, light hardcover with a decoration depicting a lion chasing Tom and Huck, probable first edition: $500.00
Tom Sawyer Abroad, 1894 Chatto & Windus, London, red hardcover with black decoration, illustrations by Dan Beard, first UK edition: $450.00
Tom Sawyer Abroad: Tom Sawyer, Detective and Other Stories, ca. 1896 Webster, illustrated by Arthur Frost. $150.00
Tom Sawyer, Detective, undated edition Grosset ca. 1940, hardcover, illustrated endpapers, Arthur Frost frontispiece. ($20.00 with dust jacket) $10.00
Tom Sawyer, related titles:
Tom Sawyer, 1931 Whitman, pictorial boards, color photograph illustrations from the Paramount movie starring Jackie Coogan as Tom and Junior Durkin as Huck, with movie text on facing pages. $50.00

TOM SLADE SERIES, Percy Keese Fitzhugh, ca. 1910 – 30 Grosset, advertised as "endorsed by the Boy Scouts of America," hardcover, photo illustrated endpapers, four b/w plates by Emmett Owen, several editions with some format variations ($30.00 with dust jacket) $15.00
Whitman edition of first two titles, hardcover. ($15.00 with dust jacket) $10.00
Tom Slade, Boy Scout
Tom Slade at Temple Camp
Tom Slade on the River
Tom Slade with the Colors
Tom Slade with a Transport
Tom Slade with the Boys Over There
Tom Slade, Motor Cycle Dispatch Bearer

Tom Slade with the Flying Corps
Tom Slade at Black Lake
Tom Slade on Mystery Trail
Tom Slade's Double Dare
Tom Slade on Overlook Mountain
Tom Slade Picks a Winner
Tom Slade on Bear Mountain
Tom Slade, Forest Ranger
Tom Slade in the North Woods
Tom Slade at Shadow Isle
Tom Slade in the Haunted Cavern
Tom Slade, Parachute Jump

TOM STETSON SERIES, John Henry Cutler, Whitman Publishing, pictorial hardcover, pictorial endpapers, illustrations by Ursula Koering. $15.00
Tom Stetson and the Giant Jungle Ants, 1948
Tom Stetson on the Trail of the Lost Tribe, 1948
Tom Stetson and the Blue Devil, 1951

TOM STRONG SERIES, Alfred Mason, ca. 1915, Holt, hardcover, illustrated throughout. ($25.00 with dust jacket) $15.00
Tom Strong, Washington's Scout, 1911 ($25.00 in Boy Scout edition with logo)
Tom Strong, Boy-Captain, 1913
Tom Strong, Junior, 1915
Tom Strong, Third, 1916
Tom Strong, Lincoln's Scout, 1919

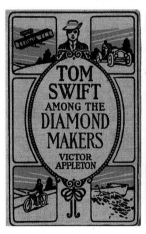 

Ca. 1910 Grosset   Ca. 1954 Grosset

TOM SWIFT SERIES, Victor Appleton (Stratemeyer syndicate pseudonym, created by Stratemeyer, the books through ca. 1932 were probably written by Howard Garis), Grosset & Dunlap, several hardcover designs. In early books, Tom invented gadgets that were just slightly ahead of their time, obviously inspired by American inventor Thomas Edison. First editions are hard-to-find, generally identified by list-to-self ads or title lists showing only titles from the original year of publication.
Tom Swift, 1910 – 1920 early editions, tan cloth hard-

cover with red/black design, b/w frontispiece: (RARE with dust jacket) $35.00
Tom Swift and His Motor Cycle, 1910
Tom Swift and His Motorboat, 1910
Tom Swift and His Airship, 1910
Tom Swift and his Submarine Boat, 1910
Tom Swift and His Electric Runabout, 1910
Tom Swift and His Wireless Message, 1911
Tom Swift Among the Diamond Makers, 1911
Tom Swift in the Caves of Ice, 1911
Tom Swift and His Sky Racer, 1911
Tom Swift and His Electric Rifle, 1911
Tom Swift in the City of Gold, 1912
Tom Swift and His Air Glider, 1912
Tom Swift in Captivity, 1912
Tom Swift and His Wizard Camera, 1912
Tom Swift and His Great Searchlight, 1912
Tom Swift and His Giant Cannon, 1913
Tom Swift and His Photo Telephone, 1914
Tom Swift and His Aerial Warship, 1915
Tom Swift and His Big Tunnel, 1916
Tom Swift in the Land of Wonders, 1917
Tom Swift and His War Tank, 1918
Tom Swift and His Air Scout, 1919
Tom Swift and His Undersea Search, 1920
Tom Swift, 1920s early editions: ($100.00 with dust jacket) $20.00
Tom Among the Fire Fighters, 1921
Tom Swift and His Electric Locomotive, 1922
Tom Swift and His Flying Boat, 1923
Tom Swift and His Great Oil Gusher, 1924
Tom Swift and His Chest of Secrets, 1925
Tom Swift and His Airline Express, 1926
Tom Swift Circling the Globe, 1927
Tom Swift and His Talking Pictures, 1928
Tom Swift and His House on Wheels, 1929
Tom Swift, 1930s and 1940s early editions: ($75.00 with dust jacket) $15.00. See also Whitman reprints.
Tom Swift and His Big Dirigible, 1930
Tom Swift and His Sky Train, 1931
Tom Swift and His Giant Magnet, 1932
Tom Swift and His Television Detector, 1933
Tom Swift and His Ocean Airport, 1934
Tom Swift and His Planet Stone, 1935.
Tom Swift, 1937, Whitman, reprints of titles previously published between 1926 – 1935, cloth hardcover with new dust jacket designs. Size and color of hardcover varies. ($20.00 with dust jacket) $10.00
Tom Swift, Whitman, Big Little Books or Better Little Books, small hardcovers with color illustrated covers, b/w drawings throughout. Hard to find, $200.00
Jack Swift and His Rocket Ship, 1934 (a copy of the Tom Swift formula)
Tom Swift and His Giant Telescope, 1939
Tom Swift and His Magnetic Silencer, 1941
New Tom Swift Jr. Adventures Series, (based on the TOM SWIFT series), Victor Appleton II (Stratemeyer pseudonym, probably a Harriet Adams idea and

written by several authors, including Jim Lawrence), Grosset & Dunlop, b/w illustrations by Graham Kaye. Once again, Tom's inventions are slightly ahead of their times. Now he invents rockets and ray guns instead of airplanes and telegraphs.

Cloth hardcover, blue and white scene endpapers (later editions use black & white endpapers): ($30.00 with dust jacket) $10.00

Tom Swift and His Flying Lab, 1954
Tom Swift and His Jetmarine, 1954
Tom Swift and His Rocket Ship, 1954
Tom Swift and His Giant Robot, 1954
Tom Swift and His Atomic Earth Blaster, 1954
Tom Swift and His Outpost in Space, 1955
Tom Swift and His Diving Seacopter, 1956
Tom Swift in the Caves of Nuclear Fire, 1956
Tom Swift on the Phantom Satellite, 1956
Tom Swift and His Ultrasonic Cycloplane, 1956
Tom Swift and His Deep-Sea Hydrodome, 1958
Tom Swift in the Race to the Moon, 1958
Tom Swift and His Solartron, 1958
Tom Swift and His Electronic Retroscope, 1959
Tom Swift and His Spectromarine Selector, 1960
Tom Swift and the Cosmic Astronauts, 1960
Tom Swift and the Visitor from Planet X, 1961

Tom Swift Jr., 1961 – 1971, blue spine (issued in 1961 only) or yellow spine, pictorial hardcover. Probable first editons: $25.00, reprints of earlier titles: $10.00

Tom Swift and the Electronic Hydrolung, 1961 (early editions had full picture wraparound on the spine).
Tom Swift and His Triphibian Atomicar, 1962
Tom Swift and His Megascopic Space Prober, 1962
Tom Swift and the Asteroid Pirates, 1963
Tom Swift and His Repelatron Skyway, 1963
Tom Swift and His Aquatomic Tracker, 1964
Tom Swift and His 3-D Telejector, 1964
Tom Swift and His Polar-Ray Dynasphere, 1965
Tom Swift and His Sonic Boom Trap, 1965
Tom Swift and His Subocean Geotron, 1966
Tom Swift and the Mystery Comet, 1966
Tom Swift and the Captive Planetoid, 1967
Tom Swift and His G-Force Inverter, 1968
Tom Swift and His Dyna-4 Capsule, 1969
Tom Swift and His Cosmotron Express, 1970
Tom Swift and the Galaxy Ghosts, 1971, hard-to-find

Tom Swift, 1981 – 1984, Simon and Schuster (Wanderer Imprint), hardcover (mostly sold to library trade) and paperback. Tom Swift's grandson goes into outer space. Hardcover hard to find: ($50.00 with dust jacket) $10.00. Ex-library hardcover ($15.00 with dust jacket) $5.00. Paperbacks: $10.00

City in the Stars
Astral Fortress
Alien Probe
War in Outer Space
Invisible Force Ark Two
Terror on Moons of Jupiter

Rescue Mission
Gateway to Doom
Crater of Mystery, paperback, $15.00
Planet of Nightmares, paperback only, $25.00

Tom Swift, 1990s, Archway (Simon and Schuster), paperback only. 13 titles plus 2 crossover "Ultra Thrillers" with the Hardy Boys. $7.00

TOMMY ROCKFORD HAM RADIO MYSTERY SERIES, Walker Tompkins, Macrae, first three titles, hardcover: ($50.00 with dust jacket) $20.00

American Radio Relay League paperback editions, all titles including revisions of the first three: $10.00

SOS at Midnight, 1957
CQ Ghost Ship, 1960
DX Brings Danger, 1962
Death Valley QTH, 1985
Grand Canyon QSO, 1987
Murder by QRM, 1988

TOMMY TIPTOP SERIES, Raymond Stone (Stratemeyer pseudonym), 1912 – 1917 Graham and Matlock, hardcover, frontispiece and seven plates. ($35.00 with dust jacket) $15.00

Tommy Tiptop and His Baseball Nine
Tommy Tiptop and His Football Eleven
Tommy Tiptop and His Winter Sports
Tommy Tiptop and His Boat Club
Tommy Tiptop and His Boy Scouts
Tommy Tiptop and His Great Show

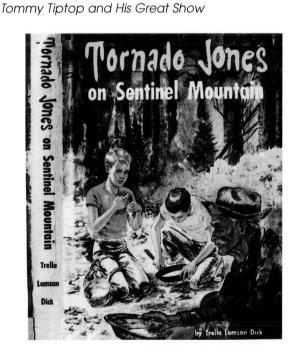

TORNADO JONES MYSTERY SERIES, Trella Dick, Follett, pictorial hardcover, b/w line drawings by Mary Stevens. ($35.00 with dust jacket) $15.00

Tornado Jones, 1953
Tornado Jones on Sentinel Mountain, 1955
Tornado Jones' Big Year, 1956

TRAIL BLAZERS SERIES, Charles Forbes-Lindsay, Charles Allen, Edward Sabin, 1907 – 1932 Lippincott, hardcover, frontispiece, various numbers of plates by different artists. $25.00
Titles include:
Buffalo Bill and the Overland Trail
Daniel Boone, Backwoodsman
David Crockett, Scout
General Crook and the Fighting Apaches
Gold Seeker of '49
In the Ranks of Old Hickory
Klondike Partners
Lost with Lieutenant Pike
Mississippi River Boy
On the Plains with Custer
Opening the West with Lewis and Clark
With Carson and Fremont
With George Washington into the West
With Sam Houston in Texas

TRAILER STORIES SERIES, Mildred Wirt, 1937 Cupples & Leon, hardcover. $15.00
Crimson Cruiser
Runaway Caravan
Timbered Treasure
Phantom Trailer

TRAVEL-TOT-TALES SERIES, 1920s Reilly & Lee, oversize picture books with color illustrated paper-on-board covers, blue/white illustrations by Bess Devine Jewell. $30.00

TREASURE SEEKERS SERIES, Edith Nesbit, popular English novels about a Victorian family of inventive children. These are easily found in paperback copies and the stories have been adapted and made popular through TV productions.
Some older editions include:
Story of the Treasure Seekers, (1899) undated Stokes, apparent first American edition, green cloth with gilt and white decoration. $100.00
Story of the Treasure Seekers, 1926 Unwin edition, blue hardcover, color frontispiece, b/w line drawings. $30.00
Wouldbegoods, ca. 1900 undated Unwin, London, gilt decoration on red hardcover, early printing: $40.00, 1901 Harper, first US edition, small decorated hardcover, Reginald Birch illustrations: $100.00
New Treasure Seekers, 1904 Unwin, first edition, gilt embossed red hardcover, engraved plates by Gordon Browne and Lewis Baumer. $100.00
Oswald Bastable and Others, 1905 Gardner Darton, red hardcover with gilt, plates by C. E. Brock and H. R. Millar, collection of 15 short stories with four about the Bastable children. First edition: $200.00
Complete History of the Bastable Family, 1928 Ernest Benn, London, red hardcover with gilt, collected edition of the three novels. $30.00

Bastable Children, 1928 Coward-McCann, first American edition, collection of three novels, preface by Christopher Morley, orange hardcover, illustrations. $150.00

TREASURE TRAILS READERS, ca. 1920s Macmillan, reprints by Doubleday, Doran, school readers with collected short stories and poems, hardcover, two color illustrations, illustrators include Maud and Miska Petersham. $20.00

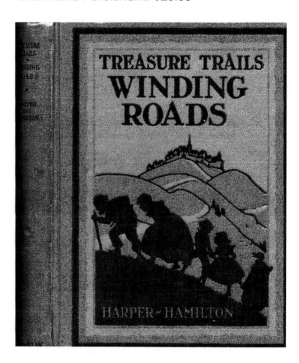

TREEGATE SERIES, Leonard Wibberley, Farrar, hardcover, historical adventure novels. ($20.00 with dust jacket) $10.00
John Treegate's Musket, 1959
Peter Treegate's War, 1960
Sea Captain from Salem, 1961
Treegate's Raiders, 1962
Leopard's Prey, 1971
Red Pawn, 1973
Last Battle, 1976

TRICK SERIES, Scott Corbett, Little, Brown, pictorial hardcover, illustrations by Paul Caldone, in humorous Corbett style, protagonist Kirby has a trick solution for every situation. $15.00
Lemonade Trick, 1960
Mailbox Trick, 1961
Disappearing Dog Trick, 1963
Limerick Trick, 1964
Baseball Trick, 1965
Turnabout Trick, 1967
Hairy Horror Trick, 1969
Hateful Plateful Trick, 1971
Homerun Trick, 1973
Hockey Trick, 1974

Black Mask Trick, 1976
Hangman's Ghost Trick, 1977

TRIG SERIES, Robert Peck, Little, Brown, hardcover, b/w illustrations by Pamela Johnson. ($20.00 with dust jacket) $10.00
Trig, 1977
Trig Sees Red, 1978
Trig Goes Ape, 1980
Trig or Treat, 1982

TRIGGER BERG MYSTERY SERIES, Leo Edwards, ca. 1930s Grosset & Dunlap, hardcover, illustrated endpapers, b/w plates by Bert Salg. Probable first edition with dust jacket: $100.00
Later editions: ($30.00 with dust jacket) $10.00
Trigger Berg and the Treasure Tree
Trigger Berg and his 700 Mouse Traps
Trigger Berg and the Sacred Pig
Trigger Berg and the Cockeyed Ghost, hard-to-find, first edition with dust jacket: $250.00

TRIPLETS SERIES, Bertha Moore, 1938 – 48 Eerdmans, small hardcover with printed illustration on cover. $15.00
Three Baers
Baers' Christmas
Triplets in Business
Triplets Go South
Triplets Over J.O.Y.
Triplets Go Places
Triplets Sign Up
Triplets Become Good Neighbors

TRIXIE BELDEN SERIES, Kathryn Kenny, pseudonyn, originated by Julie Campbell (Tatham), literary agent, first title was published in 1948 by Whit-

man. (Whitman and Golden Press are owned by Western Publishing, and the books appear under both names in different formats.) Thirty-nine books were published, written by Campbell and also by other authors who used the pseudonym Kathryn Kenny. This popular series was printed in several formats.

Trixie Belden, Whitman, plain hardcover with dust jacket:
Ca. 1948 – 1951, titles 1, 2, 3, illustration on hardcover with interior illustrations and wraparound illustration on dust jacket by Mary Stevens. ($45.00 with dust jacket) $15.00
Ca.1959, hardcover with dust jacket and a diamond pattern on spine, illustrations by Mary Stevens. Dust jacket illustrations by Herbert Tauss. ($20.00 with dust jacket) $10.00

Trixie Belden, Whitman, pictorial hardcovers, new titles and reprints:
Ca. 1954 – 1961, titles 1 through 10, glossy laminated pictorial hardcover, interior illustrations and cover by Mary Stevens. $15.00
Ca. 1961 – 70, pictorial hardcover by Larry Frederick, illustrated endpapers, books 1 through 8 plus 16. $10.00
Ca. 1962 – 1964, titles 1 through 13, "cameo" picture of Trixie appears in white or ivory-colored oval. Cover picture printed directly on cloth hardcover. Illustrations by Mary Stevens or Paul Frame. $15.00
Ca. 1965, titles 1 thru 15, oversized "deluxe" books, color illustration printed directly on cloth hardcover. Interior illustrations by Paul Frame or Haris Petie. $20.00
Ca. 1970s, titles 1 through 16, printed illustration on paper-over-board hardcover, illustrations by Larry Frederick. $15.00

Trixie Belden, London edition, pictorial hardcover:
1970s reprints, Dean & Son Ltd, London, cameo and illustration on yellow glossy hardcover. $15.00

Trixie Belden, Golden Press, hardcover:
1977 – 1980 titles 1 through 34, library binding editions using the paperback illustrations by Jack Wacker. $15.00
1980s, small hardcover library bindings, partial list of titles. $15.00

Trixie Belden, Golden Press, paperback:
1977 – 1980, titles 1 to 34, paperback with oval picture on tan cover, illustrated by Jack Wacker. $10.00
1984 – 1986, titles 1 to 39, paperback with yellow cover, illustrated by Jody Lee. Books 1 through 34: $10.00
Books 35 through 39 had short print runs which make them hard-to-find: $40.00
1. *Secret of the Mansion,* 1948
2. *Red Trailer Mystery,* 1950
3. *Gatehouse Mystery,* 1951
4. *Mysterious Visitor,* 1954
5. *Mystery Off Glen Road,* 1956
6. *Mystery in Arizona,* 1958

7. *Mysterious Code*, 1961
8. *Black Jacket Mystery*, 1961
9. *Happy Valley Mystery*, 1962
10. *Marshland Mystery*, 1962
11. *Mystery at Bob-White Cave*, 1963
12. *Mystery of the Blinking Eye*, 1963
13. *Mystery on Cobbett's Island*, 1964
14. *Mystery of the Emeralds*, 1965
15. *Mystery on the Mississippi*, 1965
16. *Mystery of the Missing Heiress*, 1970
17. *Mystery of the Uninvited Guest*, 1977
18. *Mystery of the Phantom Grasshopper*, 1977
19. *Secret of the Unseen Treasure*, 1977
20. *Mystery Off Old Telegraph Road*, 1978
21. *Mystery of the Castaway Children*, 1978
22. *Mystery at Mead's Mountain*, 1979
23. *Mystery of the Queen's Necklace*, 1979
24. *Mystery at Saratoga*, 1979
25. *Sasquatch Mystery*, 1979
26. *Mystery of the Headless Horseman*, 1979
27. *Mystery of the Ghostly Galleon*, 1979
28. *Hudson River Mystery*, 1979
29. *Mystery of the Velvet Gown*, 1980
30. *Mystery of the Midnight Marauder*, 1980
31. *Mystery at Maypenny's*, 1980
32. *Mystery of the Whispering Witch*, 1980
33. *Mystery of the Vanishing Victim*, 1980
34. *Mystery of the Missing Millionaire*, 1980
35. *Mystery of the Memorial Day Fire*, 1984
36. *Mystery of the Antique Doll*, 1984
37. *Pet Show Mystery*, 1985
38. *Indian Burial Ground Mystery*, 1985
39. *Mystery of the Galloping Ghost*, 1986

TRUDY AND TIMOTHY SERIES, Bertha Porter, 1917 – 33
Penn, hardcover, illustrated by May Aiken. $10.00

Trudy and Timothy, 1917
Trudy and Timothy Out-of-doors, 1919
Trudy and Timothy and the Trees, 1920
Trudy and Timothy, Foresters, 1922

TRUDY SERIES, Mary Alice Faid, 1950s – 60s, Pickering & Inglis, London, hardcover. ($15.00 with dust jacket) $10.00
Trudy Takes Charge
Trudy's Island Holiday
Trudy's Uphill Road
Trudy's College Days
Schoolma'am Trudy
Trudy's Small Corner
Trudy on Her Own
Trudy Married

TUCKER FAMILY SERIES, Jo Mendel, ca. 1965 Whitman, pictorial hardcover, 280+ pages, illustrated endpapers, one-color drawings by Jackie Tomes. $15.00
Adventures of Plum Tucker, 1961
Special Secret, 1961
Trouble on Valley View, 1961
Turnabout Summer, 1963
Tucker Family Big Tell-a-Tale books, ca. 1965, small, color illustrated hardcover, illustrated endpapers, color illustrations by Betty Fraser. $15.00
Tuckers: One Big Happy Family
Toby Tucker
Here Come the Tuckers
Tom Tucker and Dickie-Bird

TUCKER TWINS SERIES, Nell Speed, ca. 1915 Hurst, illustrated cloth-over-board cover, illustrated by Arthur Scott. Dust jackets all have same wrap-around illustration. ($30.00 with dust jacket) $10.00
At Boarding School with the Tucker Twins
Vacation with the Tucker Twins
Back at School with the Tucker Twins
Tripping with the Tucker Twins
House Party with the Tucker Twins
In New York with the Tucker Twins

TWINS SERIES, Dorothy Whitehill, ca. 1925 Barse Hopkins, gray cloth-over-board cover, b/w illustrations by Mary Ludlam. Same wraparound illustration on all dust jackets. ($15.00 with dust jacket) $10.00
Janet, a Twin
Phyllis, a Twin
Twins in the West
Twins in the South
Twins Summer Vacation
Twins and Tommy Jr.
Twins at Home
Twins' Wedding
Twins Adventuring
Twins at Camp
Twins Abroad
Twins A-Visiting
Twins and Tim

Japanese Twins, 1912
Eskimo Twins, 1914
Cave Twins, 1916
Belgian Twins, 1917
Spartan Twins, 1918
French Twins, 1918
Scotch Twins, 1919
Italian Twins, 1920
Mexican Twins, 1921
Puritan Twins, 1921
Filipino Twins, 1923
Colonial Twins, 1924
American Twins, 1926
Indian Twins, 1930

TWO LITTLE FELLOWS SERIES, Josephine Lawrence, ca. 1920s Barse, cloth-over-board cover, b/w illustrations. ($20.00 with dust jacket) $10.00
Two Little Fellows
Two Little Fellows Start School
Two Little Fellows Go Visiting
Two Little Fellows Secret
Two Little Fellows in April

TWO LITTLE WOMEN SERIES, Carolyn Wells, ca. 1915 Grosset, cloth-over-board cover, illustrated endpapers, about 270 pages. ($20.00 with dust jacket) $10.00
Two Little Women
Two Little Women and Treasure House
Two Little Women on a Holiday

TWINS OF THE WORLD SERIES, Lucy Fitch Perkins, 1911 – 35 Houghton, 25 books, this was an educational series for schools. ($50.00 with dust jacket) $25.00
Dutch Twins, 1911

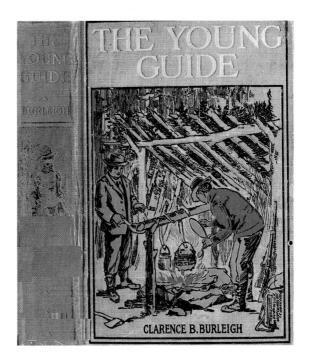

TWO LIVE BOYS SERIES, Clarence Burleigh, 1906 – 1910 Lothrop, Lee & Shepard, pictorial hardcover with gilt lettering, 8 b/w plates by Bridgman or 16 b/w photo plates by H. D. Edwards. $40.00

Camp on the Letter K, or Two Live Boys in Northern Maine
Raymond Benson at Krampton, or Two Live Boys at Preparatory School
Kenton Pines, or Raymond Benson at College
All Among the Loggers, or Norman Carver's Winter in a Lumber Camp
With Pickpole and Peavey, or Two Live Boys on the East Branch Drive
Young Guide, or Two Live Boys in the Maine Woods

TWO WILD CHERRIES see DICK AND JANET CHERRY

U

UNCLE BILL SERIES, Will James, Scribner, hardcover, color frontispiece, b/w illustrations throughout by author. First edition with dust jacket: $300.00
Later reprints: ($30.00 with dust jacket) $15.00
Uncle Bill, 1933
In the Saddle with Uncle Bill
Look-See with Uncle Bill, 1938

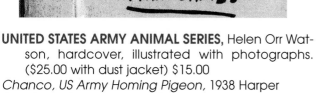

UNITED STATES ARMY ANIMAL SERIES, Helen Orr Watson, hardcover, illustrated with photographs. ($25.00 with dust jacket) $15.00
Chanco, US Army Homing Pigeon, 1938 Harper
Top Kick, US Army Horse, 1942 Houghton, Mifflin
Trooper, US Army Dog, 1943 Houghton, Mifflin
Shavetail Sam, US Army Mule, 1944 Houghton, Mifflin

UNITED STATES MARINE SERIES, Giles Bishop, 1921 – 1922 Penn Publishing, blue hardcover with paste-on-pictorial, frontispiece and four plates by Donald Humphreys. $50.00
Marines Have Landed
Marines Have Advanced

Lieutenant Comstock, U S Marines
Captain Comstock, U S Marine Corps

UNITED STATES MIDSHIPMAN SERIES, Lt. Com. Yates Stirling, 1908 – 1913 Penn Publishing, green illustrated hardcover, white lettering, illustrated endpapers, frontispiece and plates by Ralph Boyer. First edition with dust jacket: $85.00
Later printings: ($30.00 with dust jacket) $20.00
United States Midshipman in China
United States Midshipman in the Philippines
United States Midshipman in Japan
United States Midshipman in the South Seas

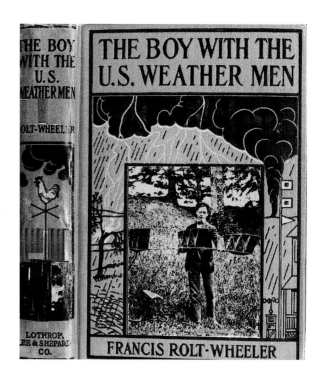

UNITED STATES NAVAL SERIES, see RALPH OSBORN
Francis Rolt-Wheeler, 1909 – 1929 Lothrop, Lee and Shepard, hardcover with photo paste-on-illustration, illustrations include photographs, maps. ($35.00 with dust jacket) $15.00
Boy with the US Survey
Boy with the US Foresters
Boy with the US Census
Boy with the US Fisheries
Boy with the US Indians
Boy with the US Explorers
Boy with the US Life-Savers
Boy with the US Mail
Boy with the US Weather Men
Boy with the US Naturalists
Boy with the US Trappers
Boy with the US Inventors
Boy with the US Secret Service
Boy with the US Miners
Boy with the US Diplomats
Boy with the US Radio

Boy with the US Red Cross
Boy with the US Marines
Boy with the US Navy
Boy with the US Aviators

—————— V ——————

VERONICA GANZ SERIES, Marilyn Sachs, Doubleday, hardcover, b/w illustrations throughout by Louis Glanzman, teenager in the Bronx. First edition: ($30.00 with dust jacket) $15.00
Veronica Ganz, 1968
Peter and Veronica, 1969
Marv, 1970
Truth about Mary Rose, 1973
Veronica Ganz, related titles: Veronica first appears in *Amy and Laura.* These three titles deal with the Bronx children when they are in grade school.
Amy Move In, 1964
Laura's Luck, 1965
Amy and Laura, 1966

VICARAGE CHILDREN SERIES, Lorna Hill, 1961 – 1966 Evans, hardcover, 3 titles. See also MARJORIE, DANCING PEELS, PATIENCE, and SADLER'S WELLS. ($25.00 with dust jacket) $10.00
Vicarage Children, 1961
More About Mandy, 1963
Vicarage Children in Skye, 1966

VICARAGE FAMILY SERIES, Noel Streatfeild, Collins, UK, and Watts, US, fictionalized stories of the author's childhood. First edition: ($30.00 with dust jacket) $15.00
Vicarage Family, 1963
Away from the Vicarage, 1967
Beyond the Vicarage, 1971

VICKI BARR FLIGHT STEWARDESS SERIES, Helen Wells and Julie (Campbell) Tatham, Grosset, advertised as the Flight Stewardess Series, *"fly to adventure with Vicki Barr."*
Pictorial hardcover reprints, illustrated endpapers, frontispiece: $15.00
Silver Wings through *Clue of the Gold Coin,* 1947 – 1958, plain hardcover: ($40.00 with dust jacket) $15.00
Silver Wings for Vicki, 1947
Vicki Finds the Answer, 1947
Hidden Valley Mystery
Secret of Magnolia Manor
Clue of the Broken Blossom
Behind the White Veil
Mystery at Hartwood House
Peril Over the Airport
Mystery of the Vanishing Lady, 1954
Search for the Missing Twin, 1954
Ghost at the Water Fall, 1956

Clue of the Gold Coin, 1958
Silver Ring Mystery, 1960, hard-to-find, Grosset tweed hardcover, first edition with dust jacket: $75.00 and up
Clue of the Carved Ruby, 1961, hard-to-find, Grosset tweed hardcover, first edition with dust jacket: $100.00 and up
Mystery of Flight 908, 1962, hard-to-find, Grosset tweed hardcover, first edition with dust jacket: $150.00 and up

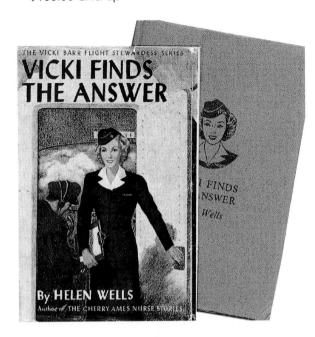

VICTORY BOY SCOUTS SERIES, Capt. Alan Douglas, ca. 1915 Donohue, tan hardcover, brown lettering. A put-together list of twelve Boy Scout adventures previously printed in other series, including Hickory Ridge Boy Scouts and a Boy Scout series by Ralphson, advertised as "stories by a writer who possesses a thorough knowledge of this subject," but with no author identification in the ads. $15.00
Campfires of the Wolf Patrol
Woodcraft
Pathfinder
Great Hike
Endurance Test
Under Canvas
Storm-bound
Afloat
Tenderfoot Squad
Boy Scouts in an Airship
Boy Scout Electricians
Boy Scouts on Open Plains

VIRGINIA DAVIS SERIES, Grace May North, ca. 1915 Burt, hardcover, illustrated. ($20.00 with dust jacket) $10.00
Virginia of V. M. Ranch
Virginia at Vine Haven

Virginia's Adventure Club
Virginia's Ranch Neighbors
Virginia's Romance

————— **W** —————

WALT DISNEY'S ANNETTE SERIES, Doris Schroeder, Whitman glossy hardcover with wraparound illustration, line drawing illustrations. Character based on actress Annette, star of Disney films and television productions. Titles through 1963 by Doris Schroeder. $15.00
Sierra Summer, 1960
Desert Inn Mystery, 1961
Mystery at Moonstone Bay, 1962
Mystery at Smugglers' Cove, 1963
Mystery at Medicine Wheel, 1964, Barlow Meyers

WALT HENLEY SERIES, Alfred Fullerton Loomis, 1927 – 1929 Ives Washburn, blue hardcover, yellow lettering, frontispiece, US Navy adventures, World War I. ($20.00 with dust jacket) $10.00
Walt Henley, D. S. M. A.
Walt Henley, Overseas
Walt Henley, Skipper

WALTON BOYS SERIES, Hal Burton, 1948 – 1952 Whitman, plain hardcover, pictorial endpapers, frontispiece plus b/w illustrations. Adventures of three brothers out West, not part of the TV Walton series. ($30.00 with dust jacket) $10.00
Glossy illustrated hardcover edition: $10.00
Walton Boys and Gold in the Snow
Walton Boys and Rapids Ahead
Walton Boys in High Country

WALTONS SERIES, novels by several authors based on the TV series of a Depression era family, 1975 Whitman, pictorial hardcover art by Maxine McCaffrey. $10.00

Waltons: The Bird Dog
Waltons: The Puzzle
Waltons: The Penny Sale
Waltons: The Treasures
Waltons: Up She Rises!
Waltons: The Accident
Related book:
Waltons' Birthday Present, 1975 Little Golden Books, small, pictorial hardcover. $5.00

WAR OF 1812 SERIES, Everett Tomlinson, 1894 – 1913 Lee & Shepard, pictorial hardcover, six to eight b/w plates. $15.00
Search for Andrew Field
Boy Soldiers of 1812
Boy Officer of 1812
Tecumseh's Young Braves
Guarding the Border
Boys with Old Hickory
Boy Sailors of 1812

WAR OF THE REVOLUTION SERIES, Everett Tomlinson, 1895 – 1902 Wilde, yellow hardcover with "War of the Revolution Series" in gilt, frontispiece and four plates by Charles Copeland. $15.00
Later edition by Grosset & Dunlap: ($25.00 with dust jacket) $10.00
Three Colonial Boys
Three Young Continentals
Washington's Young Aids
Two Young Patriots, or Boys of the Frontier
In the Camp of Cornwallis

WARD HILL SERIES, Everett Tomlinson, ca. 1897 Rowland Press, hardcover with baseball items in silver gilt, eight b/w plates in earliest editions. $30.00
Goldsmith: ($15.00 with dust jacket) $10.00
Ward Hill at Weston
Ward Hill the Senior
Ward Hill at College
Ward Hill the Teacher

WE WERE THERE SERIES, Grosset & Dunlap, Sears Book Club, hardcover, illustrated endpapers, b/w illustrations by various artists. ($20.00 with dust jacket) $10.00
Titles include:
We Were There on the Oregon Trail, Steele, 1955
We Were There at the Battle of Gettysburg, Alida Malkus, 1955
We Were There at the Boston Tea Party, Robert Webb, 1956
We Were There with Byrd at the South Pole, Charles Stanley Strong, 1956
We Were There with the Mayflower Pilgrims, Robert Webb, 1956
We Were There with the California Forty-niners, Stephen Holt, 1956

We Were There with Ethan Allan and the Green Mountain Boys, Robert Webb, 1956

We Were There with the Pony Express, William Steele, 1956

We Were There at the Klondike Gold Rush, Benjamin Appel, 1956

We Were There with Jean Lafitte at the Battle of New Orleans, Iris Vinton, 1957

We Were There at the Oklahoma Land Rush, Jim Kjelgard, 1957

We Were There at the Battle for Bataan, Benjamin Appel, 1957

We Were There at Pearl Harbor, Felix Sutton, 1957

We Were There with Richard the Lion Hearted in the Crusades, Robert Webb, 1957

We Were There at the Battle of the Alamo, Margaret Cousins, 1958

We Were There with Lewis and Clark, James Munves, 1959

We Were There when Grant Met Lee at Appomattox, Earl Schenck Miers, 1960

We Were There at the Battle of Britain, Clayton Knight, 1959

We Were There with Cortes and Montezuma, Benjamin Appel, 1959

We Were There with the California Rancheros, Stephen Holt, 1960

We Were There at the First Airplane Flight, Felix Sutton, 1960

We Were There with Charles Darwin on H.M.S Beagle, Philip Eisenberg, 1960

We Were There at the Driving of the Golden Spike, David Shepherd, 1960

We Were There at the Opening of the Atomic Era, James Munves, 1960

We Were There with the Lafayette Escadrille, Clayton Knight, 1961

We Were There on the Nautilus, Robert Webb, 1961

We Were There with Lincoln in the White House, Earl Schenck Miers, 1963

WEBSTER SERIES, Frank V. Webster, ca. 1920s Cupples and Leon, hardcover, various formats. ($25.00 with dust jacket) $15.00

Titles include:

Airship Andy
Pen Hardy's Flying Machine
Bob Chester's Grit
Bob the Castaway
Boy from the Ranch
Boy Pilot of the Lakes
Boy Scouts of Lenox
Boys of Bellwood School
Boys of the Wireless
Comrades of the Saddle
Cowboy Dave
Darry the Life Saver
Dick the Bank Boy
Harry Watson's High School Days

High School Rivals
Jack of the Pony Express
Jack the Runaway
Newsboy Partner
Only a Farm Boy
Tom Taylor at West Point
Tom the Telephone Boy
Two Boy Gold Miners
Two Boys of the Battleship
Young Firemen of Lakeville
Young Treasure Hunter

WELLWORTH COLLEGE SERIES, Leslie Quirk, 1912 – 1916 Little, Brown, hardcover, b/w plates by Henry Watson, earliest editions had gilt lettering. $35.00

Fourth Down
Freshman Eight
Third Strike
Ice-boat Number One

WEST POINT, CLINT LANE SERIES, Red Reeder, Duell, Sloane and Pearce, gray hardcover, map endpapers. First edition: $75.00 with dust jacket

1960s Meredith reprints: ($25.00 with dust jacket by Charles Andres) $10.00

West Point Plebe, 1955
West Point Yearling, 1956
West Point Second Classman, 1957
West Point First Classman, 1958
2nd Lieutenant Clint Lane: West Point to Berlin, 1960
Clint Lane in Korea, 1961

WEST POINT, MARK MALLORY SERIES, Lt. Frederick Garrison (Upton Sinclair), 1903 Street and Smith;

later editions by McKay; Federal Book; brown hardcover with gilt, frontispiece, collected stories from earlier magazine serials. $60.00

Off for West Point, or Mark Mallory's Struggle
Cadet's Honor, or Mark Mallory's Heroism
On Guard, or Mark Mallory's Celebration
West Point Treasure, or Mark Mallory's Strange Find
West Point Rivals, or Mark Mallory's Strategem

WEST POINT SERIES, General Paul Malone, Penn Publishing, hardcover, illustrated endpapers b/w plates. $30.00

Winning His Way to West Point, 1904
Plebe at West Point, 1905
West Point Yearling, 1907
West Point Cadet, 1908
West Point Lieutenant, 1911

WEST POINT SERIES see DICK PRESCOTT

WESTERN INDIAN SERIES, Elmer Russell Gregor, 1917 – 1930 Appleton, hardcover. $20.00

White Otter, 1917
War Trail, 1921
Three Sioux Scouts, 1922
Medicine Buffalo, 1925
War Chief, 1927
Spotted Pony, 1930

WESTY MARTIN SERIES, Percy Keese Fitzhugh, ca. 1920s Grosset, cloth-over-board cover, a Boy Scout series. ($30.00 with dust jacket) $15.00

Westy Martin
Westy Martin in the Yellowstone
Westy Martin in the Rockies
Westy Martin on the Santa Fe Trail
Westy Martin on the Old Indian Trail
Westy Martin in the Land of the Purple Sage
Westy Martin on the Mississippi
Westy Martin in the Sierras

WHITEY SERIES, Glen Rounds, Holiday House, hardcover, illustrations by author. ($25.00 with dust jacket) $15.00

Grosset editions, b/w illustrations by author $15.00

Whitey's First Round Up, 1942
Whitey and Jinglebob, 1946
Whitey Looks for a Job, 1944
Whitey's Sunday Horse, 1942
Whitey Takes a Trip, 1954
Whitey Ropes and Rides
Whitey and the Wild Horse, 1958
Whitey and the Colt-Killer, 1962

WHITMAN AUTHORIZED EDITIONS, ca. 1940s – 1970s Whitman, various authors, standard size plain hardcover, illustrated endpapers, b/w illustrations, colorful dust jackets often using photos of the movie star featured in the fictional adventure/mystery story. ($25.00 with dust jacket) $15.00

Titles include:

Ann Rutherford and the Key to Nightmare Hall
Ann Sheridan and the Sign of the Sphinx
Annie Oakley in Danger at Diablo
April Kane and the Dragon Lady
Betty Grable and the House with Iron Shutters
Blondie and Dagwood's Adventure with Magic
Blondie and Dagwood's Snapshot Clue
Blondie and Dagwood's Secret Service
Bonita Granville and the Mystery of Star Island
Boots and the Mystery of the Unlucky Vase
Brenda Starr, Reporter
Captain Midnight Adventure: Joyce of the Secret Squadron
Dale Evans and Danger in Crooked Canyon
Deanna Durbin and the Adventure of Blue Valley
Deanna Durbin and the Feather of Flame
Dick Tracy, Ace Detective
Dick Tracy Meets the Night Crawler
Don Winslow and the FBI
Don Winslow and the Scorpion's Stronghold
Dorothy Lamour and the Haunted Lighthouse
Gene Autry and the Badmen of Broken Bow
Gene Autry and Golden Ladder Gang
Gene Autry and the Big Valley Grab
Gene Autry and the Ghost Riders
Gene Autry and Arapaho Drums
Gene Autry and the Thief River Outlaws
Gene Autry and the Redwood Pirates
Ginger Rogers and the Riddle of the Scarlet Cloak
Gregory Peck and the Red Box Enigma
Invisible Scarlet O'Neil
Jane Withers and the Hidden Room,
Jane Withers and the Phantom Violin
Jane Withers and the Swamp Wizard
John Payne and the Menace at Hawk's Nest
Judy Garland and the Hoo-doo Costume
King of the Royal Mounted
Little Orphan Annie and the Gila Monster Gang
Lone Rider and the Treasure of the Vanished Men
Nancy Craig and the Fire Opal of Guatemala
Nina and Skeezix, The Problem of the Lost Ring
Patty O'Neal on the Airways
Peggy Parker, Girl Inventor
Polly the Powers Model and the Puzzle of the Haunted Camera
Quiz Kids and the Crazy Question
Roy Rogers and the Gopher Creek Gunman
Roy Rogers and the Ghost of Mystery Rancho
Roy Rogers and the Brasada Bandits
Roy Rogers and the Enchanted Canyon
Roy Rogers, King of the Cowboys
Roy Rogers and the Rimrod Renegades
Roy Rogers and Dale Evans in River of Peril
Roy Rogers and the Raiders of Sawtooth Ridge
Roy Rogers and the Outlaws of Sundown Valley
Sandra of the Girl Orchestra

Shirley Temple and the Spirit of Dragonwood
Shirley Temple and the Screaming Specter
Smilin' Jack and the Daredevil Girl Pilot
Son of the Phantom
Sylvia Sanders and the Tangled Web
Tammy, Adventure in Squaw Valley
Tillie the Toiler and the Masquerading Duchess
Tom Harmon and the Great Gridiron Plot
Tom Stetson and the Giant Jungle Ants
Van Johnson, the Luckiest Guy in the World
Winnie Winkle and the Diamond Heirlooms

WHITMAN CLASSICS SERIES, ca. 1930s, 1940s, reprints using earlier editions and illustrations, and some new illustrations $10.00

Titles include:
Robinson Crusoe
Treasure Island
Kidnapped
Tom Sawyer
Heidi
Hans Brinker
Swiss Family Robinson
Eight Cousins
Little Women
Little Men
Gulliver's Travels
Robin Hood
Black Beauty
Dickens' Christmas Stories
Huckleberry Finn
Bible Stories
Alice in Wonderland
Three Musketeers
Fifty Famous Fairy Tales
Fifty Famous Americans

WHITMAN TELEVISION FAVORITES SERIES, also referred to as Whitman Authorized TV Series, ca. 1950s – 1970, glossy pictorial hardcover, no dust jackets issued, b/w illustrations. There are overlaps in the Whitman TV-related books, some numbered, some with different cover designations as formats were updated, most based on TV programs but some simply featuring a TV personality as the hero or heroine of an adventure. There are numbers on the book spines, but occasionally the same number appears on different titles. $15.00

Series and titles include:
Bonanza
Treachery Trail, 1968
Heroes of the Wild West, 1970
Dragnet
Case Histories from the Popular Television Series, 1957
Dr. Kildare
Dr Kildare: Assigned to Trouble, 1963
Dr. Kildare and the Magic Key, 1964
F Troop
F Troop, the Great Indian Uprising, 1967 Whitman
Garrison's Gorillas
Fear Formula, 1968
Gunsmoke
Showdown on Front Street, 1969
Hawaii Five-O
Top Secret, 1969
I Love Lucy
Lucy and the Madcap Mystery, 1963
Ironside
Picture Frame-up, 1969
Land of the Giants
Flight of Fear, 1969
Leave it to Beaver
Leave it to Beaver, 1962
Man from U.N.C.L.E.
Gentle Saboteur
Gunrunners' Gold
Mission Impossible
Priceless Particle, 1969
Mod Squad
Assignment: The Arranger, 1969
Monkeys
Who's Got the Button?, 1968
Munsters
Munsters and the Great Camera Caper, 1965
Munsters and the Last Resort, 1966
Real McCoys
Real McCoys and the Danger at the Ranch, 1961

WILDERNESS MYSTERY SERIES, Troy Nesbit (pseudonym of Franklin Brewster Folsom), Harvey House, hardcover, illustrated by John Joseph Floherty. Some titles appear to have been published in earlier editions by Whitman with different illustrators. $15.00
Mystery at Rustler's Fort, 1960

Sand Dune Pony Mystery, 1960
Indian Mummy Mystery, 1962
Mystery at Payrock Canyon, 1962
Diamond Cave Mystery, 1962
Forest Fire Mystery, 1963
Hidden Ruin, 1966

WILLIAM BROWN SERIES, (also called JUST WILLIAM), Richmal Crompton. Crompton worked as a school teacher until forced to retire by the onset of polio. This school series is based on her experiences and on the character of her brother, Jack, also an author.

George Newnes, UK, hardcover, illustrations by Thomas Henry and Henry Ford, gilt titles and gilt picture of William on spine.

William Brown, 1920s and 1930s, first editions: $300.00 and up with dust jacket.

1950s Newnes reprints, hardcover with black lettering, b/w illustrations throughout: ($30.00 with dust jacket) $15.00

1950s Australian reprints, Dymocks hardcovers: $15.00

*Just William,*1922
*More William,*1922
*William Again,*1923
William the Fourth, 1924
Still William, 1925
William the Conqueror, 1926
William the Outlaw, 1927
William in Trouble, 1927
William the Good, 1928
William, 1929
William the Bad, 1930
*William's Happy Days,*1930
William's Crowded Hours, 1931
William the Pirate, 1932
William the Rebel, 1933
William the Gangster, 1934
William the Detective, 1935

Sweet William, 1936
William the Showman, 1937
William the Dictator, 1938
William and the A.R.P., (also issued as *William's Bad Resolution*) 1939

William, 1940s first editions: First edition with dust jacket: $200.00 and up

1950s Newnes reprints, hardcover with black lettering, b/w illustrations throughout: ($30.00 with dust jacket) $15.00

1950s Australian reprints, Dymocks hardcovers: $15.00

*William and the Evacuees,*1940 (also issued as *William the Film Star*)
William Does His Bit, 1941
William Carries On, 1942
William and the Brains Trust, 1945
Just William's Luck, 1948

William, 1950s and most 1960s first editions: George Newnes, UK, hardcover, illustrations by Thomas Henry and Henry Ford, gilt titles and gilt picture of William on spine. First edition with dust jacket: $50.00 and up

The last three titles are harder to find and usually priced first edition with dust jacket: $100.00 and up

1950s Newnes reprints, hardcover with black lettering, b/w illustrations throughout: ($20.00 with dust jacket) $15.00

1950s Australian reprints, Dymocks hardcovers: $15.00

William the Bold, 1950
*William and the Tramp,*1952
William and the Moon Rocket, 1954
William and the Space Animal, 1956
William's Television Show, 1958
William the Explorer, 1960
William's Treasure Trove, 1962
William and the Witch, 1964
*William and the Pop Singers,*1965
William and the Masked Ranger, 1966
William the Superman, 1968
William the Lawless, 1970

William, 1980s Macmillan, London, reprints, glossy illustrated hardcover, b/w illustrations: $10.00

WIN HADLEY SPORT SERIES, Mark Porter, 1960 Simon and Schuster, hardcover. ($15.00 with dust jacket) $10.00

Winning Pitcher
Keeper Play
Overtime Upset
Set Point
Slashing Blades
Duel on the Cinders

WINDEMERE SERIES, Rand McNally, reprints of classics ca. 1910 – 1930, pictorial paste-on cover, gilt lettering and spine trim, full-page color illustrations, early printings: ($60.00 with dust jacket) $45.00

Titles include:

Dust jacket

Paste-on-illustration hardcover

Adventures of Perrine, Hector Malot, illustrations by Milo Winter

Adventures of Remi, Hector Malot, illustrations by Mead Schaeffer

Alice's Adventures in Wonderland, Lewis Carroll, illustrations by Milo Winter

Andersen's Fairy Tales, Hans Christian Andersen, illustrations by Milo Winter

Arabian Nights, illustrations by Milo Winter

Grimms' Fairy Tales, J & W Grimm, illustrations by Hope Dunlap

Gulliver's Travels, Swift, 1912, illustrations by Milo Winter

Hans Brinker, Mary Mapes Dodge, illustrations by Winter

Heidi, Johanna Spyri, 1921, illustrations by Maginal Wright Barney

Ivanhoe, Sir Walter Scott, illustrations by Milo Winter

Jungle Babies, Edyth Kaigh-Eustace, illustrations by Paul Bransom

Kidnapped, Robert Louis Stevenson, illustrations by Winter

King Arthur and His Knights, edited by Philip Allen, illustrations by Schaeffer

Pinocchio, Carlo Collodi, illustrations by Esther Friend

Robin Hood, Edith Heal, illustrations by Dan Content

Robinson Crusoe, Daniel Defoe, illustrations by Winter

Swiss Family Robinson, Johann Rudolf Wyss, 1916, illustrations by Milo Winter

Tales of India, Rudyard Kipling, illustrations by Paul Strayer

Tanglewood Tales, Nathaniel Hawthorne, 1913, illustrations by Milo Winter

Three Musketeers, Alexandre Dumas, illustrations by Milo Winter

Treasure Island, R. L. Stevenson, illustrations by Milo Winter

Twenty-Thousand Leagues Under the Sea, Jules Verne, illustrations Winter

A Wonder Book, Nathaniel Hawthorne, 1913, illustrations by Milo Winter

WINDY FOOT THE HORSE SERIES, Frances Frost, Whittlesey House, hardcover. ($15.00 with dust jacket) $10.00

Windy Foot at the County Fair, 1947

Sleigh Bells for Windy Foot, 1948

Maple Sugar for Windy Foot, 1950

WINGS SERIES, Patricia O'Malley

Wings for Carol, 1941 Dodd, cloth-over-board cover. $20.00

Wider Wings, 1942 Jr. Literary Guild, b/w illustrations. $15.00

War Wings for Carol, 1943 Dodd, cloth-over-board cover. $15.00

WINNER SERIES, Everett Tomlinson, 1903 – 1905 Griffith and Rowland, hardcover, college sports novels. $25.00

Goldsmith reprints: ($20.00 with dust jacket) $10.00

Winner

Winning His W

Winning His Degree

WINONA SERIES, Margaret Widdemer, 1915 – 23 Lippincott, hardcover: $15.00

Burt edition, hardcover with printed illustration and gilt lettering, two b/w plates: ($25.00 with dust jacket) $10.00

Winona's War Farm
Winona of the Camp Fire
Winona's Way
Winona's of Camp Karonya

WIRELESS PATROL see YOUNG WIRELESS

WITH THE STARS AND STRIPES OVER THERE SERIES, William James, 1919 Platt & Nourse, hardcover, World War I novels. $35.00

Corporal Kelly of the Fighting Fifth
Gunpointer Steward of the Naval Militia
Barrage Fire Barnes of the Field Artillery
Trooper Sharpe of the First Cavalry
Barbed-Wire Grant of the Engineers

"WOHELO" CAMP FIRE GIRLS see WINONA

WONDER ISLAND BOYS SERIES, Roger Finlay, 1914 – 1915 New York Book Co., hardcover. $20.00

Castaways
Exploring the Island
Mysteries of the Caverns
Tribesmen
Capture and Pursuit
Conquest of the Savages
Adventures of Strange Islands
Treasures of the Islands

WOODCRAFT SERIES, Lillian Elizabeth Roy 1868 – 1932, ca. 1920s Doran, 1930s Grosset & Dunlap, crossover titles used in Grosset GIRL SCOUTS series, hardcover. $35.00

Woodcraft Boys in the Rockies
Woodcraft Girls in the City,
Woodcraft Boys at Sunset Island
Woodcraft Girls at Camp
Woodcraft Girls Camping in Maine

WOODRANGER TALES SERIES, G. Waldo Browne, (ca. 1900) ca. 1907 editions Wessels, N. Y., red cloth-over-board cover w/ impressed illustration on cover, b/w plate illustrations. $15.00

Woodranger
Young Gunbearer
Hero of the Hills
With Rogers' Rangers

WORLD WAR SERIES, Joseph Altsheler, 1915 Appleton, hardcover. Early editions: ($150.00 with dust jacket) $50.00

Guns of Europe, 1915
Hosts of the Air, 1915
Forest of Swords, 1915

WORLD'S END SERIES, Monica Dickens, Doubleday and Heinemann, hardcover. Stories of an old inn that becomes home to a family and the many animals they befriend and protect. Tie-in with a Yorkshire TV series. First edition: ($25.00 with dust jacket) $10.00

House at World's End, 1970
Spring Comes to World's End, 1971
World's End in Winter, 1972
Summer at World's End, 1972

WORLD'S WAR SERIES, Col. James Fiske, ca. 1915 – 1920 Saalfield. Boy Scout novels from other series under different pseudonyms, put together again in a World War I series. ($20.00 with dust jacket) $10.00

Fighting in the Clouds for France
Facing the German Foe
On Board the Mine-Laying Cruiser
Under Fire for Servia
Belgians to the Front
In Russian Trenches
Fighting in the Alps
Shelled by an Unseen Foe
At the Fall of Warsaw
With the Hero of the Marne
With Pershing for France
Fighting the U-Boat Menace

WORRALS SERIES, W.E. Johns, Lutterworth Press. Johns created Worrals, a teenage female pilot, to encourage women to join the war effort in World War II. Worrals joins the Women's Auxiliary Air Force (WAAF) and defeats various Nazi plots. When WWII ended, Worrals and her younger friend Frecks continued to solve mysteries and have adventures. See also BIGGLES.

1940s Lutterworth editions: ($55.00 with dust jacket) $15.00 1950s Hodder editions: ($40.00 with dust jacket) $15.00

Worrals of the WAAF, 1941
Worrals Flie Again, 1942
Worrals Carries On, 1942
Worrals on the Warpath, 1943
Worrals Goes East, 1944

Worrals of the Islands, 1945
Worrals In the Wilds, 1947
Worrals Down Under, 1948
Worrals Goes Afoot, 1949
Worrals in the Wastelands, 1949
Worrals Investigates, 1950

WYNDHAM SERIES, Ralph Henry Barbour, 1924 – 1925 Appleton, hardcover, school sports. $40.00
Fighting Scrub
Bases Full
Hold 'Em, Wyndham

WYNNE AND LONNY SERIES, Eric Speed, pseudonym, (Stratemeyer Syndicate), Grosset & Dunlap, pictorial hardcover, race car stories. First five titles have green spine, last title has a white spine. $25.00 GT Challenge, 1976
Gold Cup Rookies, 1976
Dead Heat at LeMans, 1977, hard-to-find, priced to $60.00
Midnight Rally, 1978, hard-to-find, priced to $60.00

X

X BAR X BOYS SERIES, James Cody Ferris (Stratemeyer Syndicate pseudonym), ca. 1926 – 1942 Grosset, advertised as "These thrilling tales of the Great West concern the Manley boys, Roy and Teddy. They know how to ride, how to shoot, and how to take care of themselves." Several were written by Roger Garis. ($25.00 with dust jacket) $10.00
X Bar X Boys on the Ranch
X Bar X Boys in Thunder Canyon
X Bar X Boys on Whirlpool River
X Bar X Boys on Big Bison Trail
X Bar X Boys at the Round-Up
X Bar X Boys at Nugget Camp
X Bar X Boys at Rustler's Gap
X Bar X Boys at Grizzly Pass
X Bar X Boys Lost in the Rockies
X Bar X Boys Riding for Life
X Bar X Boys in Smoky Valley
X Bar X Boys at Copperhead Gulch
X Bar X Boys Branding the Wild Herd
X Bar X Boys at the Strange Rodeo
X Bar X Boys with the Secret Rangers
X Bar X Boys Hunting the Prize Mustangs
X Bar X Boys at Triangle Mine
X Bar X Boys and the Sagebrush Mystery
X Bar X Boys in the Haunted Gully
X Bar X Boys Seek the Lost Troopers
X Bar X Boys Following the Stampede

Y

Y.M.C.A. BOYS SERIES, Brooks Henderley (Stratemeyer Syndicate pseudonym), 1916 – 1917 Cupples & Leon, hardcover. $40.00
Y.M.C.A Boys of Cliffwood, or Struggle for the Holwell Prize
Y.M.C.A Boys on Bass Island, or Mystery of Russabaga Camp
Y.M.C.A Boys at Football, or Lively Doings On and Off the Gridiron

YANK BROWN SERIES, David Stone, ca. 1920s Barse, cloth-over-board cover, b/w illustrations. ($20.00 with dust jacket) $10.00
Yank Brown, Halfback
Yank Brown, Forward
Yank Brown, Cross-Country Runner
Yank Brown, Miler
Yank Brown, Pitcher
Yank Brown, Honor Man

YANKEE GIRL CIVIL WAR STORIES SERIES, Alice Turner Curtis, 1920 – 30 Penn, hardcover. $15.00
Yankee Girl at Fort Sumter, illustrated by Isabel W. Caley, 1920
Yankee Girl at Bull Run, illustrated by Isabel W. Caley, 1921
Yankee Girl at Shiloh, illustrated by Isabel W. Caley, 1922
Yankee Girl at Antietam, illustrated by Nat Little, 1923
Yankee Girl at Gettysburg, illustrated by Charles Garner, 1925
Yankee Girl at Vicksburg, 1926
Yankee Girl at Hampton Roads, 1927
Yankee Girl at Lookout Mountain, illustrated by Hattie Longstreet Price, 1928
Yankee Girl at the Battle of the Wilderness, 1929
Yankee Girl at Richmond, illustrated by Hattie Longstreet Price, 1930

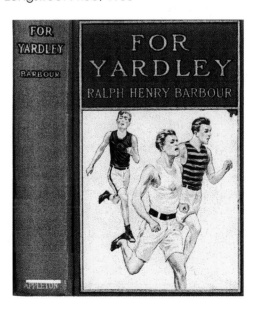

YARDLEY HALL SERIES, Ralph Henry Barbour, 1908 – 1920 Appleton, more school sports from the master of the genre, hardcover with paste-on-illustration, 4 two-color plates by Charles Relyea. First edition: $60.00 Later printings: ($35.00 with dust jacket) $20.00

Winning His "Y"
For Yardley
Change Signals
Around the End
Double Play
Forward Pass
Guarding His Goal
Fourth Down

YOUNG ALASKANS SERIES, Emerson Hough, ca. 1910 – 1920 Harper and Brothers, decorated hardcover, photo illustrations. $35.00

Young Alaskans
Young Alaskans on the Trail
Young Alaskans in the Rockies
Young Alaskans in the Far North
Young Alaskans on the Missouri

YOUNG BIRDMEN SERIES, Keith Russell, ca. 1929 Sears, hardcover, illustrated by Richard Rodgers. ($60.00 with dust jacket) $20.00

Young Birdmen on the Wing, or Rescue at Greenley Island
Young Birdmen Across the Continent, or Coast-to-Coast Flight of the Night Mail
Young Birdmen Up the Amazon, or Secrets of the Tropical Jungle

YOUNG CAPTAINS OF INDUSTRY SERIES, Hollis Godfrey, ca. 1910 Little, Brown, hardcover, b/w illustrations. $30.00

For the Norton Name
Jack Collerton's Engine
Dave Morrell's Battery

YOUNG CONTINENTALS SERIES, John Thomas McIntyre, 1909 – 1912 Penn Publishing, hardcover. Early editions: ($85.00 with dust jacket) $30.00

Young Continentals at Lexington
Young Continentals at Bunker Hill
Young Continentals at Trenton
Young Continentals at Monmouth

YOUNG DEFENDERS SERIES, Eldridge Brooks, ca. 1900 Lothrop, Lee, hardcover. $20.00

With Lawton and Roberts
In Defense of the Flag
Under the Allied Flags

YOUNG EAGLES SERIES, Harris Patton, 1932 Goldsmith, hardcover. ($20.00 with dust jacket) $10.00

Young Eagles
Riding Down
Wings of the North

YOUNG ENGINEERS SERIES see DICK PRESCOTT

YOUNG FOLK'S BOOK see ROMANCE OF KNOWLEDGE SERIES

YOUNG FOLKS LIBRARY, ca. 1900 Hall & Locke, Boston, 20 volumes, collections of stories and short pieces, cloth-over-board cover with gilt, about 390 pages, 12 color plates plus b/w illustrations, artists not credited. The fiction volumes are more popular, with little resale value for the science, history, and biography volumes alone, so that a complete set values at about $200.00. The more popular volumes sold individually are $20.00 each.

Story Teller
Merry Maker
Famous Fairy Tales
Tales of Fantasy
Myths and Legends
Animal Story Book
School and College Days
Book of Adventure
Famous Explorers
Brave Deeds
Wonders of Earth, Sea and Sky
Famous Travels
Sea Stories
Book of Natural History
Historic Scenes in Fiction
Famous Battles by Land and Sea
Men Who Have Risen
Book of Patriotism
Leaders of Men
Famous Poems

YOUNG FOLKS TREASURY, 12 volumes, edited by Hamilton Wright Mabie and Edward Everett Hale, c. 1910 – 20, University Society NY, color plate illustrations. $35.00 each

YOUNG KENTUCKIANS SERIES, Byron Archibald Dunn, 1898 – 1903 McClurg, hardcover. $15.00

General Nelson's Scout
On General Thomas' Staff
Battling for Atlanta
From Atlanta to the Sea
Raiding with Morgan

YOUNG MINERALOGIST SERIES, Edwin James Houston, 1910 – 1912 Griffith & Rowland, hardcover. $40.00

Chip Off the Old Block, or At the Bottom of the Ladder
Land of Drought, or Across the Great American Desert
Jaws of Death, or In and Around the Canyons of the Colorado
Yellow Magnet, or Attracted by Gold

Land of Ice and Snow, or Adventures in Alaska

YOUNG MISSOURIANS SERIES, Byron Archibald Dunn, 1910 – 1914 McClurg, hardcover, several editions. $15.00
With Lyon in Misouri
Scout of Pea Ridge
Courier of the Ozarks
Storming of Vicksburg
Last Raid, 1914

YOUNG PIONEERS see PIONEER BOYS

YOUNG PURITAN SERIES Mary Wells Smith, 1897 – 1900 Little, Brown, hardcover. $15.00
Young Puritans of Old Hadley
Young Puritans in King Philip's War
Young Puritans in Captivity
Young Puritans of Hatfield

YOUNG REPORTER see LARRY DEXTER

YOUNG WIRELESS OPERATOR SERIES, Lewis Theiss, ca. 1920 – 1924 Wilde, hardcover with paste-on-illustration of steamer, photo frontispiece. $20.00
Young Wireless Operator Afloat, or How Roy Mercer Won His Spurs in the Merchant Marine
Young Wireless Operator — as a Fire Patrol, or Story of a Young Wireless Amateur Who Made Good as a Fire Patrol
Young Wireless Operator with the Oyster Fleet, or How Alan Cunningham Won His Way to the Top in the Oyster Business
Young Wireless Operator with the Secret Service, or Winning His Way in the Secret Service
Young Wireless Operator with the US Coast Guard

Z

ZAN AND RINEHART SERIES, R. R. Knudson, Delacorte and Harper, hardcover, high school sports themes. First edition: ($25.00 with dust jacket) $10.00
Zanballer, 1972
Zanbanger, 1977
Zanboomer, 1978
Zan Hagen's Marathon, 1984
Rinehart Lifts, 1980
Rinehart Shouts, 1987

ZIGZAG JOURNEYS SERIES, Hezekiah Butterworth, ca. 1880s Estes, Boston, travels of the fictional Zigzag Club, oversize, dark cloth with gilt decoration, also issued with colorfully illustrated paper-over-board hardcovers, some with gilt, 300+ pages, map endpapers, numerous b/w illustrations. The stories were written originally for *Youth's Companion* periodical, than published in book format. The price range is extremely wide for these books, probably because the books are heavy and the covers are often torn away from the spine, making it difficult to find books in good condition. $65.00
Zigzag Journeys in Classic Lands, 1882
Zigzag Journeys to Europe, 1882
Zigzag Journeys in the Occident, 1882
Zigzag Journeys in the Orient, Adriatic to Baltic, 1882
Zigzag Journeys in the Levant, 1885
Zigzag Journeys in Europe, 1885
Zigzag Journeys in Northern Lands, 1885
Zigzag Journeys in the Sunny South, 1886
Zigzag Journeys in the Antipodes, 1888
Zigzag Journeys in the Great Northwest, 1890
Zigzag Journeys on the Mississippi, 1892
Zigzag Journeys on the Mediterranean, 1893
Zigzag Journeys Around the World, 1895

GLOSSARY

Annuals: Books issued once a year that collected the works published in a magazine or newspaper comic strip.

Backlist: Refers to a publisher's catalog of titles in-print or out-of-print. Often the most valuable asset of a publisher's business, backlists were often sold to pay off debts or reorganize a business. Frontlist refers to the books that a publisher has bought but has not published or is in the process of publishing.

Board: Paste-boards were covered with another material to form the hardcover of a book, leading to terms such as "cloth bound" or "paper over board."

Board books: These were originally designed for very small children. Each page is made of a stiff "board" material that babies and toddlers can handle without tearing.

Cloth binding, cloth hardcover, clothbound: Cloth wrapped around a "board" (usually paste-board or another stiff base) and glued on the edges to form a cover. See also pictorial cover and laminated cover.

Color plate: Color plates are colored pictures printed on a glossy paper that is different from the paper used for the text.

Copyright date: The copyright date indicates when the publisher or author registered the copyright for a work, but not necessarily the date that the book was printed. For example, most Grosset & Dunlap series books show the original date that the book was copyrighted and not necessarily the date that it was issued. See also first edition.

Copyright page: Generally, the copyright page is located on the back of the title page. However, this term will be used for any page that shows the copyright information. Some publishers, such as Garden City, put this information on the title page. Picture books may have this information on the title page, the endpapers, or hidden somewhere in the back depending on the design of the book.

Dust jacket, dust wrapper, dust cover: The loose paper cover used to both protect and advertise the book's contents. See also pictorial cover and laminated cover.

Edition: See first edition.

Endpapers: The double leaves (pages) added at the front and back during the binding process. The outer leaf is pasted down to the inner surface of the cover, while the inner leaf forms the first or last page of the book. Endpapers can be plain or form a double page illustration related to the text. Sometimes they are called endleaves. See also fly-leaf.

Errata: Errors made in the printing or binding of the book. Sometimes, the errata can be used to identify first editions as such mistakes are usually corrected by the publisher as soon as possible.

Ex-library: This term applies to a book that has been removed from the collection of a public library. Ex-library editions are usually priced far less than originals because they have been altered or marked by the library. They might be rebound by the library, have cards pasted over the endpapers, or be stamped with the library's name throughout the text. See also library binding.

First edition: A first edition is generally defined to be the first time that a book appeared in print. (See IDENTIFYING FIRST EDITIONS in *Collector's Guide to Children's Books*, Volume 3 for more information.)

Flyleaf: The blank loose page found in the front or back of the book is often described as the flyleaf. See also endpaper.

Folio: The largest size of a paper sheet used by printers to make a book. The term is also used by book dealers to designate books that are over 13 inches in height. See also size.

Frontispiece: This illustration faces the title page of the book.

Gilt edges, gilt lettering: When the letters are printed with gold-colored, metallic ink, the book has

gilt lettering. Gilt lettering usually appears on the cover. Gilt edges refer to pages with gold decoration on the edge of the paper.

Hardcover, hardback: A book with stiff cover created from pasteboard. Almost all the prices in this guide refer to hardcover editions of a title.

ISBN: The International Standard Book Number (ISBN) system was adopted between 1967 and 1969 by publishers in Great Britain and North America. Each book is assigned an unique series of digits, such as 0-89145-717-8 (the ISBN for our first book). This information was usually printed on the copyright page and also the dust jacket. The number is changed when the publisher changes the binding (a paperback is assigned a different number from the hardback edition). The number will also be changed when the book is reprinted by another publisher (the Macmillian edition would have a different number from the Grosset & Dunlap edition of the same title). A new ISBN will be assigned if the book goes through a re-write or other changes that make the book a new edition from the publishers' point-of-view. The ISBN does not usually change between printings. R.R. Bowker assigns and tracks the ISBN for American publishers. The Standard Book Numbering Agency Ltd. in the United Kingdom tracks the British ISBN. See also Library of Congress and SBN.

Laminated covers : Pictorial hardcovers laminated with a shiny clear gloss coating. Many of the Whitman books were issued with laminated covers. See also pictorial cover.

Library binding: As books become worn by library patrons, they may be rebound. These library bindings replace the original binding and often require the page edges to be trimmed slightly from the original size. Library bindings are usually easy to spot as they are of a thicker, more durable material than regular book covers (bright orange seems a popular color). The library bindings do not have the usual publisher marks on the spine and cover. They also considerably reduce the price of the book (see also ex- library). Sometimes, library binding may also refer to the reinforced binding used by the publishers — this type of binding does not reduce the value of the book as it generally looks just like the regular trade edition.

Library of Congress catalog card number, LOC number: The card number assigned by the Library of Congress started appearing regularly in books around 1960. Eventually this information was replaced by the Library of Congress Cataloging-in-Publication Data (a paragraph that looks like a library card) in the late 1970s. This information appears on the copyright page and is just one of the many clues that can be used to date a book when the date of printing is unclear. Publishers of childrens' books were very inconsistent during the early days of this system (and the SBN), so these dates should be used as a general guideline only.

Limited edition: An edition of a book issued in a limited number of copies.

List-to-self or List-to-title: On the dust jacket flap or on an interior advertising page in a series book, titles of other books in the series may be listed. If the book's title is the last title on the list, this is called a "list-to-self" book. Because this information is not 100% reliable, collectors and dealers refer to such a book as a "probable first."

List-to-year: Like list-to-self, this is method of determining a probable first edition of a series book. The titles on the dust jacket or advertising page may go past the volume's title, but only to include other titles released the same year, and therefore the book may still be a probable first. If titles for other series are included on the dust jacket or advertising pages, and their titles end with titles publlished the year of the volume's release, this is another helpful hint.

No date: In this guide and most dealer catalogs, no date means a book that has no date of publication printed on the copyright or title page.

Paper boards, paper covered: The paper boards are the stiff material that forms the outer cover of a book. Generally, these are made from paste boards (layers of paper). When used by a dealer to describe the cover of a book, this generally means that the boards are plain and not covered by cloth. This is different from a paperback (see softcover).

Paperback: A small book issued with a soft cover is usually called a paperback. The standard size is approximately 4.25 inches by 6.5 inches, but children's books, such as the Scholastic paperbacks, may be slightly larger. Unless specifically noted, we did not price paperbacks in this guide. See also softcover.

Picture book: In this text, a picture book is a book that relies mostly on pictures to convey the story to very young readers.

Pictorial hardcover: A hardcover, usually issued

without a dust jacket, decorated with a printed picture on the front cover. The 1960s Nancy Drew books were issued as pictorial hardcovers. Many picture books were printed as pictorial hardcovers but issued with a dust jacket. If the dust jacket and cover have the same illustration, the hardcover is often referred to as "same as" pictorial cover. See also "laminated covers" and "dust jackets."

Price clipped: In many cases, dust jackets had the price clipped off them before being given as gifts. Some collectors are looking for completely intact dust jackets, some don't care if the price is clipped as long as it doesn't affect the look of the dust jacket. Generally this is considered a minor fault on dust jackets, but something that should be noted if you are selling a book.

Printer: The company that actually operates the press or other equipment need to print a book. Many early publishers operated as both printers and publishers.

Provenance: The pedigree of a book's ownership presented by a dealer. We did not look at the provenance of books when creating this guide and this type of information should be treated like an author's signature — something that takes the book outside the normal realm of pricing.

Publisher: The company that purchases the rights to print and market a book. Some early publishers started out as printers, but by the mid-20th century, most publishers farmed out their printing to other companies.

Re-backed: When the spine or backstrip of a book has been replaced, the book has been re-backed.

SBN: Standard Book Number (SBN) was the forerunner of the ISBN and appeared on copyright pages mostly in the mid-1960s. See also ISBN.

Series: A set of books with an on-going theme, or a continuation of stories about specific characters, or a label put on a set of books by a publisher, can be defined as a series.

Set: Several books meant to be sold together , typically in sets of six or twelve volumes.

Size: In this guide, we've tried to stay with general terms like "oversize" or "small." Some dealers use "folio" or "quarto" to refer to size. These terms originally referred to the size of the paper sheet on which the book was printed and the number of times that sheet was folded to form the book. There is much debate over the proper use of these terms, so we have avoided them whenever possible. See also abbreviations on pages 1999 and 200.

Softcover: A softcover book is one that is issued with a soft outer cover but is larger than the standard paperback (this book is a softcover). Today, booksellers and publishers may use the term trade paperback to refer to softcovers of a medium size (Approximately six inches by nine inches). Unless specifically noted, we did not price softcovers in this guide.

Spine: The spine is the part of the book which is visible when the book is closed and placed on the shelf.

Volume: As used in this guide, a volume generally means one book in a set, such as a single book in a set of encyclopedias.

ABBREVIATIONS

Many dealers use abbreviations to describe books and their conditions in their catalogs and Internet listings. The abbreviations listed here seem to be the most commonly used, but be aware that dealers often invent their own abbreviations or use a standard abbreviation for another meaning. When in doubt, query first, especially if this information makes a difference in the desirability of the book for you.

4to – Quarto, usually meaning quarto sized (approximately 12" tall).

8to – Octavo, usually meaning octavo sized (approximately 9" tall).

12mo – Twelvemo or duodecimo, usually meaning approximately 7" tall.

16mo – Sixteenmo, usually meaning 5½" tall.

(Special note on sizes: librarians, bibliographical references, and many antiquarian booksellers use 4to, etc., to refer to the original size of the paper and the number of folds taken by the printer, rather than the height of the book. It is wise to check how a particular dealer is using the term.)

Anon., anony. – Anonymous author.

BCE – Book club edition.

Bndg. – Binding.

BW, b/w – Black-and-white, as in black-and-white illustrations.

C. – Copyright date (c. 1967) or circa, meaning about that time (c. 1970s). One of those abbreviations that you want to doublecheck. To avoid confusion, we have used ca. to mean circa.

Ca. – Circa (approximate date or era).

CP – Copyright page.

Cond. – Condition, as in good cond.

DJ, dw, dc – Dust jacket, dust wrapper, or dust cover.

Ed. – Editor or edited by, as in short stories ed. Andre Norton.

Ex. lib., exlib, ex–lib – Ex-library.

F. – Fine, as in f. condition.

FAE – First American edition.

FE – First edition rather than fine edition (but doublecheck if unsure).

Fly, fr. fly, r. fly - Flyleaf, front flyleaf, rear flyleaf.

Fr. – Front or frontispiece.

G, gd – Good, as in g. condition.

Ill., illus. – Illustrated or illustrations: e.g., illus. by M Sendak.

Lg., lge. – Large.

Lt. – Light, as in Lt. marks on dust jacket.

Ltd. – Limited, as in ltd. edition

Med. – Medium size.

NAP – No additional printing, i.e., no additional printings shown on copyright page.

ND, nd – No date, usually means no date of printing available

Obl. – Oblong, as in a book that is wider than it is tall.

O.P., OOP – Out of print.

PC, p.c. – Price clipped, as in dust jacket pc.

Phots., photos – Photographs, as in illustrated w/phots.

Pg., pgs. – Page, pages.

Pub., pu. – Published, as in pu. 1967, or publisher, as in pub. Random House.

Prtg. – Printing, such as first prtg.

Qto. – Quarto, often used for quarto-sized (approx. 12" tall)

Rev. – Revised, as in rev. edition.

Rpt. – Reprint or reprinted as in rept. by G&D (reprint by Grosset & Dunlap).

Sigd., sgd., /s/ - Signed, as in sigd. by author. May also use sig. for signature.

Sm. – Small.

Sp. – Spine, as in dust jacket sp torn.

SS, ss – Short stories, as in ss by various authors.
TP – Title page.

Trans. – Translator or translated by.

V., v. – Very.

VG, vg – Very good, as in vg dust jacket.

VG/VG, G/VG, etc. – Refers to condition of book and dust jacket. The first is used for a very good edition, very good dust jacket. A reference like VG/0 usually means that there is no dust jacket available, but this is one of those abbreviations that it is wise to double check.

Vol. – Volume, as in 8 vol. set.

W/ or w/o – With or without as in w/dust jacket or w/o dust jacket.

See series on page 135

RESOURCES

Fan Clubs, Newsgroups, Websites, and Other Resources

For collectors, there are a variety of resources to help find used bookstores, chat with other collectors, research titles, and swap want lists. Below you'll find Internet resources, fan clubs, newsletters, and some other research tools that we've enjoyed or that have been recommended to us by other collectors.

Most libraries now offer Internet access for their patrons, and many offer free training classes for anyone interested in research on the web.

Websites do change. However, we post changes and updates on our links page listed at the end of this chapter.

If you have found another resource for children's book collectors, we would like to hear from you. You can reach us at lostlvs@aol.com or write to Rosemary Jones, PO Box 9432, Seattle, WA 98109.

Fan Clubs & Super Fans

Every year, more and more fans of series books build their own websites to talk about their favorite characters, show off their collections, and share detailed bibliographical information. Some sites are linked to official fan clubs that even have a "real world" address and newsletters. The following is just a sampling of sites that we've visited. Be sure to check our web page (listed at the end of this chapter) for new sites over the year. See also the section on magazines and newsletters at the end of this chapter.

Betsy-Tacy Society
http://www.betsy-tacysociety.org
Incorporated in 1992, the Betsy-Tacy Society has attracted more than 1,000 members from the U.S., Canada, Europe, Asia, and Africa. Members receive the *Betsy-Tacy Society Journal* twice a year. For current membership rates, check their website or contact the Betsy-Tacy Society, c/o The Heritage Center/BECHS, 415 Cherry Street, Mankato MN 56001, USA.

Biggles
http://www.biggles.au.com/
This fan site includes information on all of W.E. Johns' series, lots of book pictures, and a terrific list of the various planes that Biggles flew. A great site for anyone interested in the aviation history behind Big-gles and great starting place for any Biggles-related search including links to several other sites.

Black Stallion
http://www.theblackstallion.com/
Maintained by Steven Farley who has written new novels for the series, this site gives basic background on the series, Walter Farley, new media projects based on the books, and a list of horse shows around the country.

Horatio Alger Society
http://www.ihot.com/~has/
Society members receive the bi-monthly *Newsboy* as well as an invitation to the annual convention. The website contains information about Alger's life, many series, book formats, and much more. For current membership fees, check the website or write to Horatio Alger Society, P.O. Box 70361, Richmond, VA 23255.

Judy Bolton
http://www.judybolton.com/
Here's all-things-Judy as well links to other sites devoted to girls' series books; information about the Phantom Friends' gatherings (see also *Whispered Watchword* under magazines); and information about the real places used by Sutton for the books.

Laura Ingalls Wilder Memorial Society
http://www.liwms.com/
If you've ever wondered about the places that Laura lived, visit this website and then plan your trip to South Dakota. The Laura Ingalls Wilder Memorial Society works to preserve the original homesteads of the Ingalls and Wilder families. The Society web page lists places open to visitors, special events, and links to other sites dedicated to the Little House books. You can also write or call the Laura Ingalls Wilder Memorial Society, Inc. P.O Box 426, De Smet, South Dakota 57231, 1-800-880-3383.

Nancy Drew
http://www.mysterynet.com/nancydrew
Primarily a commercial site devoted to selling the current crop of Nancy Drew novels, this web page does have a list of reference works and some short articles on the historical Nancy. Also, for those with a

speedy Internet connection, there's a Nancy Drew sleuthing game.

Stratmeyer Syndicate
http://www.stratemeyer.net/
http://www.keeline.com/stratemeyersyndicate.html

Two great sites for fans of the Stratemeyer Syndicate books (Hardy Boys, Nancy Drew, Tom Swift, and many others). Stratemeyer.net catalogs many series, gives title lists, and has lots of extra resources listed for Statemeyer fans. Book dealer James Keeline (www.keeline.com) has spent years researching the syndicate. His scholarly articles about the printing history of the syndicate and probable authors of various series have appeared in various fan newsletters and magazines. Copies of several articles are stored in pdf format at his site.

Yahoo Directory: Children's Series
http://dir.yahoo.com/Arts/Humanities/Literature/Genres/Children_s/Series/

Yahoo is one of the oldest search engines on the web. You can use the extremely long address above to find fan pages and other information about series books. Or just go to http://www.yahoo.com and type "Children's Series" into the search box. We also recommend Google (http://www.google.com) for quick searches of the web. An author's name or a series name will generally bring up a dozen resources.

Internet Newsgroups

Book Collecting
rec.books.collecting

This very busy Internet newsgroup spends most of its time discussing issues of interest to collectors. Everything from getting musty smells out of old books to identifying first editions can turn up during the day. The group strongly protests any type of "for sale" or "for auction" notice being posted. The FAQs (frequently asked questions) are posted on a regular basis and contain many useful tips for book collectors (see also RBC FAQs website listed later in this chapter).

Children's Books
rec.arts.books.childrens

This Internet newsgroup discusses everything from new titles to collecting various series books. Members are extremely helpful in identifying books, and this is one of our favorite places to describe that book that we read in childhood but can't remember the title or author. Like most Internet newsgroups, advertising is not welcome, and you should read a few messages before posting, or check the group's FAQ file. "For Sale" (FS) notices have been actively discouraged by many partcipants.

Nancy Drew & Other Series
alt.books.nancy-drew

Besides discussing everybody's favorite girl sleuth, members of this newsgroup are very knowledgable about series books, Hardy Boys, and other topics of interest to fans of the Stratmeyer Syndicate.

Internet Sites For Research

Book Collecting FAQs
http://www.rcbfaq.com/

The FAQs (frequently asked questions) of the rec.books.collecting newsgroup have been gathered into one place.

Library of Congress
http://www.loc.gov/

The Library of Congress offers an on-line version of their catalog. This is a useful tool for searching for more information about books if you don't have the full name of the author or have only the title. Many collectors use it for finding other titles written by a favorite author.

Internet Sites For Buying and Sellling Books

Many collectors now use the Internet as a major source for books. Following we've listed websites that we use or have had recommended to us by other collectors. There are always new sites being created (and a few going bust), but the ones here have been in business for several years and seem very stable.

Some websites are professional services where dealers pay to list their catalogs. The customer makes arrangements directly with the bookseller, usually a store, for payment and shipping. Others, like Bookfinder, help you search through all the services and compare prices. Auction sites like e-Bay give collectors a chance to buy and sell directly with fellow enthusiasts.

Addall
http://www.addall.com/

Like Bookfinder, Addall allows you to search multiple sites and compare prices. If you can't find what you're looking for, do try the individual sites as well. Both Addall and Bookfinder seem to miss listings at times, and we often get different search results when we go directly to ABE. Still, this is an easy way to do a first look at resources on the web.

Advanced Book Exchange
http://www.abe.com/

At ABE, you can search for out-of-print books by author, title, or other factors such as illustrators or category through the on-line catalogs of thousands of book dealers. Searches are free, and you can leave free want lists on the database. You will receive direct e-mail notification if a match occurs any time that a dealer posts a book that you wanted. When ordering books, you deal directly with the bookstore rather than the web service so there is no middleman mark-up. If you want to use a credit card through ABE's on-line secure service, there is a small fee.

Alibris
http://www.alibris.com/

Unlike ABE, when you order a book from Alibris, you pay the web service directly, they order the book from the dealer for you, ship it into their warehouse to check condition, and then ship it out to you. Recently, Alibris also started buying and stocking certain used books to improve their delivery time. The service may cost you a little more, but if you're nervous about buying through the Internet, this site offers all sorts of security features and guarantees.

Amazon Auctions
http://auctions.amazon.com/

Like eBay's auctions, Amazon provides a forum for individual sellers to offer items for auction. The terms of payment, shipping, and so on are arranged directly between seller and buyer. Amazon also started a "z-shops" for collectors or small businesses to sell books and other collectibles at a fixed price.

Antiquarian Booksellers Association of America
http://www.abaa-booknet.com/

The homepage of the Antiquarian Booksellers Association of America serves as a great launching place for searching for antiquarian book dealers or bookfairs in your area. The ABAA site maintains links to their member booksellers with catalogs on the Web, information about book fairs throughout the country, a directory of member booksellers by region or speciality, and links to international organizations of booksellers.

Bookavenue
http://www.bookavenue.com/

Like ABE, Bookavenue lets you search for free through the on-line catalogs of their members. Once you find a book, you deal directly with the member bookstore.

Bookfinder.com
http://www.bookavenue.com/

Bookfinder searches through a variety of Internet databases such as ABE. This is a good way to do some quick comparision shopping. Like Addall, Bookfinder tends to miss listings at certain times (gremlins on the Web?), so it's always a good idea to search directly on ABE or others if you don't find what you want.

eBay
http://www.ebay.com/

This popular auction site has literally hundreds of children's books for sale every day including a special section on children's series books. If you "win" an auction by having the highest bid, you are responsible for making arrangements with the seller for payment. Anybody can offer books for sale through this service. This site is also connected with half.com, which offers used books (usually newer books) at a fixed price.

Pacific Book Auction Galleries
http://www.pacificbook.com/

This San Francisco auction house specializes in books. Auctions may be one famous collection from a single source or several small collections grouped around a theme. In 1999, PBA started offering on-line bidding. When purchasing books, you deal directly with the auction house. The terms of sales and guarantees on book descriptions are fully explained on their site. The site also contains information on their regular auctions and how to sell large collections through their services.

Library Research

If you're doing research in a public or university library, ask if they subscribe to the CD-ROM called Children's Reference Plus. This CD is updated annually and contains information from several Bowker reference works including *Fiction, Folklore, Fantasy and Poetry for Children 1876 – 1985; Children's Books in Print; and Books Out of Print* (children's section).

See also our bibliography for a listing of favorite reference books available through most public libraries.

Magazines and Newsletters

Avonlea Spectacle
http://www.avonlea.net/

A magazine devoted to the works of L.M. Montgomery, the *Spectacle* has published reviews, articles about Prince Edward Island, new works of fiction based on Montgomery's characters, and more. For subscription information, write to Avonlea Spectacle, Moonrise Hollow Inc. P.O. Box 513, Dexter, Michigan 48130 USA.

Friends of the Chalet School

The Friends publish a newsletter four times a year for members interested in learning more about Brent-Dyer's series. For information on the club and newsletter, write to Friends of the Chalet School, 4 Rock Terrace, Coleford, Bath, Somerset BA3 5NF, United Kingdom.

Martha's KidLit Newsletter
http://www.kidlitonline.org/

This monthly printed newsletter covers a wide variety of topics concerning children's books including auction news, exhibitions, biographies of authors and illustrators, and tips for collectors. The website contains sample articles as well as links to other sites. For current subscription rates, check the website or write to: *Martha's KidLit Newsletter*, Box 1488, Ames, IA 50014, USA.

Whispered Watchword

The magazine of the Phantom Friends is devoted to girls' series books. Subscription information is available from Phantom Friends, Attn: Kate Emburg, PO Box 1437, N. Highlands, CA 95660-1437, USA.

Updates

Collector Guide's Link Page
http://members.aol.com/lostlvs/links.htm

This is the website where the authors of this guide maintain links to the various websites mentioned. Check here for updates and new resources. To add a link, just e-mail us at lostlvs@aol.com.

See Anne Shirley Series, page 25, and Avonlea Spectacle, page 203.

BIBLIOGRAPHY

Anderson, Vicki, *Fiction Sequels for Readers 10 to 16*, McFarland, 1998.

Axe, John, *Secret of Collecting Girls' Series Books*, Hobby House Press, 2000.

Billman, Carol, *Secret of the Stratemeyer Syndicate*, Ungar Publishing, 1986.

Blanck, Jacob, *Harry Castlemon, Boys' Own Author*, Bowker, limited edition, 1941.

Dartt, Captain Robert L., USNR/R, *G. A. Henty, A Bibliography*, Dar-Web Incorporated, 1971.

Doyle, Brian, *Who's Who of Children's Literature*, Schocken Books, 1968.

Feaver, William, *When We Were Young: Two Centuries of Children's Book Illustration*, Holt, Rinehart and Winston, 1977.

Gale editorial staff, *Yesterday's Authors of Books for Children*, Gale Research.

Jacobs, Larry, *Big Little Books*, Collector Books, 1996.

Johnson, Deidre, *Stratemeyer Pseudonyms and Series Books*, Greenwood Press, 1982.

Kismaric, Carole and Marvin Heiferman, *Growing Up With Dick and Jane*, Collins, 1996.

Madison, Charles A. *Book Publishing in America*, McGraw-Hill, 1966.

Meyer, Susan E., *America's Great Illustrators*, H. N. Abrams, NY.,1978.

Miller, Betha E. Mahoney ed., *Illustrators of Children's Books, 1744 – 1945*, Horn Book, 1947.

Mott, Frank Luther. *Golden Multitudes: Story of Best Sellers In the United States*, Macmillan, 1947.

Plunkett-Powell, Karen, *Nancy Drew Scrapbook*, St. Martin's Press, 1993.

Reynolds, Quentin, *The Fiction Factory (100 Years of Publishing at Street and Smith)*, Random House, 1955.
Santi, Steve, *Collecting Little Golden Books*, Books Americana, 1989.

Silvey, Anita (ed.), *Children's Books and Their Creators*, Houghton Mifflin, 1995.

Tebbel, John. *History of Book Publishing in the United States* (4 volumes), R.R. Bowker Company, 1981.

Zillner, Dian, *Collecting Coloring Books*, Schiffer Publishing Ltd., 1992.

BARNEY JUNIOR MYSTERY SERIES, see page 28

COLLECTOR BOOKS

Informing Today's Collector

For over two decades we have been keeping collectors informed on trends and values in all fields of antiques and collectibles.

DOLLS, FIGURES & TEDDY BEARS

4707	A Decade of **Barbie Dolls** & Collectibles, 1981–1991, Summers	$19.95
4631	**Barbie Doll** Boom, 1986–1995, Augustyniak	$18.95
2079	**Barbie Doll** Fashion, Volume I, Eames	$24.95
4846	**Barbie Doll** Fashion, Volume II, Eames	$24.95
3957	**Barbie** Exclusives, Rana	$18.95
4632	**Barbie** Exclusives, Book II, Rana	$18.95
5672	The **Barbie Doll** Years, 4th Ed., Olds	$19.95
3810	**Chatty Cathy** Dolls, Lewis	$15.95
5352	Collector's Ency. of **Barbie** Doll Exclusives & More, 2nd Ed.,Augustyniak	$24.95
2211	Collector's Encyclopedia of **Madame Alexander** Dolls, Smith	$24.95
4863	Collector's Encyclopedia of **Vogue Dolls**, Izen/Stover	$29.95
5821	**Doll Values**, Antique to Modern, 5th Ed., Moyer	$12.95
5829	**Madame Alexander** Collector's Dolls Price Guide #26, Crowsey	$12.95
5833	**Modern Collectible Dolls**, Volume V, Moyer	$24.95
5689	**Nippon Dolls** & Playthings, Van Patten/Lau	$29.95
5365	**Peanuts Collectibles**, Podley/Bang	$24.95
5253	Story of **Barbie**, 2nd Ed., Westenhouser	$24.95
5277	**Talking Toys** of the 20th Century, Lewis	$15.95
1513	**Teddy Bears & Steiff** Animals, Mandel	$9.95
1817	**Teddy Bears & Steiff** Animals, 2nd Series, Mandel	$19.95
2084	**Teddy Bears, Annalee's & Steiff** Animals, 3rd Series, Mandel	$19.95
5371	**Teddy Bear** Treasury, Yenke	$19.95
1808	Wonder of **Barbie**, Manos	$9.95
1430	World of **Barbie** Dolls, Manos	$9.95
4880	World of **Raggedy Ann** Collectibles, Avery	$24.95

TOYS, MARBLES & CHRISTMAS COLLECTIBLES

2333	Antique & Collectible **Marbles**, 3rd Ed., Grist	$9.95
5353	**Breyer Animal** Collector's Guide, 2nd Ed., Browell	$19.95
4976	**Christmas Ornaments**, Lights & Decorations, Johnson	$24.95
4737	**Christmas Ornaments**, Lights & Decorations, Vol. II, Johnson	$24.95
4739	**Christmas Ornaments**, Lights & Decorations, Vol. III, Johnson	$24.95
4559	Collectible **Action Figures**, 2nd Ed., Manos	$17.95
2338	Collector's Encyclopedia of **Disneyana**, Longest, Stern	$24.95
5038	Collector's Guide to **Diecast Toys** & Scale Models, 2nd Ed., Johnson	$19.95
4651	Collector's Guide to **Tinker Toys**, Strange	$18.95
4566	Collector's Guide to **Tootsietoys**, 2nd Ed., Richter	$19.95
5169	Collector's Guide to **TV Toys** & Memorabilia, 2nd Ed., Davis/Morgan	$24.95
5360	**Fisher-Price Toys**, Cassity	$19.95
4720	The **Golden Age** of **Automotive Toys**, 1925–1941, Hutchison/Johnson	$24.95
5593	Grist's Big Book of **Marbles**, 2nd Ed.	$24.95
3970	Grist's Machine-Made & Contemporary **Marbles**, 2nd Ed.	$9.95
5267	**Matchbox Toys**, 1947 to 1998, 3rd Ed., Johnson	$19.95
5830	**McDonald's** Collectibles, 2nd Edition, Henriques/DuVall	$24.95
5673	Modern **Candy Containers** & Novelties, Brush/Miller	$19.95
1540	Modern **Toys** 1930–1980, Baker	$19.95
3888	**Motorcycle Toys**, Antique & Contemporary, Gentry/Downs	$18.95
5693	**Schroeder's Collectible Toys**, Antique to Modern Price Guide, 7th Ed.	$17.95

FURNITURE

1457	American **Oak** Furniture, McNerney	$9.95
3716	American **Oak** Furniture, Book II, McNerney	$12.95
1118	Antique **Oak** Furniture, Hill	$7.95
2271	Collector's Encyclopedia of **American** Furniture, Vol. II, Swedberg	$24.95
3720	Collector's Encyclopedia of **American** Furniture, Vol. III, Swedberg	$24.95
5359	Early **American** Furniture, Obbard	$12.95
1755	Furniture of the **Depression Era**, Swedberg	$19.95
3906	**Heywood-Wakefield** Modern Furniture, Rouland	$18.95
1885	**Victorian** Furniture, Our American Heritage, McNerney	$9.95
3829	**Victorian** Furniture, Our American Heritage, Book II, McNerney	$9.95

JEWELRY, HATPINS, WATCHES & PURSES

1712	Antique & Collectible **Thimbles** & Accessories, Mathis	$19.95
1748	Antique **Purses**, Revised Second Ed., Holiner	$19.95
1278	Art Nouveau & Art Deco **Jewelry**, Baker	$9.95
4850	Collectible **Costume Jewelry**, Simonds	$24.95
5675	Collectible **Silver Jewelry**, Rezazadeh	$24.95
3722	Collector's Ency. of **Compacts**, Carryalls & Face Powder Boxes, Mueller	$24.95
4940	**Costume Jewelry**, A Practical Handbook & Value Guide, Rezazadeh	$24.95
1716	Fifty Years of Collectible **Fashion Jewelry**, 1925–1975, Baker	$19.95
1424	**Hatpins** & Hatpin Holders, Baker	$9.95
5695	**Ladies' Vintage Accessories**, Bruton	$24.95
1181	100 Years of Collectible **Jewelry**, 1850–1950, Baker	$9.95
4729	**Sewing Tools** & Trinkets, Thompson	$24.95
5620	Unsigned Beauties of **Costume Jewelry**, Brown	$24.95
4878	Vintage & Contemporary **Purse Accessories**, Gerson	$24.95
5696	Vintage & Vogue Ladies' **Compacts**, 2nd Edition, Gerson	$29.95

INDIANS, GUNS, KNIVES, TOOLS, PRIMITIVES

1868	Antique **Tools**, Our American Heritage, McNerney	$9.95
5616	Big Book of **Pocket Knives**, Stewart	$19.95
4943	Field Guide to Flint **Arrowheads** & **Knives** of the North American Indian	$14.95
2279	**Indian Artifacts** of the Midwest, Book I, Hothem	$14.95
3885	**Indian Artifacts** of the Midwest, Book II, Hothem	$16.95
4870	**Indian Artifacts** of the Midwest, Book III, Hothem	$18.95
5685	**Indian Artifacts** of the Midwest, Book IV, Hothem	$19.95
5687	**Modern Guns**, Identification & Values, 13th Ed., Quertermous	$14.95
2164	**Primitives**, Our American Heritage, McNerney	$9.95
1759	**Primitives**, Our American Heritage, 2nd Series, McNerney	$14.95
4730	Standard **Knife** Collector's Guide, 3rd Ed., Ritchie & Stewart	$12.95

PAPER COLLECTIBLES & BOOKS

4633	**Big Little Books**, Jacobs	$18.95
4710	Collector's Guide to **Children's Books**, 1850 to 1950, Volume I, Jones	$18.95
5153	Collector's Guide to **Chldren's Books**, 1850 to 1950, Volume II, Jones	$19.95
5596	Collector's Guide to **Children's Books**, 1950 to 1975, Volume III, Jones	$19.95
1441	Collector's Guide to **Post Cards**, Wood	$9.95
2081	Guide to Collecting **Cookbooks**, Allen	$14.95
5825	Huxford's **Old Book** Value Guide, 13th Ed.	$19.95
2080	Price Guide to **Cookbooks** & Recipe Leaflets, Dickinson	$9.95
3973	**Sheet Music** Reference & Price Guide, 2nd Ed., Pafik & Guiheen	$19.95
4654	**Victorian Trade Cards**, Historical Reference & Value Guide, Cheadle	$19.95
4733	**Whitman Juvenile Books**, Brown	$17.95

GLASSWARE

5602	Anchor Hocking's **Fire-King** & More, 2nd Ed.	$24.95
4561	Collectible **Drinking Glasses**, Chase & Kelly	$17.95
5823	Collectible **Glass Shoes**, 2nd Edition, Wheatley	$24.95
5357	Coll. **Glassware** from the 40s, 50s & 60s, 5th Ed., Florence	$19.95
1810	Collector's Encyclopedia of **American Art Glass**, Shuman	$29.95
5358	Collector's Encyclopedia of **Depression Glass**, 14th Ed., Florence	$19.95
1961	Collector's Encyclopedia of **Fry Glassware**, Fry Glass Society	$24.95
1664	Collector's Encyclopedia of **Heisey Glass**, 1925–1938, Bredehoft	$24.95
3905	Collector's Encyclopedia of **Milk Glass**, Newbound	$24.95
4936	Collector's Guide to **Candy Containers**, Dezso/Poirier	$19.95
4564	**Crackle Glass**, Weitman	$19.95
4941	**Crackle Glass**, Book II, Weitman	$19.95
4714	**Czechoslovakian Glass** and Collectibles, Book II, Barta/Rose	$16.95
5528	Early American **Pattern Glass**, Metz	$17.95
5682	**Elegant Glassware** of the Depression Era, 9th Ed., Florence	$19.95
5614	Field Guide to **Pattern Glass**, McCain	$17.95
3981	Evers' Standard **Cut Glass** Value Guide	$12.95
4659	**Fenton Art Glass**, 1907–1939, Whitmyer	$24.95
5615	Florence's **Glassware Pattern Identification** Guide, Vol. II	$19.95

COLLECTOR BOOKS
Informing Today's Collector

4719	**Fostoria**, Etched, Carved & Cut Designs, Vol. II, Kerr	$24.95
3883	**Fostoria Stemware**, The Crystal for America, Long/Seate	$24.95
5261	**Fostoria Tableware**, 1924 – 1943, Long/Seate	$24.95
5361	**Fostoria Tableware**, 1944 – 1986, Long/Seate	$24.95
5604	**Fostoria**, Useful & Ornamental, Long/Seate	$29.95
4644	**Imperial Carnival Glass**, Burns	$18.95
5827	**Kitchen Glassware** of the Depression Years, 6th Ed., Florence	$24.95
5600	Much More Early American **Pattern Glass**, Metz	$17.95
5690	Pocket Guide to **Depression Glass**, 12th Ed., Florence	$9.95
5594	Standard Encyclopedia of **Carnival Glass**, 7th Ed., Edwards/Carwile	$29.95
5595	Standard **Carnival Glass** Price Guide, 12th Ed., Edwards/Carwile	$9.95
5272	Standard Encyclopedia of **Opalescent Glass**, 3rd Ed., Edwards/Carwile	$24.95
5617	Standard Encyclopedia of **Pressed Glass**, 2nd Ed., Edwards/Carwile	$29.95
4731	**Stemware Identification**, Featuring Cordials with Values, Florence	$24.95
4732	**Very Rare Glassware** of the Depression Years, 5th Series, Florence	$24.95
4656	**Westmoreland Glass**, Wilson	$24.95

POTTERY

4927	**ABC Plates & Mugs**, Lindsay	$24.95
4929	**American Art Pottery**, Sigafoose	$24.95
4630	**American Limoges**, Limoges	$24.95
1312	**Blue & White Stoneware**, McNerney	$9.95
1958	So. Potteries **Blue Ridge Dinnerware**, 3rd Ed., Newbound	$14.95
1959	**Blue Willow**, 2nd Ed., Gaston	$14.95
4851	Collectible **Cups & Saucers**, Harran	$18.95
1373	Collector's Encyclopedia of **American Dinnerware**, Cunningham	$24.95
4931	Collector's Encyclopedia of **Bauer Pottery**, Chipman	$24.95
4932	Collector's Encyclopedia of **Blue Ridge Dinnerware**, Vol. II, Newbound	$24.95
4658	Collector's Encyclopedia of **Brush-McCoy Pottery**, Huxford	$24.95
5034	Collector's Encyclopedia of **California Pottery**, 2nd Ed., Chipman	$24.95
2133	Collector's Encyclopedia of **Cookie Jars**, Roerig	$24.95
3723	Collector's Encyclopedia of **Cookie Jars**, Book II, Roerig	$24.95
4939	Collector's Encyclopedia of **Cookie Jars**, Book III, Roerig	$24.95
5748	Collector's Encyclopedia of **Fiesta**, 9th Ed., Huxford	$24.95
4718	Collector's Encyclopedia of **Figural Planters & Vases**, Newbound	$19.95
3961	Collector's Encyclopedia of **Early Noritake**, Alden	$24.95
1439	Collector's Encyclopedia of **Flow Blue China**, Gaston	$19.95
3812	Collector's Encyclopedia of **Flow Blue China**, 2nd Ed., Gaston	$24.95
3431	Collector's Encyclopedia of **Homer Laughlin China**, Jasper	$24.95
1276	Collector's Encyclopedia of **Hull Pottery**, Roberts	$19.95
3962	Collector's Encyclopedia of **Lefton China**, DeLozier	$19.95
4855	Collector's Encyclopedia of **Lefton China**, Book II, DeLozier	$19.95
5609	Collector's Encyclopedia of **Limoges Porcelain**, 3rd Ed., Gaston	$29.95
2334	Collector's Encyclopedia of **Majolica Pottery**, Katz-Marks	$19.95
1358	Collector's Encyclopedia of **McCoy Pottery**, Huxford	$19.95
5677	Collector's Encyclopedia of **Niloak**, 2nd Edition, Gifford	$29.95
3837	Collector's Encyclopedia of **Nippon Porcelain**, Van Patten	$24.95
1665	Collector's Ency. of **Nippon Porcelain**, 3rd Series, Van Patten	$24.95
4712	Collector's Ency. of **Nippon Porcelain**, 4th Series, Van Patten	$24.95
5053	Collector's Ency. of **Nippon Porcelain**, 5th Series, Van Patten	$24.95
5678	Collector's Ency. of **Nippon Porcelain**, 6th Series, Van Patten	$29.95
1447	Collector's Encyclopedia of **Noritake**, Van Patten	$19.95
1038	Collector's Encyclopedia of **Occupied Japan**, 2nd Series, Florence	$14.95
4951	Collector's Encyclopedia of **Old Ivory China**, Hillman	$24.95
5564	Collector's Encyclopedia of **Pickard China**, Reed	$29.95
3877	Collector's Encyclopedia of **R.S. Prussia**, 4th Series, Gaston	$24.95
5679	Collector's Encyclopedia of **Red Wing Art Pottery**, Dollen	$24.95
5618	Collector's Encyclopedia of **Rosemeade Pottery**, Dommel	$24.95
5841	Collector's Encyclopedia of **Roseville Pottery**, Revised, Huxford/Nickel	$24.95
5842	Collector's Encyclopedia of **Roseville Pottery**, 2nd Series, Huxford/Nickel	$24.95
4713	Collector's Encyclopedia of **Salt Glaze Stoneware**, Taylor/Lowrance	$24.95
3314	Collector's Encyclopedia of **Van Briggle Art Pottery**, Sasicki	$24.95
4563	Collector's Encyclopedia of **Wall Pockets**, Newbound	$19.95
2111	Collector's Encyclopedia of **Weller Pottery**, Huxford	$29.95
5680	Collector's Guide to **Feather Edge Ware**, McAllister	$19.95
3876	Collector's Guide to **Lu-Ray Pastels**, Meehan	$18.95

3814	Collector's Guide to **Made in Japan Ceramics**, White	$18.95
4646	Collector's Guide to **Made in Japan Ceramics**, Book II, White	$18.95
2339	Collector's Guide to **Shawnee Pottery**, Vanderbilt	$19.95
1425	**Cookie Jars**, Westfall	$9.95
3440	**Cookie Jars**, Book II, Westfall	$19.95
4924	Figural & Novelty **Salt & Pepper Shakers**, 2nd Series, Davern	$24.95
2379	Lehner's Ency. of **U.S. Marks** on Pottery, Porcelain & China	$24.95
4722	**McCoy Pottery**, Collector's Reference & Value Guide, Hanson/Nissen	$19.95
5691	**Post86 Fiesta**, Identification & Value Guide, Racheter	$19.95
1670	**Red Wing Collectibles**, DePasquale	$9.95
1440	**Red Wing Stoneware**, DePasquale	$9.95
1632	**Salt & Pepper Shakers**, Guarnaccia	$9.95
5091	**Salt & Pepper Shakers** II, Guarnaccia	$18.95
3443	**Salt & Pepper Shakers** IV, Guarnaccia	$18.95
3738	**Shawnee Pottery**, Mangus	$24.95
4629	Turn of the Century **American Dinnerware**, 1880s–1920s, Jasper	$24.95
3327	**Watt Pottery** – Identification & Value Guide, Morris	$19.95

OTHER COLLECTIBLES

5838	Advertising **Thermometers**, Merritt	$16.95
4704	Antique & Collectible **Buttons**, Wisniewski	$19.95
2269	Antique **Brass & Copper** Collectibles, Gaston	$16.95
1880	Antique **Iron**, McNerney	$9.95
3872	Antique **Tins**, Dodge	$24.95
4845	Antique **Typewriters & Office Collectibles**, Rehr	$19.95
5607	Antiquing and Collecting on the **Internet**, Parry	$12.95
1128	**Bottle** Pricing Guide, 3rd Ed., Cleveland	$7.95
3718	Collectible **Aluminum**, Grist	$16.95
4560	Collectible **Cats**, An Identification & Value Guide, Book II, Fyke	$19.95
5060	Collectible **Souvenir Spoons**, Bednersh	$19.95
5676	Collectible **Souvenir Spoons**, Book II, Bednersh	$29.95
5666	Collector's Encyclopedia of **Granite Ware**, Book 2, Greguire	$29.95
5836	Collector's Guide to **Antique Radios**, 5th Ed., Bunis	$19.95
5608	Collector's Gde. to Buying, Selling & Trading on the **Internet**, 2nd Ed., Hix	$12.95
4637	Collector's Guide to **Cigarette Lighters**, Book II, Flanagan	$17.95
3966	Collector's Guide to **Inkwells**, Identification & Values, Badders	$18.95
4947	Collector's Guide to **Inkwells**, Book II, Badders	$19.95
5681	Collector's Guide to **Lunchboxes**, White	$19.95
5621	Collector's Guide to **Online Auctions**, Hix	$12.95
4862	Collector's Guide to **Toasters** & Accessories, Greguire	$19.95
4652	Collector's Guide to **Transistor Radios**, 2nd Ed., Bunis	$16.95
4864	Collector's Guide to **Wallace Nutting Pictures**, Ivankovich	$18.95
1629	**Doorstops**, Identification & Values, Bertoia	$9.95
5683	**Fishing Lure** Collectibles, 2nd Ed., Murphy/Edmisten	$29.95
5259	**Flea Market Trader**, 12th Ed., Huxford	$9.95
4945	**G-Men and FBI Toys** and Collectibles, Whitworth	$18.95
5605	**Garage Sale & Flea Market Annual**, 8th Ed.	$19.95
3819	**General Store** Collectibles, Wilson	$24.95
5159	Huxford's Collectible **Advertising**, 4th Ed.	$24.95
2216	**Kitchen Antiques**, 1790–1940, McNerney	$14.95
5686	**Lighting Fixtures** of the Depression Era, Book I, Thomas	$24.95
4950	The **Lone Ranger**, Collector's Reference & Value Guide, Felbinger	$18.95
2026	**Railroad** Collectibles, 4th Ed., Baker	$14.95
5619	**Roy Rogers and Dale Evans** Toys & Memorabilia, Coyle	$24.95
5692	**Schroeder's Antiques Price Guide**, 19th Ed., Huxford	$14.95
5007	**Silverplated Flatware**, Revised 4th Edition, Hagan	$18.95
5694	**Summers' Guide to Coca-Cola**, 3rd Ed.	$24.95
5356	**Summers' Pocket Guide to Coca-Cola**, 2nd Ed.	$9.95
3892	**Toy & Miniature Sewing Machines**, Thomas	$18.95
4876	**Toy & Miniature Sewing Machines**, Book II, Thomas	$24.95
5144	Value Guide to **Advertising Memorabilia**, 2nd Ed., Summers	$19.95
3977	Value Guide to **Gas Station Memorabilia**, Summers & Priddy	$24.95
4877	Vintage **Bar Ware**, Visakay	$24.95
4935	The **W.F. Cody Buffalo Bill** Collector's Guide with Values	$24.95
5281	**Wanted to Buy**, 7th Edition	$9.95